VISUAL QUICKSTART GUIDE

Reason 3

FOR WINDOWS AND MAC

Joe Lyford

Peachpit Press

Visual QuickStart Guide

Reason 3 for Windows and Macintosh

Joe Lyford

Peachpit Press
1249 Eighth Street
Berkeley, CA 94710
510/524-2178
800/283-9444
510/524-2221 (fax)

Find us on the World Wide Web at: http://www.peachpit.com
To report errors, please send a note to errata@peachpit.com

Peachpit Press is a division of Pearson Education

Editor: Kate McKinley
Production Coordinator: Gloria Marquez
Copyeditors: Carol Henry and Liz Welch
Compositor: Owen Wolfson
Indexer: Joy Dean Lee
Cover design: The Visual Group

ISBN 0-321-26917-9

9 8 7 6 5 4 3 2 1

Printed and bound in the United States of America

Acknowledgements

I would like to thank Kate McKinley for getting me involved, helping me internalize the VQS format, listening to my rants, being relaxed when things were tense and tense when things got lax—for being such a great editor on such short notice, and for having the proper galoshes for wading through my sloppy sentences! I would like to thank Cary Norsworthy for her patience and support, Tage Widsell at Propellerhead Software in Sweden for answering my questions, responding to my emails, and weathering general pestering from me while steering a behemoth with his teeth. I would also like to thank the Peachpit team: Rebecca Ross, Gloria Marquez, Owen Wolfson, Carol Henry, Liz Welch, and also Marjorie Baer and Nancy Davis for their patience and willingness to do multiple U-turns.

Thanks also to Mark Hirsch and John Paul for giving me a chance, and to Michael Henry at Cryptic Studios for keeping me in the loop and "looping with me in the keep," and to Lani Minella for being the best Sorceress Gauntlet will ever have.

But most of all I would like to thank my wife, Stephanie, for the patience it took to put up with me and the faith it took to keep me going, and my daughter, Eve, for helping me keep my perspective while swimming in a 1-inch-deep pond full of sharks!

Table of Contents

1

INTRODUCTION

Figure 1.1 Reason's Rack is designed to look, feel, and sound like real studio hardware.

Welcome to Reason 3.0, a complete "virtual studio" that has all the devices and music gizmos of a $10,000–$20,000 facility—and lives in the tiny space of your computer's hard drive (**Figure 1.1**).

For half the price of a typical synthesizer, you get a sound library, samplers, drum machines, synthesizers, mixing boards that never run out of channels, and a complete set of effects processors, including mastering tools. To top it off, Reason is expandable as long as you've got computer processing power to spare.

What's in the box?

On just three CDs, Reason gives you a wealth of samplers, synthesizers, drum machines, mixers, effects, beat loop players, and a number of other gizmos. In addition to the Reason program with all its devices, you get a number of sound banks, with enough samples, patches, and loops to keep you busy for quite a while.

As this book is written, a typical PC or Mac can run as many devices as a music studio. Your studio's potential for growth depends only on how fast your computer processor is. As computer speeds increase, so does your studio capacity.

Who Is This Book For?

This book is meant to get new users up and running quickly. No previous experience with Reason and music-composition software is necessary.

Working with Reason requires a knowledge of synthesizers and how they work, which is what this book is designed to give you. If you don't have any background in music, this book will guide you quickly through the basic concepts needed to use Reason, and set you on the path to exploring Reason's possibilities on your own.

I hope reading this book will give you enough knowledge to get yourself moving boldly forward. An inquisitive ear will be your ultimate guide for getting the sounds you want out of Reason. With imagination and dedication, you'll soon be mixing music down to CD-quality audio that can stand alongside a professional CD.

What Does Reason Do?

You write the music; Reason performs it. You're the writer and producer—Reason is the orchestra, conductor, and control room all wrapped up in one package, ready for a performance. Reason performs your music, then captures the performance on your hard drive as an audio file. Not bad for one program.

How do I use Reason?

Although Reason can do a lot of complicated things, it's remarkably easy to use. A project in Reason never has to be more complicated than you want it to be: If you don't need a gizmo, just don't put it in and you never have to think about it! With Reason, these are your basic tasks:

1. Set up a studio. Create your studio by loading it with gear, instruments, and effects. Hook it up any way you want—or let Reason take care of all the cables for you.

2. Start writing. Add as many instruments as you need, whenever you need them. If you get in over your head, use Reason's tools to help manage your hefty studio setups, keeping them simple so you can stay productive and inspired.

3. Fine-tune everything and mix it. Reason gives you control over every mixing fader and instrument knob, then "conducts" and mixes the performance until everything sounds exactly the way you want it.

4. "Master" your music (put the finishing touches on) for whatever format or production specs you're using.

5. Save your music as an audio file that can be burned to CD.

Can I write my style of music in Reason?

Reason's synthesizers, drum machines, and samplers can be set up to compose any kind of music you want—from writing parts to mixing them, and saving your music to digital sound files that can be burned to CD. Reason is versatile enough to use for any music style, and ships with a huge library of sounds to use in your instruments, including an orchestral bank of more than 700 MB.

The back panel gives Reason's virtual instruments the flexibility of their hardware counterparts, because you can take any output and plug it into any input. This means you can hook things together any way you want. The drawbacks of hardware studios—like shorted-out connection cables, electrical interference, and crawling into crannies to follow a cable to its input—are things of the past. Reason makes studio configuration fast, painless, and reversible (just click Undo).

Reason's advantages

Digital music programs typically trade the hands-on control, configuration, and quality of studio hardware in favor of the micro-control, space-saving, and pricing advantages of software. But with Reason there is no trade-off—you keep the knobs, levers, and even the custom setup advantages of hardware.

Figure 1.2 Here, Steinberg's multi-track recording program, Nuendo, shows Reason tracks using ReWire bussing.

Using Reason with Other Programs

If you want to expand your studio to record live instruments, Reason integrates very easily with all the major recording software. It does this using a program called ReWire.

Think of ReWire as a 64-channel audio cable (or "internal audio bus") in your computer, connecting Reason to your other programs. Reason can pipe up to 64 audio channels into ReWire so they show up as active tracks in your setup (**Figure 1.2**).

A list of ReWire-compatible programs is available on the Propellerhead's Web site (www.propellerhead.se) under "ReWire Product Index."

Recording "Outside" Sound

If you plan to use Reason with a typical sound card and want to use your computer to record stereo sound that can be imported into Reason, you will need additional recording software.

The good news is that a lot of programs will record audio and allow you to edit it. They're called *audio editing* programs. Many are shareware and freeware; check the Internet. And there are many inexpensive commercial audio editors that are easy to use. For Windows, Cool Edit, Audacity, Audio Blast, Soliton II, and Encounter 2000; for Macintosh, Amadeus II, Audacity, Jasmine, D-Sound Pro, and GarageBand—just to name a few.

What you will need for multi-track recording

If you do want to record more than one stereo input at a time, you'll need to purchase a "hardware (or "audio") interface, *and* a multi-track recording program.

An *audio interface* is an audio input box (like the four-input MBox for the Mac) that converts incoming audio signals (such as those from a microphone or guitar cord) to digital signals and then writes them onto your hard drive.

To play back and mix together multiple music tracks of recorded audio, or to record more than one stereo track at a time, you'll need another program. Pro Tools, Cubase (Mac/Win), GarageBand (Mac), Digital Performer (Mac/Win), Nuendo (Win), and Sonar Live! are just a few designed for this task. A multi-track recorder isn't cheap, but it's well worth the investment if you're serious about live recording.

Reason Does Not Record Live Sound!

Reason can take any audio sample, load it into an instrument, and play it back. With its virtual synthesizers, Reason can also create sound, process it with virtual effects, write instrument parts in tracks, and set up mixers to layer them all together—**but Reason is *not* a multi-track recorder.**

What's the difference? Sound-recording and audio-editing software capture live instruments and other sources, whereas Reason plays back existing "samples" or creates its own audio signals internally using its own instruments. In other words, multi-track recorders record and mix live sound; Reason generates its own sound and mixes that.

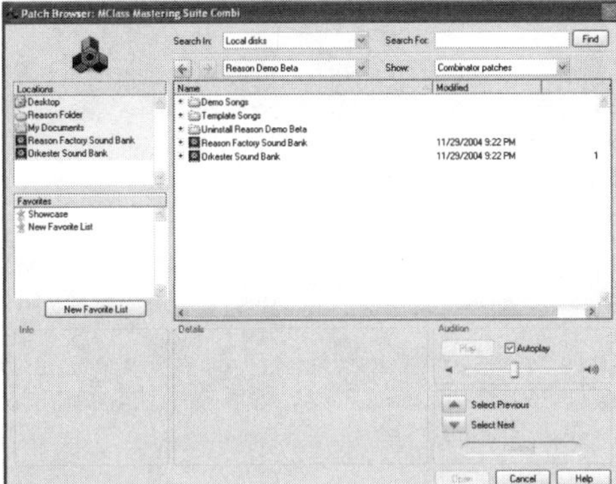

Figure 1.3 Reason's redesigned browser makes finding and auditioning patches easier.

Figure 1.4 The 6:2 Line Mixer saves space in your Rack display.

What's New in 3.0

If you have used earlier versions of Reason, this book will introduce you to a new browser, a line mixer, a mastering suite (four new devices), an improved interface for external control boards and mixing consoles, and even a new macro device called the *Combinator*, which holds any setup as a studio-within-a-studio, fitting neatly into one small Rack device.

The 3.0 browser

The redesigned browser (**Figure 1.3**) now allows you to

- Store as many shortcuts as you want
- Search patches by instrument type, regardless of synthesizer, and audition them using your keyboard
- Create devices from the browser, using a new "Create device by browsing patches" option

The 6:2 Line Mixer

A new six-channel Mixer (**Figure 1.4**) allows you to save Rack and window space. Use it in situations where you don't need the full Mixer and you'll keep your Rack more organized.

The MClass Mastering Suite

Four new sound processors have been introduced in Reason 3.0. Now you have all the tools needed to take your music from the first notes to final production.

The MClass Compressor (Figure 1.5) is an industry-quality dynamic compression unit with all the controls you need.

The MClass Stereo Imager (Figure 1.6) allows you to enhance the stereo spread of a mix, and gives you independent control over high- and low-frequency spread. Use this to enhance and optimize a stereo mix without destroying the bass.

The MClass Equalizer (Figure 1.7) is a top-notch multiband paragraphic equalizer, with a graphic display that helps you to see what you're hearing.

The MClass Maximizer (Figure 1.8) now allows you to create high-gain, distortion-free mixes and keep up with the competition.

Figure 1.5 The MClass Compressor is new in Reason 3.0.

Figure 1.6 The MClass Stereo Imager

Figure 1.7 The MClass Equalizer

Figure 1.8 The MClass Maximizer

Figure 1.9 The Combinator is a MIDI control center, and a studio-in-one device (full view).

Figure 1.10 The Combinator can also save you a lot of Rack space (folded view).

The Combinator

With the brand-new Combinator (**Figure 1.9**), you can save an entire studio setup as a patch, loaded inside one Rack device.

- Save visual Rack "real estate" (**Figure 1.10**).
- Keep your studio manageable, even with extremely complex configurations.
- Create submixes quickly.
- Control multiple devices with a single pattern player or Sequencer track, without complicated cabling.
- Create "mega-instruments."
- Get instrument controls to talk to one another in ways that were previously impossible.

Digital Audio Basics

To operate Reason's synthesizers, you'll need to understand at least one key concept: *waveforms*.

Though invisible, sound waves are just like any other kind of wave. They can be described by their length, height (amplitude), and speed (frequency), and no two waves are exactly alike. The unique combination of length, amplitude, and frequency makes up a sound wave's shape, or *waveform*.

As you can imagine, sounds bouncing around and interacting in the real world can have some pretty complex waveforms. That's why we use *samplers* in Reason to capture the character of not just the unusual, but of even the everyday sounds we want to use in our music.

But Reason and other synthesizers are also able to generate very simple, or "pure," waveforms (sine, sawtooth, triangle, and so on) that can't be found anywhere in nature. Using these pure waveforms has come to be known as *FM* or *analog synthesis*. This synthesized sound has a distinctive character that's become almost synonymous with techno music, and is typically described as "warm" and "rich."

Reason's instruments use both kinds of sounds, allowing you to combine sampled sounds and generated (synthesized) sounds to produce your own unique ones.

Digital audio and sampling

Before you jump into creating sounds in Reason and storing them on your hard drive, you also should understand a little about how audio samples are converted from sound to computer data.

Converting sound waves to digital information means taking a series of "snapshots" of a wave—its length and height at a particular time. These snapshots, or *samples*, are stored together and can then be played back to re-create the sound. The more individual samples you take, the better your re-creation will be.

Sampling rates

Faster sampling can store higher frequencies and produces more-faithful sound reproduction. Sampling formats and rates can vary in digital music, and you will have some choice as to what quality you want to use to store your audio. For example, CD audio means sampling 44,100 times a second (44.1 kHz), and then playing back at the same rate.

The trade-off with very high sampling rates is that better quality means bigger files to store and more processor speed consumed for playback. But if you have space on your hard drive (and most computers come with multigigabyte drives), high sampling rates are well worth it. Many of today's audio cards and hardware can even capture and play back at up to 96 kHz. Keep in mind, though, for burning an audio CD of your music you will need to "downsample" your music to 44.1 kHz at some point, and this may not justify the storage space and processor load required by higher rates.

Dynamics and bit depth

Dynamics are louds and softs over time, and even the most complex waveforms have peaks and valleys (louds and softs). *Bit depth* represents how many different louds and softs your sample contains. Think of bit depth as vertical notches measuring waveform height as a sound plays. The more notches, the more smoothly the louds and softs get captured by the sampler.

Bit depth, or sample size, is just as important as sampling rate in preserving audio quality: Louds and softs get forced to the closest value allowed at a given bit depth. So at a low bit depth, the original sound gets squished to a fairly uniform height, which makes for noise and distortion. CD-quality audio has a bit depth of 16, which does little or no damage; most people don't even notice a difference. However, 8-bit sampling will add significant, noticeable noise and distortion. Lower bit depths do result in much smaller files, but these days that isn't an issue for most people.

If you're finicky about holding on to as much fidelity as you can, you should archive your audio at the highest possible sampling rate and bit depth, even if you later have to downsample for output to CD. If your sound card and driver settings are optimized (see Chapter 2, "Installation"), you can capture your Reason tunes at bit depths of up to 24 and sampling rates up to 96 kHz.

2

INSTALLATION

Although installing Reason is simple enough if you follow the onscreen directions, you need to consider a few factors before you get started. Taking the time to figure out in advance what kind of setup you want for your virtual studio can save you a lot of time later.

In this chapter, we'll go over what you need to get started, as well as a few additional things you may want, such as external controllers. Then we'll look at basic installation and how to configure your Reason settings to get you going.

Before You Start

Take a moment to make sure your system is ready to install Reason, and that you have all the necessary software.

First check to make sure that your system is fast enough and that you have sufficient RAM to run Reason.

Mac OS X system requirements

- G3 or better processor
- System 10.2 or higher
- 256 MB of RAM
- 2 GB of free hard disk space
- CD-ROM drive
- MIDI interface and keyboard recommended

Windows system requirements

- Intel Pentium 3 or better; 300 MHz or faster
- Windows 2000/XP or later
- 256 MB of RAM
- 256-color, 800x600 resolution monitor or better
- 16-bit Windows-compatible audio card; Audio Stream Input/Output (ASIO) or DirectX driver recommended
- MIDI interface and keyboard recommended

Next, make sure that you have a complete Reason 3.0 package.

Reason 3.0 package

- A Program CD
- A Factory Sound Bank CD
- An Orkester Sound Bank CD
- Printed documentation
- An authorization card

Audio Hardware

Now it's time to make sure that your sound system is set up properly so that you can hear.

Mac users

Since Macintosh computers have built-in sound cards, Mac users just need to make sure they have speakers, headphones, or some other monitoring system attached to their computer and that their computer volume control is not off or set to Mute.

Windows users

Windows PCs come with a range of sound cards, so you'll first need to confirm that your card is playing sound properly, and that speakers or headphones are connected properly to your sound card's audio outputs.

If you are installing a new sound card or other hardware, follow the directions provided in your hardware documentation *before* installing Reason on your system. This will minimize confusion as you start configuring Reason.

Users with custom hardware

If you are using a multiple audio input-output interface, check any hardware control panels to make sure that the sound is working before installing Reason.

Windows compatibility

It is recommended you use hardware that is ASIO or Direct X compatible. It is possible to use hardware that is Windows compatible using Microsoft multimedia extensions (MMEs), but doing so will limit your use of Reason to rendering audio files at much slower speeds, making real-time playback difficult or impossible.

To set up audio hardware:

1. Make sure your card or interface drivers are up-to-date and follow your hardware system's instructions for installation.
2. Connect your hardware's stereo outputs to whatever speakers, headphones, or other equipment you plan to use.
3. If possible, test your hardware setup to ensure that audio works before starting Reason (those using Direct X or MME can test with Windows Media Player).

✔ Tip

- If your hardware supports multiple audio outputs, see Appendix A, "ReWire, ReCycle!, ReBirth," to find out how to use Reason in ReWire mode. In ReWire mode you can route all 64 audio interface outputs to tracks in a host application such as Pro Tools, Logic, Digital Performer, Nuendo, or Sonar.

Setting Up MIDI

It is strongly recommended that you use Reason with at least one MIDI keyboard to enjoy its full potential. A MIDI interface with two or more ports is ideal, since you can use both a keyboard to play notes and a control surface for knobs, faders, and buttons.

Before connecting a keyboard, make sure that any MIDI interface you are using is installed with the correct drivers and connected properly.

To connect a keyboard:

◆ Connect the USB cable from your keyboard to your computer (the simpler of the two methods).

or

◆ Connect your keyboard's MIDI out cable to a MIDI in port on your MIDI interface.

You should also connect the keyboard's MIDI in cable to the interface's MIDI out port.

✔ Tip

■ If you want to use multiple keyboards or control surfaces, you should use separate MIDI ports. If you have USB-compatible keyboards or surfaces, connect them directly to your computer's USB ports (see "Setting Up Control Surfaces" later in this chapter).

Installing Reason

Insert the Reason CD labeled "Program Disc" into your CD-ROM drive. What you'll do next depends on whether you are installing on a Windows computer or a Mac.

To install in Windows:

1. The installer may start automatically when you insert the Program CD. If not, find the Install Reason program and double-click it.
2. The Reason setup wizard will launch, asking you to close other programs before clicking Next (**Figure 2.1**).
3. Specify an install location, and indicate whether you want a desktop shortcut/alias added (**Figure 2.2**).
4. At the prompt, click Install to continue (**Figure 2.3**).

   The setup wizard will begin installation (**Figure 2.4**).
5. When the installer is finished, check the Launch Reason box if you want to launch Reason to finish the installation, and click Finish.

To install in Mac OS:

1. Double-click the `Reason.dmg` file on the CD. When the disc image loads, drag the `Reason` file to the `Applications` folder on your hard disk.
2. Go to the `Applications/Reason` folder, select the Reason 3.0 icon, and press Cmd+M to create an alias.
3. Move the Reason alias to your desktop or Dock.

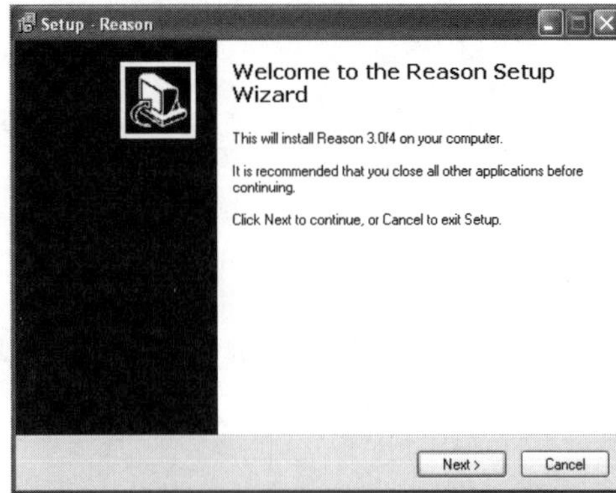

Figure 2.1 The Reason setup wizard will guide you through installation.

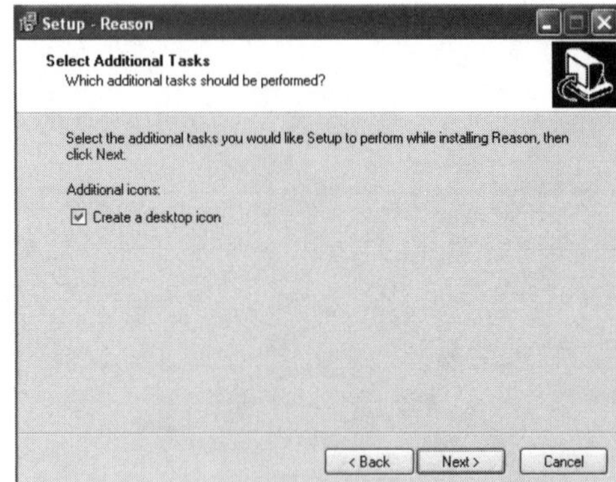

Figure 2.2 Choose whether you want a desktop alias.

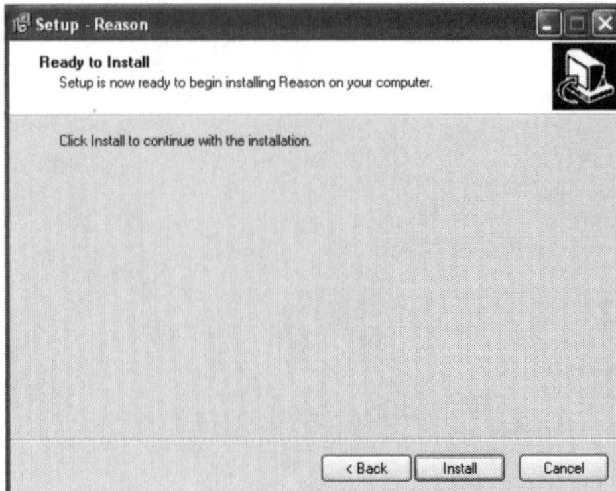

Figure 2.3 Click Install to begin installing.

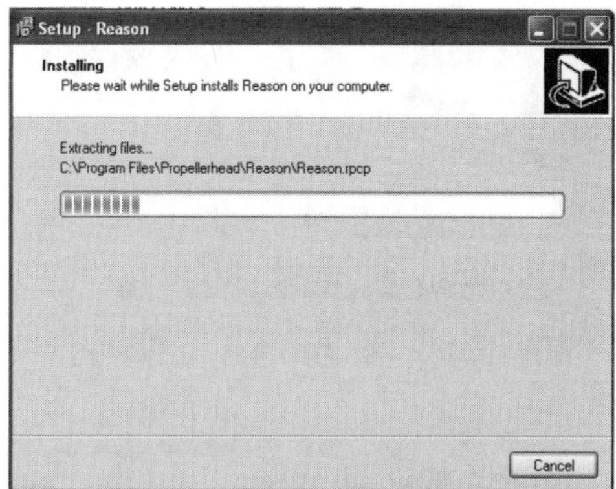

Figure 2.4 The install status bar gives you an idea of how much longer you'll have to wait.

Figure 2.5 When launching Reason for the first time, you will be prompted to insert the Orkester Sound Bank CD.

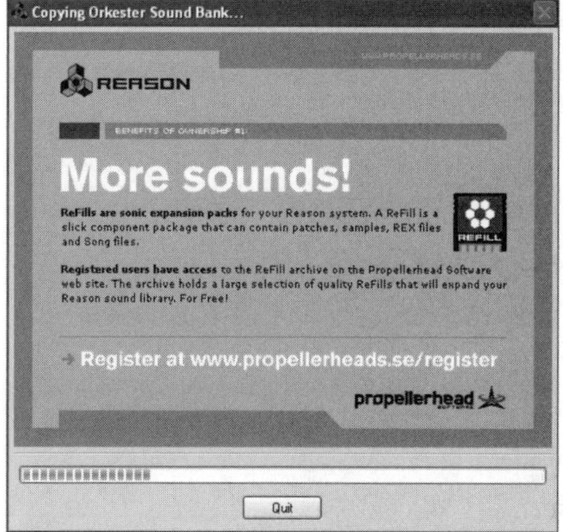

Figure 2.6 The screen will display information about Reason while the sound bank copies to your drive.

Installing the sound banks

The first time you launch Reason, you will be asked to insert the Factory and Orkester sound bank CDs. These each contain one large file, or sound bank, that will need to be copied to your local drive.

This process takes a few minutes—on the bright side, keep in mind that nearly 1.5 GB of sounds are being installed to your hard drive.

To launch Reason the first time:

1. Open and read any read-me files in the Reason folder; they may contain important information for the build version you are running.
2. In Windows, if you did not check the Launch Reason box, you will need to select Reason from the Start menu or double-click the Reason icon on your desktop or in the program folder.

   or

   Mac users, you will need to click the Reason alias in your Dock, or double-click your Reason 3.0 alias or program icon.
3. Read the licensing agreement and accept by clicking Agree before proceeding.
4. When prompted, insert the Orkester Sound Bank CD (**Figure 2.5**).

   The Orkester Sound Bank will copy to your Reason program folder, and a meter will display the task progress (**Figure 2.6**).

continues on next page

5. When prompted, insert the Factory Sound Bank CD.

   The Factory Sound Bank will copy to your Reason folder (**Figure 2.7**).

6. Type in the license number on the authorization card included in your package (**Figure 2.8**).

7. If you have an Internet connection and want access to additional sounds and upcoming program updates, click Register Now.

   You can also skip registration by clicking Later. You can register any time using the Product Registration command in the Help (Win) or Contact (Mac) menu, or at www.propellerhead.se/register.

8. Click Continue and the Reason setup wizard will guide you through basic settings.

Using the Reason setup wizard

Once you have finished installation, it's time to start up Reason. The setup wizard appears the first time you run Reason, to help you set up your preferences. If you don't like the settings, you can always change them in the preferences later (which we cover in the next section).

To use the setup wizard:

1. In the Reason setup wizard, click Next to continue. (If you already know your way around Reason's preferences, you can go ahead and click Open Preferences Dialog.)

2. You will be prompted to choose an audio driver and a sampling rate from a drop-down list.

   Reason will select the first compatible driver it detects, and a default sample rate of 44,100 (CD quality). If your hardware supports higher sampling rates, you can choose one from the drop-down list (**Figure 2.9**).

Figure 2.7 Insert the Factory Sound Bank CD when prompted to do so.

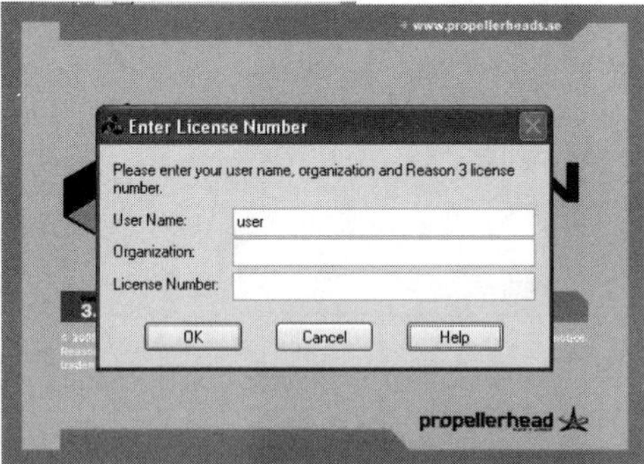

Figure 2.8 At the Reason 3.0 authorization window, you'll need to type in your name and license number.

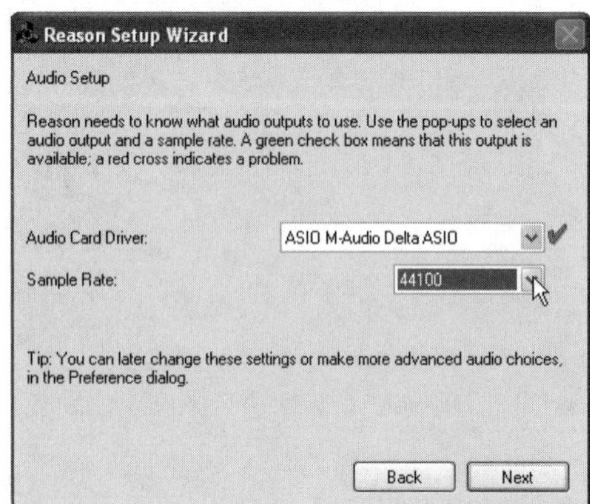

Figure 2.9 Choose a higher sampling rate, if your system supports it.

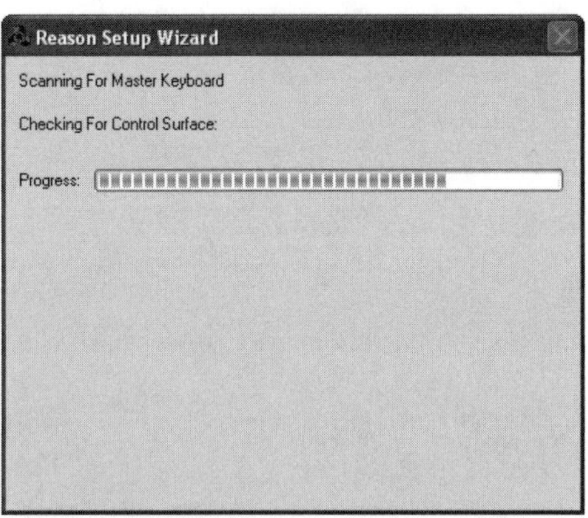

Figure 2.10 Reason will scan your system for your master keyboard.

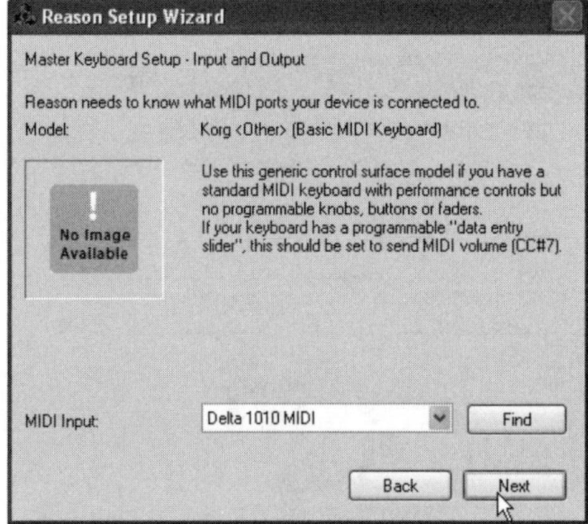

Figure 2.11 Choose a MIDI port from the list of those detected.

3. Click Next when you are done.

   or

   If your audio driver isn't displayed, see the sidebar "Troubleshooting Drivers."

4. The setup wizard will start scanning for a master keyboard (**Figure 2.10**). Choose a detected MIDI keyboard manufacturer and model (if yours is not detected or listed, select Other); click Next when you're done.

   Reason only detects keyboards with two-way communication. If your keyboard/surface is connected to the computer via USB, you should have two-way communication. If it's connected to the computer through a MIDI interface box, you'll have two-way communication only if both a MIDI out and MIDI in cable are joining the keyboard and the MIDI interface.

5. Choose a MIDI port from the MIDI Input list (**Figure 2.11**); click Next to continue.

continues on next page

Troubleshooting Drivers

If your audio driver isn't showing up in the Reason setup wizard, first check your connections. Shut the wizard down by clicking Cancel; then double-check that your audio hardware is working properly.

If your hardware *is* working, try starting up Reason and the setup wizard again. If the driver you want is still not listed, you may need to use a different driver that is compatible with Reason, or download a more recent driver update from your hardware manufacturer. Look in your hardware manual for support information.

You can find a list of hardware supported by Reason on the Propellerhead Web site (www.propellerhead.se) in the Support area. Be sure you have your authorization card handy, as you'll need that number to access the support articles.

6. If no MIDI port is listed, click Find (**Figure 2.12**).

   The Find option allows you to set a MIDI port by playing a few notes on your keyboard (**Figure 2.13**).

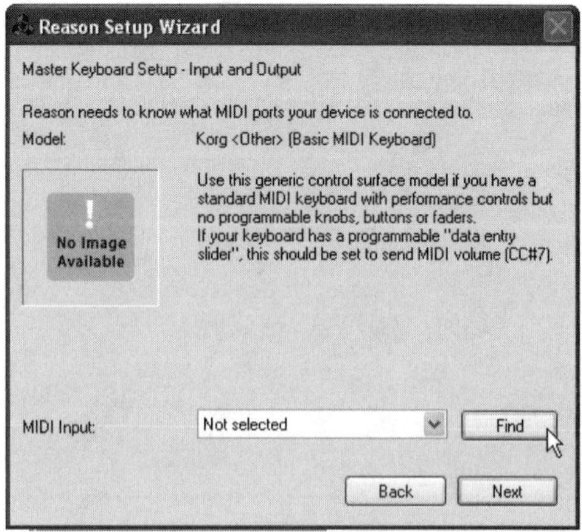

Figure 2.12 If no MIDI port is listed, click Find.

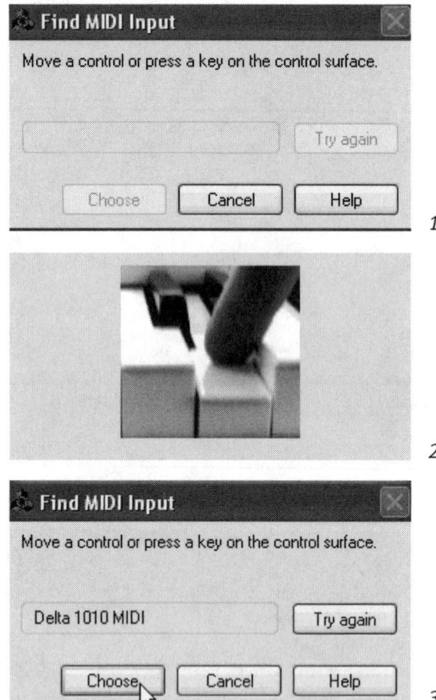

Figure 2.13 The Find MIDI Input window lets you play a few notes to set up your keyboard for use with Reason.

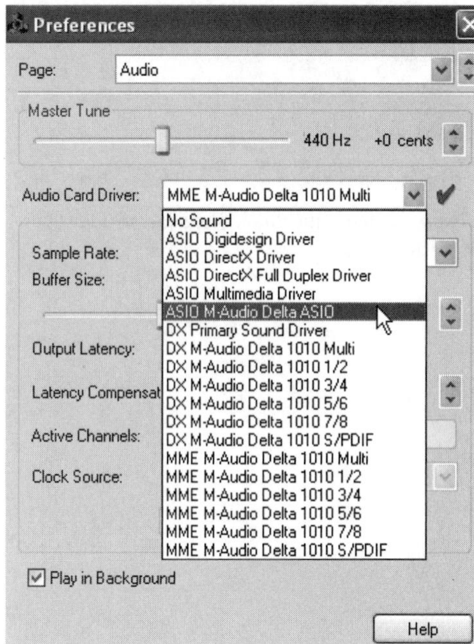

Figure 2.14 Whenever possible, choose an ASIO driver that is tailored to your hardware.

Changing Preferences

Finding the right driver may require you to go back to the Audio Preferences dialog after you begin working in Reason and change some settings.

To change the Mac OS X driver:

1. To choose a different driver, select Reason > Preferences > Audio.
2. Select a driver from the Audio Card Driver drop-down list. Options not applicable to your setup will be grayed out.

To change the Windows driver:

1. To choose a driver go to Preferences > Audio.
2. Select a driver from the Audio Card Driver drop-down list. Options not applicable to your setup will be grayed out.

   The best possible driver will be one that is both specific to your hardware and ASIO (**Figure 2.14**).
3. If no ASIO driver is available for your hardware, select a Direct Sound driver. Select the MME driver only if you can't use ASIO or Direct Sound drivers.

✔ Tip

- With Direct Sound, Reason uses Microsoft DirectX to communicate with your hardware. To use it, DirectX must be installed on your computer.

Optimizing latency with buffer size

Besides drivers, the most important audio setting is Buffer Size. How this setting affects output latency is critical.

If you have to use the MME driver, expect a significant lag (called *latency*) between when a control or note is triggered and the resulting sound. It is possible to slightly decrease the latency in the Audio Preferences dialog.

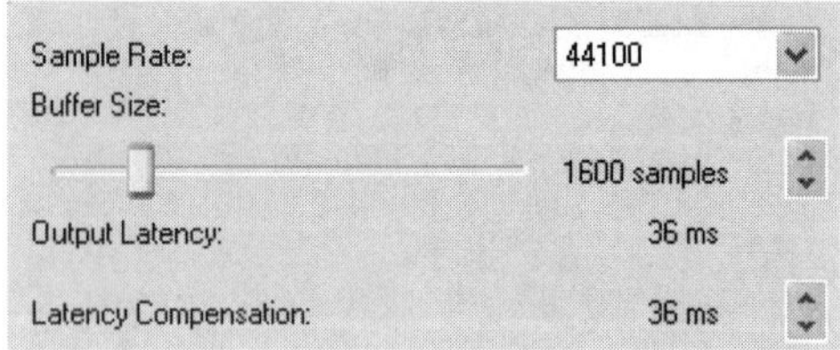

Figure 2.15 Move the Buffer Size slider to adjust the latency.

To adjust latency with buffer size:

1. Go to Preferences > Audio and select the driver you want to adjust the buffer size for.
2. Move the Buffer Size slider to lower the latency (**Figure 2.15**). Some drivers won't allow you to adjust this. If the Buffer Size slider is grayed out for a particular driver, try selecting another.

   A smaller buffer size means less latency, but smaller buffers also rely more on processor speed. The trick is to find the smallest buffer size possible without breaking up the sound.
3. When you've adjusted the buffer size, close the Preferences dialog and play the Demo Song to see if your audio is smooth sounding.

   If you have a keyboard set up, use that to test the sound.
4. If the Buffer Size slider is grayed out, you may be able to adjust it in your hardware controls. You can access these controls from Reason's Audio Preferences dialog by clicking the Control Panel button.
5. If latency on your system is still a problem, look on the Internet for recent ASIO or Direct Sound drivers for your hardware setup. If none are available, you may have to purchase a more compatible sound card or hardware setup.

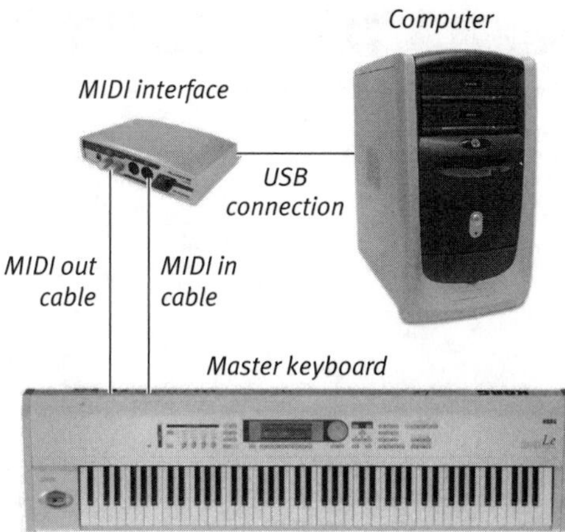

Figure 2.16 This bidirectional MIDI setup connects a keyboard to a computer via a MIDI interface box.

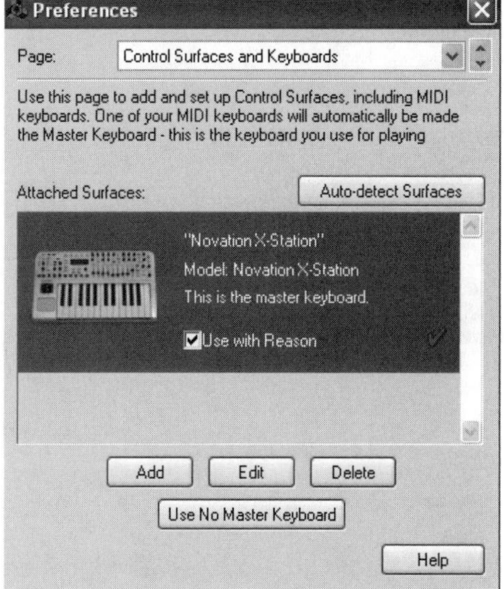

Figure 2.17 Click the Auto-detect Surfaces button in the Preferences dialog.

Figure 2.18 Activate a surface in Reason by clicking the Use with Reason check box.

Setting Up Control Surfaces

Reason supports many major brands of control surfaces, allowing you to automatically map the knobs, faders, and buttons to the most-often-used controls on the Reason devices.

A typical control surface will look similar to a mixer, and will have a number of knobs, faders, and buttons on it that can be used to control the virtual knobs, faders, and buttons in Reason.

For Reason to detect a control surface, it must be a supported brand, and must be connected either directly to your computer via a USB cable or bidirectionally through a MIDI interface, with both MIDI in and out cables properly attached (**Figure 2.16**).

To detect control surfaces:

1. Select Preferences > Control Surfaces and Keyboards (in Mac, that's a submenu of the Reason menu).
2. Click Auto-detect Surfaces (**Figure 2.17**).
3. To activate a surface for use in Reason, select the surface icon in the Attached Surfaces pane and click the Use with Reason check box (**Figure 2.18**).

If you are not using a supported surface, or are using a unidirectional MIDI setup (MIDI out from your keyboard only), you can manually add your control surface.

To manually add a control surface:

1. From the Control Surfaces and Keyboards page in the Preferences dialog, click the Add button (**Figure 2.19**).

   This will bring up the Control Surface edit window (**Figure 2.20**).

2. Choose a manufacturer from the drop-down list, or select Other.

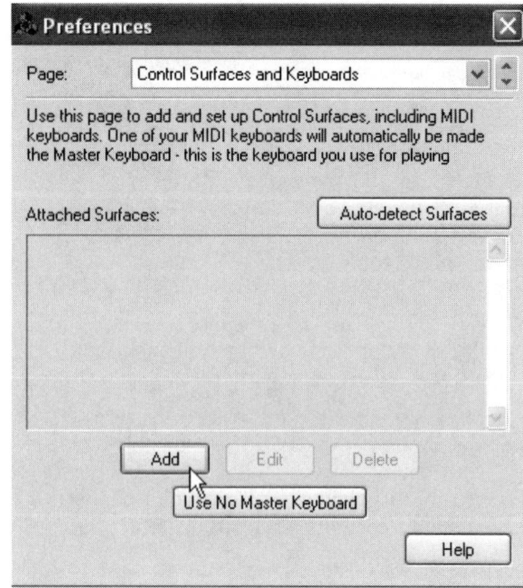

Figure 2.19 Add a surface manually by clicking the Add button.

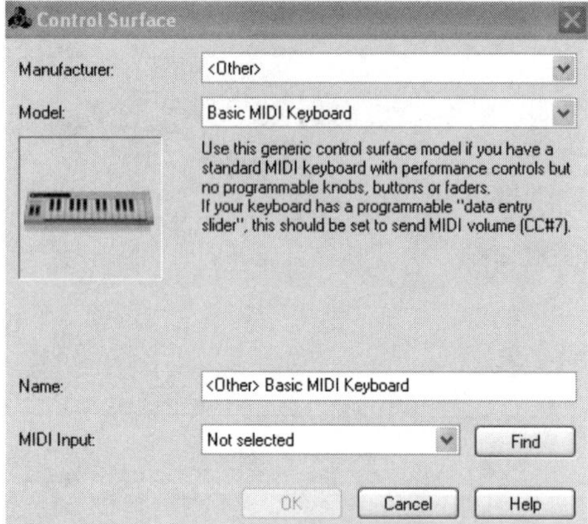

Figure 2.20 The Control Surface edit window lets you manually configure your control surface.

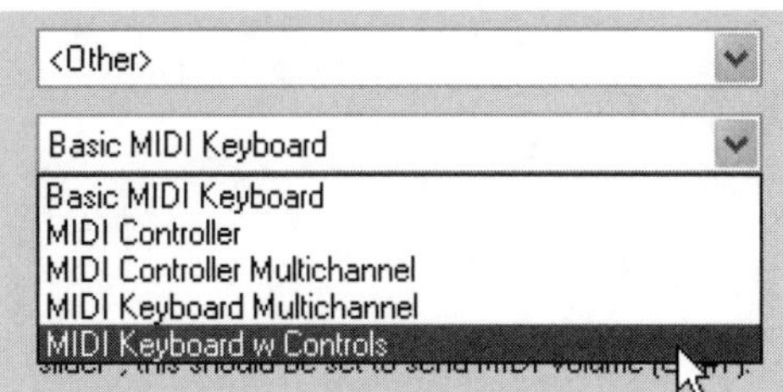

Figure 2.21 Choose a generic keyboard type for an unsupported manufacturer.

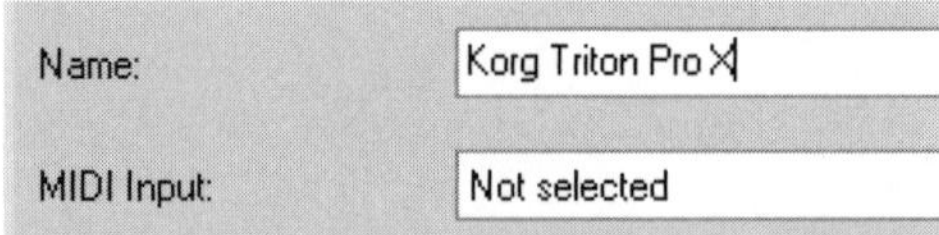

Figure 2.22 Type whatever you want in the Name field.

Figure 2.23 Pick a MIDI input port from the list.

3. Choose from the list of keyboard types, or choose Other (**Figure 2.21**).
4. If you are using Other, type in a name for your device (**Figure 2.22**).
5. Choose an input port for this device from the MIDI Input drop-down list (**Figure 2.23**).
6. If no MIDI input ports have been detected, follow the Find MIDI input procedure in the section "Using the Reason setup wizard" earlier in this chapter.

   If no MIDI in ports are shown, make sure your keyboard is connected properly. If it is, you should be able to click Find and use the Find MIDI Input window again.

✔ Tip

- Reason control surface drivers are constantly being developed, so check the Propellerhead Web site to download the latest ones.

Reason Overview

In this chapter we'll take a quick look around the Reason interface and get an overview of what working in Reason will be like.

If Reason is your first music studio, chances are the interface looks to you like a mad scientist's lab. Don't panic; this chapter will help you get your lab in order before starting to create your first monster project.

Getting Around in Reason

The first thing you'll see when you launch Reason is the Demo Song (**Figure 3.1**). Anytime you have Reason running, you're looking at a *song*—the Reason file format. We'll use the Demo Song to see and hear what Reason instruments sound and look like, and to see how music looks after it's recorded.

The Demo Song is a typical finished Reason project, with stacks of knob-plastered devices and a host of music tracks.

Figure 3.1 The Demo Song

Introduction to the Rack and Sequencer

The Reason interface has two windows: One reads music, and the other one plays it.

The lower window is your writing workspace and is called the *Sequencer*. Think of it as sheet music. The upper window, your studio, is called the *Rack*. It plays the notes and makes the sound—your orchestra (albeit a shiny modular one with lots of knobs!).

The Sequencer and Rack are invisibly connected and work together.

Start a new song by setting up the Rack. It's a one-step process, and you'll build your studio one instrument at a time as you write, adding more gear as it's needed. The Rack can be as complex or simple as you want it to be; it's up to you.

For now, let's look at the Rack used by the Demo Song (**Figure 3.2**).

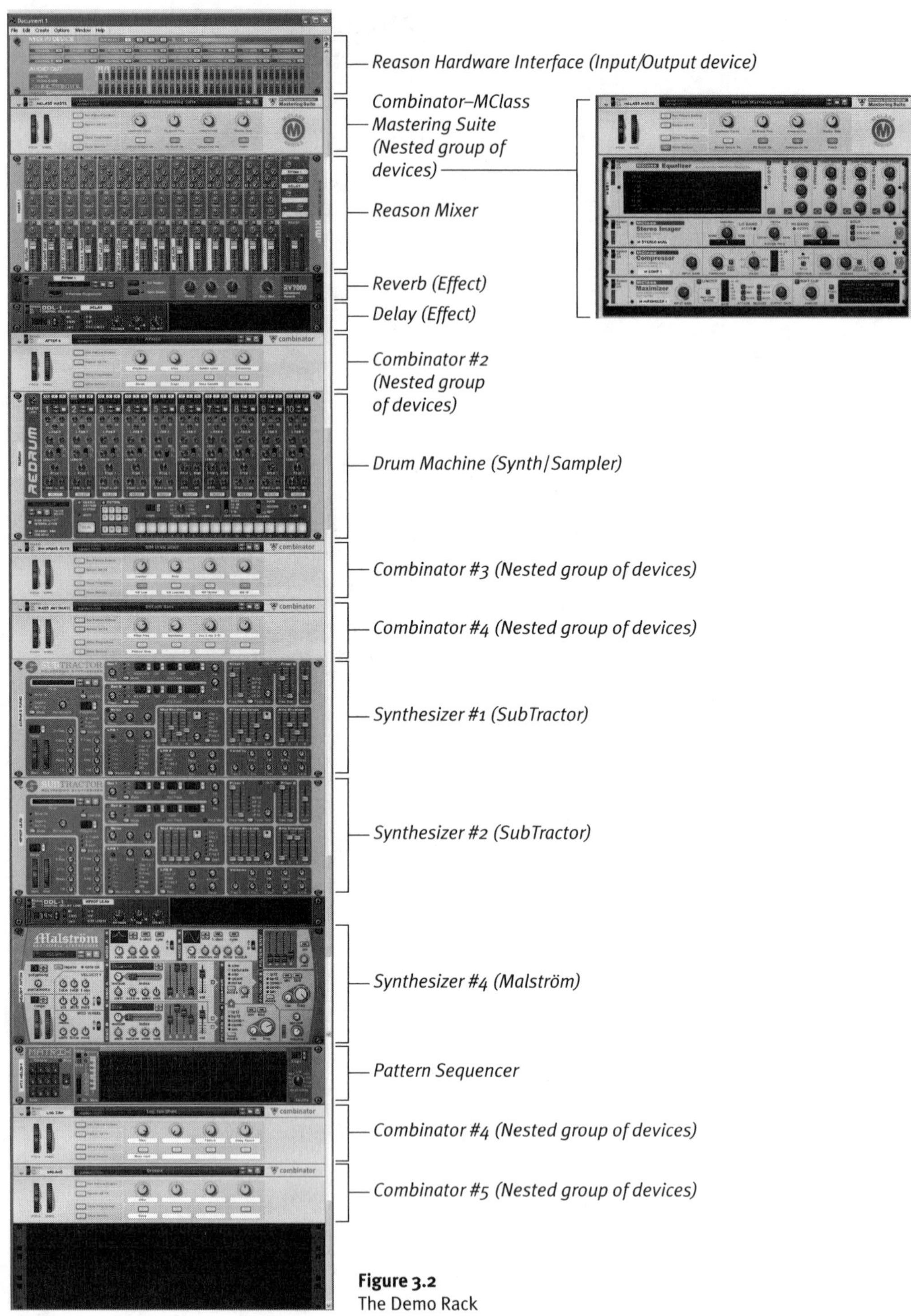
Reason Hardware Interface (Input/Output device)
Combinator–MClass Mastering Suite (Nested group of devices)
Reason Mixer
Reverb (Effect)
Delay (Effect)
Combinator #2 (Nested group of devices)
Drum Machine (Synth/Sampler)
Combinator #3 (Nested group of devices)
Combinator #4 (Nested group of devices)
Synthesizer #1 (SubTractor)
Synthesizer #2 (SubTractor)
Synthesizer #4 (Malström)
Pattern Sequencer
Combinator #4 (Nested group of devices)
Combinator #5 (Nested group of devices)

Figure 3.2
The Demo Rack

To play a song in Reason:

1. To listen to the song, press the spacebar, or click the play button on the transport bar at the bottom of the screen, under the Sequencer (**Figure 3.3**).

   As the song plays, a *position bar* scrolls from left to right in the Sequencer.

2. To stop the song, press the spacebar again or click the stop button on the transport bar.

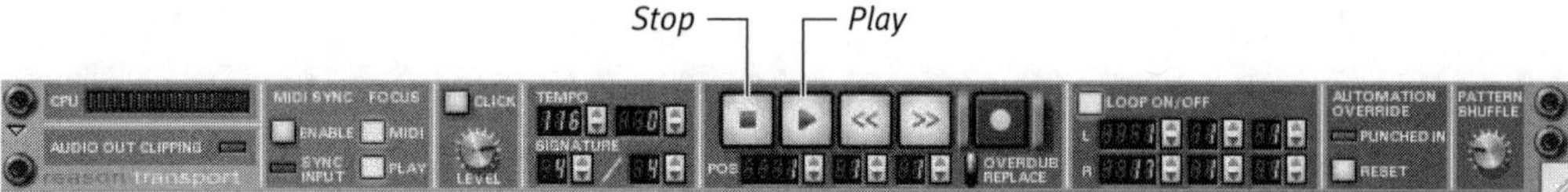

Figure 3.3 The transport bar's play controls

Meet the Mixer

Now look at the Rack (top window) to see the Mixer (**Figure 3.4**). From the Mixer you can control the volume levels of all the instruments that are playing in the song.

Each vertical strip on the Mixer represents the sound coming from a particular instrument, and represents a Mixer audio *channel*. As the song plays, signal levels go up and down on the channel indicators. The Mixer funnels all these channels into one stereo sound coming through your speakers.

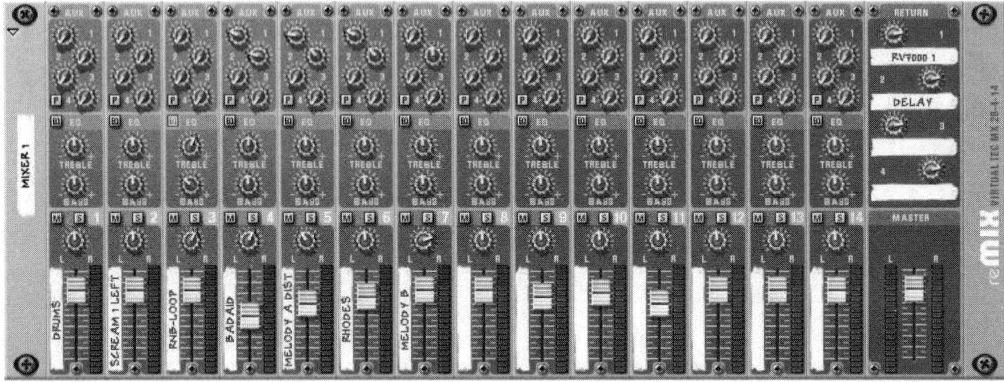

Figure 3.4 The Rack Mixer

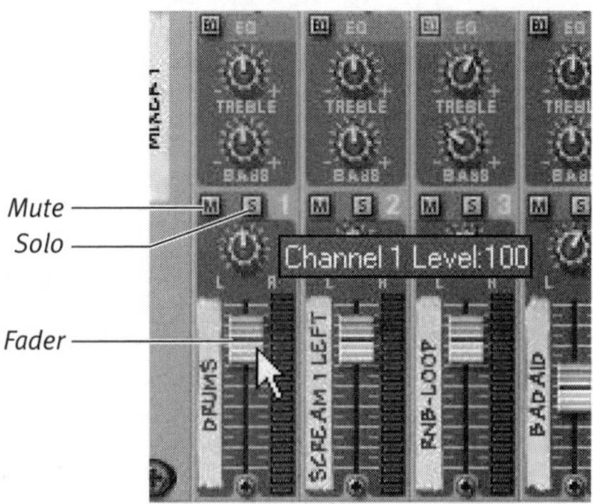

Figure 3.5 Moving channel faders

To use the Mixer:

1. With a song playing, move the channel fader on the Mixer up and down to change the volume for an instrument (**Figure 3.5**).
2. Hit the *Solo* button on a Mixer channel to hear that channel by itself. You can solo as many channels as you want—Solo just mutes the un-soloed channels.
3. Hit the *Mute* button to silence a channel. (Solo overrides mute; you don't have to "unmute" in order to solo.)

The Reason Work Process

For a typical project in Reason, you'll create a Mixer, add a device such as a drum machine or a synth, record the parts, listen to them, edit them, add more devices or parts as needed, fine-tune them, add effects, arrange the tracks, mix the song, master the final version, and save the results as an audio file that can be burned to an audio CD.

Here's what the process can look like in slightly more detail:

- **For a brief setup, start with a Mixer.** The Mixer is where the instruments in your studio (such as a drum machine or a synthesizer) plug in so that you can hear them (more on this in Chapter 4, "Getting Started"). Once the Mixer is created, all the instruments will plug into it automatically (**Figure 3.6**).

Figure 3.6 A basic setup using a Mixer and a drum machine

- **Write a music track.** Create your first instrument; then move to the Sequencer window to write and edit the instrument's part (discussed in Chapter 4). Input the notes using a typical music keyboard, or just use your mouse. Working on one track at a time, you'll add some notes, play them back, and move on to the next track (**Figure 3.7**). Add another instrument and repeat the process.

continues on next page

Figure 3.7 Write a drum track using the Sequencer.

- **Mix sparingly.** After two or more parts are written, you'll start adjusting the balance between the parts (**Figure 3.8**). Keep the mix rough, though—every added instrument changes the way the other instruments sound against one another. The real mixing work comes at the end (more on this in Chapter 10, "Arranging and Mixing").
- **Tweak some knobs.** Once you have your basic tracks, it's time to experiment with the knobs and control levers on your instruments (**Figure 3.9**). Later you may decide to write knob movements during recording; we'll get to this in Chapter 6, "Working with Samplers." You can even input pinpoint-accurate controller tracks in your track, using the Pencil tool (**Figure 3.10**).

Figure 3.8 Balance instrument levels in the Mixer.

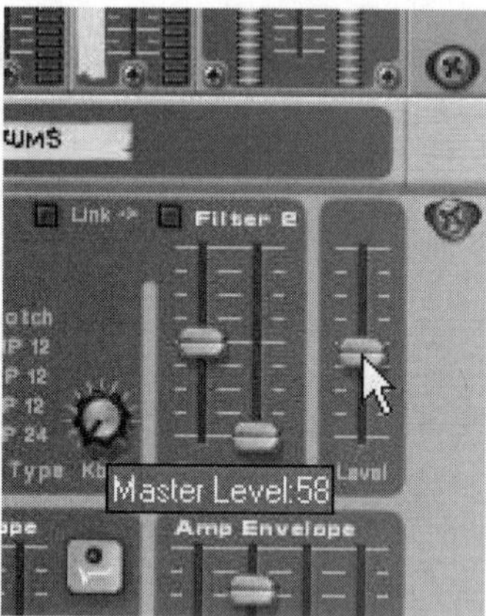

Figure 3.9 Create exact volume changes for a synthesizer.

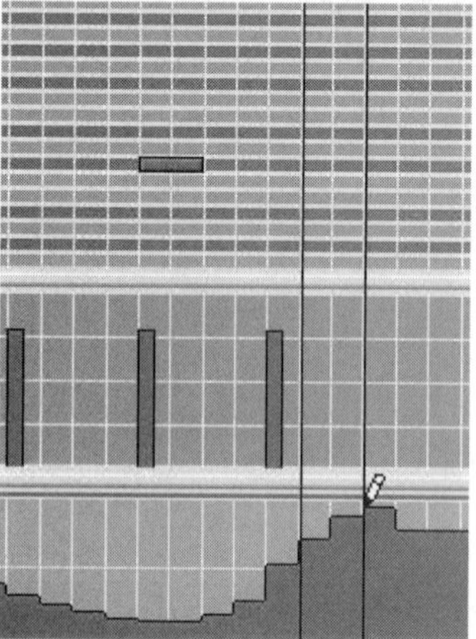

Figure 3.10 Quickly record synth knob movements directly in the Rack.

Preset Sounds: The Factory Sound Bank

You can make music in Reason without ever touching a control knob, using instrument presets from Reason's *Factory Sound Bank*. Audition or switch sounds during playback using Reason's redesigned *patch browser*. You'll use these *patches* to start exploring the different instruments, and learn how to tweak the controls to make your own patches later.

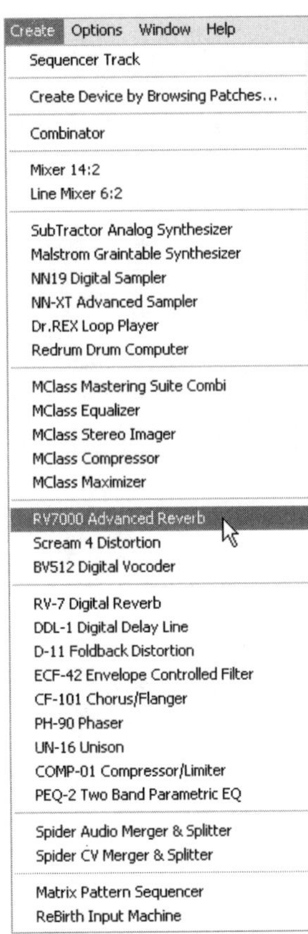

Figure 3.11 Add effects devices.

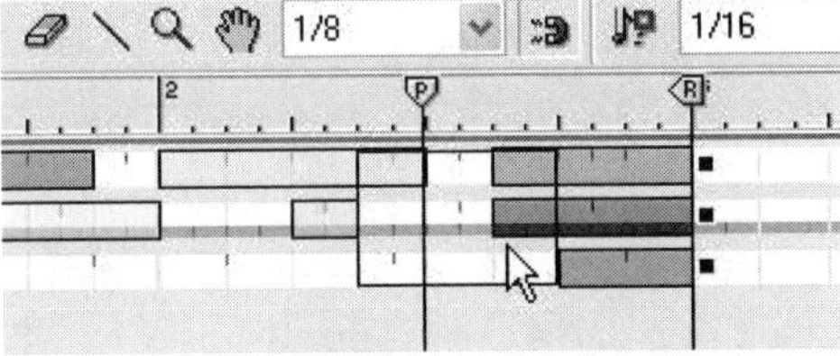

Figure 3.12 Drag selected sections from three adjacent tracks to a new location.

- **Add effects.** After recording and tweaking, you'll want to experiment with some effects (more on this in Chapter 8, "Effects"). Creating effects works just like creating instruments (**Figure 3.11**). And Reason's effects can do much more than add ambience—they can help you finalize a mix, bring instruments to the forefront, or make crazy otherworldly sounds with just a tiny bit of experimenting.
- **Arrange tracks.** Don't like your song the way it is? Move parts around, repeat sections, or add breaks and additional ornamental parts easily in Reason's *Arrange view* in the Sequencer (discussed in Chapter 10). Arrange view lets you shuffle parts, move or repeat song sections, and polish the overall construction of the song (**Figure 3.12**).

- **Fine-tune the mix.** Zero in on your final version by fine-tuning the mix without fussing with your instrument sounds. Make adjustments to the tone and balance of your tracks easily using Reason's powerful tone equalizing tools (EQs).
- **Master your song.** Use Reason's MClass *mastering tools* to smooth out or boost the levels of your tracks and optimize them for CD. Fine-tune the overall EQ, adjust the stereo spread, or add compression. Make the final version jump out in an audition by making it as loud as it can be without distortion.
- **Burn your music to CD and test it out.** Pop out multiple versions of your song as separate .wav files (**Figure 3.13**) and burn them to CD (more on this in Chapter 11, "Mastering").
- **Wrap up.** Burn a CD.

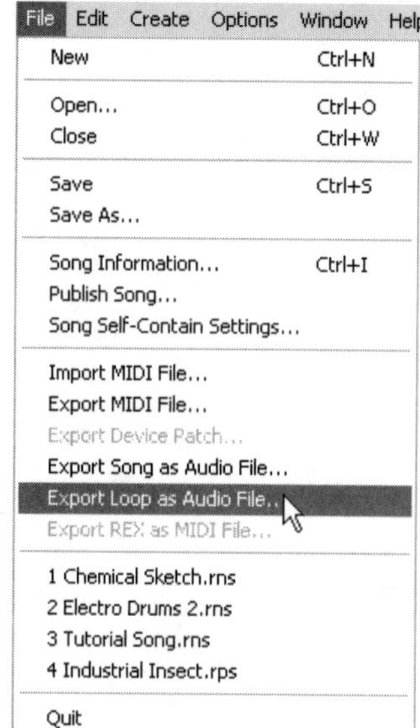

Figure 3.13 Export a song as an audio file.

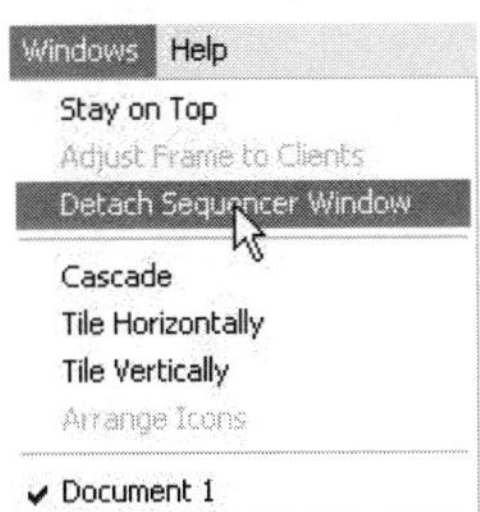

Figure 3.14 Detach the Sequencer window.

Switching Windows

Working with Reason will involve a lot of switching between the Rack and the Sequencer windows. Switching is faster when they are detached.

To detach the windows:

- From the Windows menu, select Detach Sequencer Window (**Figure 3.14**). Or click the Detach button at the top-right of the Rack window.

Now you can see more in both windows, or move your Sequencer to a second monitor. Switch between them by clicking the window you want, or choosing it from the Windows menu. Faster still, hitting Ctrl+Tab in Windows switches you between the Rack and Sequencer; on a Mac, Cmd+1 brings up the Rack and Cmd+2 moves to the Sequencer.

What's in the Sequencer?

Let's look at where you will write "tracks," or parts (**Figure 3.15**).

The Sequencer window starts off with an overview of all the tracks in the song (the Arrange view). The Rack instruments are listed in the left column, and the parts are to the right.

Arrange view lets you drag parts around and decide how you want them all to fit together. The instrument column lets you create new tracks (you can send more than one track to the same instrument) or switch devices for a given track.

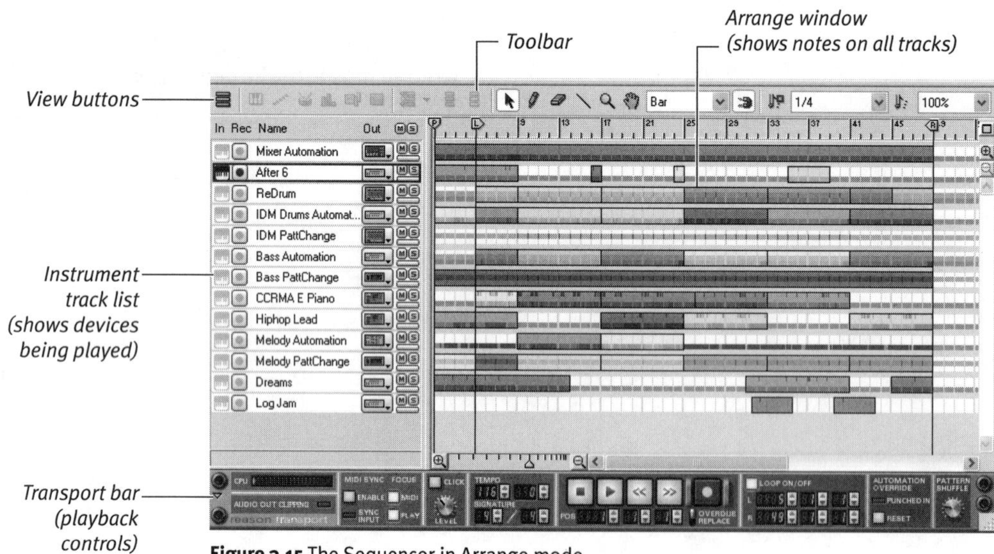

Figure 3.15 The Sequencer in Arrange mode

What Is a Sequencer?

Anything that can store a series of notes and then read them back is a sequencer.

One low-tech analogy for a sequencer is a player piano holding sheet music. A sequencer does both tasks. It stores the parts and then plays them back. The Rack is the piano that makes the sound.

When you write in the Reason Sequencer window, you are essentially writing a score to be performed; you're not creating the actual musical performance. The music is not created until the Sequencer sends your score to the Rack, where your instruments perform it.

The advantage of Reason over our low-tech player-piano example is that any performance can be sent to any instrument. Want to hear how that bass line sounds playing a vocal sample? Send the same performance to a different instrument with just a click of the mouse.

MIDI: Computer Music Notation

Your Reason Sequencer speaks a language called MIDI (musical instrument digital interface). It records nuances of a performance without storing the actual sound, keeping track of "note on," "note off," "note length," "note strength," and more.

If you are using an external music keyboard to control Reason, chances are you're sending MIDI data into Reason via a five-pin MIDI cable.

For now, don't worry too much about the MIDI language because Reason translates it for you, in much the same way that Microsoft Word handles the code when you type a letter.

The Sequencer Edit Mode

Edit mode is where you get in close and tell an instrument what to play. Unless you use alternative "Rack sequencing" (see Chapter 7, "Patterning"), Edit mode is where you'll spend most of your writing time.

To use Edit mode:

1. In the Sequencer, select the eighth track down ("CCRMA E Piano") in the left column of the Demo Song.
2. Click the Edit mode display button in the upper-left corner (**Figure 3.16**) to look at the track, or press Alt+Tab (Win)/Ctrl+Cmd+E (Mac).

   You should now see a graph showing the notes in Track 8 (CCRMA E Piano), arranged on a grid (**Figure 3.17**).

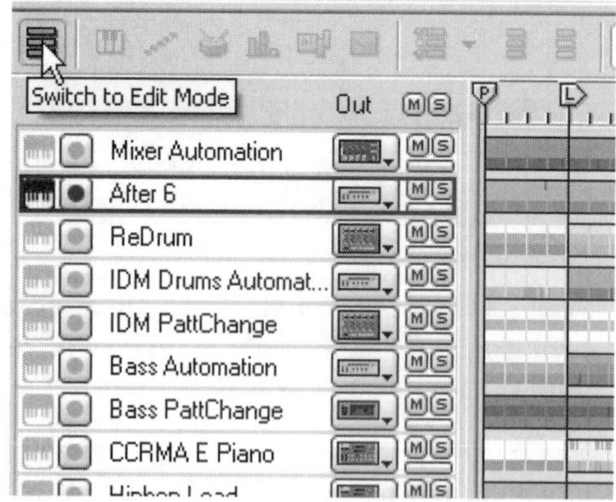

Figure 3.16 The Edit mode display button

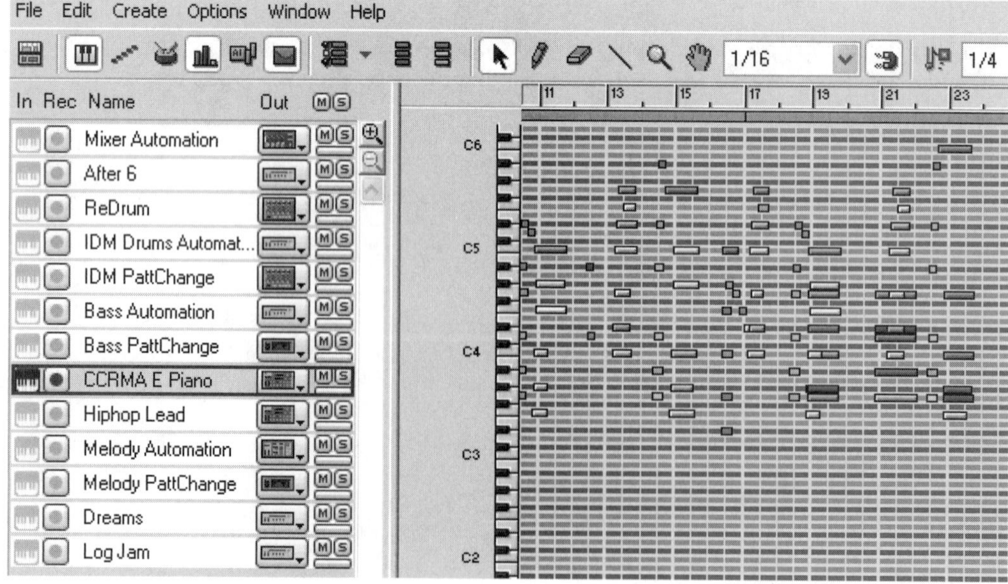

Figure 3.17 A track displayed in Edit mode

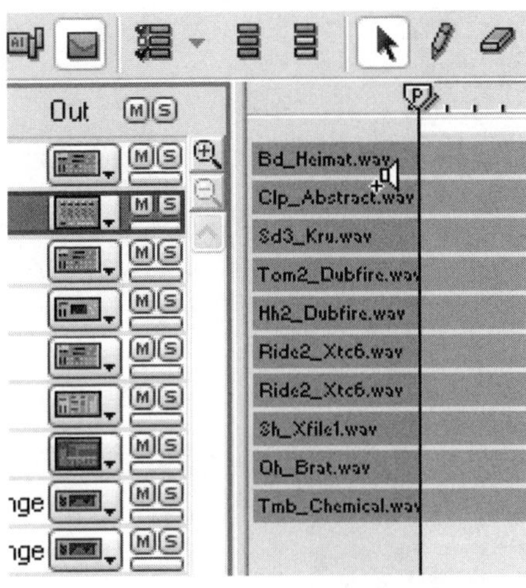

Figure 3.18 Audition notes on the keyboard ruler.

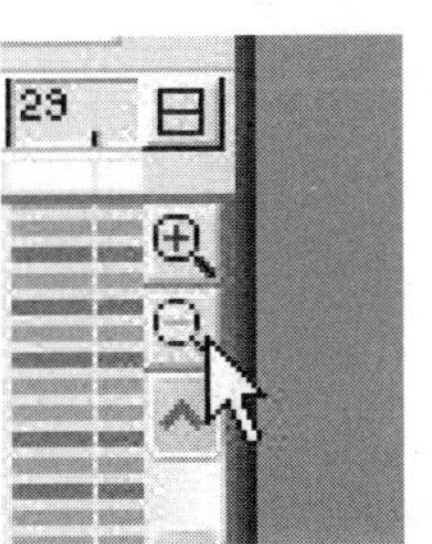

Figure 3.19 The vertical zoom buttons

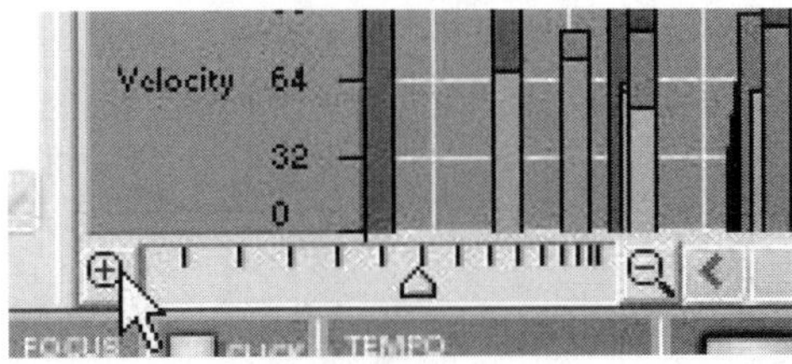

Figure 3.20 The horizontal zoom buttons

3. If necessary, use the scroll bar at the side of the window to scroll up or down and see the notes, or resize your Sequencer window.
4. Move your cursor over the keyboard ruler at the left margin of the track display; when the cursor changes to a speaker icon, click the mouse to audition notes (**Figure 3.18**).
5. To see more or less of the track, use the zoom buttons. Vertical zoom is at the upper-right (**Figure 3.19**) and horizontal zoom is at the lower-left (**Figure 3.20**).

continues on next page

6. Hit the play button on the transport bar (or press the spacebar) to watch the track play. You'll see the display scroll to the right as the song advances.

   Longer notes sustain (**Figure 3.21**) and short notes are staccato (**Figure 3.22**). Soft notes appear in a lighter shade of red than those played very hard and loudly (**Figure 3.23**).

7. Look below the note grid, and you'll see red vertical bars arranged under the notes. This is the *Velocity lane;* the bars represent the strength of the attack, or *velocity,* for each note.

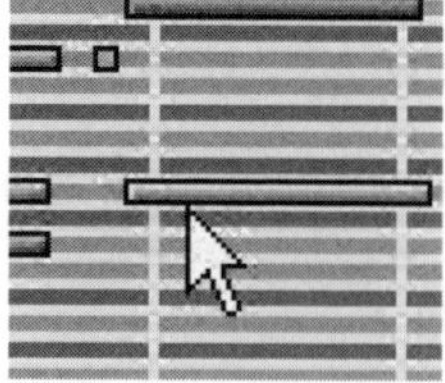

Figure 3.21
A sustained note

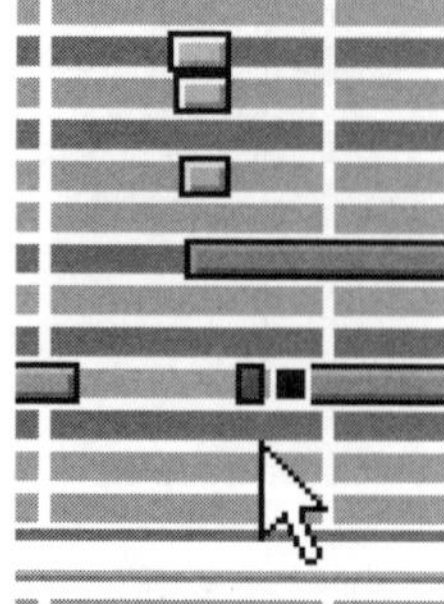

Figure 3.22
A staccato (short) note

✔ Tip

- Velocity is a note's speed of attack, not its volume. (*Volume* is another parameter that has its own controls.) If you're not sure what the difference is, see the sidebar "Velocity vs. Volume."

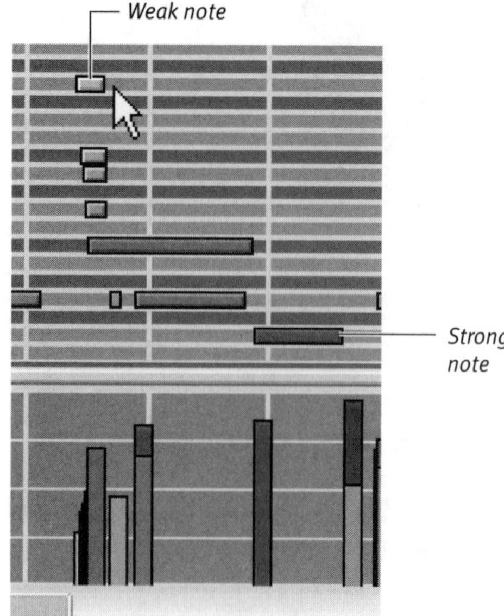

Figure 3.23 Strong vs. light notes

Velocity vs. Volume

Velocity is "relative note strength" and volume is "instrument level."

The term *velocity* comes from the way music keyboards keep track of how hard the performer is hitting a note. Though a piano responds directly to finger pressure, an electronic keyboard only measures how fast a key is struck, or how quickly the key moves between a high and a low sensor when played.

Measuring a key's speed is an economical and stable alternative to measuring pressure, because it minimizes the number of potential moving parts that can wear out; and speed is just as accurate as pressure as an indicator of the strength of note attack.

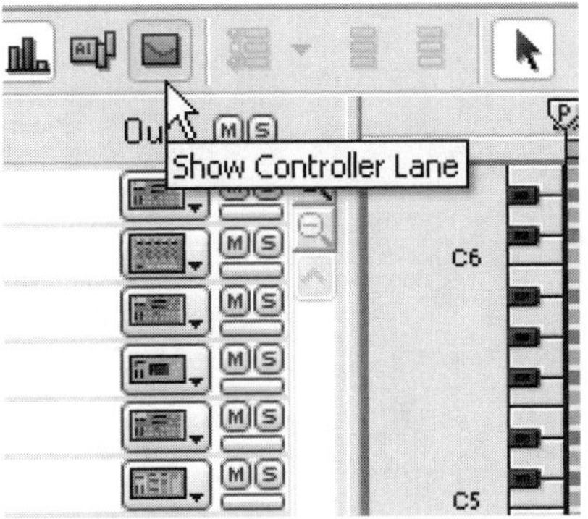

Figure 3.24 Click the Show Controller Lane button.

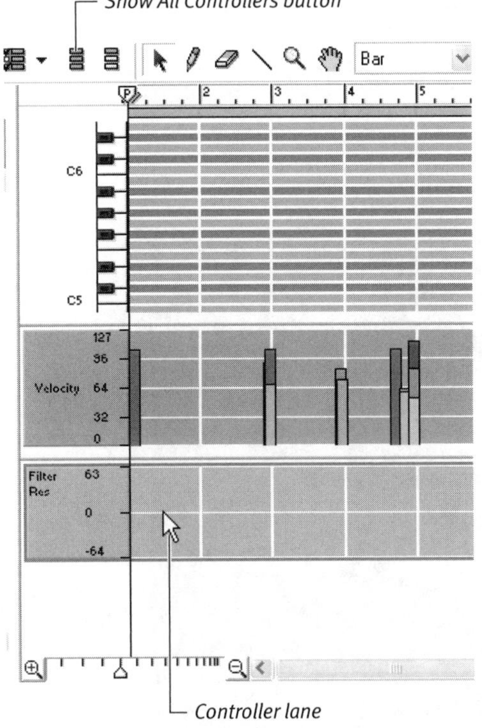

Figure 3.25 The Controller lane

Introducing Controllers

Now that you've looked closely at a track of music in Reason, let's go deeper and get a glimpse into one of Reason's most powerful features: control over instruments.

You can actually record nearly any movement of any knob, lever, or button on a Rack device. The movements are stored in the instrument's Sequencer track and then get sent to the Rack during playback. If you want to see what controller information looks like in a track, you must first tell Reason to display it.

To view Controller lanes:

1. Make sure your Sequencer is in Edit mode.
2. Click the Show Controller Lane button at the top of the Sequencer window (**Figure 3.24**).

   This adds the Controller lane to the bottom of the Sequencer and activates the three controller buttons at the top of the window (**Figure 3.25**). (For details on Controller lane editing, see "Controller Automation" in Chapter 6.)

The Back of the Rack

Reason has the potential to get very complicated when you know enough to get greedy about piling up Rack gear. What if you forget how all your devices are hooked up? What if you run out of Mixer channels? There's a whole other Rack view that we haven't explored—it's the back panel view showing how each device is connected.

To see the back of the Rack:

1. With the Rack window active, press Tab. Voilà! You can see all the cables (**Figure 3.26**).
2. Hold your mouse cursor over one end of a cable; after a short delay, a tool tip pops up, telling you where the other end of the cable is plugged in.

Figure 3.26 The Rack's rear panel

If you haven't tinkered much with real music hardware, this back view may look like spaghetti. Just remember that you'll add the Rack devices one at a time as you build up the tracks of your own song, and Reason takes care of most of the cabling for you.

The back panel really sets Reason apart from other music software: Reason instruments function just like real studio gear—you can hook them up any way you want, and the cables are easy and fast to move! (And you will never have to crawl behind a patch bay in a cramped studio while holding a flashlight in your teeth.)

So if you are using Reason for the first time, take heart. Reason automatically takes care of the rear panel for you in the same way it handles controllers: You don't have to mess with it if you don't want to.

Doing your own cabling is easy, and you can do some amazing things by cabling instruments and effects to one another. For a few samples of what can be done, see Chapter 9, "Cabling Setups."

Understanding Control Voltage (CV)

Now that we know the difference between audio signals and MIDI signals, let's talk about the other kind of signal that Reason uses extensively: control voltage. *Control voltage (CV)* is an electronics term that refers to the way synthesizers communicated in the days before MIDI and computer technology.

Before computers and digital language, synthesizers used electronic control voltages to relay anything from knob movements to "note on" and "note off" messages. Synthesizers were well established when computers arrived, so the new digital instruments were designed to fit the established electronic conventions.

As you start working with synthesizers, you'll become familiar with lots of electronic synth terms, such as *envelope, filter, resonance, LFO*, and others.

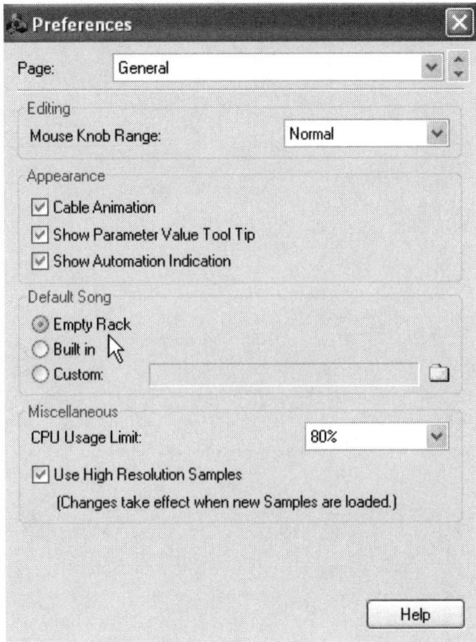

Figure 3.27 Change the Preferences to get rid of the Demo Song.

Getting Rid of the Demo Song

Now that you've had a basic tour of the Reason interface, it's time to get rid of the Demo Song so you can start your first project!

To get rid of the Demo Song:

1. Select Edit > Preferences (Win)/ Reason > Preferences (Mac).
2. Under Default Song, select Empty Rack (**Figure 3.27**).
3. Close the Preferences dialog box and close the Demo Song Rack window.
4. Select File > New.

   A new, empty Rack and Sequencer open, and you're ready to start your first song from scratch.

Getting Started

Now that you've seen an overview of Reason, you're ready to start your first song. In this chapter, you'll learn how to set up your first project by creating a custom Rack and a workspace for writing notes into a track.

Most songs are constructed on top of a rhythm track, so to begin you'll create a beat and fine-tune it a bit. Once you have a beat, you'll have a foundation for adding melodies, bass lines, and ambient sounds to your song.

You'll also learn how to correct timing inaccuracies using Reason's rhythmic grid settings—how they work, when to apply them in your tracks, and some ways to preserve and even enhance a sense of natural "feel" or human timing.

Finally, you'll learn how to save your creation as an audio loop.

Starting Your First Song from Scratch

At the end of the last chapter, you learned how to turn off the Demo Song and set Reason to start with an empty Rack. If you haven't done this yet, you'll need to do it before continuing here.

This chapter assumes you're not using Reason with any other programs and want to set it up as a stand-alone music production program.

Now it's time to set up a new Rack and begin working with Reason's drum computer to write beat loops.

To start a new song:

1. Launch Reason.
2. Select File > New, or Ctrl+N (Win) / Cmd+N (Mac).

   You'll be presented with an empty Sequencer and a Rack containing only the hardware interface (**Figure 4.1**).

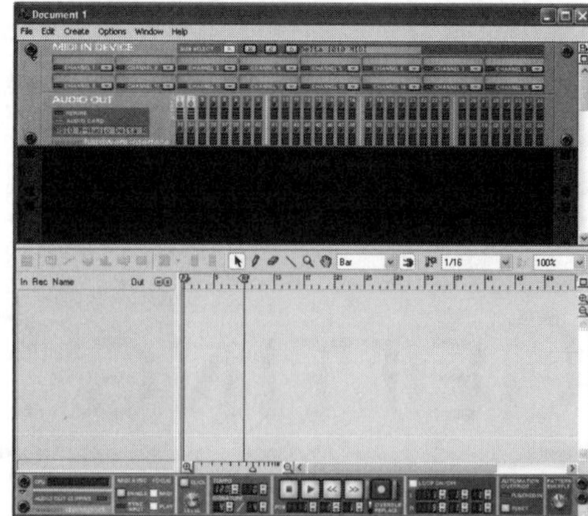

Figure 4.1 An "empty" Rack isn't really empty. All songs in Reason include a hardware interface device.

Figure 4.2 Create a 14:2 Mixer.

Figure 4.3 The Mixer back panel, connected to the hardware interface audio inputs 1 and 2.

The Reason 14:2 Mixer

Now you'll learn how to build up a Rack, and how to set it up so you can start writing.

You'll need to add a Mixer before doing anything else. The first time you create a Mixer, Reason will automatically connect it to your Reason hardware interface. Once this is done, the Mixer will function as a control center for most of the instruments you'll create in the examples of this book.

The Mixer has the capability to independently lower and raise the volumes of all the instruments connected to it, and has tone controls for each channel that will help you further balance these instruments as your song develops and your studio grows.

To create a Mixer:

1. Go to the Create menu and select Mixer 14:2 (**Figure 4.2**).

   A new Mixer appears in your Rack.

2. Press Tab to see the back panel. Reason has automatically connected the Mixer to audio inputs 1 and 2 of the hardware interface (**Figure 4.3**).

✔ Tip

- Using interface audio inputs 3 through 64 only works if you're planning to route Reason's audio signals to another program, or you've set up Reason to route additional audio outputs to a multi-output audio interface.

As you begin adding instruments to your project, you'll want to make more window space in your Rack so you can see what you're doing. All of Reason's instruments and virtual hardware devices can "fold" into a minimized view.

To fold and unfold your devices:

1. Click the down arrow in the upper-left corner of the hardware interface (**Figure 4.4**) to fold the interface and make more visual room (**Figure 4.5**).
2. Click the arrow again to unfold the interface and see it in full view.

   For the time being, leave the hardware interface in a maximized (unfolded) view.

✔ Tip

- You can fold and unfold all the devices in your Rack at once by holding the Alt (Win) / Opt (Mac) key when clicking the fold/unfold arrow.

Figure 4.4 Use the fold arrow to minimize/maximize a piece of Rack hardware. The arrow points right when a device is folded, and down when it's unfolded.

Figure 4.5 The hardware interface in its folded (minimized) state

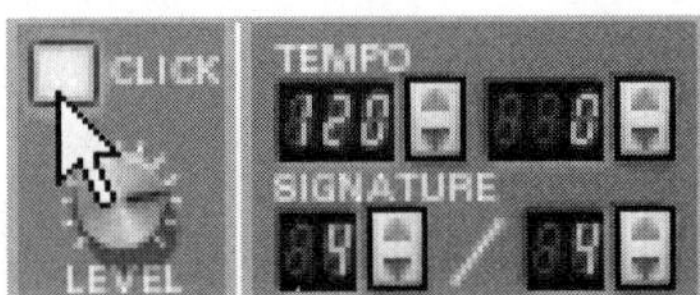

Figure 4.6 The Reason metronome clicks out beats at the selected tempo. To toggle it on or off, just press the Click button.

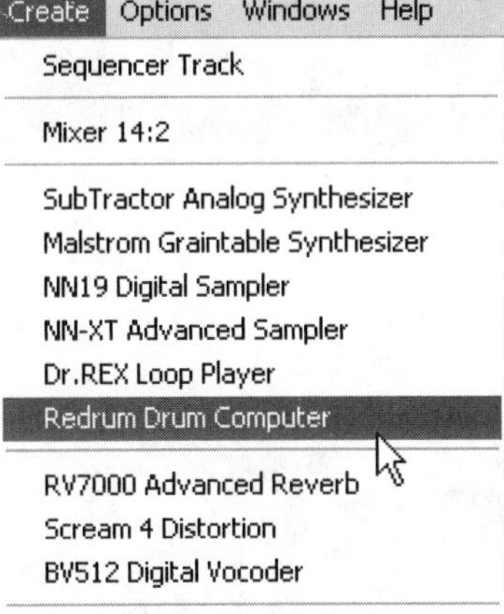

Figure 4.7 Create a Redrum Drum Computer.

The Redrum Machine

The Redrum Drum Computer is a practical choice as the first addition to your Rack. This device allows you to lay a basic beat for your new song.

Why start with the drums? Writing a beat first can help simplify the writing of bass and melody parts later. On the other hand, it's not the only way to start a song.

Some may want to avoid writing drum parts altogether—if this includes you, Reason's Dr. Rex Loop Player allows you to enhance, or even skip the process of sequencing drums by using breakbeats or drum loops instead (see Chapter 6, "Working with Samplers"). If you plan to have no drums at all, you can use the Reason metronome to keep time in your first tracks (**Figure 4.6**).

To create a drum machine:

1. Select Create > Redrum Drum Computer (**Figure 4.7**).

   You'll see a new device in your Rack, and a new track in your Sequencer titled Redrum 1.

continues on next page

2. Press Tab to look at the back panel, and check that Reason has automatically connected the Redrum to Channel 1 of your Mixer (**Figure 4.8**).

3. Press Tab again to return to the front panel and look at the Redrum's basic features (**Figure 4.9**).

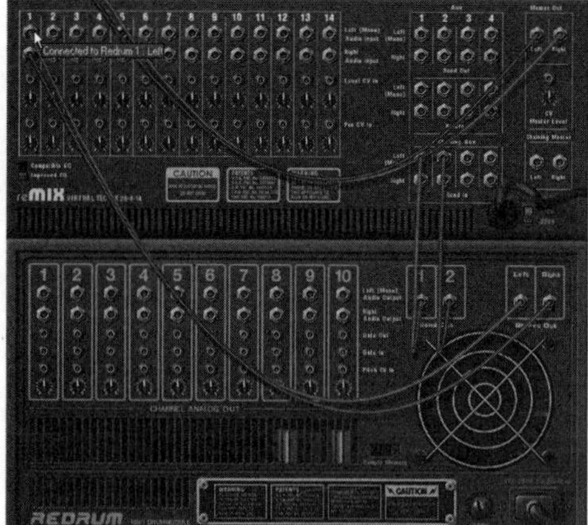

Figure 4.8 Check the Redrum back panel. The Stereo Out jacks of the Redrum Drum Computer should be connected to the Left and Right Channel 1 inputs of the Mixer.

Figure 4.9 The Redrum Drum Computer front panel

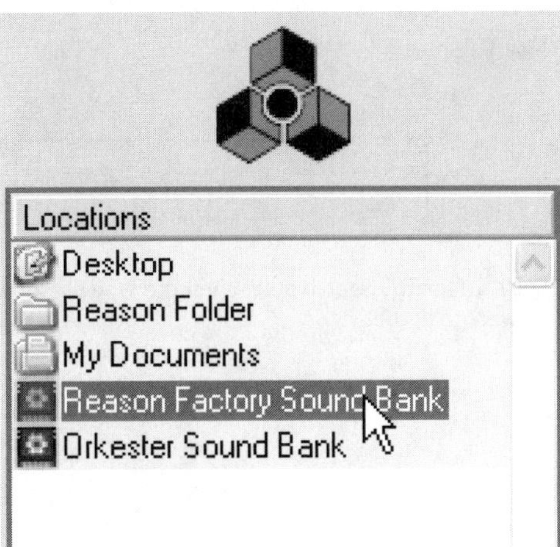

Figure 4.10 Use the Locations window to browse to the Factory Sound Bank.

Figure 4.11 The Redrum's patch display should now show a loaded Redrum (.drp) patch.

Loading Samples

The Redrum Drum Computer is a 10-part drum machine that plays samples. This means it stores a different drum sound on each channel and can play 10 different drum sounds at once.

Although its 10 channel strips may resemble the Mixer, the Redrum only puts out sound. In other words, it doesn't receive audio. It sends the audio, one sound from each of its 10 channels.

Since a new Redrum is always empty when you first add it to the Rack, you'll need to load it with samples before it can play any sounds. A *Redrum patch* (.drp file) typically consists of a couple of kick drums, a couple of snare drums, some toms, a couple of hi-hats, and a cymbal or percussion sample. The Reason Factory Sound Bank has scores of patches, so you should be able to find just what you need.

To load Redrum sounds:

1. On the front panel of your Redrum Drum Computer, click the Browse Patch button to open the Patch Browser.
2. In the Locations window (upper-right), double-click the Factory Sound Bank (**Figure 4.10**).
3. Open the `Redrum Drum Kits` folder.
4. Choose the style of drum kit you want and open that folder. For this example, I chose `Rock Kits`.
5. Choose a kit and click Open to load it. For this example, I chose `Groovemasters Rock Kit 2`.
6. Now go to your Rack and look at the Redrum's front panel. Notice that at the top of each drum channel there are samples loaded, with their names displayed in red. Also, you should see a patch name in the Patch field of the Redrum master controls panel (**Figure 4.11**).

You can also browse a list of all .drp files, regardless of what folder they're in.

To view all available drum kits:

1. Open the Patch Browser and select Factory Sound Bank in the Locations window.
2. In the browser's Search For field, type `drp` to search for drum patches.
3. From the Show pull-down menu, select All Instruments (**Figure 4.12**).
4. Click the Find button, and the browser will list all drum patches in the Factory Sound Bank.

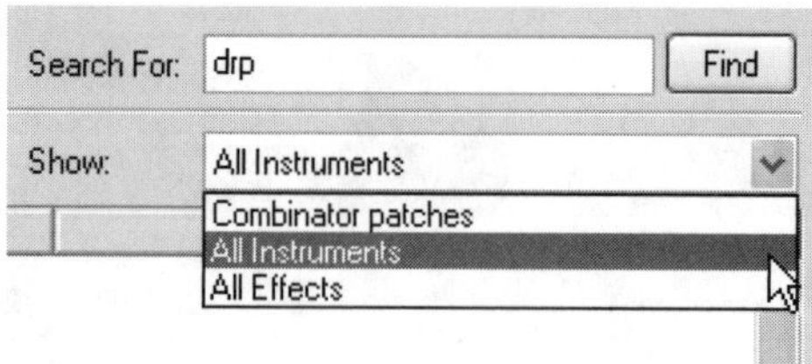

Figure 4.12 In the Search field, enter the type of patch you want to find.

Patches vs. Samples

Patches are different from samples. What's the difference?

Patches contain many different sounds and any accompanying virtual knob settings. For example, a Redrum patch has 10 different drum sounds, one for each of the 10 drum channels of one track. Patches are loaded from the Redrum master controls panel.

Samples are audio files (individual sounds) stored on your hard drive. Often they are of very short duration—an excerpt of a song or phrase, or even a single note. When you installed Reason, you installed hundreds of samples in your Factory Sound Bank, and you can add even more samples to your collection from third-party sellers.

Figure 4.13 Click the Browse Sample button on a Redrum channel.

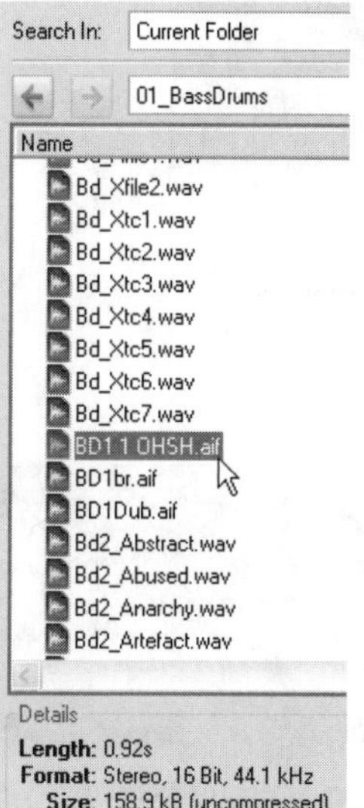

Figure 4.14 Select a drum sample in the Reason Factory Sound Bank from the xclusive drums-sorted folder.

Although loading a patch is the quickest way to set up your drum sounds, loading samples individually into the Redrum's channels allows you to create a custom drum set that can be saved as a custom patch.

To create a custom drum set:

1. Go to a Redrum channel strip and click the Browse Sample button (**Figure 4.13**).
2. In the Locations window of the Sample Browser, double-click the Factory Sound Bank, and open the `Redrum Drum Kits` folder.
3. Open the folder named `xclusive drums-sorted`; then open the folder for the type of drum you want to add. For this example, I chose `01_BassDrums` (**Figure 4.14**).

continues on next page

4. Check the Autoplay box in the Sample Browser to audition the drum samples (**Figure 4.15**), and select the one you want. For this example, I chose the sample `BD1 1 OHSH.aif`.
5. Click Open to load the sample. The name of the sample will appear at the top of your Redrum drum channel.
6. Use the up and down arrow buttons under the sample name in the Redrum channel (**Figure 4.16**) to scroll through the sounds quickly.
7. Repeat steps 1 through 6, choosing drums for the different channels until you have created the kit you want.
8. Click the Save Patch button (**Figure 4.17**) in the Redrum master controls and save the Redrum patch to a location where you want to store your future patches.

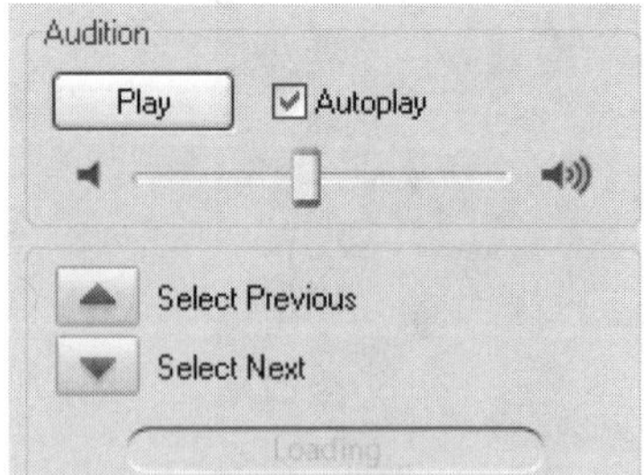

Figure 4.15 Audition samples in the sample browser. Check Autoplay to hear each sample as it is selected, or manually trigger the sound using the Play button.

Figure 4.16 Click the up or down arrows to swap the currently loaded sound with the preceding or next sound in the directory.

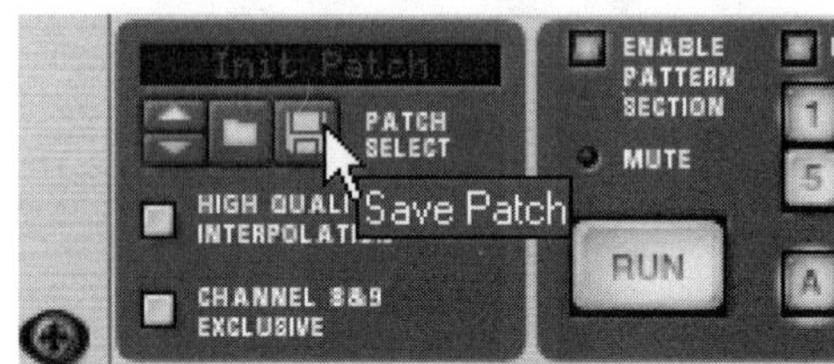

Figure 4.17 Save a drum patch from the Redrum master controls panel.

✔ Tips

- Set up a file structure on your hard drive that lets you easily find your custom patches and keep them backed up.
- If you decide later that you want to work with more than 10 drum sounds, no problem. Just create a second Redrum instrument, add it to your Mixer, and load it with additional sounds. A new drum track will be created in your Sequencer, where you can write a second drum track or copy an existing track to layer various sounds over the same part.

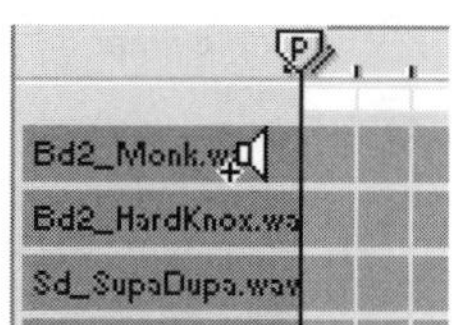

Figure 4.18 The cursor changes to an audition tool when you pass it over the sample name column in your drum track.

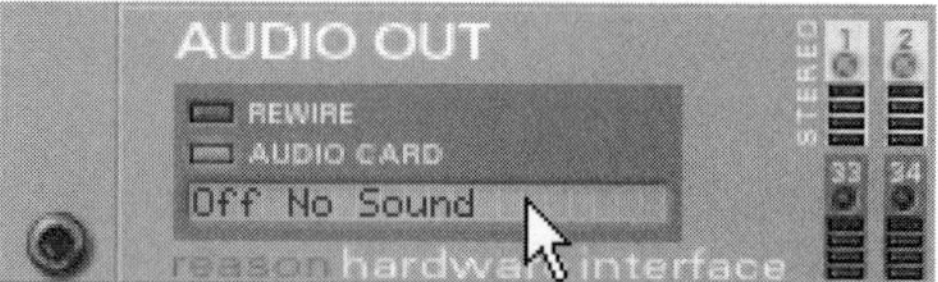

Figure 4.19 If your hardware interface says "No Sound," you need to choose a sound card in Reason Preferences.

Getting the Redrum to Play

In the following examples, you're going to be writing a drum track in Reason's Sequencer. You'll open a drum track in the Sequencer and hear your first drum sounds.

If you've created your Redrum, you already have a drum track ready to go; Reason creates a track in the Sequencer every time you add a device to your Rack.

To audition your drum sounds:

1. Move the mouse over the sample list to the left of the Sequencer's Edit mode grid.

   The cursor will change to a speaker icon—your mouse is now an audition tool (**Figure 4.18**).

2. Click a sample name to hear it.

Troubleshooting: No Sound?

If you're not hearing anything when you play a sample, here are several things to check before you throw your computer out the window:

The hardware interface. Does the green field under Audio Out display a sound card, or does it say No Sound (**Figure 4.19**)? If it displays No Sound, you need to go to your Reason Preferences and select a sound card.

The Mixer. Is there a Redrum 1 label on Channel 1? If not, you need to manually cable the left and right stereo outs from your drum machine to the Channel 1 audio inputs of the Mixer.

Volumes. Are the Channel 1 or Master Volume faders all the way down? Are any of the Mixer channels muted?

Computer volume settings. You might have a desktop audio control that is set to zero or muted. Check the volume controls in the computer's Control Panel in Windows, or the Volume slider and Mute check box in the Sound panel of Mac OS X System Preferences.

Making a Beat Loop

Before you start writing, you should create a small working area (perhaps two measures) that repeats in a loop while you create your song. By default, Reason will set up an eight-bar work area, which is a bit long for your first pattern. Keep it short and simple until you're familiar enough with sequencing that you're comfortable inputting longer sections in one go.

If you haven't worked with loops before, a *loop* is a section of a song that you designate to repeat. Looping is a fast way to work with small sections of a track, because it allows you to hear your work immediately as you add and change your first notes.

Setting up a loop means adjusting your *loop markers*. These tell Reason where to begin playback, when to loop back, and where to loop back to. These markers are located at the top of the position ruler (**Figure 4.20**), tagged with the letters L (left, or "begin loop"), R (right, or "end loop"), and P (play).

Let's set up a two-bar work area now.

To create a loop:

1. In the Sequencer, click and drag the L marker to the beginning of the sequence (measure 1), or Ctrl+click (Win) / Opt+click (Mac) in the ruler at measure 1.
2. Click and drag the R marker to the beginning of measure 3, or Alt+click (Win) / Cmd+click (Mac) in the ruler at the beginning of measure 3.
3. Set the P marker by clicking the ruler.
4. Adjust the zoom controls so you can see the whole work area (**Figure 4.21**).
5. Make sure the Loop On/Off button is active in the transport bar (**Figure 4.22**).

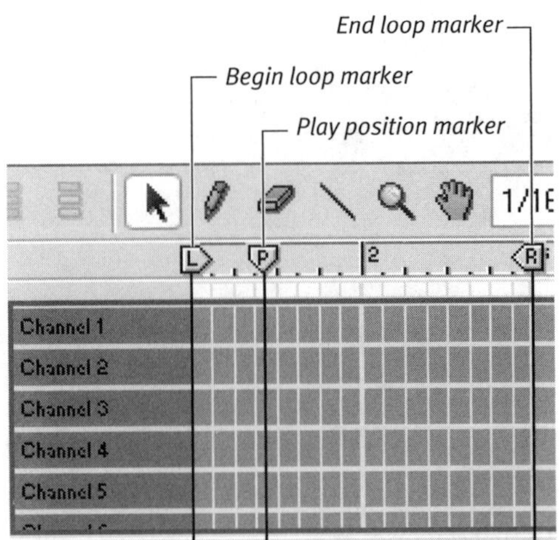

Figure 4.20 Reason's loop markers set the play and record area.

Figure 4.21 The two-bar working section should now fill the screen.

Figure 4.22 This button enables loop mode.

MAKING A BEAT LOOP

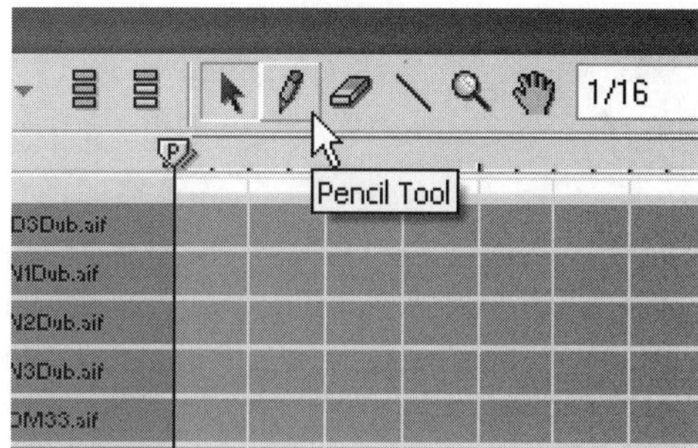

Figure 4.23 The Pencil tool makes it possible to input notes by clicking the mouse anywhere on the track grid.

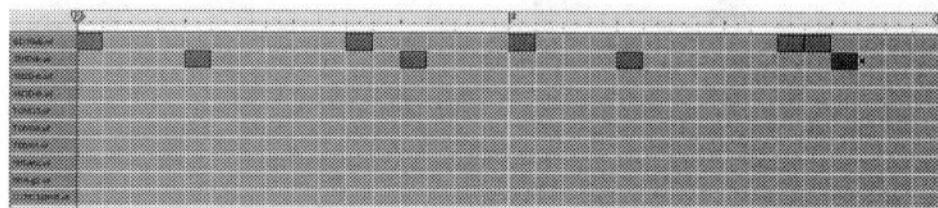

Figure 4.24 In this example, notes have been added for the samples BD3Dub.aif and SN1Dub.aif in a basic rock pattern.

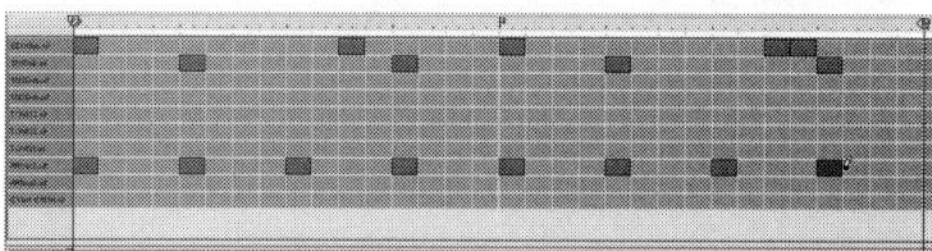

Figure 4.25 In this example, the hi-hat is sounding every half-beat (eighth note).

Writing a Drum Track

After setting up your work area and zooming in for a good view, you're ready to start writing drum notes. In the following example, you'll learn how to input a basic snare drum and kick drum pattern. If you haven't the faintest clue how to write a kick-and-snare pattern, don't despair—just copy the examples if you get stumped!

To input a basic drum pattern:

1. In the Sequencer, select the Pencil tool (**Figure 4.23**).
2. To input notes, click with the Pencil tool on the grid next to the desired drum sound. In this example, I've put some kick and snare notes into the track (**Figure 4.24**).
3. Click the play button (press spacebar) to hear your drum pattern.
4. Add some additional notes in another row. In this example I've added notes in the hi-hat row (**Figure 4.25**).
5. If you need to delete some of your notes, select the Erase tool and click them.

Enhancing your beat

Adding variety to a beat can be done with techniques such as fills, hits, and note attack. These should all work together to lead the listener from one point in the song to another. Most drummers have a sense of this phrasing, but getting good beat phrasing into your MIDI tracks can be frustrating.

Adding fills: Additional notes, or "fills," are easy to add to a pattern and can add or build a lot of energy into your beat. Even very simple fills can accelerate one measure into or through another (**Figure 4.26**).

Adding hits: Loud bright sounds, or "hits" (for instance, crash cymbals and sound effects like slamming car doors) can powerfully announce or emphasize the beginning of a loop (**Figure 4.27**).

Together with fills, hits can make a loop much more dramatic, and can provide a clean and punchy structure on which to add melodic instruments.

Accenting notes: Adding accents to some notes by changing the note attack strength (velocity) in the Velocity lane is another way to add variety (**Figure 4.28**).

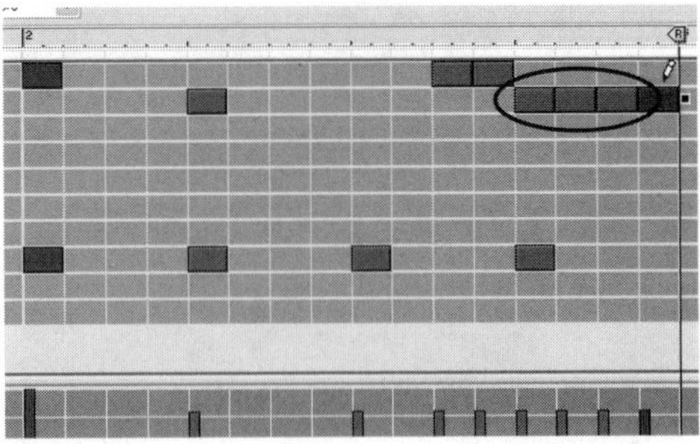

Figure 4.26 Drum fills add energy. Here, some consecutive snare hits at the end of the second measure accelerate the beat back into the beginning of the loop.

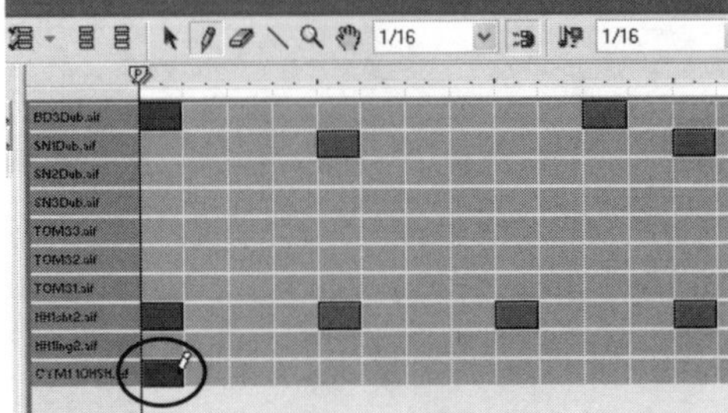

Figure 4.27 Creating a cymbal hit at the beginning of the loop "announces" or emphasizes the beginning of the pattern.

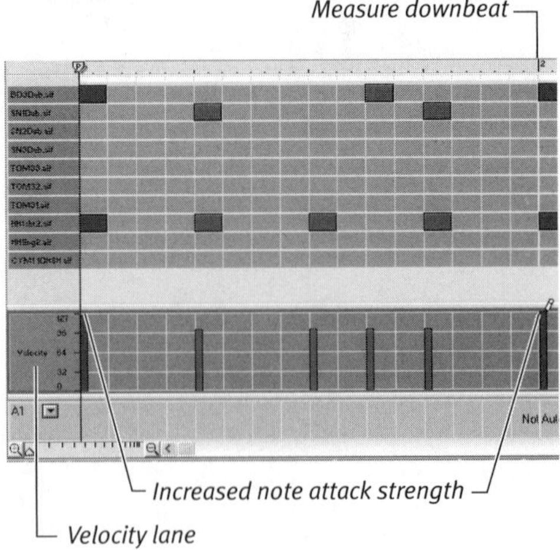

Figure 4.28 Velocity bars display attack strength. In this example, note strength was raised at the beginning of each measure.

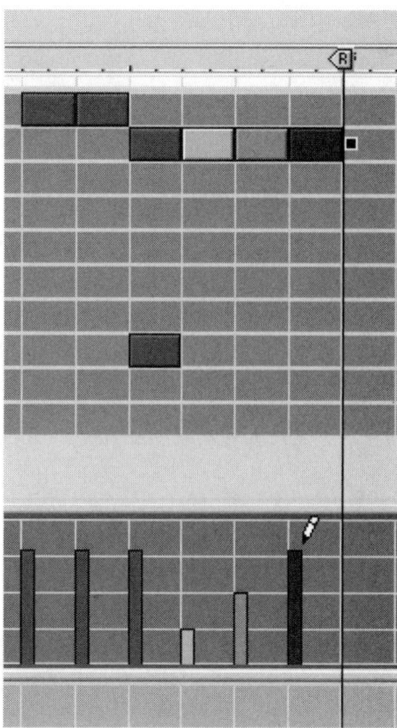

Figure 4.29 Adding a velocity crescendo to a snare drum fill magnifies the acceleration created by the snare hits.

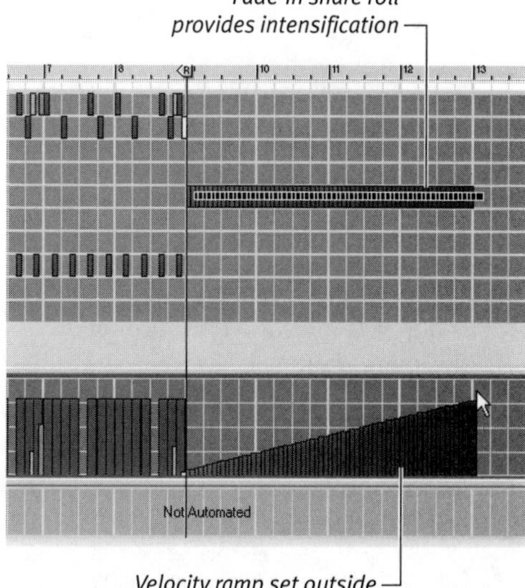

Figure 4.30 When notes are simultaneous or close together, you may need to move them outside your loop in order to work with their velocity.

To edit velocity:

1. In the Sequencer, hold down the Alt (Win)/ Cmd (Mac) key. The Select tool automatically becomes the Pencil tool.
2. Click the Pencil tool in the Velocity lane below the note you want to edit.
3. Click higher or lower on the velocity bar to alter the note attack value. Reason lightens or darkens the color of the note and raises or lowers the velocity bar indicator to show the strength of the note attack (**Figure 4.29**).

✔ Tip

- Since Reason layers the velocity bars of simultaneous notes on top of each other in the Velocity lane, it is often necessary to make velocity adjustments *outside* of the work area (**Figure 4.30**) before moving the notes to their intended place.

Mixing the Drums

In this section you'll walk through the process of using the various Redrum channel knobs (**Figure 4.31**) to adjust everything from volume levels to length and decay. The channel level knobs on the Redrum control the volume of the sound playing on each channel, enabling you to mix the various drum sounds in your beat against each other.

However, when people refer to a song's "mix," they are talking about more than just volume balance. The mix also includes the way different sounds are spread (panned) across the left and right channels, and how well the sounds balance tonally (are equalized) against each other. In short, mixing consists of taking a number of tracks and using every tool at your disposal to make them sound good together.

The Redrum does not have the same controls on every channel. Some channels are optimized for toms (notice the pitch sensitivity controls on the bottom of Channels 6 and 7), and others work better for drums that sound brighter when hit hard (notice the tone sensitivity controls on Channels 1, 2, and 10).

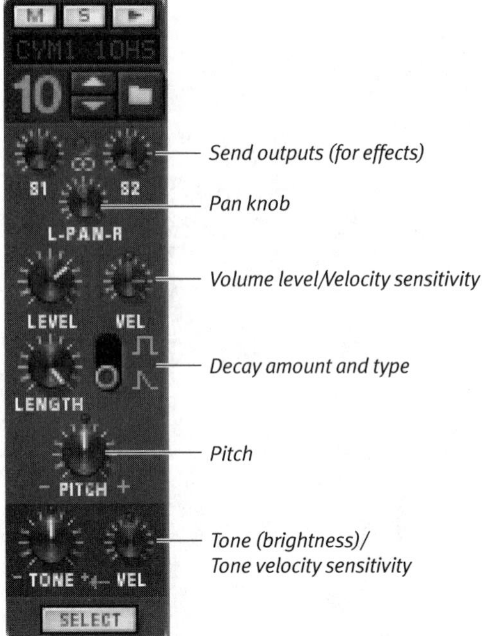

Figure 4.31 The Redrum channel controls affect only the sample playing on that channel, and are optimized for different sounds.

Mixing Tips for Drums

- Turn up the Level knob on the kick channel for a heavier bottom.
- Depending on what your snare sound is like, you may find that turning up the snare channel gives your beat more of a loud rock vibe.
- Emphasizing the hi-hat can be useful for funk styles, especially if you are using complicated patterns.
- Cymbal crashes often need to be turned down in the mix because their bright, noisy sound can easily overpower the other drum sounds.

Figure 4.32 Turn up the kick drum using Channel 1's Level knob.

Figure 4.33 Turn up the snare drum using Channel 2's Level knob.

To adjust levels:

1. With looping enabled in the Sequencer, click the play button.
2. In the Rack, choose a Redrum drum channel and drag the Level knob counterclockwise to lower the volume, or clockwise to raise it (**Figure 4.32**).
3. Adjust the other channels' Level knobs to get an overall balance (**Figure 4.33**).

✔ Tip

- Click a knob while pressing Ctrl (Win) / Cmd (Mac) to reset it to its default position.

Velocity sensitivity

Right next to the Level knob in all the channels is the Vel knob, which controls level velocity sensitivity. This knob determines the drum level's sensitivity to note attack.

To adjust velocity sensitivity:

1. In the Sequencer, in Edit mode, find a channel with a lot of activity and many different attack strengths, such as the hi-hat.
2. In the Rack, turn the Vel knob clockwise. This makes hard attacks sound louder, and soft attacks softer.
3. Turn the Vel knob counterclockwise to make soft attacks sound louder, and hard attacks sound softer.

✔ Tips

- Though not always useful, the "reversible" velocity sensitivity control can add some interesting variety to your beat.
- You can even disconnect note attack from volume altogether by setting the Vel knob at 12 o'clock.

Panning

The Redrum Pan knobs allow you to separate sounds between the right and left speakers. Turning the Pan knob clockwise puts more sound out the right side, and turning the Pan knob counterclockwise puts more sound out the left side.

To adjust panning:

1. With the loop playing, select a drum channel and turn the Pan knob counterclockwise.
2. Pick a second drum channel and turn its Pan knob clockwise (**Figure 4.34**).

   You should hear the first sound coming out the left speaker, and the second sound coming out the right side.

✔ Tip

- If you're concerned with creating an interesting stereo space, you may want to pan some sounds hard left and others hard right to separate them as much as possible. If you're looking for "realism" or "live" sound quality, pan the channels closer together (**Figure 4.35**).

Figure 4.34 These channels' Pan knobs are turned hard left and hard right for dramatic separation.

Figure 4.35 When the channels' Pan knobs are turned to similar positions, the listener's ear will perceive the sounds as coming from the same location.

Panning Stereo Samples

Reason handles stereo and mono samples differently.

With mono samples, Reason passes two copies of the signal through the outputs—one to the left and one to the right. This means when the sound is panned center, both left and right sides have equal volume.

A stereo sample, on the other hand, already has left and right channels. Reason passes the left channel through the left output, and the right channel through the right output.

Panning a stereo sample left and right can cause drop-outs or fade-ins if the stereo sample is already panned heavily to one side. How? If a stereo drum sound is recorded panned hard to the left, the right channel will have very little signal (**Figure 4.36**). So when you pan that sample hard right, there's almost no sound.

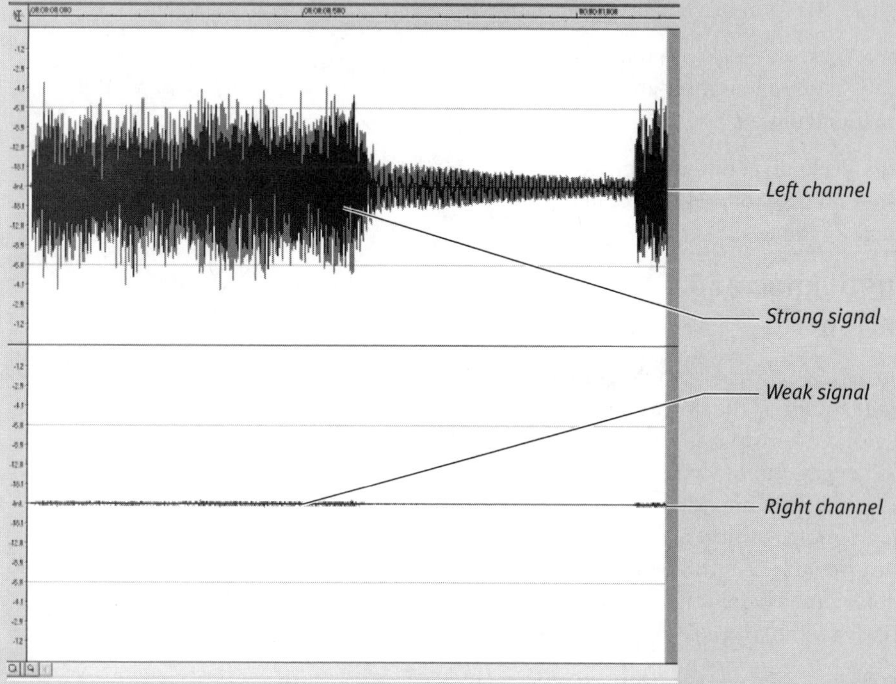

Figure 4.36 A stereo file with heavy panning, displayed as a waveform. This sample would produce little or no signal on the right channel, even when panned dead center.

Tone control and accents

Channels 1, 2, and 10 are typically used for kick, snare, and cymbals in many preset patches in your sound bank. Conveniently, Reason has tone controls for these channels—tone controls can be an even more powerful tool than level volume for creating dramatic accents. The Tone knob sets brightness level, and the adjacent Vel knob sets brightness sensitivity to note attack.

To control tone:

1. With your loop playing, boost the Tone knob setting on Channel 1 in the Redrum to brighten the sound.
2. Turn the Vel knob clockwise to make hard attacks sound brighter and soft attacks sound darker.
3. Turn the Vel knob counterclockwise to make soft attacks sound brighter and hard attacks sound darker.

The Length knob and articulation

Articulation is the musical term describing how slurred or punchy the notes sound, and technically that means the spaces between notes. The Length and Mode controls on the Redrum channel strip directly affect the articulation of notes by altering the length of the drum sounds (Length knob) and the way the notes decay before the next note is played (Mode switch).

The Length knob shortens the drum sound by applying a volume cutoff, or *gate*, to the end (the *decay*) of the sound. The Redrum has two types of gates for cutting off a note: Mode 1, *square* mode, cuts off the drum sound instantaneously. Mode 2, *ramp* mode, fades out.

Figure 4.37 The shape or gate mode switch determines how the Redrum cuts off a drum sound. The gate does not function unless the Length knob is at a short setting.

Since every sample is different, these modes will create different results for every sound, so the easiest way to understand length and gate modes is to start tweaking them and listen to the result.

To control the length and mode:

1. With the loop playing, choose a drum channel with a lot of activity and click the Solo button on the top of the Redrum channel strip.
2. Drag the Length knob counterclockwise to shorten the drum sound.
3. Reset the Length knob to midrange.
4. Flip the Mode switch to the right of the Length knob, switching it from the lower, triangle icon to the upper, square icon (**Figure 4.37**).
5. Listen to how these two ways of cutting off a sound affect the sound's quality.

   Mode 1 (square) cuts off sharply, creating more separation between notes. As a result, this setting often sounds louder and more aggressive than mode 2 (ramp), which fades out.

Changing Drum Sounds

Reason is packed with drum samples, and choosing the right one for your kit is easy. You may find another drum set (patch) that you like better, or you may find that changing just one or two drum samples gives you more ideas.

You can browse through the Reason sound banks while your beat is playing, allowing you to swap drum sounds on the fly.

To change drum sounds:

- With your loop playing, click the arrow buttons on your drum channel Sample Browser to switch to the next sound in the same folder.

  or

- Click and hold on the sample name in a drum channel to choose a sound from the pop-up list (**Figure 4.38**).

  Since drum samples are stored in folders with similar sounds, this is a fast and easy way to find sounds.

The Patch Browser works the same way as the Sample Browser, allowing you to audition different drum sets and change them on-the-fly.

To change drum patches:

1. With your loop playing, click the Browse Patch button in the Redrum master controls and choose a new patch from the same directory or switch directories and choose a patch.
2. To surf through the current patch directory, use the arrow keys below the patch name.

   or

   Click and hold on the patch name display in the Redrum master controls to select from the pop-up menu of recent patches. If no patch has been loaded, you can only choose Open Browser.

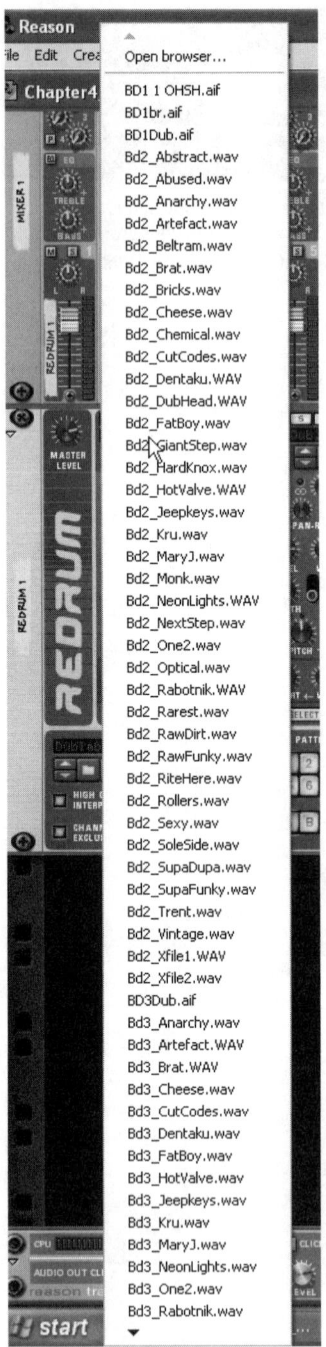

Figure 4.38 Swapping sounds is easy. Click the sample display for a menu of all other samples that are in the same directory as the currently loaded sample.

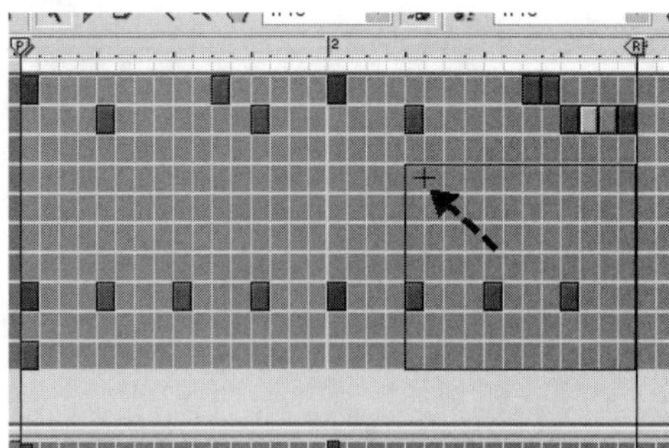

Figure 4.39 Drag-selecting creates a rectangular select zone around a group of notes. Selected notes are darker in color.

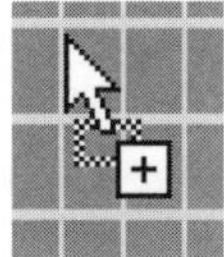

Figure 4.40 Ctrl-click (Win) or Opt-click (Mac) to drag-copy selected notes.

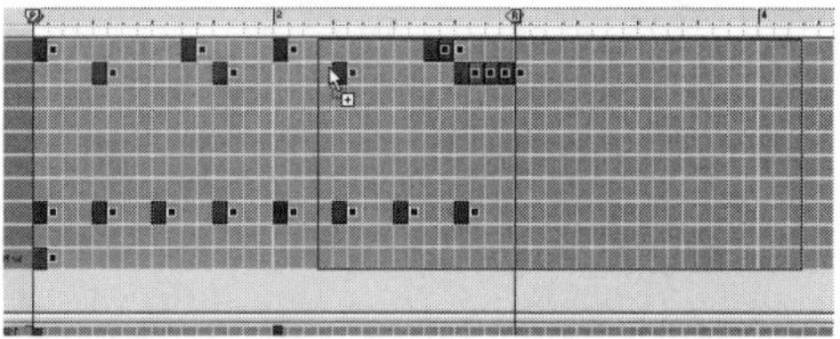

Figure 4.41 When drag-copying a series of selected notes, a new selection zone appears at the target location.

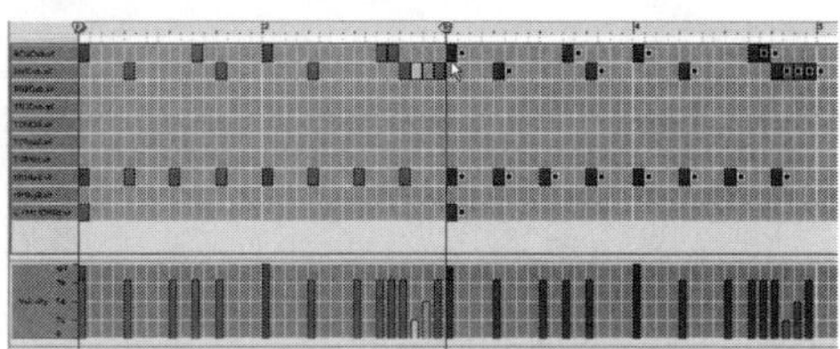

Figure 4.42 This four-bar phrase was created by cloning (drag-copying) a two-bar section to measure 3.

Copying and Moving Notes

Let's assume that you want a longer track than the one you've made. You can save time by copying an existing phrase and altering it to make a new one.

To double the size of a phrase:

1. Zoom out in the Sequencer so that you can see more of the track, by clicking the horizontal zoom out button.
2. Using the Select tool, click and drag over the notes you want to copy. The cursor will draw a rectangular selection zone. Release the mouse button (**Figure 4.39**).
3. Hold down the Ctrl (Win) or Opt (Mac) key and click one of the selected notes. Notice that the cursor changes to a box with a plus (+) sign, and a selection zone appears (**Figure 4.40**).
4. Still holding the mouse button, drag to the right until the zone is where you want the copied notes to be (**Figure 4.41**).
5. Release the mouse button, and the copied notes appear in your track (**Figure 4.42**).

✔ Tip

- Be sure to hold down the Ctrl (Win) / Opt (Mac) key until *after* you have released the mouse button, or you will disable the drag-copy feature and the notes will be moved instead of copied.

Repeated series of notes become bland quickly. If you use them throughout your song, they can squash your own creativity and keep your song from developing. You can add some variety by changing the velocity or adding some fills.

To add small variations to a phrase:

1. Adjust the end loop marker to the end of the new section.
2. Create variations by adding or moving some notes to differentiate your new section from the preceding one.
3. Adjust velocity to intensify the new section (**Figure 4.43**). This example simply adds some subtle, low-velocity snare hits. We also shift one snare hit to the left one grid space from the fill in measure 4. And we add some boosted velocities in the middle of the measures.

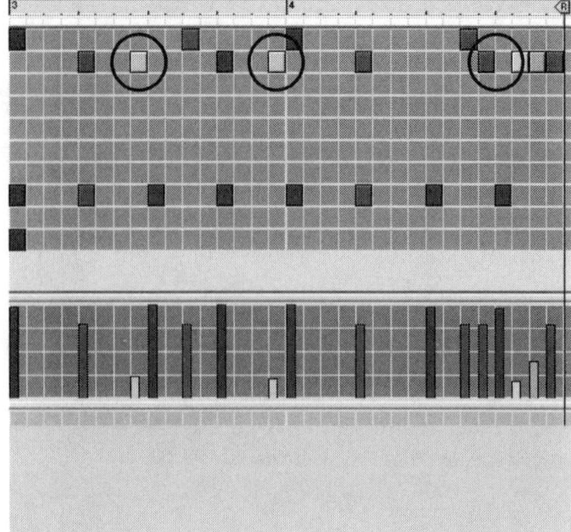

Figure 4.43 Variations don't have to be extreme to help build a little interest. Notice the low-velocity "ghost notes" on the upbeats, and the fill note moved just one grid space.

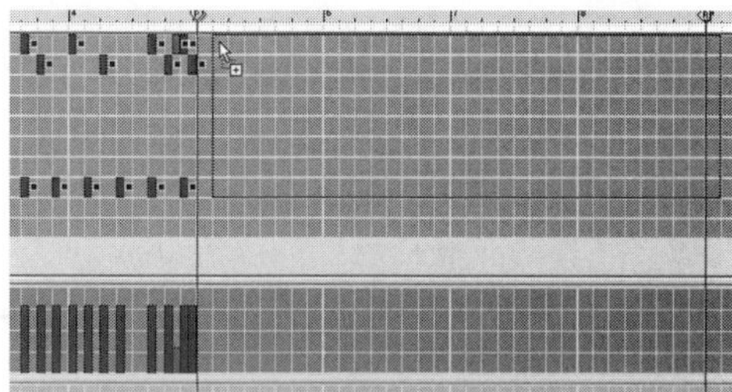

Figure 4.44 Clone the previous section to create a new one using the copy-drag function.

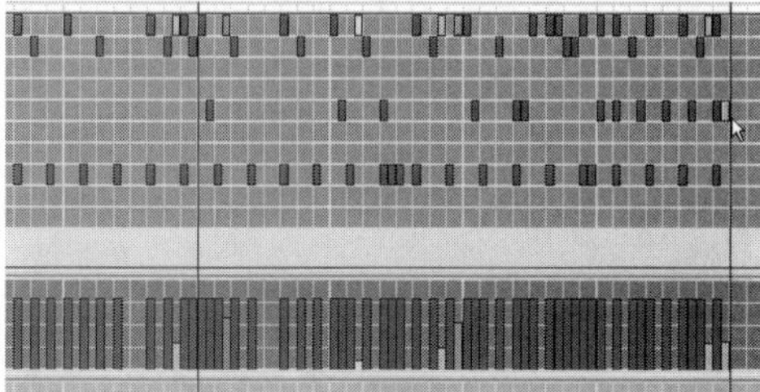

Figure 4.45 Alter and add to cloned material to differentiate the new section from the old. Here, new material intensifies the old section.

Figure 4.46 The Line tool is handy for drawing straight lines across dense sections of data—in this case, velocity bars.

Moving Beyond the Loop

You've now learned how to build up a basic pattern from scratch, how to copy and paste material to create a new section without reinventing the wheel, and how to alter the existing material to create new material.

Assuming that you don't want to simply repeat your existing rhythm track throughout the rest of your song, it's time to move forward into some new material. You'll start by creating a new loop.

If you haven't already created a clear plan for your song, it may help if you consider these simple categories:

- **Intensification:** Continue with the current feel, either to extend or build toward a section later on.
- **Breakdown:** Create a sparse open section that introduces a new pattern or basic idea.
- **Transition:** Add a short break for a drum fill or other instrument, to propel the song into another feel or go back into a refrain of the previous section.

Though there is no "right" way to build a song, these examples will help you work loops to your advantage and write music that fits together as a whole.

To intensify a previous section:

1. In the Sequencer, copy-drag an earlier section into a new loop area (**Figure 4.44**).
2. Add new notes or drum sounds (**Figure 4.45**).
3. Consider introducing a longer drum phrase that builds up to a new section.

   In this example, the Pencil tool was changed to the Line tool (**Figure 4.46**) to draw a one-measure velocity ramp that peaks at the end of the measure.

To add a breakdown section:

1. Make a new loop area.
2. Create a new basic pattern using sounds not emphasized in the earlier section.

   In this example, I dropped out the beat, created a four-note (one beat) hi-hat pattern, cloned it to last four bars, and altered the note velocities for accents (**Figure 4.47**). Through the introduction of additional layers (the clap part), the new section begins to build.

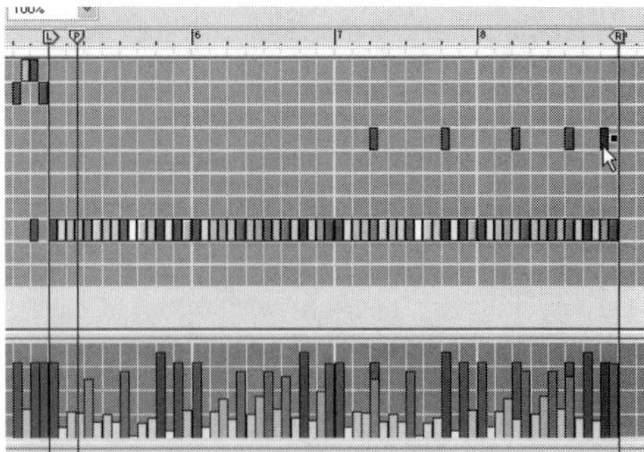

Figure 4.47 In this breakdown example, the beat drops out completely, leaving only a heavily accented hi-hat. The new section builds through the introduction of additional layers (claps).

✔ Tip

- Breakdowns work on the principle of *contrast* to the previous section. Using sounds not emphasized in the previous section can increase contrast.

To add a transition:

1. Make a new loop area in the Sequencer.
2. Write a fill or short pattern to use as a break or a bridge between sections (**Figure 4.48**).

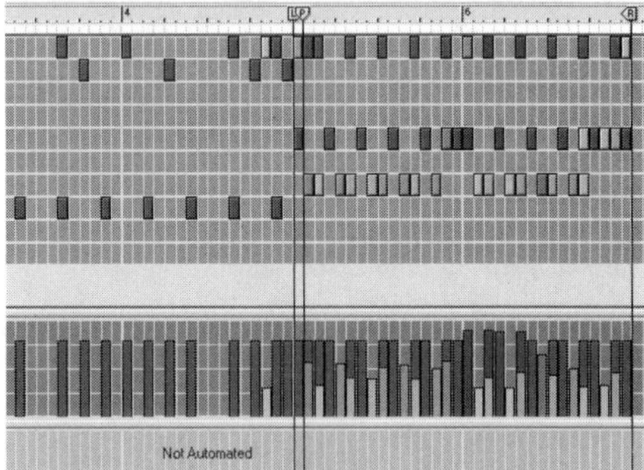

Figure 4.48 A transition section serves as a bridge from one section into another. This transition section is a break beat using a short, repeating phrase.

Editing Timing in Reason

If you are performing on a MIDI keyboard to record tracks, you may want to clean up the timing of your performance. In the old days, this task was a nightmare and usually meant either retaking an entire part, or splicing multiple takes together with tape and a razor blade.

Using *quantization,* Reason makes it easy to input perfectly timed notes or to alter mistimed notes without any fuss. Quantization corrects timing, conforming it to a grid that's set to a specific value, such as eighth notes, sixteenth notes, or quarter notes.

Notes that do not fall precisely on a grid boundary are moved to the nearest grid slot, or "time-corrected."

✔ Tip

- Adjusting grid resolution can be a powerful tool for writing parts with your mouse—it's easy to switch from one grid value to another for more complex drum parts.

Understanding Note Values

A note's "value" is simply its percentage of a four-beat measure. For example, a whole note lasts one measure (four beats), a half note lasts half a measure (two beats), a quarter note lasts a quarter measure (one beat), and so on.

So when you count the beats of a measure, you are counting quarter notes.

There is, however, still the matter of triplets, which break the rules a bit. A triplet is three notes that get squashed into the space of two—the triplet still carries the same note value but is slightly faster. Thus, quarter-note triplets are faster than quarter notes but slower than eighth notes.

Understanding note values doesn't mean you have to do math on-the-fly! Just remember that the higher the number, the more rapid the note. The rest will become clear as you work more with various notes.

Snap-to-Grid and Quantization

To help make timing adjustments easy, Reason has a number of quantization controls located on top of the Sequencer window.

Reason has three ways of cleaning up timing: snapping notes to a grid, record quantize, and quantization edit. Let's look at snap-to-grid first.

Snapping notes to a grid allows you to input perfectly timed notes with the mouse. The timing of your notes is set in the grid resolution menu. By default, Reason snaps all the notes you input to the nearest sixteenth note. At most tempos, sixteenth notes are rapid and a challenge for most performers to execute with precision. For sequencing notes in time, it is a good middle-of-the-road value for beat making.

To snap a note to grid using the mouse:

1. In Edit mode in the Sequencer, open up a track and select the Pencil tool.
2. Make sure that the Snap to Grid button is enabled (**Figure 4.49**).
3. Click the mouse anywhere on the grid to make the note fit perfectly on the grid. Perfect timing!
4. Select a different value in the grid resolution pull-down menu, such as 1/8 (eighth notes). You will see the grid change—the slots for notes will now be longer.
5. Click the Pencil tool anywhere on the grid to see what a longer-duration eighth note looks like.
6. To turn off grid snapping, click the Snap to Grid button again.

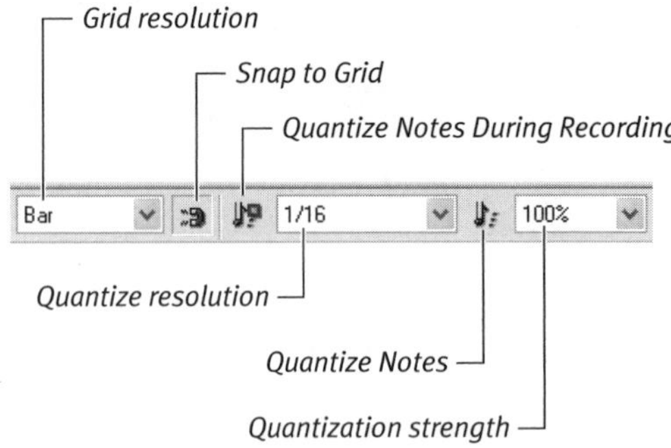

Figure 4.49 Reason's quantization controls

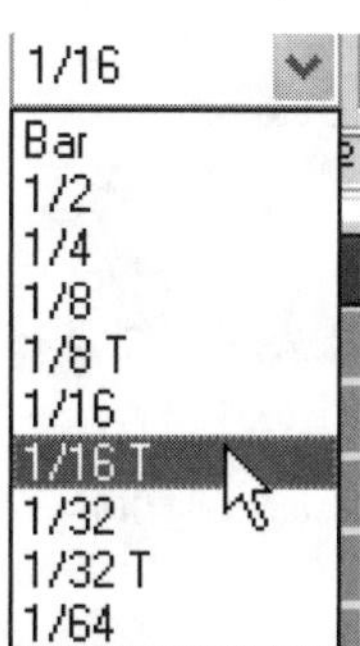

Figure 4.50 Triplet values for grid resolution are marked with a T.

To add triplets:

1. With your Sequencer track open, make sure the Pencil tool is selected.
2. Change the grid resolution to 1/16 T (sixteenth-note triplets) and watch how the grid changes (**Figure 4.50**).
3. Click the Pencil tool anywhere on the grid, and click the play button to hear what a shorter-duration sixteenth-note triplet sounds like.

✔ Tip

- Once you get the hang of switching note values and hearing the result, you'll be able to use Reason's Snap to Grid function to write parts quickly.

The **record quantize** method fixes notes to a grid during recording with a MIDI keyboard, cleaning up timing *before* notes are written to a track. (You'll read more about this in the next section, "Using an External MIDI Input Device.")

And lastly, **quantize edit** is a clean-up method for notes that are already written to a track. It has the advantage of working only on the note or series of notes you select. You can record performances exactly as played and then quantize only those notes that need it.

To quantize edit:

1. With grid snapping turned off, use the Pencil tool to input notes randomly on the grid.
2. Drag-select the notes you want to quantize.
3. Click the Quantize Notes button above the Sequencer ruler and watch your notes snap to grid.

Using an External MIDI Input Device

Although it's not necessary to use a MIDI keyboard to record in Reason, this method is a faster and more convenient way to write notes than clicking with the mouse.

It's easy to use a MIDI keyboard to play/record a Redrum drum track; just keep in mind that the Redrum will only use 10 keys on your external keyboard to trigger drum sounds. To see which keys will trigger your Redrum sounds, switch out of the 10-row Drum lane editing pane and into the 127-row Key lane.

Inputting and editing notes with the mouse works the same way in the Key lane as it does in the Drum lane—the only difference is how the notes are displayed on screen.

To switch to the Key lane:

1. In Sequencer Edit mode, open a drum track with some notes recorded in it.
2. Press the Show Key Lane button at the top-left of the Sequencer (**Figure 4.51**).

   Your Sequencer will now show you a larger, blue grid—the keyboard ruler on the left side indicates which keys on your keyboard will trigger drum notes (**Figure 4.52**).

✔ Tip

- Octaves are marked at each C note with a number. If your keyboard octaves don't correspond to the keyboard ruler in Reason, check your MIDI keyboard's range setup to make sure you haven't programmed an offset.

Figure 4.51 The Show Key Lane button changes your track display to a view optimized for using a MIDI keyboard.

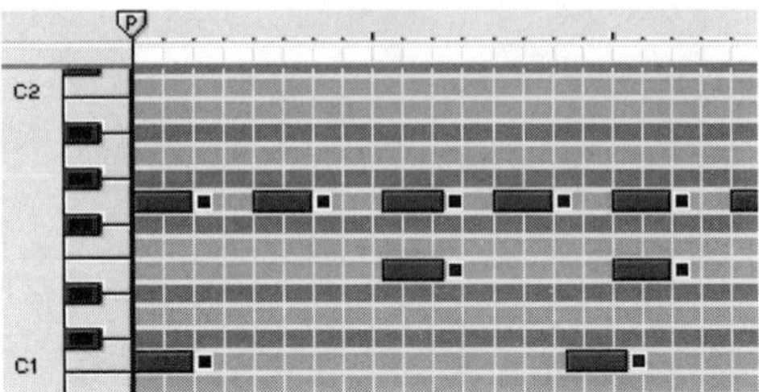

Figure 4.52 The Key lane edit view shows which notes on your MIDI keyboard are set to trigger the drum tones on the Redrum.

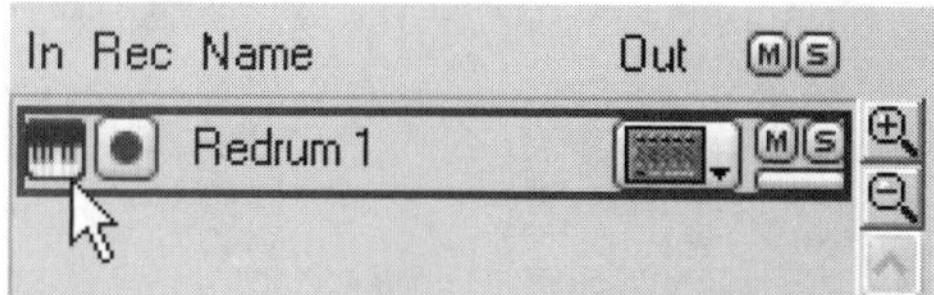

Figure 4.53 A keyboard icon next to a track signifies it is ready to receive MIDI data.

Figure 4.54 The active track is set to receive MIDI input, the Play marker is set for a two-bar count-in, and loop markers set off the section to be recorded. Click is enabled, and Record mode is active.

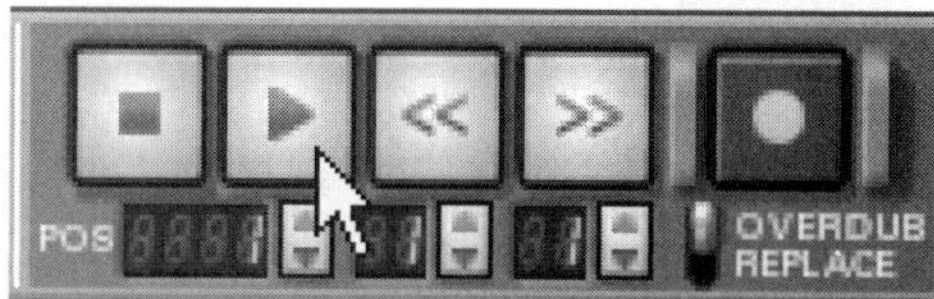

Figure 4.55 Click the play button to begin recording.

Now you should be ready to start recording.

To set up Record:

1. Open the active MIDI track in Sequencer Edit mode.
2. Click the Click button to turn on the metronome so you can play in time.
3. Set up a two-bar count-in by setting loop markers around the section you want to record, and setting the Play marker two bars before the loop starts.
4. Set the track to record by clicking the In column next to the device to which you want to record. A keyboard icon (**Figure 4.53**) appears, indicating that Reason is ready to record on that track.

To record a performance:

1. Click the record button to activate Record mode (**Figure 4.54**).
2. Click the play button (press spacebar) when you are ready (**Figure 4.55**).
3. Record your track.
4. Click the stop button (press spacebar) when you are finished.

✔ Tip

- You can enable Quantize Notes During Recording in the Sequencer, and your notes will snap to the grid as you play. However, Reason will snap the notes to the nearest grid, which may not be where you want them. Most often you will want to capture some of the feel (subtle variances) of your performance by using the Quantize Notes option instead.

No matter how good your timing is, if you are using a MIDI keyboard you will need to adjust at least some of the note timings from your performances.

The most common way of cleaning up timing in MIDI performances is to first record a performance and then quantize edit (Quantize Notes button) your tracks afterward.

To quantize a recorded performance:

1. In Sequencer Edit mode, set your loop markers around the section you want to quantize, and zoom in for a good view.
2. Listen to the track for any timing that you think needs tidying up, and select those notes for quantization (**Figure 4.56**). You can use the Shift key to select multiple notes at different locations in your track.
3. Choose a grid resolution, and click the Quantize Notes button (**Figure 4.57**).
4. Listen to your new track.
5. Adjust the grid resolution and edit any notes that should snap to slower or faster timings. For example, a triplet must be selected and quantized at the correct timing, or its note value will be changed.
6. If you like the timing of your performance better than the "corrected" version, you can use the strength pull-down menu to adjust the degree of quantization (**Figure 4.58**). Perfect timing is 100%; lower settings leave the timing less exact.

✔ Tip

- You don't have to quantize all the new notes. Just hold down the Shift key while selecting notes individually or when jumping between groups of notes to select multiple ranges.

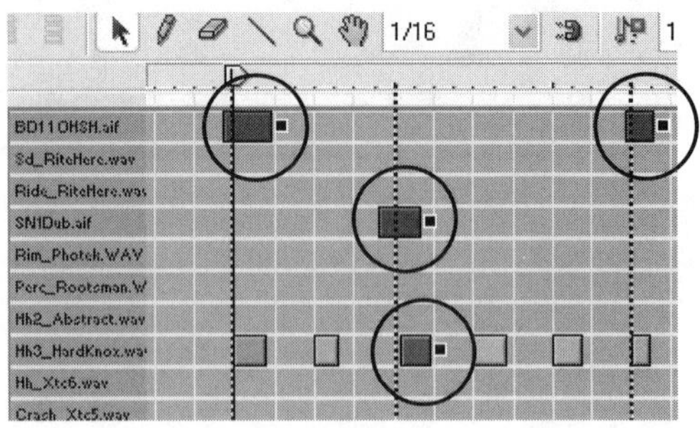

Figure 4.56 The timing of these notes has drifted perilously far from the grid resolution setting.

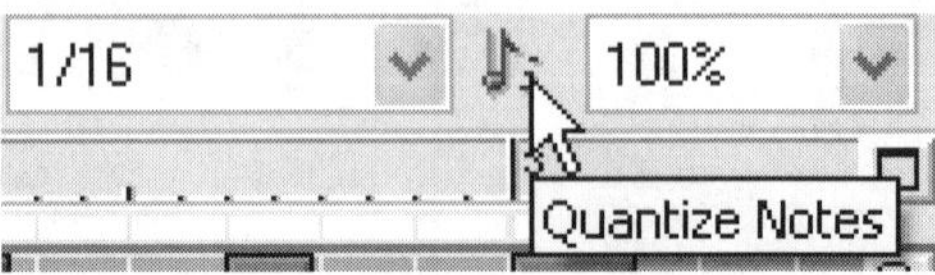

Figure 4.57 The Quantize Notes button

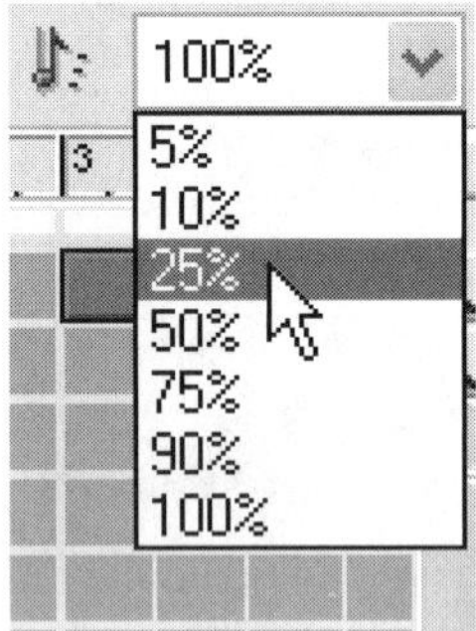

Figure 4.58 Quantization strength can be a great compromise between perfect timing and timing with "human" feel.

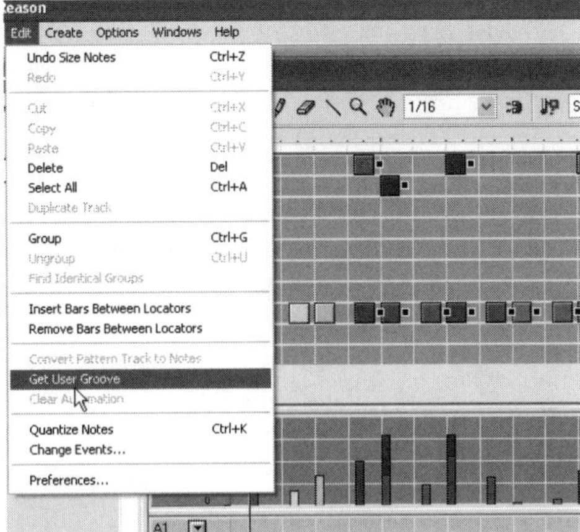

Figure 4.59 Get User Groove copies the subtle timing and velocity characteristics of a section of notes and copies it to the clipboard.

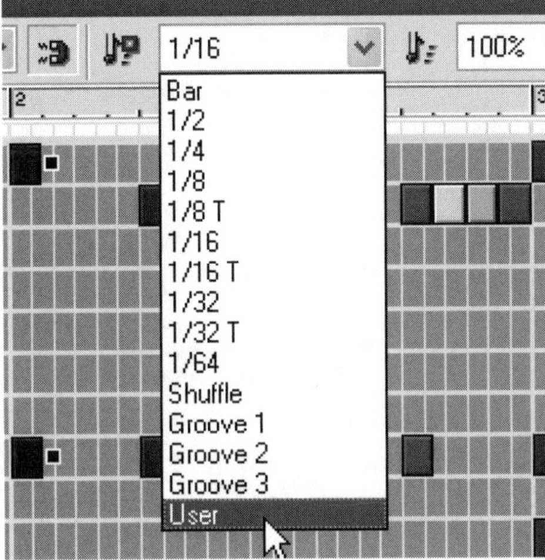

Figure 4.60 Once a groove has been defined as a user groove, it can be used to edit other groups of notes (choose User in the quantize resolution menu).

Custom Quantization: User Groove

Quantization doesn't have to sound mechanical. In fact, when used wisely, it can liven up your tracks. Quantization in Reason goes beyond correcting notes. You can use it to capture feel and apply it to a section that has little or no feel to begin with.

To copy and apply a groove:

1. In Sequencer Edit mode, select a series of notes (starting at the beginning of a measure) whose feel you want to copy.
2. Choose Edit > Get User Groove (**Figure 4.59**).

   Reason copies the groove of the notes you've selected to the quantize resolution pull-down menu (**Figure 4.60**). Until you select Get User Groove again or close down your program, this groove will remain in the User Groove memory.
3. To apply your groove, select a note or series of notes at the beginning of a measure, and then select User from the quantize resolution pull-down menu.
4. Click the Quantize Notes button.

"Feel" and the Limits of Quantization

Quantization is a great way to keep your multi-track project "clean sounding"—but clean is not always better. Track upon track of perfectly timed performances can sound mechanical and phony—without feel.

Feel is how humans play "outside the grid," also called *groove*. Groove is difficult if not impossible to calculate through quantization. Though mathematically wrong, a good groove can sound "righter than right."

Reason's User Groove feature makes it possible to analyze a series of notes and apply the timing quality of those notes to other notes in your tracks.

Copying a Groove: What Does It Mean?

Copying a groove is different from copying notes. When you copy a groove, Reason analyzes and copies the timing relationship among the notes. You can apply this groove (relationship) to any pattern, regardless of how different the notes or rhythms are. For the swing example in **Figure 4.61**, Reason copies how far the notes on/off the beat vary from the grid value. The notes on the upbeats (between the beats) lag in timing, and this accelerates the timing moving into the downbeats (counts of 1, 2, 3, or 4).

Copying a groove is more reliable when Reason has more information to analyze. If you were to copy the groove from a pattern that was already snapped to grid, you wouldn't be copying any groove data because there would be no variation information.

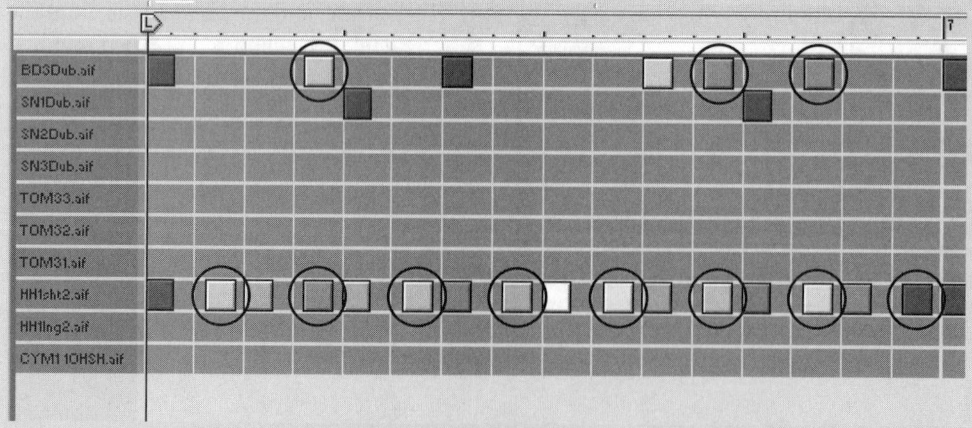

Figure 4.61 In this basic swing beat, the notes between the beats drift to the right of the default sixteenth note grid (the notes are playing "behind the beat").

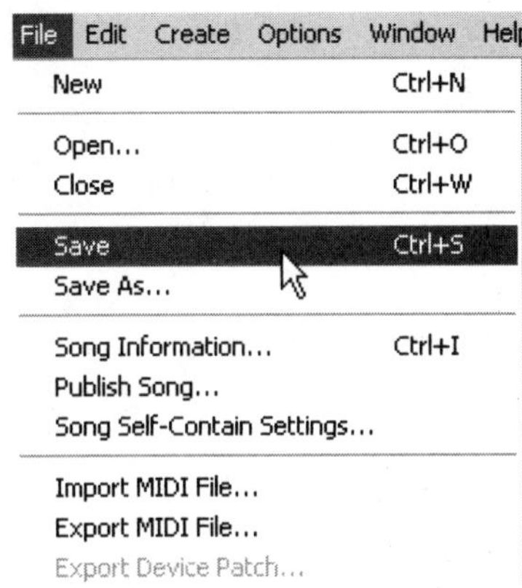

Figure 4.62 Use the File menu to save a song.

File Edit Create Options Window Hel
New Ctrl+N
Open... Ctrl+O
Close Ctrl+W
Save Ctrl+S
Save As...
Song Information... Ctrl+I
Publish Song...
Song Self-Contain Settings...
Import MIDI File...
Export MIDI File...
Export Device Patch...
Export Song as Audio File...
Export Loop as Audio File...
Export REX as MIDI File...

Figure 4.63 Export your loop as an audio file.

Saving Your Work

Now that you've created a beat in Reason, save the song so you don't lose your hard work. It's usually a good idea to save your .sng file as well as to convert, or *bounce*, your song to an audio file or CD.

To save your song:

1. Go to the File menu and select Save or Save As (**Figure 4.62**).
2. If you haven't saved your song before this, select a location for your saved file and give it a name.
3. Click Save.

To save (bounce) your beat as an audio file:

1. Switch back to Sequencer Arrange mode to get an overview of what to bounce.
2. Make sure your loop markers are placed correctly; Reason will only export audio lying between the L and R loop markers.
3. Select File > Export Loop as Audio File (**Figure 4.63**).

continues on next page

4. In the Export Loop as Audio File dialog box, choose a file format (for example, .wav or .aif) and a save location, and give your loop a name (**Figure 4.64**).
5. Click Save.
6. In the Export Audio Settings dialog box, choose a sample rate and bit depth and click OK (**Figure 4.65**).

✔ Tip

- To export a CD-compatible audio file, choose a sample rate of 44,100 Hz and a bit depth of 16.

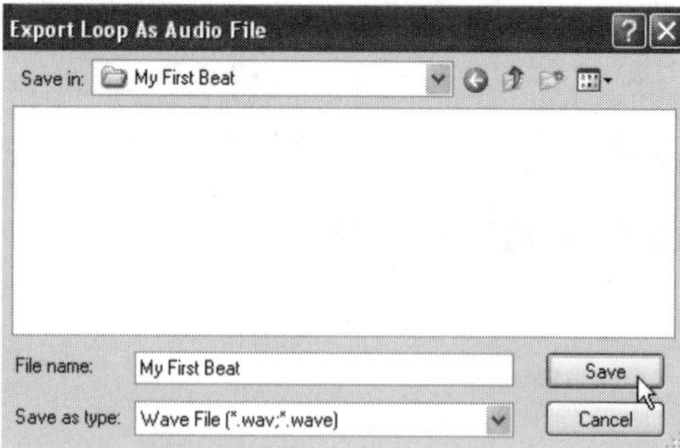

Figure 4.64 Save your loop as an audio file, in the same folder as your song.

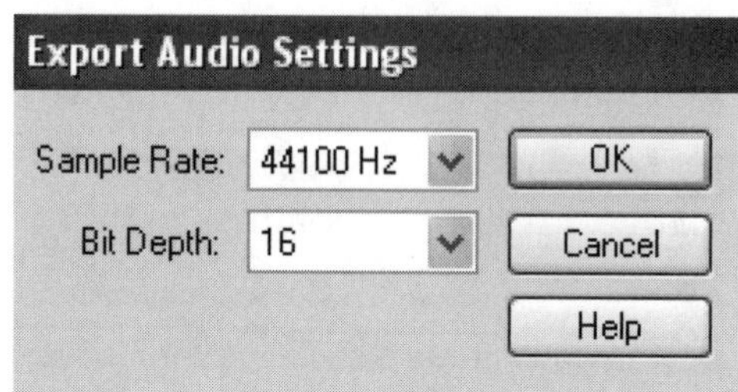

Figure 4.65 The Export Audio Settings dialog box

Staying Organized: Saving Multiple Songs

At this point, give some thought to how you want to organize your files. As you work on more and more songs, you can avoid confusion by starting with some sort of folder system to keep track of your work.

If you're unsure about how to archive your material, consider putting all patches, new samples, and audio bounces in one song-related folder. Add version numbers to the song and audio files so that you can always work your way back through the composition process if you need to make changes.

5

Building a Song

Now that you've learned how to build a beat, it's time to learn more of Reason's instruments and how to build up a complete song.

To do this you'll meet new instruments. Some are samplers like the Redrum Drum Computer and will need to be loaded with sounds in order to work. Others, like the SubTractor and the Malström, which we'll cover in this chapter, generate their own sound.

Since you started out with rhythm tracks, keep with the same "from the bottom up" strategy with the other instruments—start the rest of the song by building a bass line with the SubTractor. Then we'll add some melody with the Malström.

Adding a SubTractor

In Reason, the SubTractor Analog Synthesizer is a good instrument for writing a bass line. The SubTractor is a virtual analog synth—it generates "pure" waveform tones that are very fat-sounding for bass and techno-acid parts.

The SubTractor has an advantage over typical sampler bass patches, which pitch-shift one audio sample across the keyboard. Instead, the SubTractor generates a new (fresh) tone for each note, so you don't lose high frequencies with low notes, or low frequencies in the high register.

The SubTractor generates very simple tones, then uses a host of controls to turn those simple tones into fat, expressive, and evolving sounds.

To create a SubTractor synth:

1. Select Create > SubTractor Analog Synthesizer (**Figure 5.1**). A new device appears in your Rack: the SubTractor (**Figure 5.2**).
2. Press Tab to see the back panel and make sure that the SubTractor is now cabled to an open Mixer channel (**Figure 5.3**).
3. Press Tab to return to the front panel.

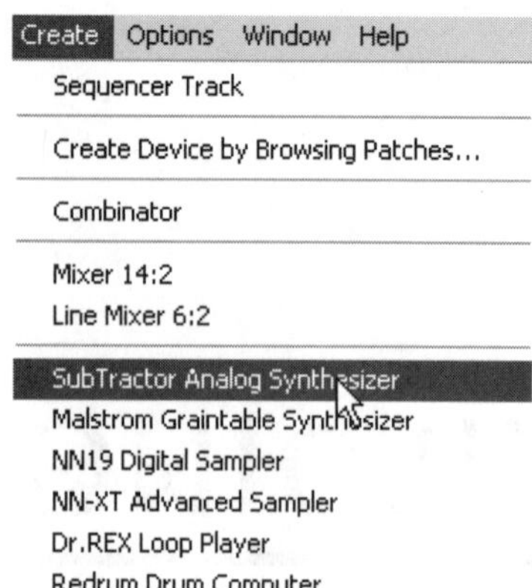

Figure 5.1 Create a SubTractor synth.

Figure 5.2 The SubTractor Analog Synthesizer

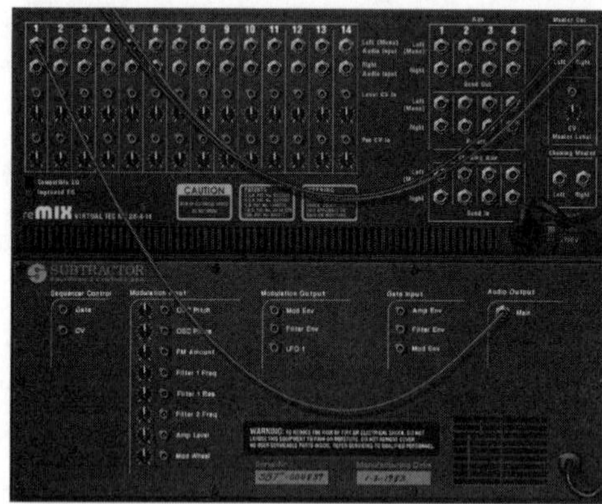

Figure 5.3 The SubTractor should be cabled to an open Mixer channel.

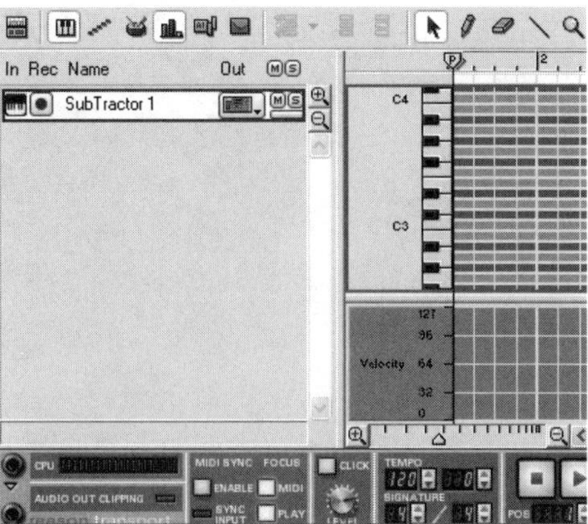

Figure 5.4 The Sequencer's Edit mode showing an empty SubTractor track

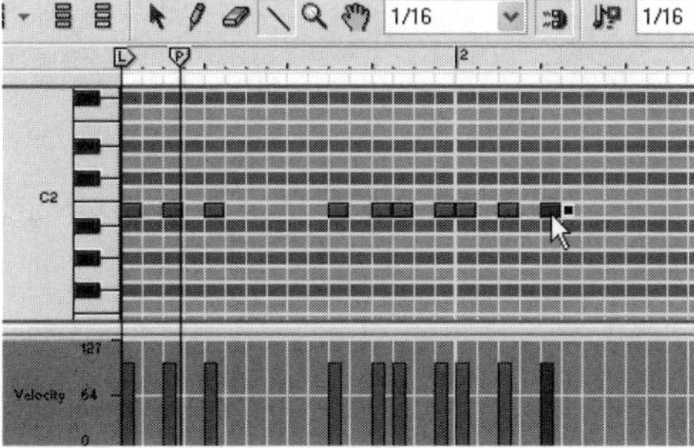

Figure 5.5 Start basic and add more notes after you play it back.

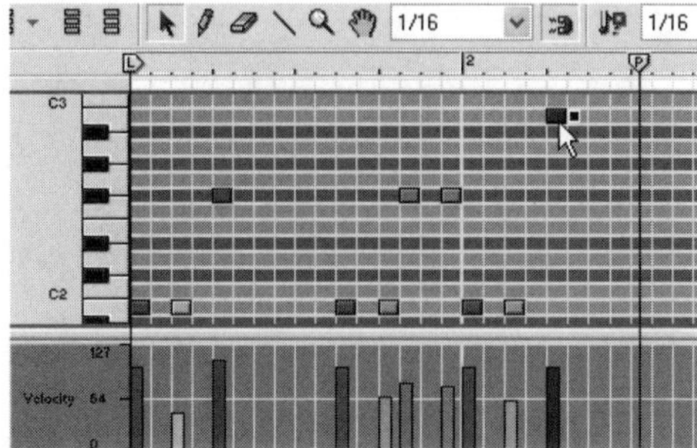

Figure 5.6 In this example, note pitches were altered for melody, and velocity was edited for accents.

The SubTractor will initialize with a very plain-sounding default, or `Init` patch. We'll change this later; first let's write some notes so we have something to work with.

To write a bass track:

1. In the Sequencer, make sure you're in Edit mode, and go to the SubTractor 1 track (**Figure 5.4**).

   By default, Reason displays new SubTractor tracks in Key lane mode.
2. Click on the keyboard ruler to audition notes for this synth, and if necessary, use the scroll bars to pick a pitch range for your window. (C1 to C3 is a good bass range.)
3. Set loop markers for two bars and input some sixteenth notes (**Figure 5.5**).
4. Play your loop, and alter the notes until you're happy with your line (**Figure 5.6**).

Loading a SubTractor patch

If you don't want to create your own bass sound, you can start listening to your bass part without further ado by loading SubTractor patches from the Factory Sound Bank.

Figure 5.7 The SubTractor patch browser

To load a SubTractor patch:

1. Click the SubTractor's Browse Patch button to open up Reason's patch browser (**Figure 5.7**).
2. Pick a bass sound to use from the Reason Factory Sound Bank/`SubTractor Patches/Bass` directory (**Figure 5.8**).
   The SubTractor's patch display now shows the name of the patch you selected.
3. Reason makes it easy to change sounds without stopping your music. With your bass line playing, open other patches or use the patch browser's arrow buttons to scroll through the current patch directory.

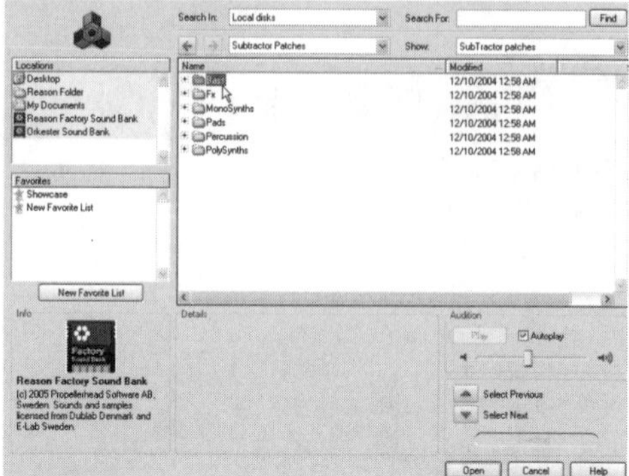
Figure 5.8 SubTractor synth patches from the Factory Sound Bank

Bass Lines for Non-Bass Players

A good bass line should play important root notes, accent the rhythm, and still leave space in the song for additional tracks.

Here are some suggestions:

- Use rhythms similar to the kick drum part, especially on strong beats.
- Keep the line simple and sparse. Busy bass lines can sound great and driving, creating a lot of energy in a song. But they also make it harder to layer parts and keep "open room" for vocals. Simple bass lines and simple drum parts can create a foundation for powerful, catchy grooves.
- Don't use too bright a bass sound unless you're sure it's what you need. In more traditional styles of music, bright bass parts can "hog" frequencies in a mix that are better used for leads or voice. Techno music breaks this rule often, using morphing bass sounds as leads.

  Also, clipped repeating bass notes are often spread out among many voices as part of the rhythmic feel in goa and other styles that go for a synth-heavy sound. Even in styles that take this approach, there is usually one primary voice that "holds down the low end."

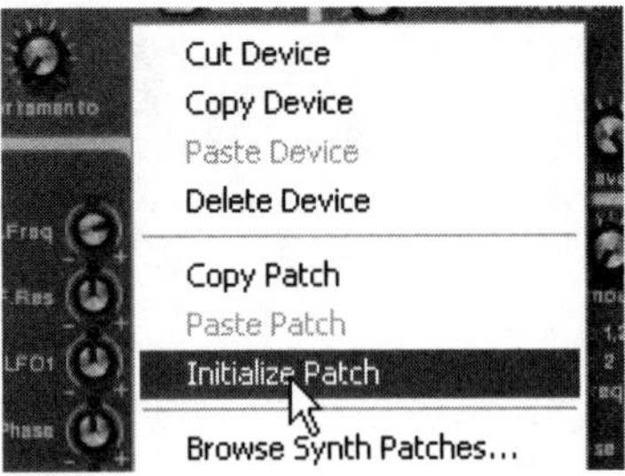

Figure 5.9 Initializing a SubTractor's patch sets all the knobs to their default settings.

Figure 5.10 Disengage the velocity section (F.Env) *before* saving a test patch.

Synth Basics

The SubTractor controls will be familiar to anyone with experience in analog synthesis, but if this isn't you, the next sections provide a crash course. This will mean a lot of new concepts and plenty of exercises illustrating how the many controls work. Take heart—learning the SubTractor will teach you most of the fundamental synthesizer concepts necessary to use Reason's other instruments, too.

The examples will focus on listening to, understanding, and adjusting different types of controls. When you're done, you'll have a working knowledge of filters, LFOs, envelopes, modulation, and play parameters.

To follow along with the exercises, you'll first need to create a patch with "neutral" settings—in other words, one that zeros out the various control sections so that we can learn about them one at a time.

To create and save a test patch:

1. Initialize your SubTractor by choosing Edit > Initialize Patch, or right-click the front panel and choose Initialize Patch (**Figure 5.9**).
2. In the Velocity section of the SubTractor's front panel, set the F.Env knob to the middle (**Figure 5.10**). The red indicator light will go out.

   The velocity knobs alter the tones, and we want to disable them to hear the oscillators in their "raw" beginning stage.
3. Click the File icon to the right of the patch name to open the Save dialog box.
4. Name your patch `test patch`, and save it somewhere that's easy to find again.

   Now we're ready to start learning about and listening to the SubTractor.

Oscillators

Oscillators are simple tone generators that sit at the very beginning of the SubTractor's virtual circuitry. Think of them as on/off switches that trigger a tone. This may seem a crude metaphor—and it is—but it'll work for now.

The SubTractor can generate two tones simultaneously (Osc 1 and Osc 2). Let's hear what the oscillators sound like through your test patch.

To adjust an oscillator:

1. With your loop playing, go to the Osc 1 section (**Figure 5.11**) in the top center of the SubTractor.
2. Click the arrow buttons next to the Waveform display until you find one you like (there are 32).

   Make sure you listen to the sawtooth, sine, square, and triangle waveforms (**Figure 5.12**). These are all "pure" analog tones and will soon become very familiar to you.

   Sawtooth is the most complex: all harmonics (bright sound, good for acid bass and leads; filters have a strong effect).

   Square is less bright, with odd harmonics (good for hollow-sounding leads and bass; filters have a strong effect).

   Triangle has very few harmonics, with a dark sound (good for flutes and other "hollow" sounds; filters have little effect).

   Sine is the simplest, with no harmonics (dark sound, good for bass and kick drums; filters have no effect).
3. Click the Oct arrow buttons to move up and down through the SubTractor's range (**Figure 5.13**).

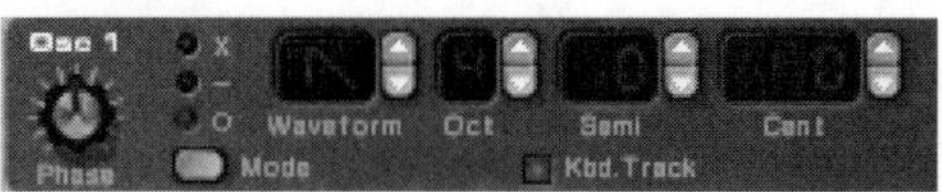

Figure 5.11 Sound begins in the SubTractor synth's oscillator section, where tones are generated.

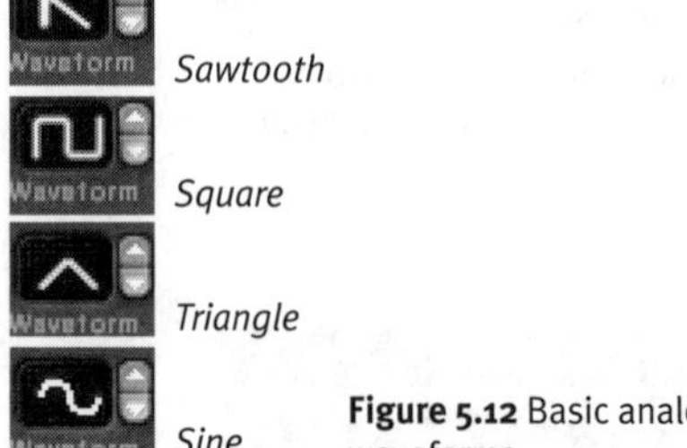

Figure 5.12 Basic analog waveforms

Figure 5.13 The oscillator's Octave arrow buttons change the octave of the generated tone.

Figure 5.14 Activate Osc 2.

Figure 5.15 The Mix knob adjusts the balance between Osc 1 and Osc 2.

4. Now click the Osc 2 On/Off button to activate the SubTractor's second tone generator (**Figure 5.14**).

   By default, both oscillators start at the same settings. So when they're first activated, they're making the same tone.

5. Find an Osc 2 tone you like by clicking the arrow buttons next to the Waveform display.

   You should now be able to hear two discrete voices playing.

Now let's try adjusting the balance between the oscillators.

To mix two oscillators:

1. With your loop playing and both oscillators active, turn the Osc Mix knob back and forth (**Figure 5.15**).

   When you move the Mix knob all the way to the right (clockwise), you're hearing just oscillator 2 (with one exception, as you'll learn shortly in "The Noise Generator"). When you move the Mix knob all the way to the left (counter-clockwise), you're hearing only oscillator 1.

2. To beef up the sound, move the Mix knob back to the middle (both oscillators at equal volume), and try raising and lowering the octave of one of the oscillators using the Oct arrow buttons.

✔ Tip

- Pressing Shift while adjusting a knob moves it in one-unit increments.

Phase Modulation

Now it's time to fatten the sound. The oscillator section of the SubTractor is very versatile—it allows you to adjust the *phase modulation* ("phase mod" for short) of each oscillator.

Huh? Well, each SubTractor oscillator can create a second tone—a copy of itself—behind the scenes. When the SubTractor combines this copy with the original tone, it creates a new, third tone. This is not the same thing as having four more oscillators. Rather, it's a process called *phase offset modulation.* What does it do? Despite its complex-sounding name, this process is simply a powerful tone-shaping tool.

The Phase knobs control the amount of the phase offset's effect, and the three-way switch next to each oscillator activates the offset and sets its type. The O position has no modulation (fat), the – position has some (fatter), and the X position has the most (fattest).

For starters, let's listen to how the phase mode controls affect the sound of just one oscillator.

To set phase mod characteristics:

1. With your loop playing and Osc 1 enabled, click the Phase Mode button, or click to select the bottom mode O (no phase offset). When set to O, the phase knobs don't do anything because the oscillator isn't making any copies of itself.
2. Select the middle phase mode (–) to hear a phase type called *waveform subtraction.* This adds high-frequency harmonics to the tone.

Phase differential affects the "thickness" of (X) and (–) phase modes.

Phase modes:
(X) multiplication (thickest)
(–) subtraction (thick)
(O) none (plain)

Figure 5.16 The oscillator Phase controls

Figure 5.17 Activate ring modulation to produce a bright, bell-like sound.

3. Drag the Phase knob left and right to thin and fatten the sound (**Figure 5.16**).

   Technically, this nudges the oscillator's "tone copies" around in relation to the original. This is called *adjusting the phase differential.* When you use the middle (–) phase offset, turning the Phase knob to its leftmost position causes the oscillator tone to cancel itself out.

4. For the most saturated, thickest-sounding phase offset, use the top (X) mode, or *waveform multiplication.*

5. Drag the Phase knob left and right again.

   When you use the X phase offset type, turning the Phase knob to either extreme position causes the oscillator tone to cancel itself out.

Ring modulation

The SubTractor has a mode called *ring modulation.* Use it to get a brighter, more bell-like sound.

Ring modulation is like the X type of offset modulation, but instead of multiplying a signal by itself, ring modulation multiplies the Osc 1 and Osc 2 tones, creating difference and sum frequencies between the two oscillators.

There are no phase type controls for ring modulation—it's either on or it's off.

To use ring modulation:

1. Make sure you have both oscillators enabled.

   The next step will increase the volume dramatically, so watch your ears!

2. Click the Ring Mod button to enable ring modulation (**Figure 5.17**).

The Noise Generator

Figure 5.18 Enable the Noise button.

Figure 5.19 The SubTractor noise generator controls

The SubTractor also has a third generator—it's for random frequencies, or *noise*. When activated while a SubTractor part is playing, the noise generator adds "grit" or distortion to a tone.

This is only half the story—when played by itself, the noise generator is a powerful analog drum and sound-effect synth!

To use the noise generator by itself:

1. With your loop playing, disable Osc 2. Click the Noise On/Off button to enable noise (**Figure 5.18**).
2. To hear just the noise signal, turn the Osc Mix knob all the way to the right (mixing out the Osc 1 tone).
3. Adjust the volume using the Noise Level knob (**Figure 5.19**).
4. Turn the Noise Color knob right and left for "white" (bright) and "pink" (dark) noise.

   Use bright noise color settings for hiss effects and hi-hat sounds. Mixed with oscillators, this adds bright distortion or bright attacks. Use dark noise color settings for analog kick drums, timpani-like percussive sounds, and thunder effects. When used with oscillators, dark noise adds a deep distortion or booming attack.
5. Use the Noise Decay knob to adjust between sustained (clockwise) and short attack (counterclockwise) sounds.

   This Decay knob works just like the Length channel knob on the Redrum (see Chapter 4). When Decay is turned all the way to the left, the noise signal disappears altogether. When it's turned all the way to the right, it lasts as long as the note that's playing.

To mix tones and noise:

1. Keep Osc 2 disabled and turn the Osc Mix knob to the middle for an equal mix between Osc 1 and the noise generator.
2. Enable Osc 2 and turn the Osc Mix knob hard right for an equal mix between Osc 2 and the noise generator.

   The noise generator is attached to Osc 2. When noise is turned up to maximum, it's at equal mix with Osc 2 (if 2 is on). Use the Noise Level knob to adjust volume, or the Color knob as a tone mute.

Keyboard Tracking

Each oscillator has a button to enable *keyboard tracking* (Kbd. Track). This shuts off and turns on the oscillator's response to your master keyboard's (or the Sequencer's) pitch.

When you have two oscillators playing at the same time, one can be set to drone "pitchlessly" while the other oscillator plays tones against it. You can still tune the "drone" oscillator using the Oct, Semi, and Cent arrow buttons—but it won't respond to your keyboard or to the Sequencer.

To turn off Osc 2 keyboard tracking:

1. With your loop playing, make sure that both Osc 1 and Osc 2 are turned on.
2. Turn off keyboard tracking for Osc 2 (**Figure 5.20**) by clicking the Kbd. Track button. Osc 2 now generates a steady tone, while Osc 1 plays your Sequencer track.

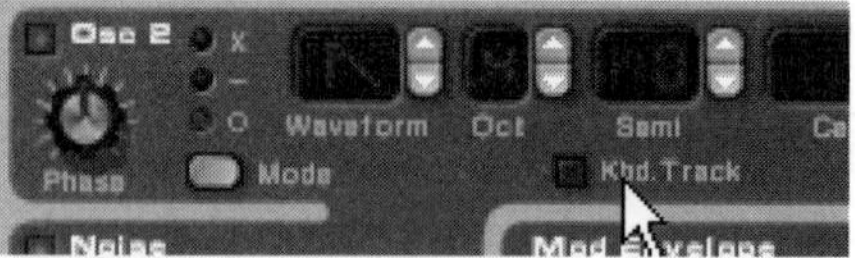

Figure 5.20 With keyboard tracking off, the oscillator ignores the Sequencer and master keyboard and plays only the pitch set with the Oct, Semi, and Cent controls.

Figure 5.21 The FM knob modulates Osc 1 with the signal from Osc 2 and/or the noise generator.

Adding Frequency Modulation

The FM (frequency modulation) knob is a fast way to modulate or achieve effects with the SubTractor's oscillators.

When both oscillators are enabled, the FM knob causes Osc 2's frequency to modulate Osc 1. This will add harmonics or interference and noise-like effects. Because it's based on frequency, the FM knob behaves differently depending on how the oscillators are tuned to each other, as you'll hear.

To FM-modulate Osc 1 with Osc 2:

1. Make sure the noise generator is turned off, and enable both oscillators.
2. With your loop playing, rotate the FM knob to the right (**Figure 5.21**).

FM has more of an effect when the oscillators play different notes. When tuned an octave, a fifth, or a fourth apart (perfect intervals), the FM knob acts very much like an "overdrive" effect, introducing high-frequency harmonic content and fattening the sound.

Knowing semitone-to-interval relationships is important for tuning in Reason. Also, knowing the right terminology for intervals can save you some embarrassment if you're planning on working with vocalists (or being one). Intervals can be *perfect, minor, major, diminished,* and *augmented.*

To modulate between perfect intervals:

1. Tune the oscillators an octave apart by setting the Osc 2 Oct value to 12.
2. Make sure both oscillators' Cent values are at zero, then tune the oscillators apart a fifth by incrementing the Osc 2 Semi value to 7 (**Figure 5.22**). (The Semi arrow buttons adjust the oscillator sound by halftones.)
3. Tune the oscillators apart a fourth by incrementing the Osc 2 Semi value to 5.

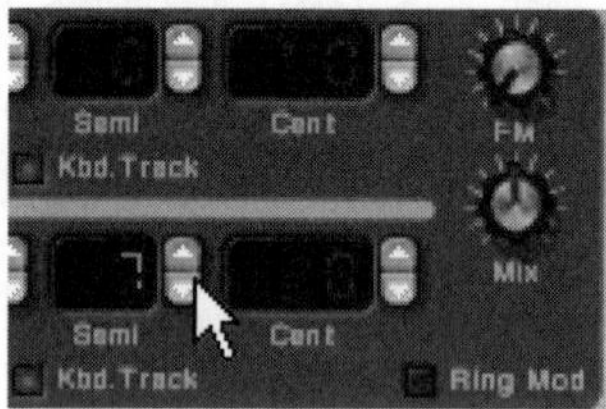

Figure 5.22 The Semi control raises and lowers pitch in half steps. At 7, the oscillator is raised a fifth.

✔ Tip

- The Cent arrow buttons fine-tune by 100ths of a half step. Detuning "shift" effects are possible when oscillators are tuned apart by 10 Cents or so.

Let's return to the subject of intervals. Perfect intervals are said to be "diminished" when lowered a half step, and "augmented" when raised a half step.

All "imperfect" intervals (anything other than fourths, fifths, octaves, and unison) get their names from the major and minor scales, and are either lowered (minor) or major.

When oscillators are tuned apart using imperfect intervals, the FM effect is more like a noise signal, or interference.

Table 5.1

Semitone-to-Interval Conversions (All 12 Tones)

Number of semitones	Interval
0	Unison
1	Minor second
2	Major second
3	Minor third
4	Major third
5	Perfect fourth
6	Diminished fifth (or augmented fourth)
7	Perfect fifth
8	Minor sixth
9	Major sixth
10	Minor seventh
11	Major seventh
12	Octave

Figure 5.23 When modulating with the noise generator, use the FM knob sparingly.

To modulate between imperfect intervals:

1. Make sure that both oscillators are active.
2. Now set the Semi counter to any interval other than 5 or 7 (see the conversion chart).

FM modulation and the noise generator

As long as the noise generator is on, it affects the Osc 2 signal's modulating of Osc 1. To hear how this affects the FM modulation knob, let's listen to it by itself.

To modulate Osc 1 with the noise generator:

1. Turn off Osc 2.
2. Turn on the noise generator.
3. Turn the FM knob to the right (**Figure 5.23**).
4. Play your loop—and cover your ears!
5. Try adjusting the Noise Color knob to see how it affects the sound.

   When the noise color is set hard left, the noise signal is fluctuating slowly and random pulses will be audible. When the color is set high, there is no pulse effect—just a uniform tonal brightness.

Using Filters

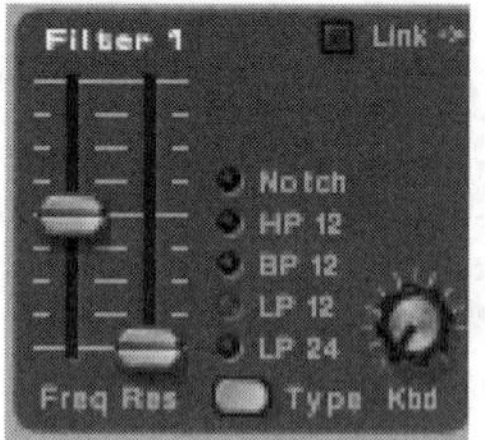

Figure 5.24 The Filter controls

Filters adjust the frequency spectrum in the sound coming out of the SubTractor's tone generators, and can amplify harmonics as well.

How do they work? As the name suggests, filters stop some sounds from being produced while letting others play. The SubTractor's Filter panel has two tone controls: the Freq (frequency) fader and the Res (resonance) fader (**Figure 5.24**).

The frequency fader controls the frequency at which harmonic content is cut off. This is sometimes called the *cutoff frequency*; it can be raised so it doesn't filter out an audible sound, or lowered so it only allows extremely low frequencies through.

By default, anything below the Freq fader position passes through the filter, and anything above the Freq fader position gets cut off. This kind of filter is called a *low-pass* filter, because low frequencies pass through it and high frequencies are filtered out.

Resonance is the part of the filter that amplifies sound. The Res fader follows the Freq fader and boosts sound at the cutoff frequency—emphasizing harmonics, or *resonating*. The Res fader has a range from 0 (no boost) to 127 (maximum). At maximum setting, the Res fader will boost certain harmonics so that additional tones get created.

The SubTractor has two low-pass modes that cut off frequencies at different speeds. LP 12 mode fades frequencies gradually (12 dB per octave) and LP 24 fades them more sharply (24 dB per octave). How sharply frequencies cut off has a big effect on how the filters sound when they are resonating. For example, the LP 24 mode has a much more focused, sharp, pronounced resonance than the LP 12. You'll easily be able to hear this for yourself.

Figure 5.25 Nudge the Freq fader down.

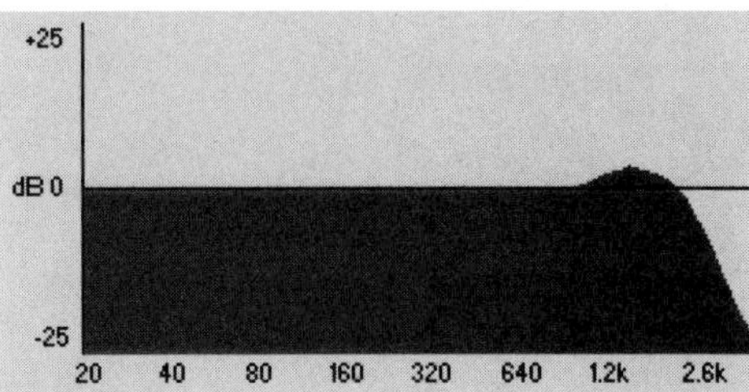

Low-pass filter 12

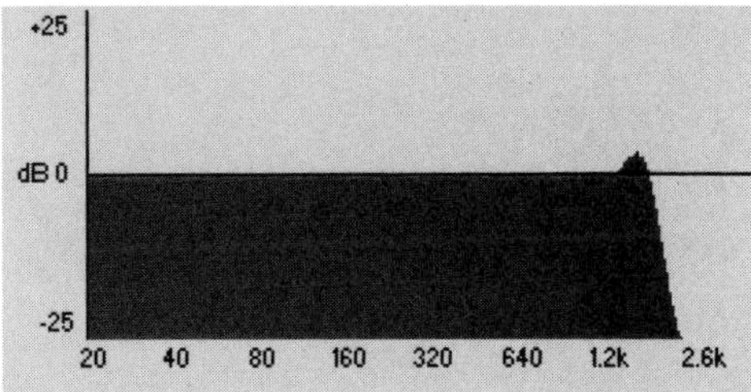

Low-pass filter 24

Figure 5.26 Compare the SubTractor's two low-pass resonant filters. Resonance is the slight bump just before the cutoff frequency.

The SubTractor also has other types of filters: *high-pass, band-pass,* and *notch.*

Filters are more useful when used on tones with a lot of frequency content, such as saw-tooth and square waves, and other bright sounds. Filters will have little if any effect on sine and triangle waveforms, which have almost no brightness at all.

Now let's hear what the filters sound like!

To adjust the low-pass filter:

1. Load your test patch.
2. With your bass loop playing, go to the Filter 1 section and move the Freq fader down to mute the sound (**Figure 5.25**).

   By itself, the frequency fader may not sound very impressive—it just rolls back high-end, like a "tone knob" that only goes down.
3. Now increase the Res fader slightly and move the Freq fader back up, to hear the boost in resonance follow the cutoff frequency.

   With resonance, the filters spring to life and become musical instruments—no doubt familiar ones you've heard in many different types of music.
4. Toggle the Filter Type button to LP 24, and repeat steps 2 and 3.

   Now you should hear how cutoff rate affects the sound of the resonators, as demonstrated by the difference between LP 12 and LP 24 sound. A steeper (24 dB) fade means a more "pointed" resonant boost, resulting in a thinner, more pro-nounced resonance (**Figure 5.26**).

✔ Tips

- Very high resonance can have unpredictable effects. The SubTractor has a master Level fader located at the far-right of the front panel (**Figure 5.27**). Nudge it down before maxing out your resonance settings.
- Filters can provide a lot of drama. Just a little resonance can sometimes turn your little Freq fader into an acid bomb. Try adjusting it as your bass line loops—filter movements sound great with reverb or delay.
- The high-pass (HP) filter lets higher frequencies through and cuts out those *below* the Freq fader, or "drops the bottom" out of the tone. As with the low-pass filter, the Res fader boosts frequencies at the cutoff point.
- Pressing Shift while adjusting a fader moves it in one-unit increments.

Figure 5.27 The SubTractor's master Level fader

Now let's try some other filter types.

A band-pass (BP) filter allows only a band of frequencies through, creating a thin spike of sound. With this filter, increasing the Res fader boosts the spike, creating sharp harmonics.

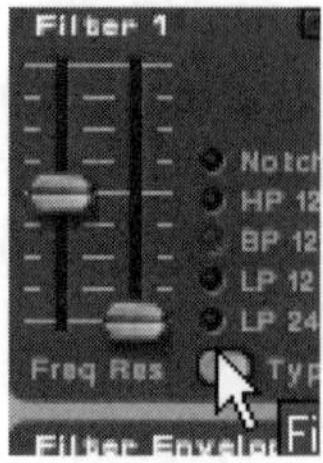

Figure 5.28 Select the band-pass filter type.

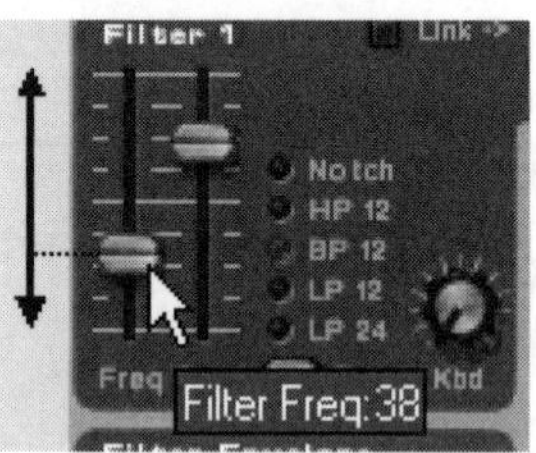

Figure 5.29 With band-pass, the frequency fader solos a small frequency band and is good for "lo-fi" effects.

To adjust the band-pass filter:

1. Click the Filter Type button until BP 12 is selected (**Figure 5.28**).
2. With the bass loop playing, boost the Res fader and move the Freq fader up and down for a "lo-fi gizmo" effect (**Figure 5.29**).

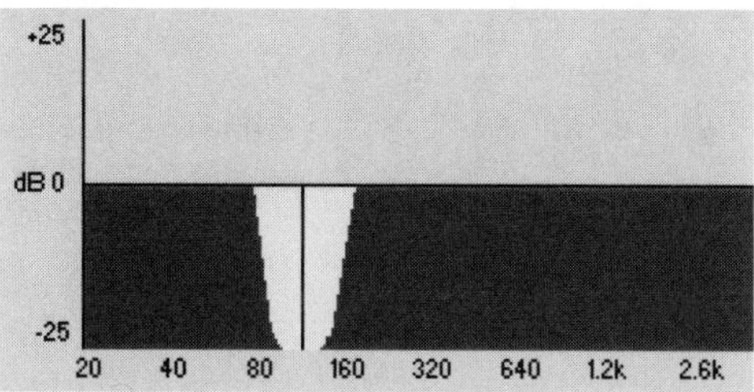

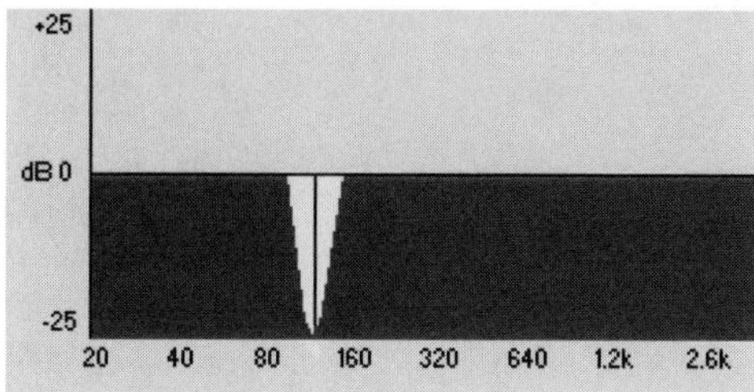

Figure 5.30 Here's how resonance works on a Notch filter.

The opposite of the band-pass filter is the notch filter: It drops out a band around the Freq fader, passing everything else through. (Notch has very little audible effect unless it's used in combination with Filter 2.)

With Notch, the Res fader narrows the band as it increases, lessening the effect (**Figure 5.30**). This can be difficult to hear and is most effective when the Freq fader is moving or when Filter 2 is enhancing the effect.

To use the notch filter:

1. Play your loop and set Filter 1 to Notch.
2. To hear how differently the notch filter works, turn Filter 1 resonance up to maximum and move the frequency fader up and down.

   Remember that the resonance works differently on the notch filter. High resonance means a narrower band being filtered out. The narrower the notch, the less sound gets filtered. The less sound getting filtered, the less noticeable the effect.
3. Now set the resonance to minimum and move the frequency fader up and down again.

   Even at low resonance (widest band/ maximum effect), the notch filter is most noticeable when moving, "shimmering" subtly as the frequency shifts.

Adding a Second Filter

Figure 5.31 Add Filter 2 to the notch filter.

Filter 2 works in low-pass 12 dB mode only, and can only be used on top of Filter 1. Filter 2 can exaggerate the more subtle filters such as the band-pass and notch, or amplify a high-pass or low-pass filter to cut through almost anything.

To add Filter 2 to the band-pass filter:

1. Set the Filter 1 type to BP.

   This setting affects a narrow frequency band that is very pronounced at high resonance.

2. Turn the Filter 1 resonance to a high setting and set the Freq fader to a good tonal position.

3. Now click the Filter 2 button (**Figure 5.31**), making sure that the Link button is not enabled.

4. Turn the Level (master volume) fader down (to protect your ears), and start your loop playing.

5. Now move the Filter 2 resonance to a high value, and move Filter 2's Freq fader up and down.

   The result is a set, resonant tone from Filter 1 being resonated a second time by Filter 2, for an amplified filter effect.

✔ Tip

- Set filters to different frequencies and boost the resonance to create an additional resonant tone.

You can make the two filters move together automatically, using Link mode.

Warning: Set your volume *low* before boosting resonance on both filters at once! When Filter 2 is at zero offset (all the way down), both filters are set to the same frequency—in this situation, high resonance is very powerful and can blow out headphones, speakers, and ears.

To link Filter 2 to Filter 1:

1. With your loop playing, set Filter 1 to BP and set both Freq and Res to about 64.
2. Enable Filter 2 with Res at 64 and Freq at 96.
3. Click Filter 2's Link button.

   The Filter 2 Freq fader now acts as an *offset* of the Filter 1 frequency setting.
4. Turn Filter 2's Freq all the way down. There is no offset now; Filter 2's frequency matches Filter 1's.
5. Turn Filter 2's Freq fader up to about 40. Because Filter 1 is in band-pass mode, the higher Filter 2 Freq setting has nothing to work with.

✔ Tips

- In Link mode, the Filter 1 Freq fader acts as a master fader for both filters. When you move the Filter 1 fader, both filters move, preserving the relative offset value.
- Filter 2 is more effective when set to a higher frequency than Filter 1. Why? Because Filter 2 is a low-pass filter—setting it below the Filter 1 frequency can mute what Filter 1 is doing (or, if Filter 1 is in BP or HP mode, can even cut off all sound).

Though the notch filter is subtle by itself, it sounds much different when you add Filter 2.

To add Filter 2 to the notch filter:

1. Play your loop, set Filter 1 to Notch, and push the Res fader to minimum.
2. Enable Link and Filter 2.
3. Set Filter 2's frequency offset to zero by moving the Filter 2 Freq fader all the way down.

   The harmonic tone you hear is Filter 2 boosting frequencies along the slope of Filter 1's notch. Filter 2 is producing the tone, but Filter 1 is focusing it.
4. Now try boosting the Filter 1 resonance.

   The Filter 1 Res fader suddenly has an audible effect, because the notch "slope"—silent before—is now exaggerating Filter 2's resonant frequency (**Figure 5.32**).

✔ Tip

- Whenever you discover some filter settings you like and that you'll want to apply to your bass line, save the bass patch again under a new name.

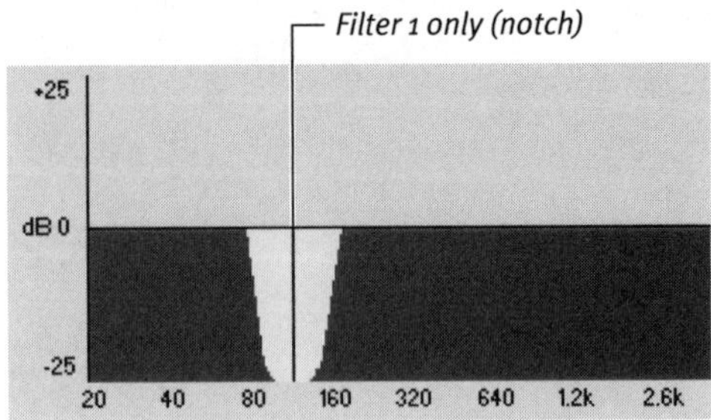

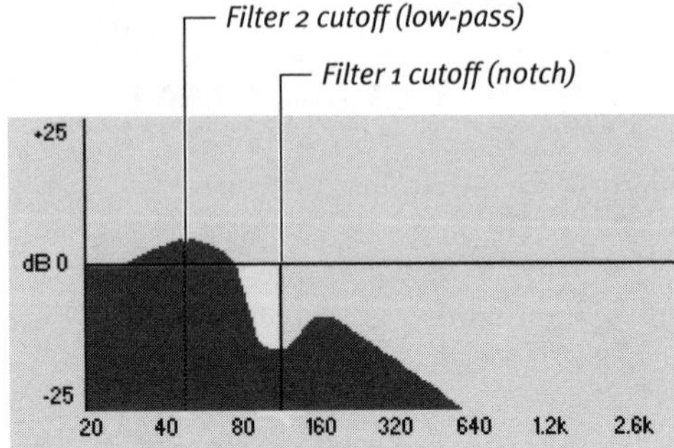

Figure 5.32 This is how Filter 2 works with Filter 1 in Notch mode.

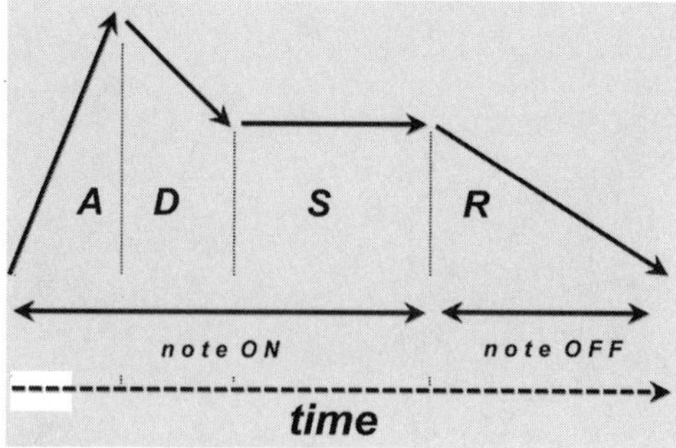

Figure 5.33 An ADSR envelope

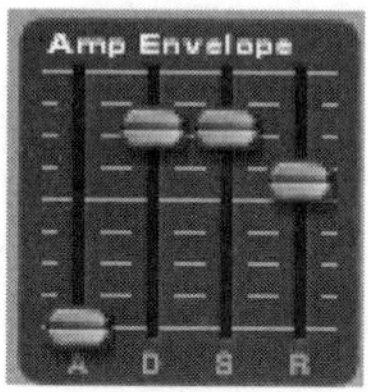

Figure 5.34 The amp envelope's attack and release faders control how your notes begin and end.

Using Envelopes

The SubTractor's *amp envelope* and *filter envelope* faders regulate how the tones behave over time. Instead of playing steady tones, the envelopes allow the oscillators to mimic many of the sound variations of real-life instruments—such as louds and softs, and bright and dark tonal variations.

The primary envelope is the amp envelope, which varies louds and softs (amplitude) from the time a note is struck until it gets released. Each time a note is played, the amp envelope opens and closes a gate in four stages: *attack, decay, sustain,* and *release*—commonly referred to as ADSR (**Figure 5.33**).

Amp envelope

Let's start with the attack and release faders. Attack (A) is how quickly a sound ramps up to maximum level, and release (R) is how long a note takes to fade out *after* it is released.

By adjusting these amp envelope faders, you can play notes with sharp attacks that fade out quickly, play sustained sounds that keep sounding long after you take your finger off the key, or make your own volume shapes.

To adjust amp envelope attack and release:

1. Load your test patch and start your loop.
2. Push up the A fader. This engages a quick fade at the beginning of each note in your bass line.
3. Now nudge the R fader up just a bit, and the notes begin to fade out slowly (**Figure 5.34**).

continues on next page

4. Nudge R farther up, and the notes begin to run together.
5. Nudge R all the way up, and the notes bleed into one another from one loop repetition to the next (until your eight-note polyphony runs out).

✔ Tips

- You can't do a long fade-in on a short note! Setting the attack stage too high on short notes will simply mute the sound, because the note will end before the ramp reaches an audible level.
- To eliminate overlapping, just set your SubTractor's Polyphony counter to 1.

The amp envelope decay (D) fader controls how long it takes for the sound to drop in volume from its attack peak to the sustain stage. The sustain (S) fader sets the volume for the main body of the sound. Sustain length is determined by the note duration in the Sequencer track.

To adjust amp envelope decay and sustain:

1. Load your test patch and set the S and the D faders all the way down.
2. Play your loop and move the D fader up and down until the notes become shorter overall.

   With sustain off, the attack becomes the only part of the note you hear.
3. To lengthen the notes again, move the S fader up and down. At this point, it may sound as if the D and S faders both do the same thing.
4. To hear the difference, first lower both the D and S faders all the way down. The bass notes become short clicks (no duration).

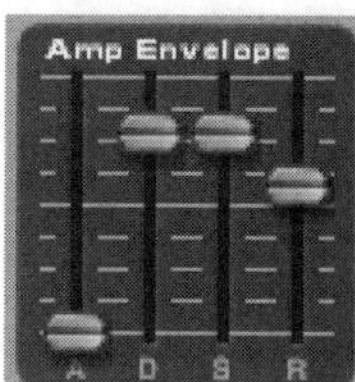

Figure 5.35 The amp envelope, set to "neutral"

5. Now bring up the D fader slightly, listening to how the notes sound as the decay becomes audible.

   The decay fader never changes volume, only how fast a note fades from attack to sustain.

6. Lower the D fader to 0 again and nudge up the S fader.

   With the decay stage off, a sudden drop in volume occurs between the attack and the sustain stages, resulting in a click. Get rid of this by boosting the D fader again.

Filter envelope

The filter envelope's ADSR faders work like those of the amp envelope, but the filter envelope increases and decreases brightness instead of volume. It moves the frequency fader up and down as an offset to your Filter 1 and 2 settings.

The filter envelope depends on the amp envelope for sound. If the amp envelope R fader is at 0, the filter envelope's R fader won't do anything. That's why, in order to test the filter envelope, you need to adjust the amp envelope faders to "neutral" positions first.

To set the amp envelope to neutral:

1. Move the A fader down to 0.
2. Move the D and S faders to 100.
3. Move the R fader to 73 (**Figure 5.35**).

   Your bass notes will now play their full sound and duration (sixteenth notes) through the release stage.

Now you're ready to work the filter envelope.

To adjust the filter envelope attack:

1. With your bass loop playing, activate the filter envelope by turning the Amt knob to the right to about 40 (**Figure 5.36**).

   The Amt knob only affects how far up and down the filter frequency is going to travel. (Turning it up won't lengthen your stages.)

2. Now slowly nudge the filter envelope A fader upward. The attack effect differs at various values:

   At about 28, the click disappears and the brightness attack ramp sounds like a synth brass attack.

   At about 42, the note attack sounds "bubbly."

   At about 50, the note is starting to sound "backwards."

   Past 66, the attack ramp is longer than the note, and the filter never kicks in at all.

Figure 5.36 Turn up the filter envelope Amt knob to activate it.

To adjust the filter envelope decay:

1. With your loop playing, drag the filter envelope's A fader down to 0, and the D fader just above the point where it causes a "pop," around 16 (**Figure 5.37**).

   Hear how the envelope decay creates a short bright period in each note that quickly dissipates into the darker sustained tones you started with.

2. Drag the D fader to 32 to lengthen the bright period into a solid pulse (**Figure 5.38**).

   Assuming you're adjusting tone on relatively short (sixteenth) notes, the decay length will probably max out at 55, and the dark sustained tone you started with will drop out (**Figure 5.39**).

Figure 5.37 At a low decay fader setting, you'll hear a "pop."

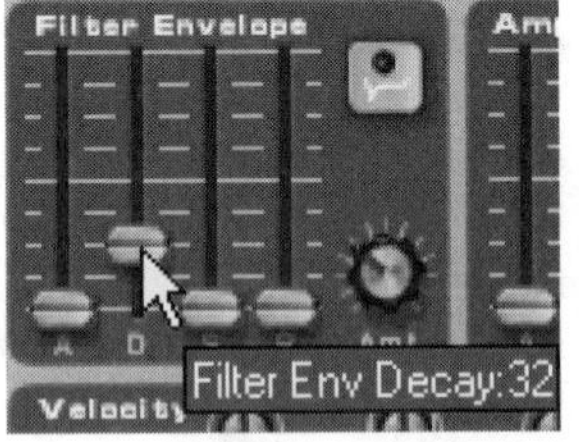

Figure 5.38 A longer decay causes a bright pulse.

Figure 5.39 When decay is longer than note length, the fader has little effect.

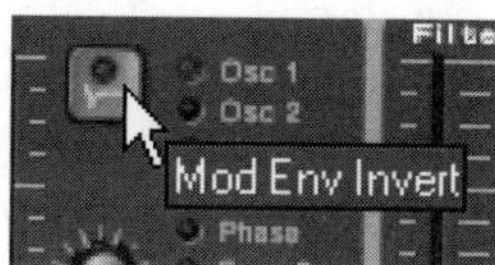

Figure 5.40 The Invert Filter button

To adjust filter envelope sustain:

1. With your loop playing, drag the filter envelope's D fader back to 0.
2. Now slowly raise the S fader.

   Filter envelope sustain works differently from amp envelope sustain: Instead of setting a volume, filter envelope sustain sets a filter frequency for the filter to rest at throughout the sustain stage of the sound. The sustain period length is still determined by holding down a key or by the note length in the Sequencer.

✔ Tips

- The R fader is not applicable with short-note-value bass lines. Why? The filter envelope release stage resets to the attack stage whenever a new note is pressed. Filter release will therefore only work when the amp envelope release is set high and there is enough space between notes for filter release to "trail" behind the note.
- The filter envelope has an Invert Filter button (**Figure 5.40**) that will invert the filter setting. When Invert Filter is enabled, the attack stage of the filter envelope will ramp down in brightness instead of up. With all the variables at work, the best way to use this feature is to simply press the button and hear what happens!

Low-Frequency Modulation

The SubTractor has two low-frequency oscillators, LFO 1 and LFO 2 (**Figure 5.41**). These low-frequency oscillators move so slowly that they don't make tones. Rather, they superimpose slow-moving waves over high-frequency ones to change their behavior. You can create vibrato by generating a very low-frequency wave and sending it to an oscillator's pitch. The result is as if the oscillator were poised on an ocean wave, making it go from high to low.

Figure 5.41 The low-frequency oscillators LFO 1 and LFO 2

That's the LFO concept in a nutshell. LFOs use some of the same waveforms used by the SubTractor's other oscillators—triangle, sawtooth, square, and noise—but at a fraction of the speed.

Figure 5.42 Enabling Sync allows you to set the LFO rate in tempo increments.

To modulate pitch using LFO 1:

1. Reload your test patch.
2. With your bass line playing, go to the LFO 1 section of the SubTractor and click the Sync button (**Figure 5.42**).

   Enabling Sync allows you to set the rate of the LFO to your song tempo.
3. If the triangle waveform shape is not selected, click the Waveform button to select it.

   The LFO shape determines the type of motion. In this case, you're selecting a triangle with a smooth, straight line.
4. Click the Dest (destination) button until it is set to Osc 1,2 (if it's not already selected).

Figure 5.43 Set the Rate knob to 2/4, meaning one cycle every two counts, or twice per measure.

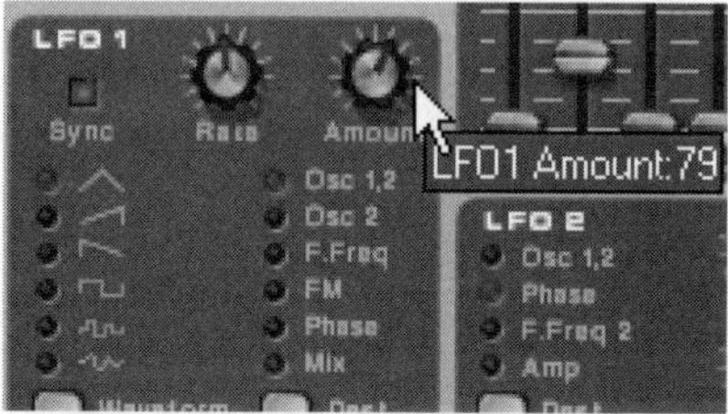

Figure 5.44 Increase the Amount to activate LFO 1 and begin pitch modulation.

Figure 5.45 The LFO wave shape switch changes how modulation occurs.

5. Place your cursor over the Rate knob and read the setting. Drag the knob left or right as necessary to set it to 2/4 (**Figure 5.43**). At a setting of 2/4 the LFO will run its triangle cycle once every two counts, or two times per measure.
6. Now comes the fun part—turn the Amount knob to the right until it is set to 79 (**Figure 5.44**). You should now hear a regular rise and fall in the pitch of your bass line.

Let's hear how different LFO waveforms or shapes change the motion effect.

To change the LFO 1 waveform:

1. Use the LFO 1 Waveform select button to get the next waveform in the column, the upwards ramp or "sawtooth" wave (**Figure 5.45**).

   Now, instead of a smooth up-and-down pitch modulation, you'll hear a half-measure ramp-up in pitch that drops back down suddenly when it gets to the top.
2. Click the LFO 1 Waveform button again to select the next shape, the reverse sawtooth wave.

   Now the pitch of your bass line starts high and ramps down every half-measure.
3. Select the next waveform, the square shape.

   The pitch of your bass line now switches back and forth between two different pitches every half-measure.
4. Select the next shape, the square noise waveform.

   This time the pitch of your bass line switches randomly between pitches every half-measure.
5. Select the final waveform, sine noise.

   This one makes the pitch of your bass line move smoothly to a random pitch every half-measure.

The LFO can also modulate parameters other than pitch by changing the LFO destination.

To change what is modulated by LFO 1:

1. With your bass line looping and LFO 1 enabled, select the LFO 1 triangle waveform.
2. Click the Osc 2 button to activate oscillator 2.
3. Click the Dest button to select the next destination, Osc 2 (**Figure 5.46**).

   Now the Osc 1 pitch is unchanged, but Osc 2 is going up and down. As these two oscillators behave differently against each other, it creates a kind of "dive bomber" effect.
4. To drastically increase the range of Osc 2's pitch changes, turn the LFO 1 Amt knob all the way to 127.
5. Turn the Amt knob back to 79.
6. To send the LFO modulation to the brightness filter, switch the Dest setting to F.Freq (filter frequency).

   Osc 2 is now dampening the brightness, causing a tremolo effect.
7. Continue experimenting. As you learn more about the sections of the SubTractor, you'll be able to do more with LFOs, as well.

✔ Tip

- With LFO 1 at maximum and going to Osc 2, try turning off Osc 2's keyboard tracking for an '80s dance siren sound.

Figure 5.46 The LFO 1 destination switch changes what is modulated.

LFOs in Everyday Life

If listening to LFO modulation is giving you a sense of déjà vu, it's because people hear LFOs every day, often without realizing it. Most police, fire, and ambulance sirens use schemes based on LFOs to vary the pitch of the siren to make them more audible.

Triangle or sine waves? Think of a fire engine's wailing siren, which goes up and down in a smooth line.

Square wave? Think of a European ambulance that switches between two tones.

Sawtooth wave? Think of a car alarm that uses tones that ramp up once and then start over when someone passes by on a Harley-Davidson.

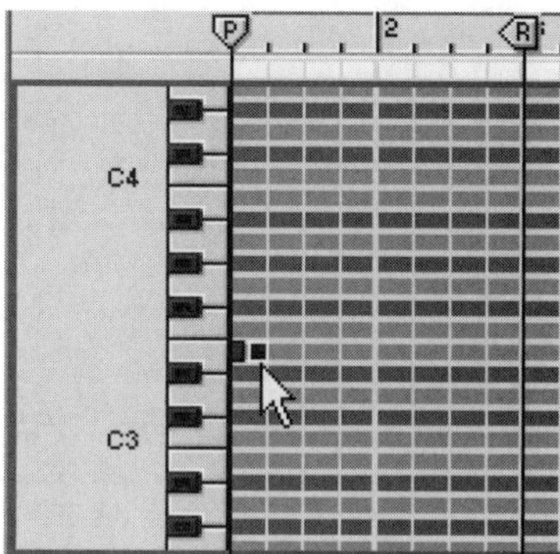

Figure 5.47 Input a note in your SubTractor Sequencer track.

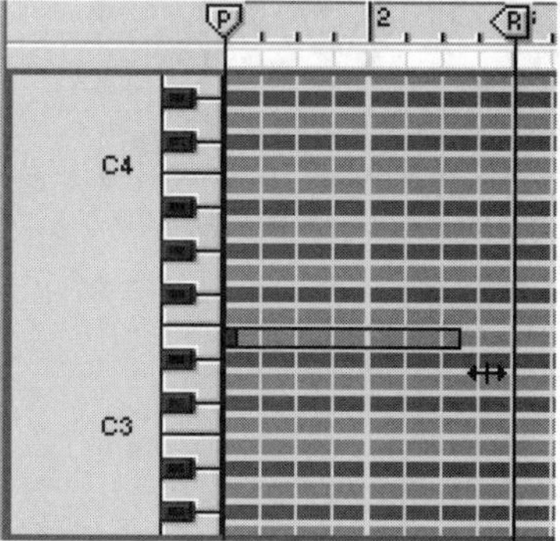

Figure 5.48 Lengthen the note by dragging its handle.

Figure 5.49 Use these knob settings to create vibrato with LFO 2.

Adding LFO 2

Because the SubTractor has another LFO, you can modulate multiple destinations at once. LFO 2 works the same way as LFO 1, but it only functions in triangle waveform mode and doesn't have a Sync function. It also has fewer Dest choices, yet it's better suited than LFO 1 for effects such as vibrato (*triangle pitch-modulation,* in synth-speak). That's because it has a Delay knob which sets a delay time before the LFO modulation is faded in.

Of course, in order to hear vibrato properly, you'll need at least one sustained note.

To use LFO 2 for vibrato:

1. Stop your loop, if it's still playing, and switch off LFO 1 by turning the Amt knob all the way to the left.
2. Go to the Sequencer window and set up a new two-bar loop in an empty section of your bass line track.
3. To make a sustained note, first use the Pencil tool to input a note at the beginning of the first measure (**Figure 5.47**). Then use the Select tool to click the right note border and drag it to the end of your two-bar section (**Figure 5.48**).
4. Now set the LFO 2 knobs: Set Dest to Osc 1,2 so that it will modulate both oscillators (**Figure 5.49**).
5. Typically, vibrato is not too fast, so set LFO 2's rate to about 80.
6. Set the Amount knob to 22—this will give you a noticeable but subtle fluctuation.
7. Most vibrato doesn't begin immediately but fades in during a sustain. To do this, set the Delay knob to 85. This sets the vibrato fade-in to be a count or two after the note begins playing.
8. Play your new loop to hear the effect.

LFO 2 keyboard tracking

The LFO Kbd knob increases the LFO 2 rate as notes go up in pitch. This is particularly helpful if you're using LFO 2 to control the oscillator's Phase knobs, which behave differently at various oscillator pitches.

To hear LFO 2 keyboard tracking:

1. In Sequencer Edit mode, drag-copy your two-bar sustained note to the next two measures and extend your loop to include it.
2. Now drag the copied note up two octaves—for example, from C2 to C4 (**Figure 5.50**).
3. With LFO 2 Dest set to Osc 1,2 and your loop playing, turn the LFO 2 Kbd knob all the way to the right (**Figure 5.51**).
4. Set your LFO 2 Amount knob high and your Delay setting short enough to allow LFO 2 to reach its full speed.

   You should now hear the LFO 2 rate accelerate as your sustained note jumps in range. (This effect will still work even if keyboard tracking is turned off on your oscillators.)

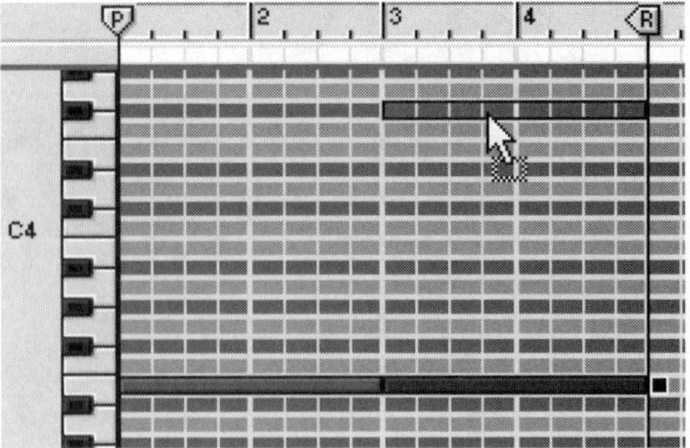

Figure 5.50 Drag a note up an octave to test the LFO 2 Kbd knob effect.

Figure 5.51 The LFO 2 Kbd knob increases the LFO rate based on note pitch.

Figure 5.52 The modulation envelope controls

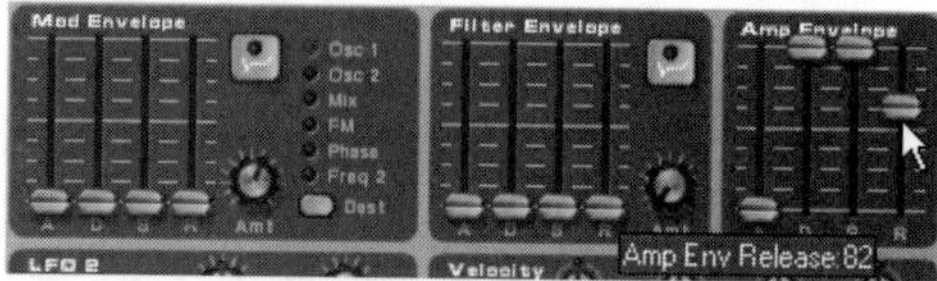

Figure 5.53 Set the amp envelope to enable all note stages so that the mod envelope can affect them.

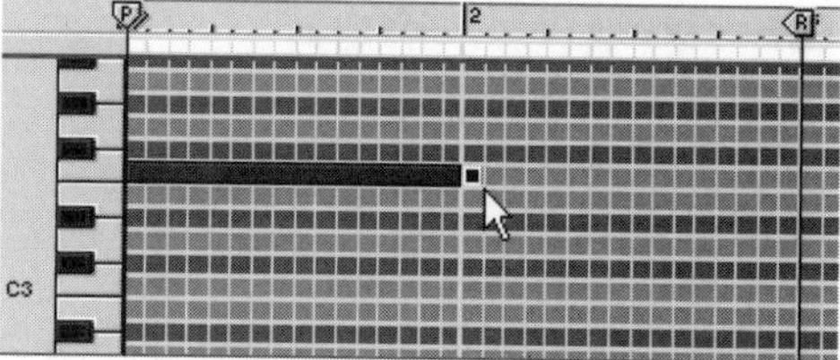

Figure 5.54 Set up a sustained note with some space after it so you can test the release stage.

Figure 5.55 Set the mod envelope attack fader above 0 to hear a pitch ramp at the beginning of a note.

The Modulation Envelope

Don't throw that sustained-note loop away just yet...we're going to use it to learn about the modulation envelope. The mod envelope works just like the amp and filter envelopes, but it accepts parameters from you to tell it what to raise and lower (**Figure 5.52**).

The mod envelope also depends on the amp envelope for signals, just as the filter envelope does. If the amp envelope release is off, there won't be an audible release stage for the modulation envelope, either.

To pitch-modulate Osc 1 with the mod envelope's attack:

1. Save any settings you may want to keep, and load the test patch.
2. Set all the mod envelope faders to 0, and set the amp envelope release fader to 82 (**Figure 5.53**). This gives your mod envelope the stages it needs for this demonstration.
3. Keep your loop length at two measures, but shorten the sustained note to one bar (**Figure 5.54**).
4. Set the mod envelope Dest to Osc 1.
5. Turn the mod envelope Amt knob to the right to about 71, and play your sustained loop.
6. To cause the Osc 1 pitch to ramp up at the attack stage, move the mod envelope A fader to 53 (**Figure 5.55**).

   The sound will now bend upward in pitch at the beginning of the note and then drop down abruptly (there is no decay stage yet).

To adjust the mod envelope D, S, and R values:

1. With your sustained loop playing and your A fader still at 53, move the mod envelope D fader to 59 (**Figure 5.56**). Now the pitch will ramp down during the decay stage.
2. Move the S fader to 44 (**Figure 5.57**).
   After the decay stage, you will hear the pitch settle to a steady tone during the sustain stage. The note will abruptly drop down to the starting pitch (there is no release stage yet).
3. Now move the R fader to 82.
   Through the second bar of your loop, you'll hear a slow ramp back down to the starting pitch as the amp envelope's release stage fades.

✔ Tip

- Try this mod envelope setting on your bass track just to see what happens. What you hear will sound more like a sound effect.

Figure 5.56 The decay stage sets the time it will take to ramp down the pitch to the level of the sustain fader.

Figure 5.57 When modulating pitch, the mod envelope's sustain stage sets a frequency. At 44, the pitch of the sustained note will settle on a high note.

Short-duration mod envelope effects sometimes behave strangely. For example, when running your bass line with the mod envelope set to Osc 1, your decay fader alone can seem to be doing three different things.

To use the mod envelope's decay stage on short notes:

1. Set up your Sequencer to play your bass line.
2. Reset all the mod envelope faders to 0 and the Dest to Osc 1.
3. Set your Polyphony count to 1 so that your notes don't overlap.
4. Play your loop, and turn up the mod envelope Amt knob.

   You should be hearing the first decay effect: a percussive pulse or noise transient. The pulse is the decay dropping the pitch at maximum rate (0 in this case) and creating an impact sound.
5. Lengthen the decay to 53 and it becomes a laser swooping sound.
6. Continue moving the D fader up. Past halfway, the decay will exceed your note length, cutting off the swoop sound. The result will be a second tone that seems to toggle off the first—like a ringing cell phone.

   The ring tone gets higher when you raise the decay fader more. This is a phantom effect, since the pitch modulation isn't really changing pitch; what's changing is just the point where the decay pitch swoop is cutting off. As the decay slope decreases, the cutoff point rises.

✔ Tip

- As you try out the mod envelope on other synth parameters, keep in mind that only the S fader in the mod envelope sets a level. The other faders adjust time.

Using the Velocity Section

The Velocity controls (**Figure 5.58**) are a powerful array of sensitivity knobs like the ones on the Redrum channel controls (see Chapter 4, "Getting Started").

Each of the Velocity knobs sets the SubTractor's various parameter reactions to velocity in your Sequencer track. When a knob is turned to the right, increases in velocity will cause an increase in that parameter. When a knob is turned to the left, increases in velocity will cause a decrease in that parameter.

Now that you know how the oscillator, filter, LFO, and envelope sections work, you're ready to use the Velocity controls to tune a track and add different types of expression to the accents.

First, let's look at how to get the SubTractor to play high-velocity notes louder. This one's important, because it's the only way to get the SubTractor to play hard notes loudly and soft notes softly!

To control volume with velocity:

1. Save any settings you want to keep, and load your test patch.
2. Make sure that the notes in your bass track have accents or some type of velocity variation (**Figure 5.59**). If they don't, use the Pencil tool to boost and drop some note velocities. (If you're not sure how to do this, refer back to Chapter 4.)

Figure 5.58 The Velocity control knobs

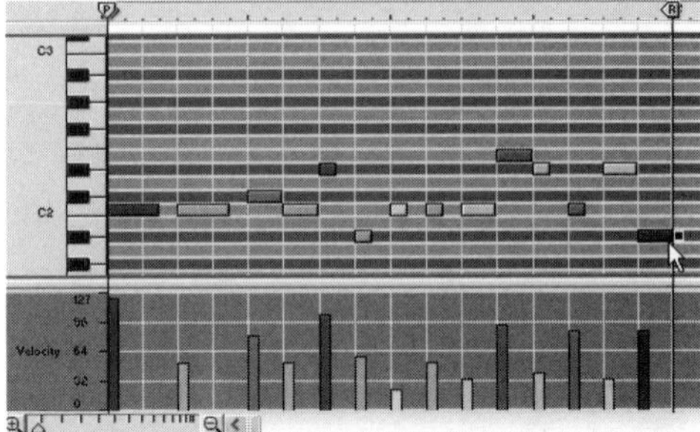

Figure 5.59 This example bass line uses note and velocity variation (accents).

Figure 5.60 The Amp velocity knob sets velocity's affect on volume.

3. With your loop playing, boost the Amp knob to the right. This makes the SubTractor respond to velocity with note volume (**Figure 5.60**).

4. Invert the velocity sensitivity by turning the Amp knob to the left of center, until strong attacks sound soft, and weak attacks sound loud.

✔ Tips

- When the Amp knob is set midway, the SubTractor will play all notes at the same volume, regardless of velocity.
- A "negative" or inverse setting for the Amp velocity knob is a useful real-time play parameter. It can change the phrasing of a music line without doing anything at all to the notes.

To control Filter 1 with velocity:

1. Turn the filter envelope on by turning up the filter envelope Amt knob.

2. Set the filter envelope's D fader up high enough to create a brightness boost.

3. In the Velocity panel, turn the F. Dec knob to the right.

   Now when note attack increases, the equivalent of a boost to the filter envelope D fader will occur.

✔ Tip

- Always remember that Velocity sensitivity knobs will have no effect on disabled controls. For example, if Filter 2 is not enabled, the Velocity sensitivity knob won't do anything for Filter 2.

Other Play Parameters

There are other controls that affect the way the SubTractor reacts to note data. You'll find them under the Patch name display (**Figure 5.61**).

Figure 5.61 The SubTractor's play parameter controls

The Legato and Retrig (or Retrigger, used with the Portamento knob) modes are slurring effects and only work when the SubTractor is limited to one voice (when Polyphony is set to 1).

Legato mode works when notes overlap, disabling envelopes until notes are no longer sounding simultaneously.

Figure 5.62 Switch to Legato key mode.

To create a legato line:

1. Initialize your patch.
2. Use the arrow buttons to set Polyphony to 1.
3. Select the Legato mode by clicking the Mode button (**Figure 5.62**).
4. Create a new one-bar loop in your SubTractor track, and input a series of consecutive notes (**Figure 5.63**).
5. Disable Snap to Grid, and select the new notes using the Selection tool (**Figure 5.64**).
6. Grab each note's length-adjustment square and drag it slightly to the right, just enough so that the notes all overlap (**Figure 5.65**).
7. In the Rack, increase the S fader on your amp envelope all the way up to 127. Press play.

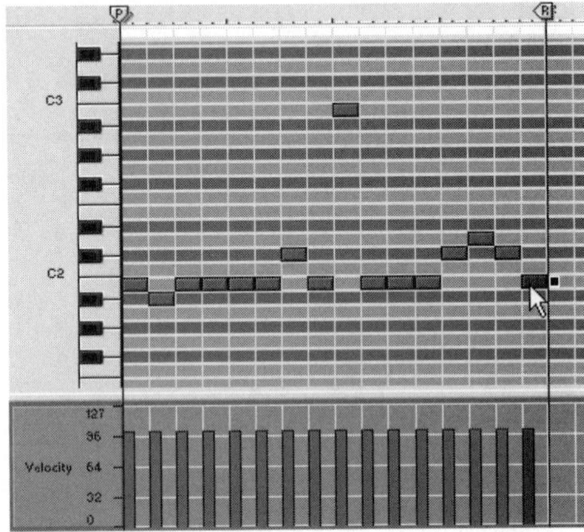

Figure 5.63 Input a series of consecutive notes for a legato line.

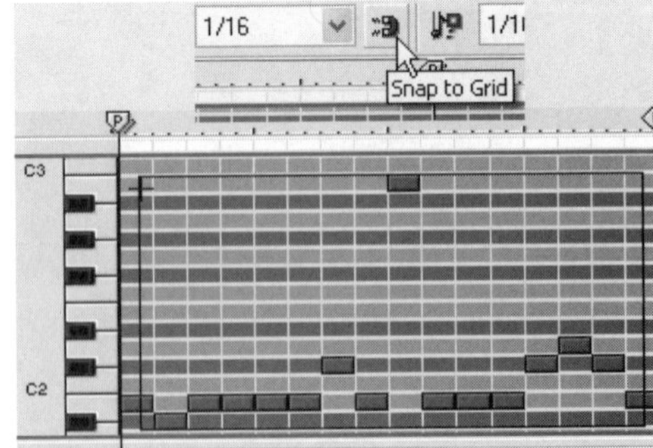

Figure 5.64 Disable Snap to Grid and select all the notes.

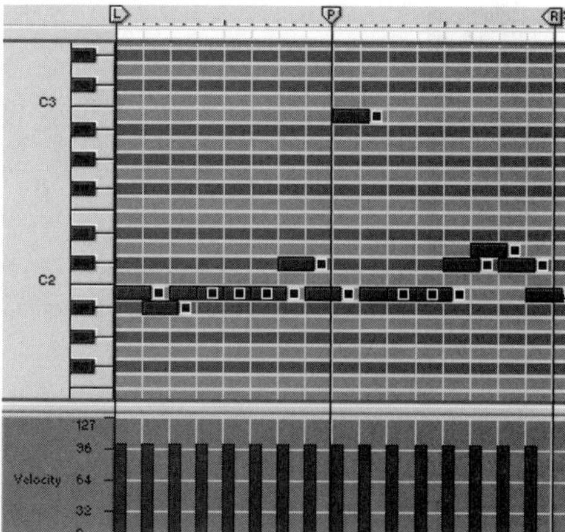

Figure 5.65 Drag all the note lengths until they slightly overlap.

Figure 5.66 The Portamento knob slurs the pitch from one note to the next, slowing down the effect at higher settings.

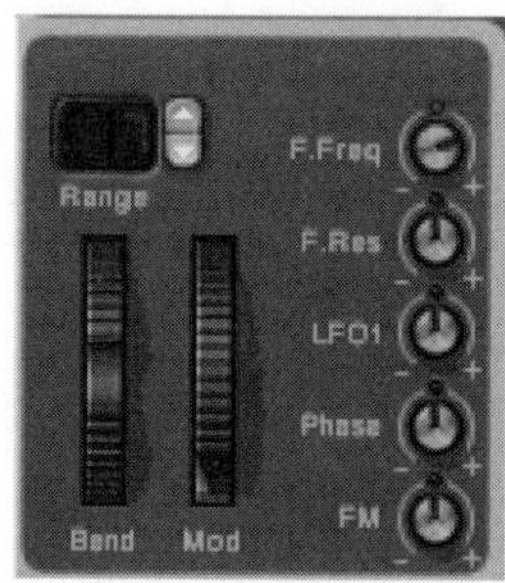

Figure 5.67 The Range setting determines how much effect the pitch Bend wheel has.

Retrigger mode slurs pitch from one note to the next. It's great for adding expression to a bass line or melody. The rate at which the pitch slurs is set by the Portamento knob (or *portamento time*) setting.

The Portamento knob can create "otherworldly" theremin effects. When the portamento time setting exceeds the note length, the slur effect will "float" without ever settling on a pitch.

To create a portamento line:

1. With your loop playing, select the Retrig mode.
2. Drag the Portamento knob to the right to increase the pitch slur time between notes (**Figure 5.66**).

MIDI control section

The SubTractor can process external controllers like the pitch bender on your keyboard. You don't have to have a keyboard to bend notes, however, because the SubTractor comes with a virtual bender of its own.

To set the Bend wheel range:

◆ Click the Range arrow keys to select the number of half steps you want the Bend wheel to bend (range is 1–24 semitones) when pushed up or down all the way (**Figure 5.67**).

✔ Tip

■ When it's set below 2, bend range can be used for very subtle fluctuations in pitch; or it can be set at maximum (24) to swoop up and down two whole octaves.

The SubTractor also has a set of Mod wheel controls that function just like the Velocity controls. The Mod wheel settings provide an excellent way to adjust many aspects of the SubTractor's sound all at once from your master keyboard, or from the front panel.

Figure 5.68 These controls determine the effect of the Mod wheel.

To set up the Mod wheel controls:

1. Turn the F.Freq knob to the right, and the Mod wheel movements will raise Filter 1's Freq value.
2. To set the Mod wheel to control the Filter 1 Res value, increase the Mod wheel's F.Res knob.
3. To set the Mod wheel to control the LFO 1 Amt parameter, increase the Mod wheel's LFO1 knob.
4. To set the Mod wheel to increase the oscillator's Phase or FM settings, increase the Mod wheel's Phase and FM knobs, respectively.

✔ Tip

- The SubTractor has a third set of Ext. Mod control knobs (**Figure 5.68**) that respond to aftertouch (additional pressure on keys after they're pressed down), expression (a pedal controller), or a breath controller.

Figure 5.69 Set the phase offset type for Osc 1.

Figure 5.70 Set the phase offset amount for Osc 1.

Figure 5.71 Accent attack using a short setting for noise decay.

Putting It All Together

Now that you've been through the various controls of the SubTractor, you may feel a bit overwhelmed. To help you understand how it fits together, following are some patch setups that use many of the controls.

Before you start, make sure that your bass line has some accents (velocity variations), because we're going to use the Velocity controls later.

Example 1: Phase bass

This is a basic techno bass that will work well for arpeggios and filter sweeps. Many of the knob settings will react strongly when altered, so this example has some tone-morphing potential if you want to tweak some knobs during playback.

To set up the oscillators:

1. Re-initialize your patch and start your bass loop.
2. For Osc 1, click the Mode switch to select the middle phase offset (–) (**Figure 5.69**). This will fatten the oscillator sound.
3. Turn the Osc 1 Phase knob down to 40 (**Figure 5.70**).
4. Turn on Osc 2.
5. To complement Osc 1, set the Osc 2 phase offset to the middle (–), and turn the Osc 2 Phase knob to 76.
6. Activate the noise generator.
7. Turn the Noise Decay knob down to 81 (**Figure 5.71**). This adds a crisp attack sound to Osc 1 and 2.

To set up the filters:

1. For a slight resonance effect, drag the Filter 1 Res fader to 20 (**Figure 5.72**).
2. To slightly mute the bass, drag the Filter 1 Freq fader to 58 (**Figure 5.73**).
3. To brighten the attack stage, set the filter envelope D (decay) fader to 48 (**Figure 5.74**).

   Why mute the filter in step 2 and brighten it in step 3? Here in step 3 we're applying a filter motion on note attack, whereas in step 2 we set a base brightness value.
4. Increase the motion effect by raising the filter envelope Amt knob to 12 (**Figure 5.75**).

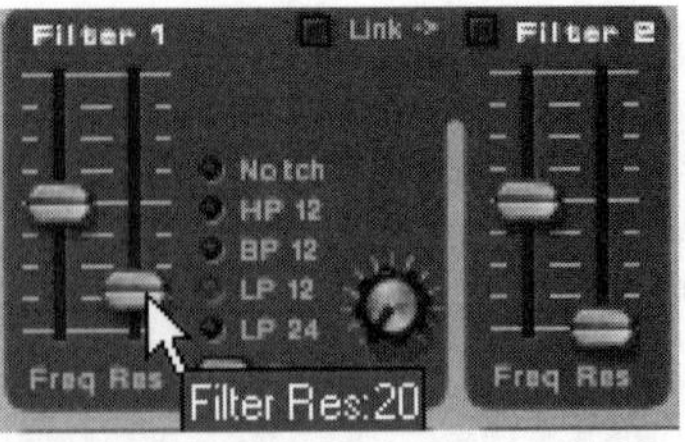

Figure 5.72 Boost Filter 1 resonance.

Figure 5.73 Mute the overall frequency by turning down the Filter 1 Freq fader.

Figure 5.74 Brighten the filter effect by increasing the Filter 1 decay time.

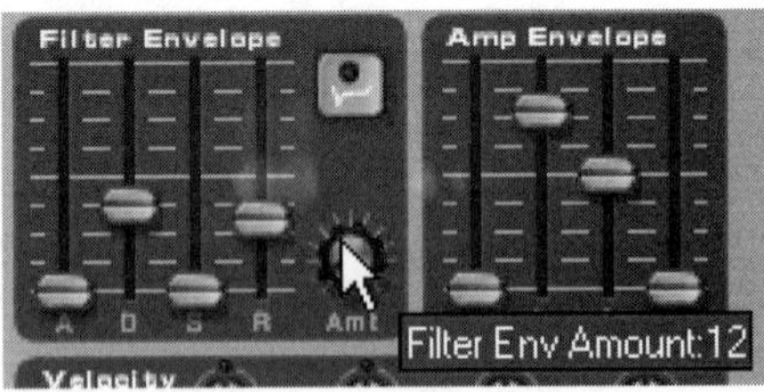

Figure 5.75 Raise the filter envelope amount.

Figure 5.76 Enable Sync to modify the LFO rate by time signatures.

Figure 5.77 Turn on the LFO with the Amount knob.

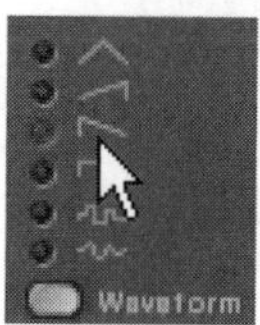

Figure 5.78 Select the downward sawtooth waveform.

Save the patch now if you like it the way it is, because next we're going to modulate some parameters.

To set up the LFO:

1. Enable Sync on LFO 1 (**Figure 5.76**) and set the Rate knob to 4/4.
2. Select the LFO 1 F.Freq destination by clicking the Dest switch.
3. Turn the LFO on by increasing the Amt knob to 30 (for a subtle modulation), or higher for a more dramatic modulation (**Figure 5.77**). This will cause the LFO filter to run one waveform cycle each measure.
4. Now select the downward-ramping sawtooth LFO waveform (**Figure 5.78**). Now the LFO filter motion is brightest at the beginning of each measure.

Lastly, we'll shape the tone using the mod envelope and Velocity controls.

To shape the tone:

1. In the mod envelope settings, turn the Amt knob to 22 and slide the decay fader to 22. This applies a slight detuning effect to the default mod envelope destination, Osc 1 (**Figure 5.79**).
2. In the Velocity controls, turn the FM knob to 10 (**Figure 5.80**). This adds a subtle distorted pulse to the line.
3. Turn the F.Dec knob in the Velocity controls to –6 (**Figure 5.81**). This tightens up the sound by causing the high-velocity notes with the most FM modulation to have the shortest bright period.
4. If you like this particular bass sound, save it as a new patch. If not, just click and hold on the patch name to return to your saved patch, or re-initialize the patch to start over from scratch.

Figure 5.79 Set the mod envelope's destination to Osc 1.

Figure 5.80 The FM velocity control makes frequency modulation respond to note velocity.

Figure 5.81 The F.Dec velocity control knob makes filter decay respond to note velocity.

Example 2: Superhero bass

This is a bright bass stack that tunes both oscillators a perfect fifth apart—it works well either as a bass or a lead.

To set up the oscillators:

1. Re-initialize your SubTractor patch.
2. Start your bass loop or write another one; this sound works the best in the range from C2 to C3.
3. Change the Osc 1 Waveform setting to 15.
4. Select the middle (–) phase offset mode.

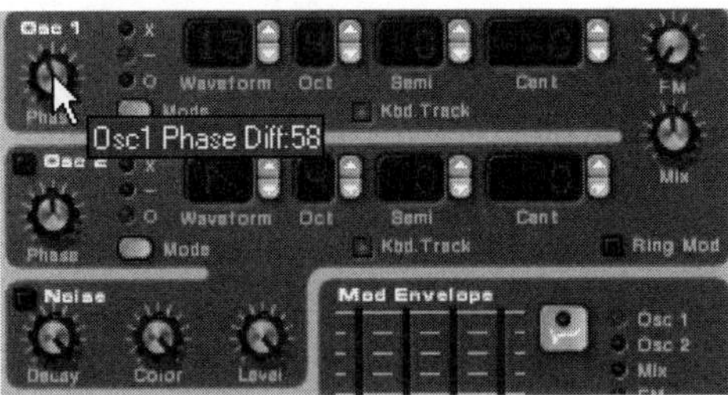

Figure 5.82 Set the Osc 1 Phase knob.

Figure 5.83 Transpose Osc 2 up a fifth using the Semi arrow buttons.

Figure 5.84 Add a bit of FM modulation.

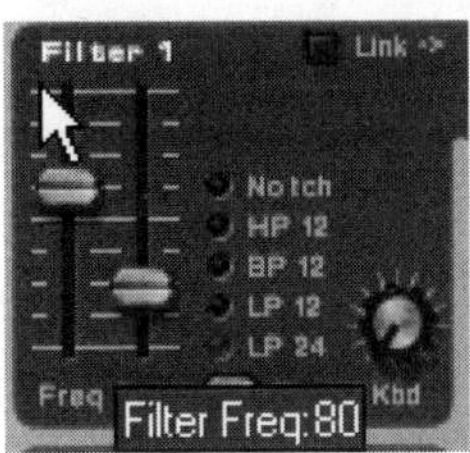

Figure 5.85 Select the LP 24 filter type for Filter 1.

5. Turn the Osc 1 Phase knob left to 58 (**Figure 5.82**).
6. Turn on Osc 2.
7. Raise the Osc 2 Semi setting to 7 (**Figure 5.83**).
8. For a tubelike distortion effect, tap the Osc 1 FM knob up to 2 (**Figure 5.84**).
9. To add a nice bright attack, turn on the noise generator and set the Noise decay to 63.

Now we'll use the filters to brighten up the sound and set high release values to add fullness.

To set up the filters and envelopes:

1. Set the Filter 1 Type to LP 24, the Res fader to 30, and the frequency to 80 (**Figure 5.85**).
2. Set the amp envelope release stage to 64 and the Polyphony somewhere between 2 and 4.

   This puts in a slight bit of overlapping that will add some low tone, but not so much as to create a wash. Feel free to drop the Polyphony count lower depending on how your bass line sounds.
3. Now set hard notes to stay bright longer, by dragging the Velocity F.Dec knob right to 6.
4. Save the patch if you want to keep it.

Adding a Malström

Although the Malström is good for percussion sounds, bass sounds, and so forth, it really shines for long, evolving, and bright sounds that cut through to the top of a mix. In this section you'll write a basic melody and then use it to get introduced to the various sound-processing controls of the Malström.

The Malström is an analog synth/sampler hybrid: Instead of generating tones, its two oscillators use samples. What makes it different from a sampler (or "wavetable" synthesizer) is that the Malström can fast-forward or play slow-motion through samples without changing the pitch. The process is called "granular synthesis" and involves chopping up the samples, processing the pieces, and then putting them back together again.

The Malström can also play from any point in a sample and use the tone characteristics from the sound at that point to create new tones. This gives the Malström a great deal of tonal variety and modulating possibilities, as you'll hear shortly.

To create a Malström:

1. If you are starting from an empty Rack, be sure to create a Mixer first.
2. Select Create > Malström Graintable Synthesizer.
3. Take a minute to look at the controls.

   The play parameter controls (**Figure 5.86**) and oscillators (**Figure 5.87**) should look familiar from your work with the SubTractor. The only significantly different area is the Shaper (**Figure 5.88**).

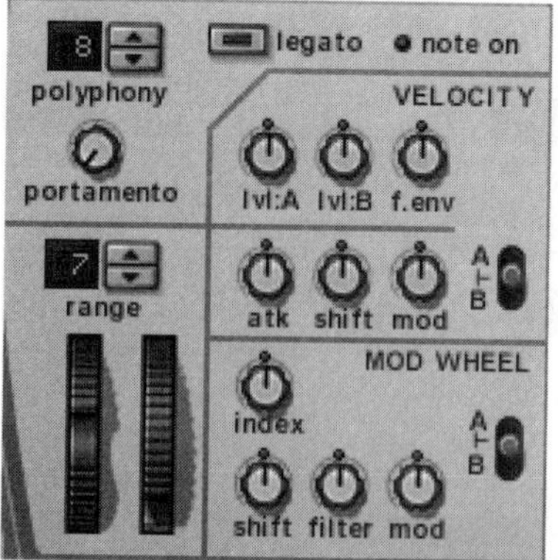

Figure 5.86 The Malström's play parameter controls are just like the SubTractor's.

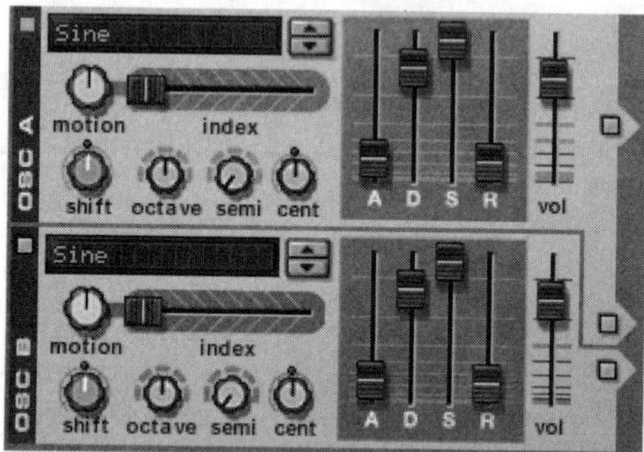

Figure 5.87 The Malström's oscillators play samples rather than simple tones.

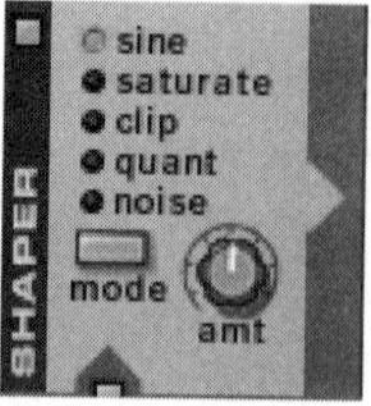

Figure 5.88 The shaper is the only significantly new control in the Malström.

ADDING A MALSTRÖM

Figure 5.89 Check the back panel of the Malström, to make sure it's cabled to an open Mixer channel.

4. Check the back panel to make sure that Reason has cabled the Malström to an empty Mixer channel (**Figure 5.89**).
5. Return to the front panel.

To write a melody track:

1. In Sequencer Edit mode, open up the Malström track Key lane. Reason adds new Malström tracks in Key lane mode by default.
2. Set up loop markers around a four-bar writing area.
3. Set the grid resolution to 1/2 (half notes; to review note values, see "Editing Timing in Reason" in Chapter 4).
4. Using the Pencil tool, input a basic two-bar melody with a long ending note (select and stretch the note duration using the Selection tool if necessary).
5. Press play.

✔ Tip

- When you know you want longer, sustained notes, changing grid resolution before drawing the notes will save you the trouble of dragging their lengths later by hand.

Changing Malström Waveforms

The Malström's `Init` patch plays a test tone (sine wave). Let's change oscillator 1 to a different waveform.

Figure 5.90 Choose the sawtooth*4 waveform for Osc A.

To change the Osc A waveform:

1. Start your melody loop and make sure your volume isn't set too high (Malström patches can be very bright).
2. Click once on the up arrow next to the Osc A waveform display. You should now see the second waveform, `sawtooth*4` (**Figure 5.90**).
3. Switch through the various waveforms to hear what they sound like. You can either right-click or click and hold on the oscillator's waveform display to see a pop-up menu of all the available choices.

Waveform index

The Malström oscillator banks are full of complex and changing waveforms. Using the sounds as they are will keep you busy for a while. However, using these types of sound with the Maelstrom's granular synth engine gives you another advantage.

The Malström indexes each oscillator tone into "snapshots." You can browse these using the Index slider to start the waveform playback at a different point. Even with a waveform as simple as `sawtooth*4`, you will see that just moving the Index slider can squeeze many different tones out of one oscillator!

Figure 5.91 Turn the Motion knob to the left for the slowest setting.

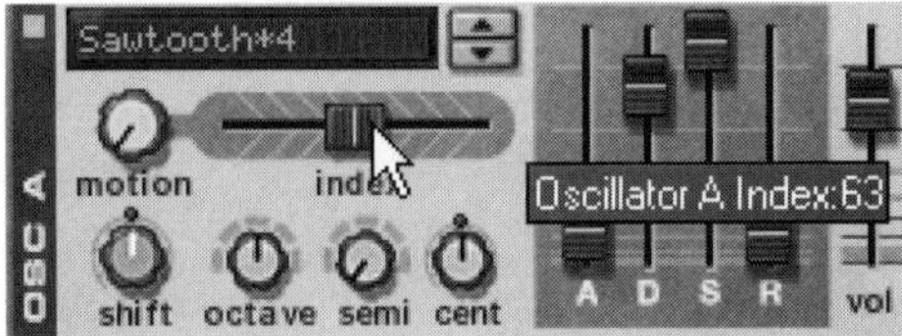

Figure 5.92 The Index slider switches through the grain table of Osc A, changing the sample's playback start point.

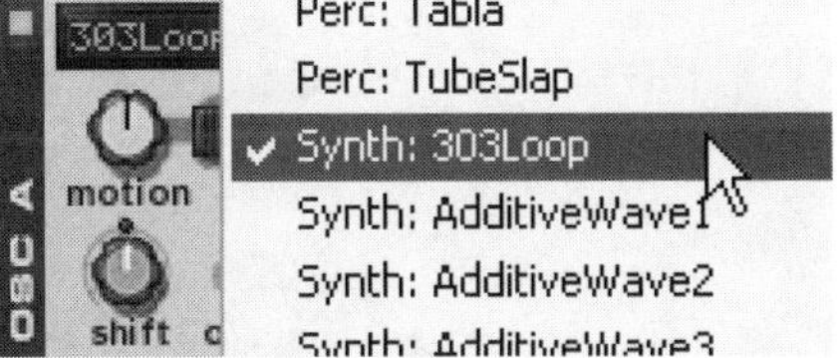

Figure 5.93 Right-click the waveform display for a pop-up menu of waveforms.

To use the index slider as a tone control:

1. With Osc A set to the `sawtooth*4` waveform, start your loop.
2. Freeze-frame the oscillator by turning the Motion knob all the way left to –64 (**Figure 5.91**). You'll hear the sound "focus" to a much simpler sound.
3. To hear all the different tonal variations along the `sawtooth*4` waveform, move the Index slider slowly to the right (**Figure 5.92**).

   The Index slider is a powerful tone control for focusing in on a tone or for varying the tone during playback.

The Index slider has different effects when the oscillator sample is in motion. Let's try it with a longer, more recognizable type of sample: a bass loop from the oscillator bank.

To adjust waveform motion:

1. Turn the Motion knob back to the middle 0. This sets the playback rate for the sample to the same rate at which it was recorded.
2. Select the `Synth:303Loop` waveform for Osc A, using the arrow buttons or by right-clicking on the oscillator's waveform display (**Figure 5.93**).

   The `303Loop` *s*ample will play a pattern on each note of your melody. This particular bass loop makes the Malström sound like a pattern player or arpeggiator, changing pitch and keeping the same rhythm. Remember that what you're hearing is still a single bass sample!

continues on next page

3. Move forward in the sample by moving the Index slider to about 34. Now the pattern starts in a different place because the sample is being played back from the middle.
4. Turn the Motion knob right to 2; this speeds up the pattern without affecting pitch.
5. Turn the Motion knob left to –2, to slow the sample down.
6. Set the Motion knob all the way left if you want to hear different parts of the loop in freeze-frame mode.
7. Now for something new—turn the Shift knob left and right to alter the formant (see sidebar, "Formant Shifting")—or to hear the sound "smaller and larger" (**Figure 5.94**).

   The Shift knob is not a pitch control. Notice that the actual notes are not rising and falling, but rather just the size or character of the bass playing them.

Figure 5.94 The Shift knob shifts the formant up and down—the effect is like enlarging and shrinking the sound.

Formant Shifting

Formants are the harmonics and frequencies that define a sound.

The Malström can shift formants by mapping a sound's defining frequencies and then shifting them up or down. This changes the "size" of a sound—without affecting the pitch.

Think of formants as frequencies that characterize the size of a speaker cabinet or resonant chamber, like the human throat. With voice, these frequencies are normally associated with gender or head size. Raising the formants of a female voice can make a woman sound like a child, but leave the note the same!

Figure 5.95 Set the Osc A amp envelope set for a smooth attack (52) and release (56)

Creating a Pad

The Malström has a number of controls that work just the same as the SubTractor controls of the same name. To find out how to work the Oct, Semi, and Cent knobs in the Malström, see "Oscillators," and for the ADSR amp envelope faders, see "Using Envelopes" earlier in this chapter—or just play with them on your own!

By now you should have an idea of how the Malström's oscillators work. Now let's try using them on a voice sample to create a "pad," or sustained voice.

To create a typical sustained voice:

1. Re-initialize the Malström patch.
2. Select the `Female Choir` waveform for Osc A.
3. Move Osc A's attack (A) fader to 52. This adds a fade that simulates vocal breath attacks.
4. Move the release (R) fader to 56 (**Figure 5.95**). This scrambles some of the non-musical artifacts (called *transients*) in the oscillator sample, and blurs the note durations, as when many voices are singing.
5. Lower the Osc A Motion knob to make the choir sample sound more like a solo instrument.

The Malström's Modulator sections work much like the SubTractor's LFOs do, but the Malström's Mods are able to work on either or both oscillators, modulators, or filters.

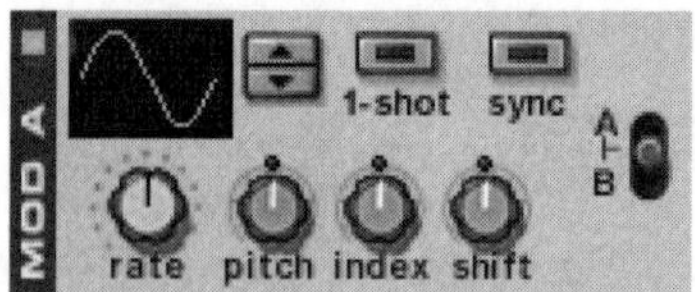

Figure 5.96 Modulator A displaying the sine waveform

To use Mod A:

1. With the `Female Choir` waveform still loaded in Osc A, turn the Motion knob back to 0 and play your loop.
2. We'll be using the default `sine` waveform for Mod A, which should already be enabled by default (**Figure 5.96**). If not, enable it and select curve 1 manually.
3. Click the 1-shot button (**Figure 5.97**). This sets the modulator to play only one waveform cycle, instead of repeating like an LFO.
4. Turn the Mod A Pitch knob to 18.

   Now you should hear a pitch slur—it will be limited to each note attack because it only modulates for one wave cycle.
5. Click the Sync enable button. Just as in the SubTractor, enabling Sync sets the Rate knob to tempo.
6. Set the Mod A Rate knob to 1/8T (eighth-note triplet) to shorten the attack slur.

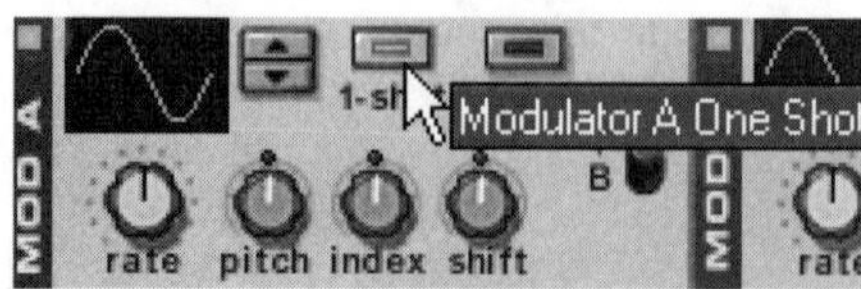

Figure 5.97 The 1-shot button forces the modulator to play only one cycle of its waveform.

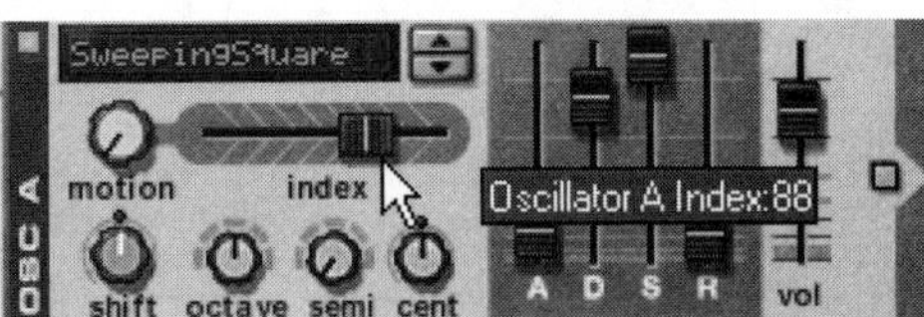

Figure 5.98 Set the Osc A index to 88.

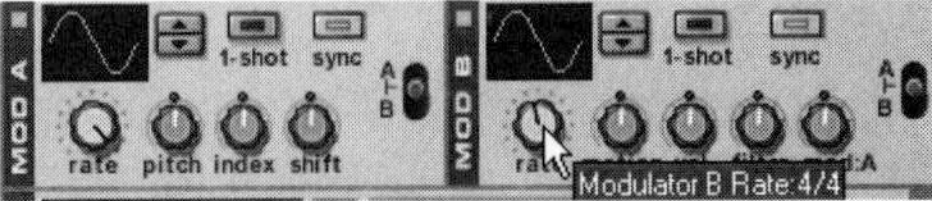

Figure 5.99 Use a slow (4/4) sine waveform on Mod B to modulate a fast (1/32) sine waveform on Mod A.

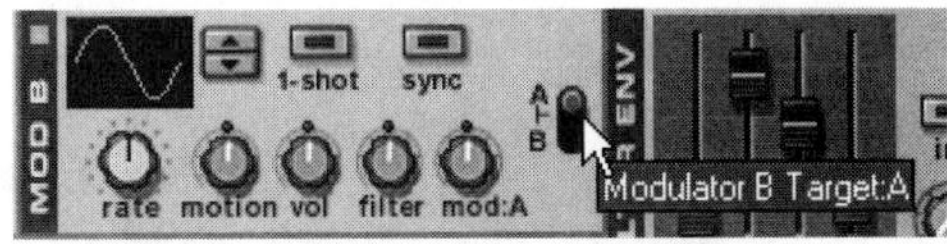

Figure 5.100 The Malström modulator destination can be set to A (up), both (middle), or B (down).

Modulation squared

When both of the Malström's modulators are active, Mod B can impose its curve on the rate at which Mod A is modulating. We'll start with a simple tone and make a "cricket" synth voice using two modulators set to different rates.

To create vibrato with Mod A and Mod B:

1. Initialize the Malström patch and start your loop.
2. Choose the `Synth:SweepingSquare` waveform for Osc A, set the Motion to zero and the Index slider to 88 (**Figure 5.98**).
3. Enable both modulators, and enable Sync for both.
4. Using the default `sine` waveforms for both modulators, set the Mod A Rate knob to maximum (1/32) and the Mod B Rate knob to 4/4 (**Figure 5.99**).
5. Set Mod A's Pitch knob to 14. This will make a very rapid vibrato.
6. Set Mod B's Mod:A knob to maximum. This causes the Mod A vibrato to fade in and out according to the Mod B waveform and rate.

✔ Tip

- The Malström's Mod B destination switch works on any A- or B-labeled control section (**Figure 5.100**). For example, when you select A for Mod B's destination, the Motion knob controls Osc A, but the Filter knob controls Filter A. In the play parameter sections (Velocity and Mod wheel), the A/B destination switches control modulators A and B, as well.

Making a Slow Pad with the Malström

Now let's use some of what we've learned to create a slow, evolving pad with just one note in our Sequencer.

Figure 5.101 Sequencer set up for a long, evolving pad

Here's an example of a creepy, evolving pad that uses one modulator on each oscillator with different shapes and very low rates. This sound uses no filtering or tone shaping. When the filters aren't being used, you can bypass the master controls altogether and run sound out the *oscillator outputs* instead of the default *main outputs.*

Figure 5.102 Change the index and motion for this Osc A pad.

First we'll set up Osc A to play a deep, low-frequency pad.

To set up and program Osc A:

Figure 5.103 Pick a lower octave and a lower formant setting for Osc A.

1. Initialize your Malström patch.
2. Make a new eight-bar loop with just one four-bar note at G3 (**Figure 5.101**), and press play.
3. At the far-right of the Malström, move the Spread knob hard right so each oscillator is coming out of a separate channel.
4. We're going to set up Osc A to be a slow metallic pad. Set Osc A to the `Voice:TibetanMonks` waveform.
5. Set the Index to 57 and the Motion to –22 (**Figure 5.102**).
6. To deepen the voice, set the Octave knob to 3 and the Shift knob down to –24 (**Figure 5.103**).
7. For infinite sustain, set the Osc A release fader to 127 (**Figure 5.104**).

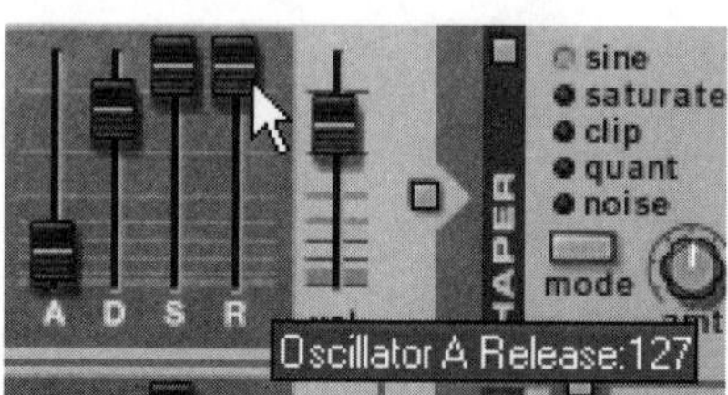

Figure 5.104 Set the Osc A release time for infinity.

Figure 5.105 Select curve 7 for Mod A.

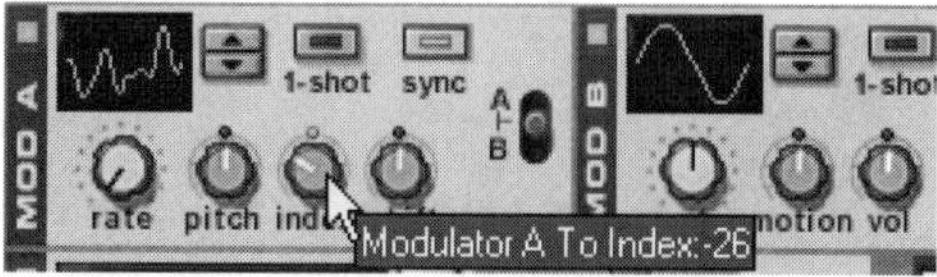

Figure 5.106 Change the Mod A Index and Motion settings.

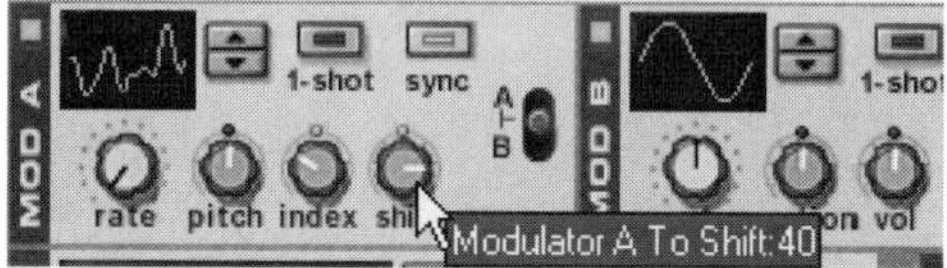

Figure 5.107 Increase Mod A's Shift.

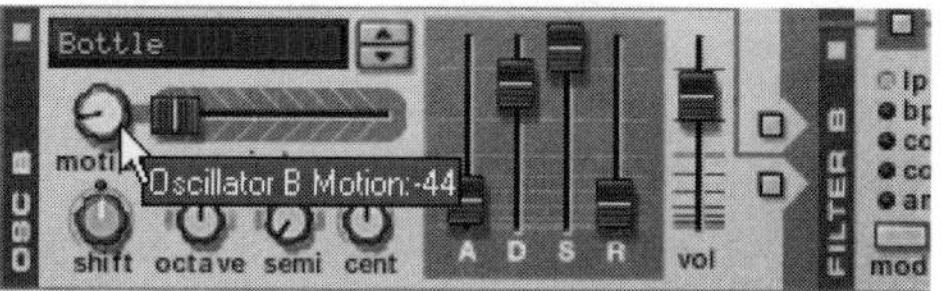

Figure 5.108 Increase the Osc B Index and decrease Motion.

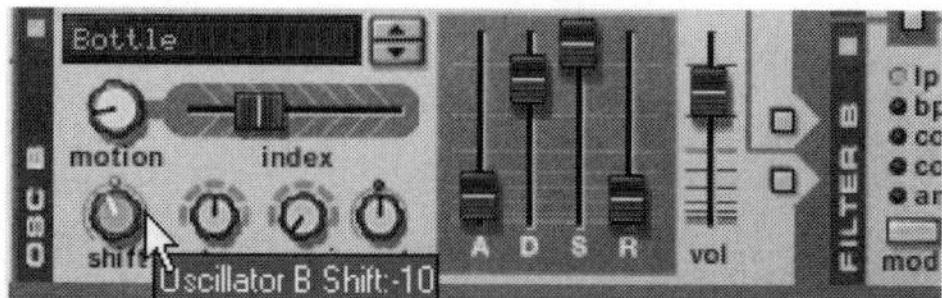

Figure 5.109 Set Osc B shift to –10 and Index to 2.

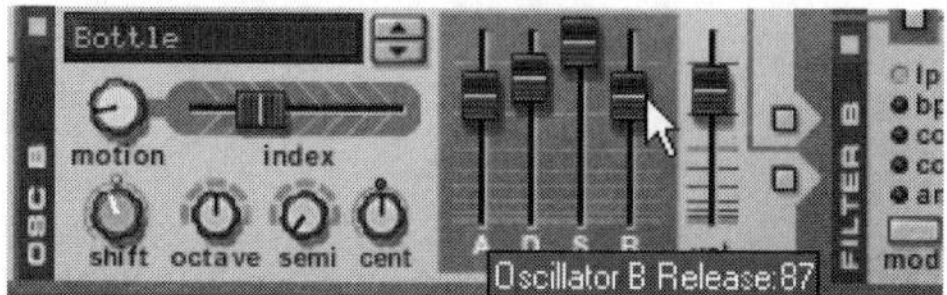

Figure 5.110 Increase attack and release for the Osc B envelope.

Now let's set up a slow-moving wave to modulate the tone of Osc A.

To set up Mod A to control Osc A:

1. Enable Mod A and set the destination switch to A (Osc A).
2. Turn on Sync for Mod A, and select curve 7 (**Figure 5.105**).
3. Slow the Mod A Rate hard left to 16/4, and the Mod A Index knob left to –26 (**Figure 5.106**).
4. Turn the Mod A Shift knob right to 40 (**Figure 5.107**).

We'll use a bottle sound in Osc B to float against Osc A.

To set up Osc B:

1. Enable Osc B and select the `Wind:Bottle` waveform.
2. Set the Motion knob left to –44 and the Index to 43 (**Figure 5.108**).
3. Set the Shift knob to –10 and turn the Octave knob left to 2 (**Figure 5.109**).
4. Set the Osc B attack and release sliders to 87 (**Figure 5.110**).

Now we'll set up a regular, sine-shaped modulation curve for Osc B.

To modulate Osc B and Mod A:

1. Enable Mod B, turn on Sync (**Figure 5.111**), and set the destination to B (Osc B).
2. Set the Mod B Rate to 16/4 and the Mod B Motion knob to –38.
3. Set the Mod B Mod:A knob hard right to 63 (**Figure 5.112**).

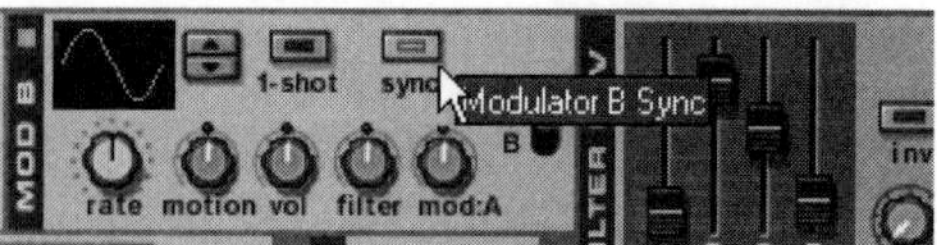

Figure 5.111 Enable Sync for Mod B.

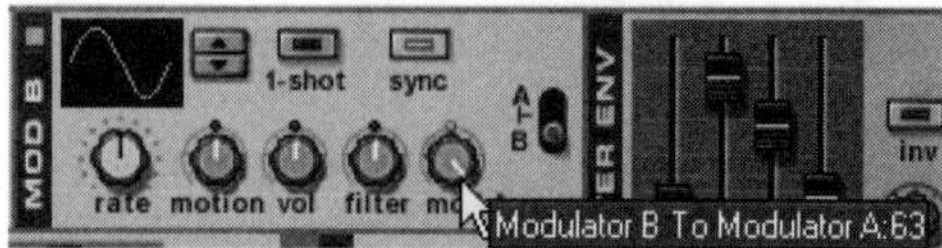

Figure 5.112 Set Mod B's Mod A control all the way right.

Figure 5.113 A path enable button

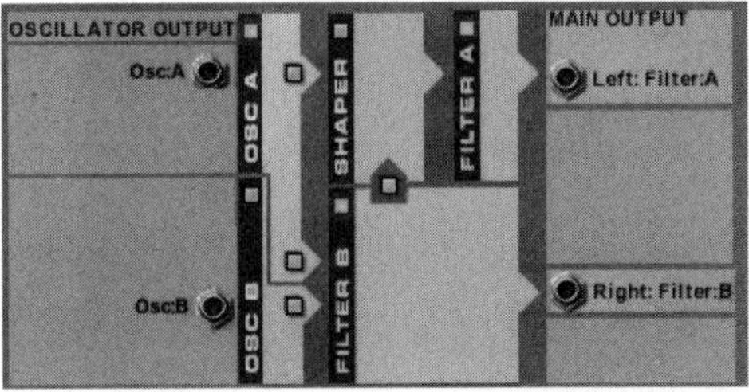

Figure 5.114 A simplified view of the Malström signal paths

Routing Signals in the Malström

One of the strengths of the Malström is that you can send, or *route*, signals from either oscillator to nearly any control. The oscillator signal paths are marked on the front panel with arrows, and can be directed a number of ways using the front panel's *path enable buttons*, marked with small connector icons (**Figure 5.113**).

The Malström can output audio directly from each oscillator, bypassing the Shaper and filter sections completely, as you can see in the simplified signal path diagram in **Figure 5.114**.

The Malström's Shaper section

The Shaper section automatically gets routed out the Left:Filter:A output. If you send Osc B to the shaper, the signal will get sent out the Left:Filter:A output even if both the shaper and the filter are disabled.

The shaper is an extension of the oscillators—it changes the shape of an oscillator's waveform at the cyclical level. Because it reshapes the wave, the shaper may not always behave the way you expect, and you'll need to do some experimenting to get comfortable with it.

For example, one would expect a "saturation" mode to simply boost gain and create more harmonics as a waveform starts clipping. However, when the shaper imposes waveform clipping on, say, a sine wave, maximum clipping isn't a noisy distortion-box type of sound—when compared to a distorted guitar, it's a perfect square wave with a fairly mellow tone.

Sometimes the shaper may have less effect than you would expect (or even no apparent effect at all). It just depends on what's feeding into the shaper and the shaper type.

To add the shaper to Osc A:

1. Initialize your patch and disable Filter A.
2. Set Osc A to play the `Wave:Sawtooth*4` sample.
3. With a melody loop playing, click the Osc A path enable button leading to the shaper (**Figure 5.115**).
4. Click the Shaper enable button (**Figure 5.116**).
5. Select the Sine mode using the shaper's Mode button, and rotate the shaper Amt knob to 65.

   Sine modulates the sound by imposing a sine wave to the oscillator. It can transform simple waveforms into more complex ones, or make complex waveforms sound smoother.
6. Drag the Amt knob to its maximum setting; the sine wave rises drastically in frequency.
7. Change the shaper mode to Saturate. This acts somewhat like a pre-amplifier or tube distortion; it can overdrive or warm up a sound, depending on the Amt knob setting.
8. Change the shaper mode to Clip. This uses digital distortion for extreme clipping.
9. Change the shaper mode to Quant. This reproduces "lo-fi" bit reduction and the resulting low-amplitude noise.
10. Change the shaper mode to Noise. This acts as a noise modulator, multiplying noise with the incoming signal.

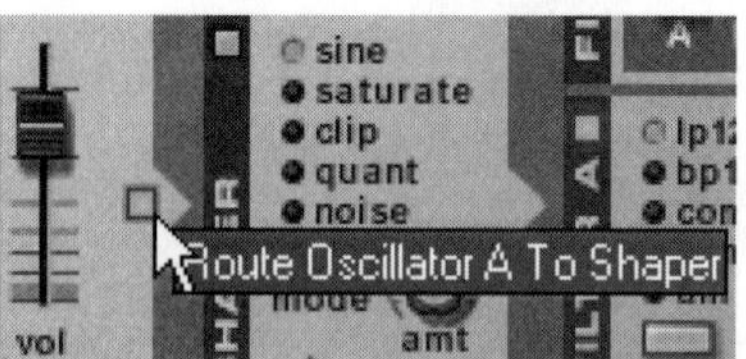

Figure 5.115 Click the Osc A path enable button to the shaper section.

Figure 5.116 Turn on the shaper.

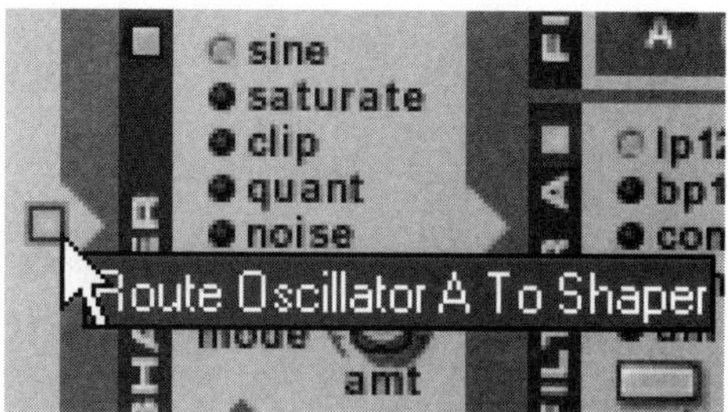

Figure 5.117 Route Osc A through the Shaper to Filter A.

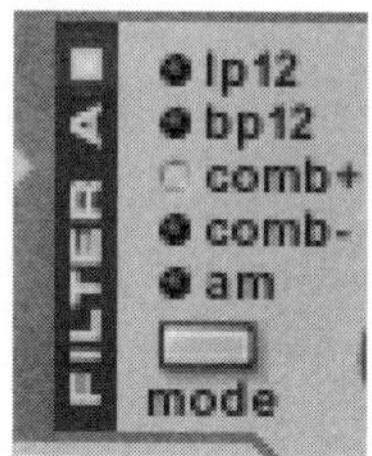

Figure 5.118 Enable Filter A.

The Malström Filters

The Malström includes some different types of filters from the SubTractor filters: a positive and negative comb filter and an AM filter.

The comb filters aren't really filters, but rather a delay effect. They duplicate an incoming signal and introduce a delay or offset, causing cancellation and interference. With comb filters, the offsets are timed so that some frequency bands get filtered out and others resonate.

Because comb filters work differently from regular filters, the Res knob doesn't work as usual, either—instead of resonating, it increases the comb effect by raising the *feedback* (number of duplications creating the comb effect).

To add a comb filter to Osc A:

1. Initialize the Malström.
2. Play a loop, and select the VSWaves waveform for Osc A.
3. Set the Osc A Motion knob to –30 and the Index slider to 37. This backs off some of the busy filter motion in this patch and sets the grain to a smoother attack.
4. Enable the Osc A path button through the Shaper to Filter A (**Figure 5.117**), and enable Filter A (**Figure 5.118**).

continues on next page

5. Choose the Comb+ mode for Filter A (**Figure 5.119**) and set the Freq knob to about 46 (**Figure 5.120**). This adds a peculiar sort of resonance to the sound, similar to a sitar.

Figure 5.119 Choose a Comb+ filter type.

Figure 5.120 Turn up the Freq knob.

6. You can hear how the comb filter is really a delay by increasing the feedback to maximum; do this by turning the Res knob to 127. Resonance will increase to a metallic ringing similar to a very short delay time with lots of feedback.

7. Just for fun, with the Res still at maximum, try dropping the Filter A Freq knob slowly down to 0.

   You should be able to hear that the Comb filter frequency is related to delay time. At lower frequencies, the ringing becomes longer and more pronounced, more like clock bells.

8. For a more melodic modulation effect, try turning Filter A's frequency to 49 and resonance to 71.

9. Save this patch as `sitar 1` so that we can come back to it.

✔ Tip

- The AM filter can sound like short-wave interference. It's a ring modulator that multiplies the oscillators entering the filter, by a sine wave produced in the filter. Resonance mixes modulated signal with clean.

Figure 5.121 Enable the envelope for Filter A.

Figure 5.122 Set up the envelope filter for a weird "plucking" effect.

You can get some interesting effects with this new `sitar 1` patch using the modulators to move some of the parameters. Let's change the settings a bit and add the filter envelope, which works just like the one on the SubTractor.

To use the filter envelope:

1. Load your `sitar 1` patch from the last exercise.
2. For a weird "plucking" effect, click the Env button to enable the envelope for Filter A (**Figure 5.121**) and set the filter envelope Amt knob to 42 (**Figure 5.122**).

To add Mod B:

1. Reload the `sitar 1` patch. (A fast way to do this is simply to click the patch name and reselect `sitar 1`.)
2. Set the Mod B destination to Osc A.
3. Set the Mod B Filter knob to 24 to make the filter swoop.

Malström Play Parameters

The Malström Mod wheel control and Velocity section work like the SubTractor's, but on the Malström these parameters can be sent to either or both of the two oscillators, two filters, and two modulators, using the A/B destination switches.

The Malström's modulation wheel can also be used to control oscillators' Shift and Index.

To hear the effects of the Mod wheel controls:

1. Load the patch Reason Factory Sound Bank/`Malstrom patches/MonoSynths/Antillator`. This patch offers a nice contrast between the up and down Mod wheel settings.
2. Move the modulation wheel with the mouse, or using your external keyboard's controller.

   On this patch, the Mod wheel works on the Filter B frequency and the Osc A Shift values (Osc B and Filter A are disabled). The result: a singing harmonic at the top wheel position, and a bright lead with a moving filter at the bottom position.

   This patch is well suited for playing with an external keyboard.

Figure 5.123 This is the default output cabling from the Malström.

Figure 5.124 The Spread knob is located with the master Volume knob in the master control section.

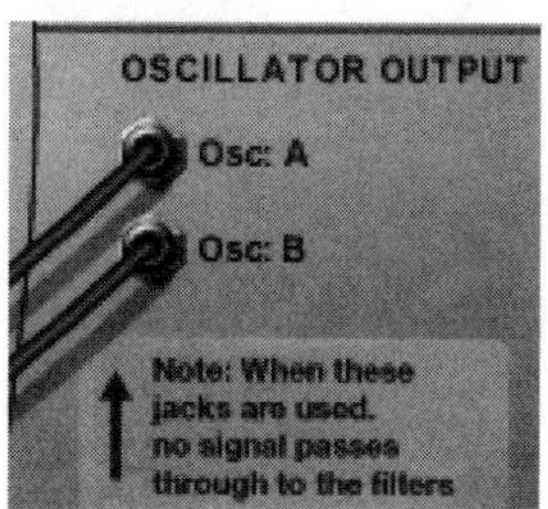

Figure 5.125 Recable the Malström to use the direct Osc A and B outputs.

The Malström Outputs

When you create a Malström, Reason automatically uses the Filter A and B outputs, whether or not filters are enabled (**Figure 5.123**). In the master control section of the Malström, you can use the Spread knob to override the default outputs.

To use the Spread knob:

1. With your loop playing and both oscillators enabled, turn the Spread knob to the left (**Figure 5.124**). You'll hear all your signals combined as one mono signal.
2. Select the `Voice:AngelChoir` waveform for Osc 1, and `Voice:TibetanMonks` for Osc 2.
3. Turn the Spread knob all the way to the right. You'll now hear the separate sounds.
4. Press Tab; on the back panel, move the output cables from the Filter A and B outputs to the Oscillator A and B outputs (**Figure 5.125**).

   This "hard-wires" a stereo spread between the two oscillators. However, these outputs will disable the main left/right filter A/B outputs. This is not a problem if you don't plan on using the filter or the shaper controls. In fact, this arrangement allows you to use the shaper and the filters for another device!

The Malström Audio Inputs

This brings us to the last example of the Malström section. It's time to try something fancier: using the Malström filter audio inputs. You can hook other devices to the shaper and to the other filter types like Comb+/- and AM.

It also means you'll need to create one new instrument for each input. To do this in the final Malström exercise, we'll use two SubTractors playing plain old `init` patches.

To hook external synths through the Malström:

1. Cable each of the Malström's oscillator outputs to a separate Mixer track (**Figure 5.126**). Just click the output and drag to the input you want.

   These will be used to play a Malström melody.

2. Write a basic two-bar sustained melody loop for the Malström (**Figure 5.127**).

3. Hold down the Shift key to disable auto-routing, and create two SubTractor synths. Without auto-routing, you'll be cabling these manually.

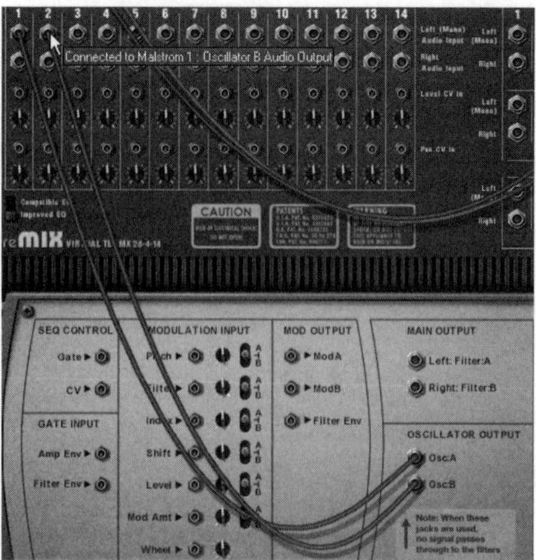

Figure 5.126 Instruments plugged into the Malström audio inputs will need the Filter A and B outputs to pass sound on to the Mixer.

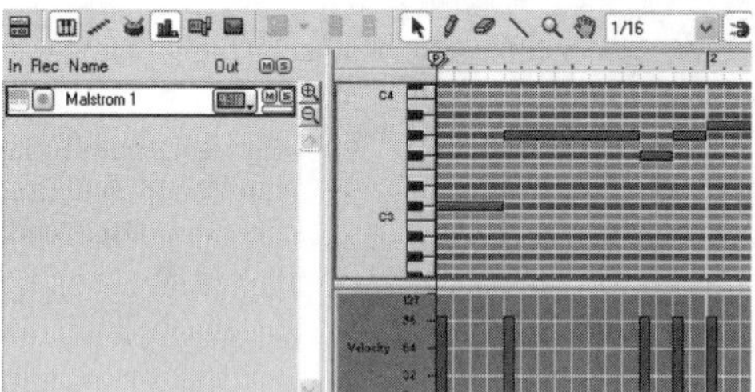

Figure 5.127 Example of a basic two-bar sustained melody loop.

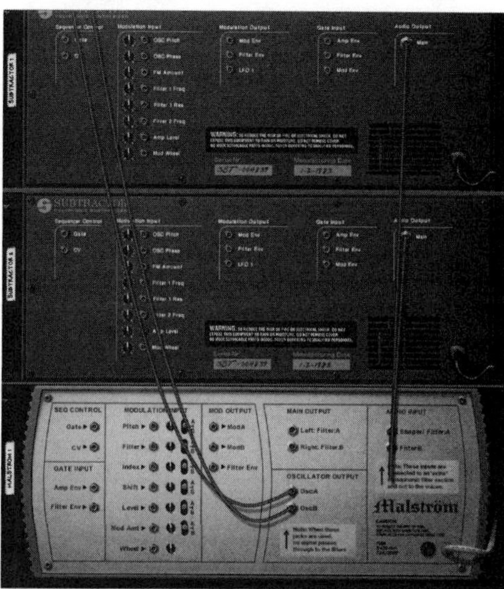

Figure 5.128 Hook two SubTractor synths to the Maelstrom's audio inputs.

Figure 5.129 Hook up the Malström Filter A and B outputs to pass the SubTractor signals out the Malström to the Mixer.

4. Go to the back panel and cable one SubTractor audio out to the Malström's Shaper/Filter:A audio input, and the other to the Malström's Filter:B input (**Figure 5.128**).
5. Minimize the SubTractors by clicking the fold/unfold arrows.
6. Now cable the Malström's main left and right outputs to separate Mixer channels (**Figure 5.129**). These will be outputting the filtered SubTractor tracks.
7. Now preserve your work by saving your song somewhere easy to find. (Saving a patch won't keep your cabling!)

Now let's set up the Malström controls to use on the SubTractor signals. We're going to use the Malström's Mod B to move Filter A and its filter envelope to move Filter B.

To run external synths through the Malström filters:

1. In your Sequencer, write a simple two-bar, sixteenth-note pulse line for SubTractor 1 (**Figure 5.130**).
2. Activate the Arrange view. Then copy and drag the SubTractor 1 track to the SubTractor 2 track (**Figure 5.131**).

   This is one fast way to get two SubTractor synths to play the same notes.
3. Return to the Rack, and in the Malström, enable Filter A.
4. Set Filter A type to Comb+, set the frequency to 52, and the resonance to 66 (**Figure 5.132**).

   This is a midrange setting good for a moving filter.

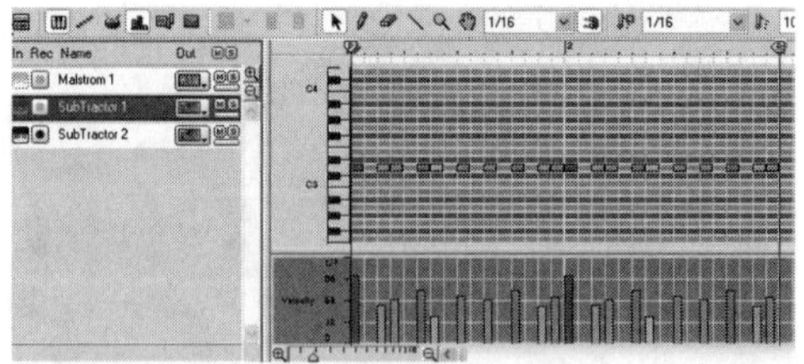

Figure 5.130 A simple, pulse bass line is sufficient for testing the Malström audio input signal.

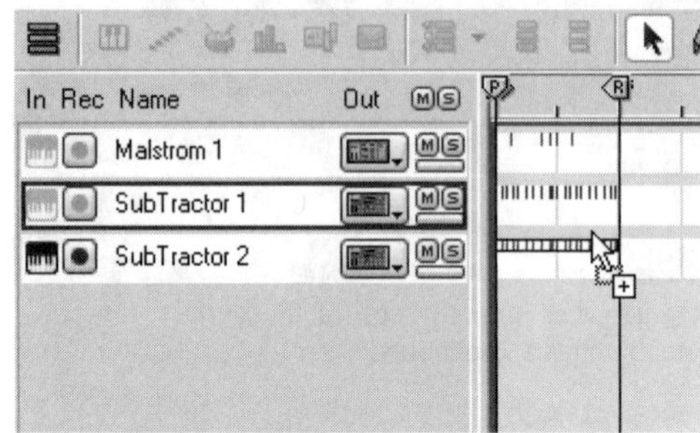

Figure 5.131 Drag-copy the bass track to the second SubTractor in the Arrange window.

Figure 5.132 This is a good setting for a moving filter.

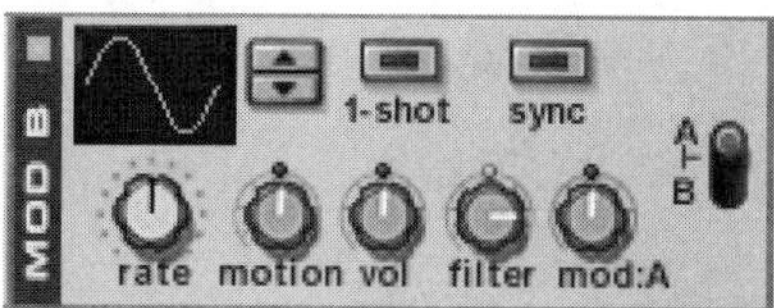

Figure 5.133 Set Mod B to move Filter A.

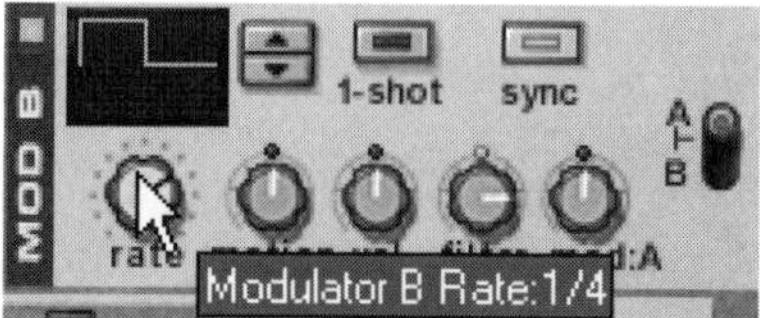

Figure 5.134 Set the Mod B curve and rate parameters.

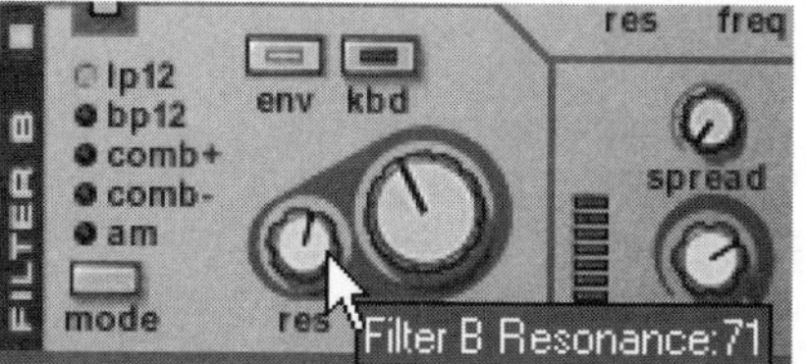

Figure 5.135 Set Filter B with a medium frequency and boost its resonance.

Figure 5.136 Filter envelope settings

5. To control Filter A with Mod B, set Mod B's destination to A and turn the Mod B Filter knob to 42 (**Figure 5.133**).

   This causes Filter A's frequency to rise according to the Mod B shape.

6. Set the Mod B curve to 4 (positive square), turn Sync on, and set the Rate knob to 1/4 (**Figure 5.134**).

   Since Filter A is set at fairly high resonance and is creating some harmonic tone, this will have the effect of imposing a ping-pong pitch shift on it.

7. Enable Filter B and set the type to LP 12.

8. To get Filter B to respond to the filter envelope, click Filter B's Env button.

9. Set the Filter B frequency to 52 and the resonance to 71 (**Figure 5.135**).

10. Set the filter envelope Amt knob to 30 (**Figure 5.136**).

    If you want more filter motion than this, try boosting the filter envelope Amt knob more and bringing the Filter B Freq knob down.

11. Save the patch in a likely, easy-to-reach spot.

For the last task, we'll set up the Malström's voice. We're already using the Malström's filters and Mod B for the SubTractor voices, which leaves us with just Mod A. That's plenty to create a long phasing effect that will sound good next to the SubTractor's pulsing lines.

Figure 5.137 Change the Osc A Index setting.

To use Mod A on the Malström oscillators:

1. Set the Malström's Osc A to `Sawtooth*4`. Turn the Motion knob to –40 and move the Index slider to a harmonically rich 57 (**Figure 5.137**).
2. Choose `Square` for the Malström's Osc B, and turn Motion to –40 (**Figure 5.138**).

   This sets up slow voices that complement each other and will respond well to Mod A Index and Shift modulations.
3. Enable Mod A.
4. Set the Mod A destination to A and B (the middle).
5. Turn the Mod A Index knob to 36.
6. Turn on the Mod A Sync and set the Rate to 8/4 (**Figure 5.139**). This sets up Mod A to give us a fairly subtle tonal change.
7. Save your patch if you think you might want to use it again!

Figure 5.138 Set Osc B's motion fairly slow.

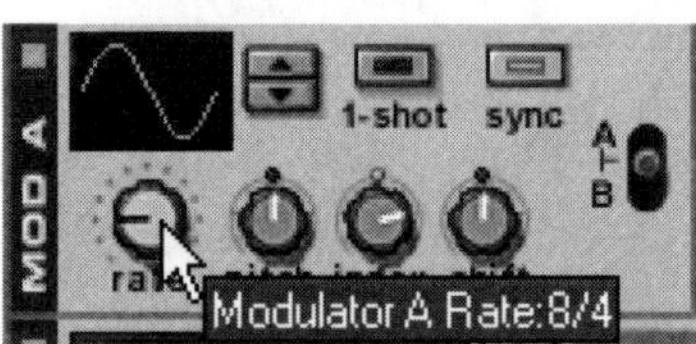

Figure 5.139 Set Mod A to a fairly slow rate for a more subtle effect.

✔ Tips

- For some nice variations on the sound created in this exercise, try changing the Filter A frequency, the Mod B Filter knob, and the filter envelope's Amt knob.
- Try loading some patches from the Factory Sound Bank into your SubTractors, or tuning the oscillators for some fatter tones.

6

Working with Samplers

Now that you've been introduced to Reason's synths, it's time to start exploring the many instruments in Reason's sound banks and using Reason's samplers to play them in your tracks.

A sampler is an empty synth that you put your own sounds in. It then maps those sounds to keys so you can play them from your keyboard or from Reason's Sequencer. From there the sampler uses the same types of filters, envelopes, LFOs, and modulation as a typical synth.

This chapter teaches you how to use Reason's NN-19, NN-XT, and Dr. Rex samplers and gives you practice in controlling them by automating knob and fader movements in your Sequencer tracks.

Creating an NN-19 Sampler

The simplest of Reason's samplers is the NN-19, which is designed to handle standard MIDI instrumentation. (If you aren't sure what counts as a *basic MIDI instrument*, look in the NN-19 `Instrument` folders in the Reason Factory Sound Bank to get an idea.) The NN-19 is also a good starting place for making your own sounds.

To create an NN-19 sampler:

1. If you're starting with an empty Rack, create a Mixer first (see Chapter 4, "Getting Started," if you need a refresher).
2. Select Create > NN-19 Digital Sampler. An NN-19 sampler appears in the Rack (**Figure 6.1**).
3. Check the back panel to make sure the L and R audio outputs are cabled to an open Mixer channel (**Figure 6.2**).
4. Return to the front panel.

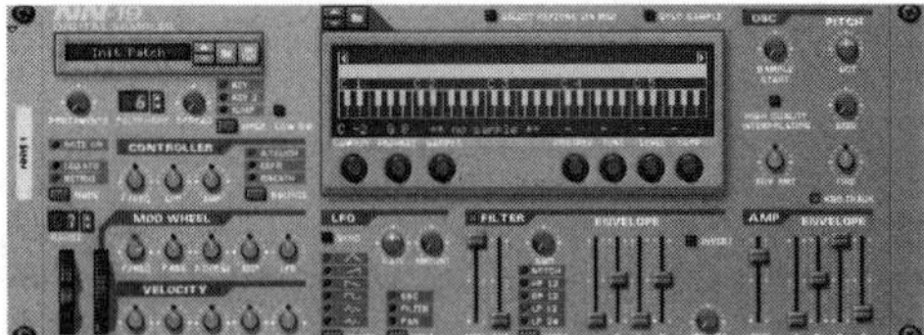

Figure 6.1 The NN-19 digital sampler's front panel

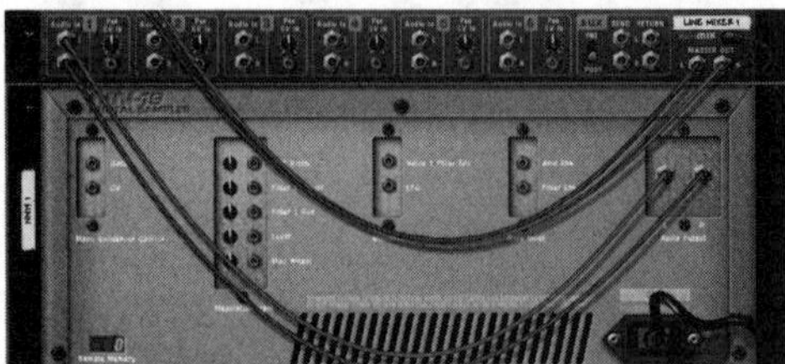

Figure 6.2 The NN-19 back panel, showing its connection to the Mixer

Figure 6.3 Click Browse Patch to bring up the NN-19 patch browser.

Figure 6.4 The Locations window is the quickest way to navigate to the Factory Sound Bank.

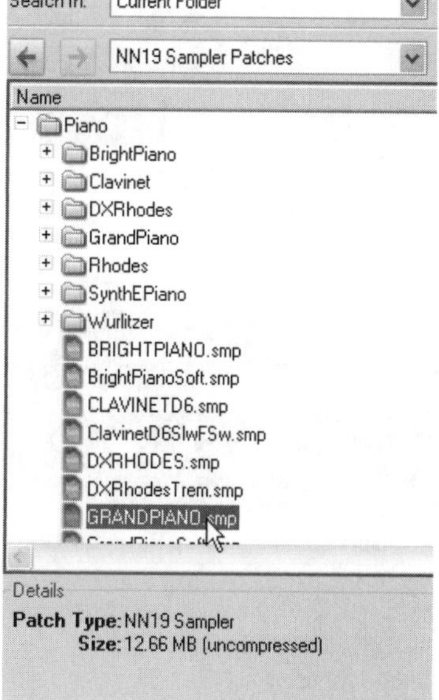

Figure 6.5 Select the GRANDPIANO patch.

Writing Your First Sampler Track

All the NN-19 instruments are stored in your Factory Sound Bank (the Reason Orkester bank does not contain NN-19 patches). Let's start by writing a piano part.

To load a sampler patch:

1. Click the patch browser icon on your NN-19 front panel (**Figure 6.3**) to bring up the Reason patch browser.
2. From the Locations window of your browser, open the Factory Sound Bank (**Figure 6.4**)
3. Go to the `NN-19 Patches/Piano` folder, select the `GRANDPIANO` patch (**Figure 6.5**), and click OK.

   The NN-19 patch display should indicate that the `GRANDPIANO` instrument is loaded (**Figure 6.6**).

Figure 6.6 The patch display shows the loaded patch.

To write a piano part:

1. If you are using a master keyboard, check your interface to make sure your keyboard's MIDI channel is routed to the NN-19 (**Figure 6.7**) and that the current Sequencer track is set to record (**Figure 6.8**).
2. Go to the NN-19 1 track in the Sequencer, open up Edit mode, and record or input some notes.

   In this example, I wrote a part for each hand: a "right hand" melody (selected) and a "left hand" bass part (**Figure 6.9**).
3. Click play, or press the spacebar to hear your track played on the NN-19's grand piano.

✔ Tip

- When a part is finished, save Rack space by clicking the fold arrow on devices that won't need further adjustment (**Figure 6.10**).

Figure 6.7 Set MIDI input from an external keyboard using the Reason hardware interface.

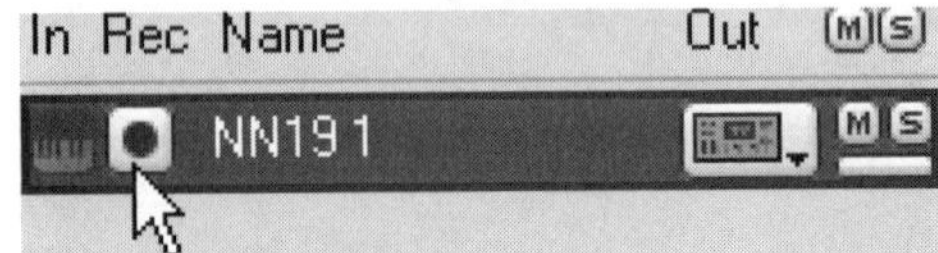

Figure 6.8 Set the Sequencer track to record note input.

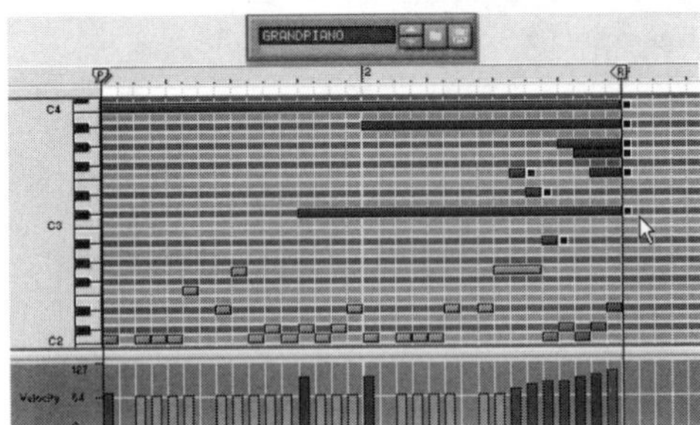

Figure 6.9 A piano part in the NN19 1 Sequencer track, with the melodic voice highlighted

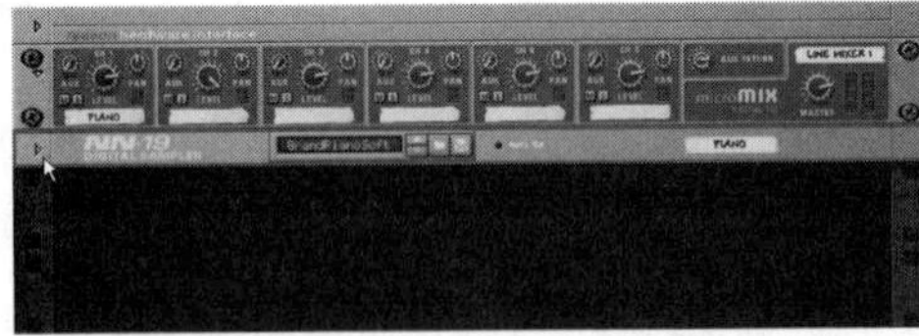

Figure 6.10 To conserve space, fold up Rack devices that you're done with.

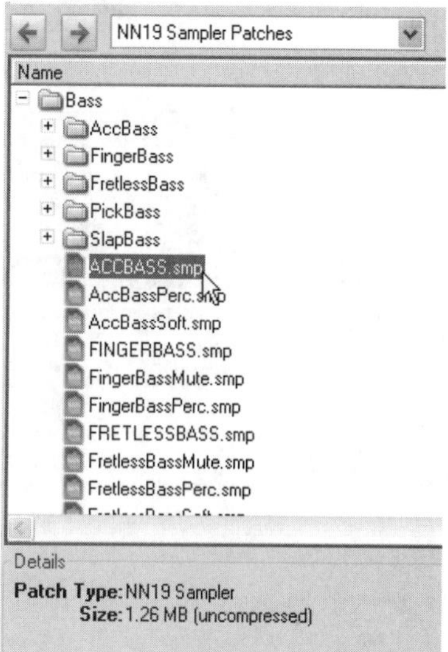

Figure 6.11 Choose a patch from the Reason Factory Sound Bank.

Figure 6.12 Write a bass accompaniment for the piano part.

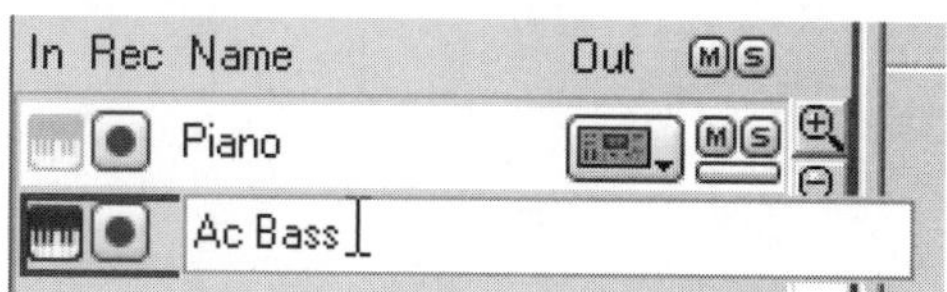

Figure 6.13 Edit the default track name.

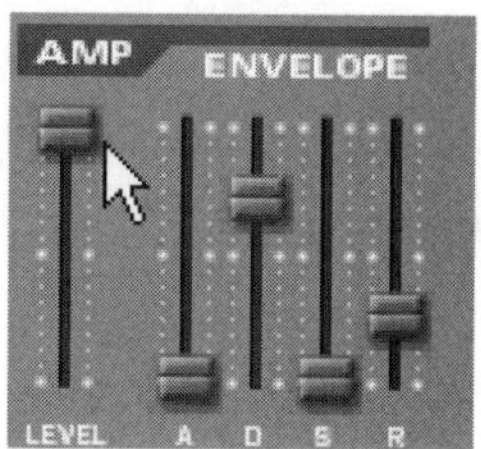

Figure 6.14 The amp envelope Level fader increases the NN-19's volume.

Writing Multiple Parts

To add more parts, simply create more instruments and record or write on the corresponding tracks. In the following examples, I add bass, trumpet, and nylon string guitar to the piano.

To add a bass part:

1. Create a new NN-19 device and load the `NN-19 Patches/Bass/ACCBASS` patch (**Figure 6.11**).
2. Write a bass part to complement the piano (**Figure 6.12**).
3. Double-click track names to change them from the default device names, to help you tell them apart quickly (**Figure 6.13**).
4. Click play or press the spacebar to hear your loop, and make any necessary adjustments.
5. If you need to boost the bass volume, either raise the Amp Level fader on the NN-19 (**Figure 6.14**), or raise the Mixer's Level knob/fader.

To add additional parts:

1. Create more NN-19s—each will have its own Mixer channel and Sequencer track.
2. Load an instrument patch into each NN-19.

   For this example, I loaded `Brass and Woodwinds/Trumpets` and `Guitar/NYLONGTR` from the `NN-19 Patches` folder.
3. Write more tracks, playing and adjusting as necessary.

   For the trumpet part, I set the grid value to 1/32 so I could input very short notes to create a slur (**Figure 6.15**).

   For the nylon string guitar part, I selected all the notes and lengthened them to create a legato "open-string" effect.

✔ Tip

- Writing parts that mimic the way instruments unfamiliar to you play may take some thought and experimentation. When in doubt, let your ear guide you.

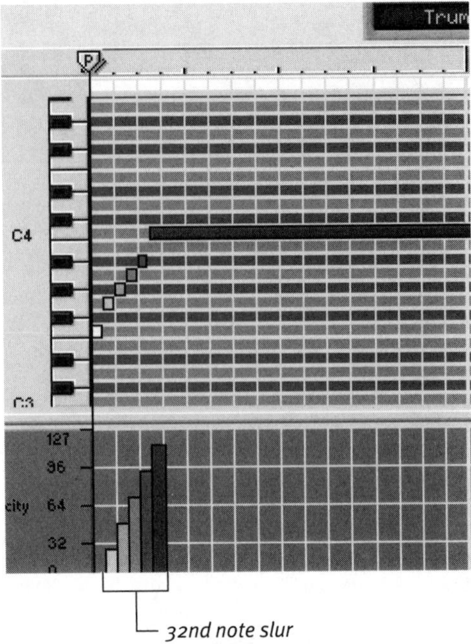

Figure 6.15 My trumpet part begins with a slur.

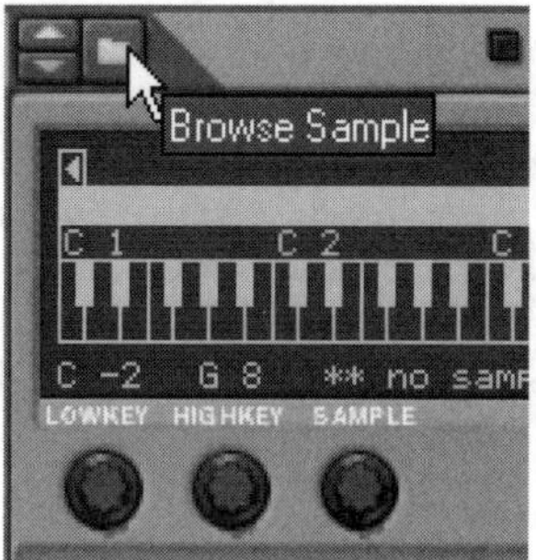

Figure 6.16 Click Browse Sample to open the NN-19 sample browser.

Brass and woodwind

Name

- Bassoon
- BrassEns
  - BrSeCompA1x.wav
  - BrSeCompA2x.wav
  - BrSeCompA3xx.wav
  - BrSeCompA4x.wav
  - BrSeCompC2x.wav
  - BrSeCompC3xx.wav
  - BrSeCompC4x.wav
  - BrSeCompC5x.wav
  - BrSeCompD#3xx.wav
  - BrSeCompD#4x.wav
  - BrSeCompF#1x.wav
  - BrSeCompF#3xx.wav
  - BrSeCompF#4x.wav

Details

Length: 2.30s

Format: Stereo, 16 Bit, 44.1 kHz

Size: 395.7 kB (uncompressed)

Figure 6.17 Choose a sample from the Factory Sound Bank.

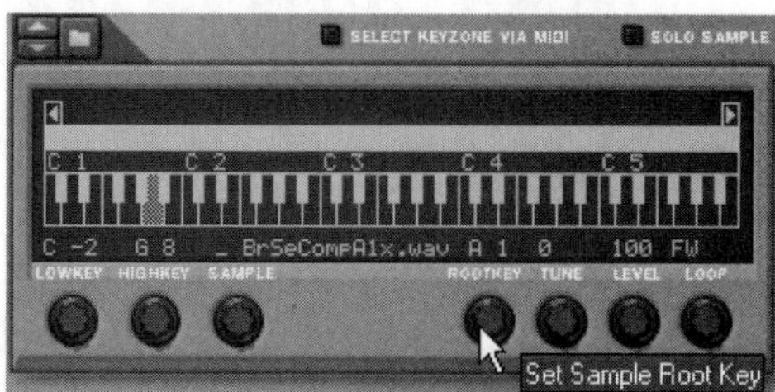

Figure 6.18 The NN-19's Rootkey knob sets the place on the keyboard where a sample will play back at its recorded pitch.

Creating Your Own Instruments

The simplest way to make your own patch is to load a single sample and start writing. The NN-19's sample browser lets you do this yourself. Though slower than loading patches from the Factory Sound Bank, loading your own instruments breaks the NN-19 instrument barrier—giving you access to Redrum drum samples and Orkester instruments.

Synths, pads, and abstract sounds will usually work as single-sample patches.

To create a single-sample instrument:

1. Click the Browse Sample button above the NN-19's sample map display (**Figure 6.16**).
2. Use the NN-19's sample browser to locate and load a sample (**Figure 6.17**).

   The sample appears in the NN-19 sample map display (**Figure 6.18**). The horizontal bar at the top shows the sample's *key zone,* which is the notes that will trigger the sample to play—by default, the NN-19 sets the sample to play from all 128 keys (C2 to G8).
3. Select the key zone to see the sample's root key (recorded pitch) highlighted on the keyboard display underneath. By default, the NN-19 sets the sample's root key at C3.
4. To change the selected sample's root key, drag the Rootkey knob to the left for a lower pitch, or to the right for a higher pitch.
5. Click the Save Patch button next to the patch name display; in the Save dialog box, name your patch, pick a save location, and click Save.

You can add additional samples to your patch manually—as many as you need or have the patience for. For example, you could load two or more abstract sounds in a single patch and have them triggered by different keys. (For more on this, see "Using Unpitched Instruments" later in this chapter.)

To add an additional sample:

1. With your single-sample patch loaded, drag the Sample knob (**Figure 6.19**) left until the sample field reads `** no sample **`. This is the blank sampler memory area. This ensures that the new sample won't overwrite the loaded sample.

2. Click the Browse Sample button, navigate to the desired sample, and click OK. The new sample appears in the sample map display, with the default root key (C3) and default key zone (all keys).

3. Select Edit > Split Key Zone (**Figure 6.20**), or right-click the sample map and select Split Key Zone from the context menu.

   The key zone is split in half, and the sample field once again reads `** no sample **` (**Figure 6.21**). New zones are always empty, with no sample assigned.

4. With the new, unassigned key zone still selected, drag the Sample knob to the right until the sample field shows the name of the sample you want these keys to trigger.

5. Select the other key zone to make sure your first sample is still assigned to those keys. If necessary, use the Sample knob to reassign the sample.

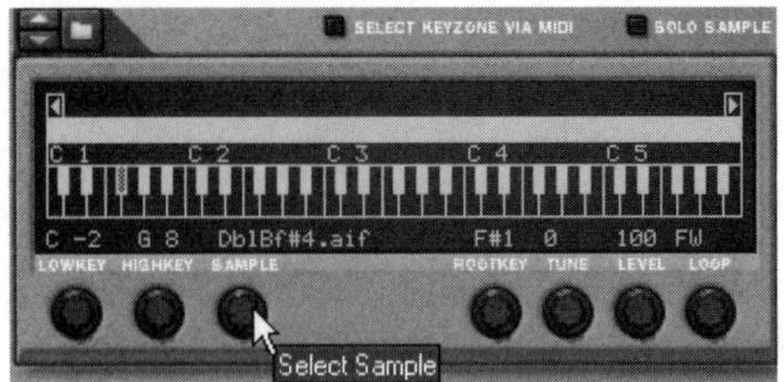

Figure 6.19 The Sample knob scrolls through the NN-19's bank of loaded samples.

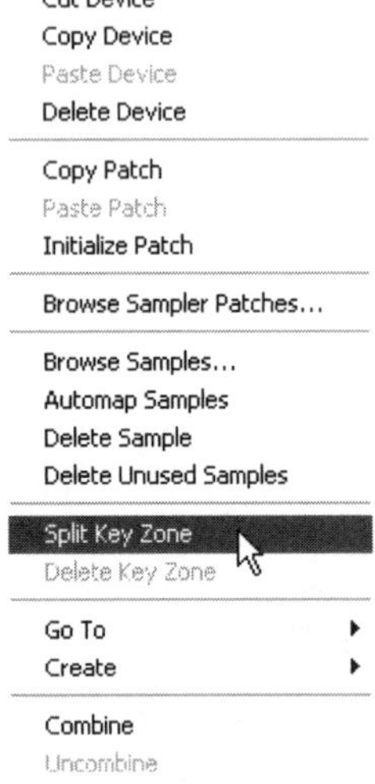

Figure 6.20 The Split Key Zone command evenly divides the selected key zone.

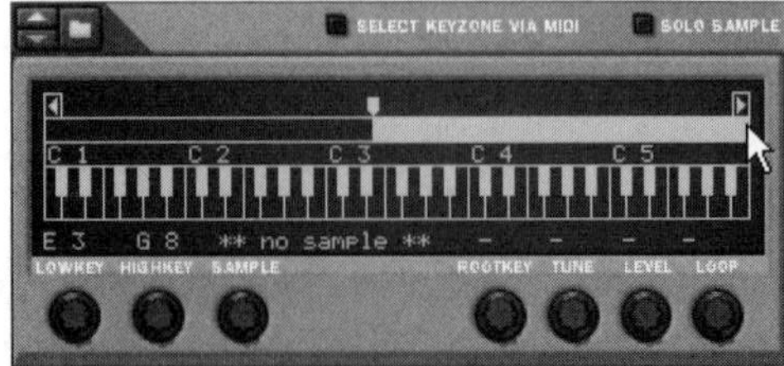

Figure 6.21 The newly created key zone has no sample assigned to it.

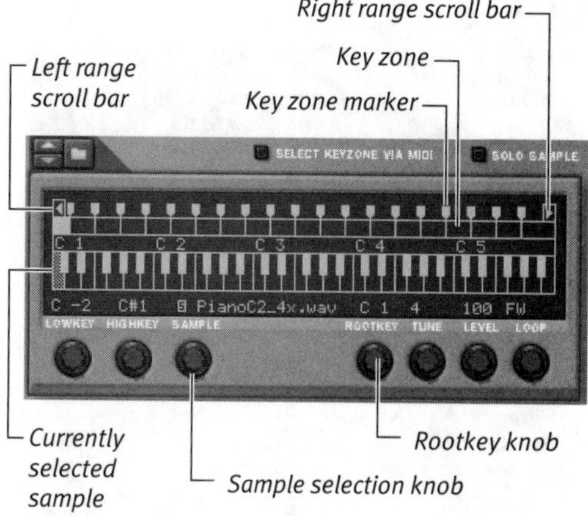

Figure 6.22 The NN-19 sample map display

Multisampled Instruments

Once you've gained familiarity with the basic instrument patches, the next step is to learn how to use the sampler so that it sounds more like a live instrument.

This brings us to *multisampling*—the technique of spreading multiple samples across the keyboard. Each sample in a patch has one recorded pitch, called the *root key*. Multisampled patches are more complicated, but they can safeguard instruments from pitch-shifting beyond their "comfort zones." The result is that multisampled instruments sound more realistic up and down the keyboard.

To load and check a multisampled patch:

1. Using the sample browser, load a patch, such as `NN-19 Sampler Patches/Piano/GRANDPIANO` from the Reason Factory Sound Bank.
2. Look at the sample map display of the patch (**Figure 6.22**).

   On the top row of the virtual LED, you'll see dividing lines with handles on top. These represent the key zones, or areas of the keyboard assigned to a particular sample. Each key zone represents a different piano note sample.

continues on next page

3. Select a key zone on the top of the display, to see the root key of the sample highlighted on the virtual keyboard (**Figure 6.23**).

   Note that correct root keys should sit on the keyboard ruler at the midpoint beneath the key zone of the selected sample.

4. To listen to a sample, press Alt (Win) / Opt (Mac) and click the key zone.

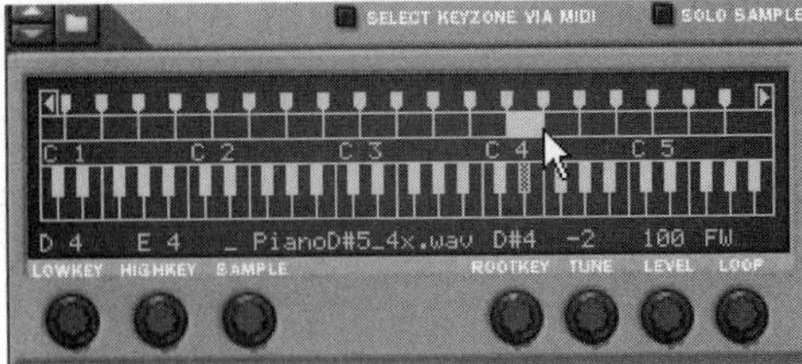

Figure 6.23 The root key of the selected key zone is displayed on the keyboard ruler.

✔ Tip

- When you select a sample, the NN-19 will display its name, key, loop status, and pitch (**Figure 6.24**).

Figure 6.24 When a sample's key zone is selected, the NN-19 displays information about it.

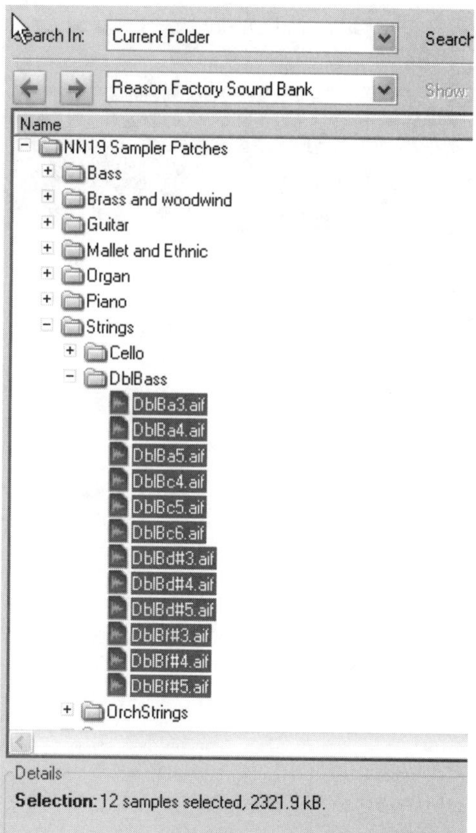

Figure 6.25 Select multiple samples to load all at once.

Creating Multisampled Instruments

Although the Reason Factory Sound Bank's `NN-19 Sampler Patches` folder contains many multisampled instruments, you may want to create your own—for example, using samples for other devices.

First you'll need to load the samples you want to use. You could load them individually, but there is a faster way.

To load multiple samples at once:

1. If necessary, right-click your NN-19 and select Initialize Patch.
2. Click the Browse Sample button, and in the sample browser, navigate to a directory of samples you want to load.
3. Hold Shift and select all the samples you want to load.

   In this example, I selected all the samples in the `NN-19 Sampler Patches/Strings/DblBass` directory (**Figure 6.25**).

continues on next page

Beyond Reason's Sound Library

Reason's Factory and Orkester banks contain all the sounds you'll need for most types of music. But if you do want more, you can expand your sounds using third-party libraries formatted for Reason. See Appendix B, "Resources," for sample library links.

There's a wealth of Reason-formatted sample libraries on the Internet for free, and most top-quality professional libraries are Reason-compatible. What's more, Reason can convert Akai-format sample CDs using Reload, an application that is free to Reason owners (see "Reload" in Appendix A).

4. Click OK. After a short delay (depending on the number of samples you selected), all the samples will appear in the sample map display, with no key zones set.

5. Scroll through memory using the Sample knob to confirm that all your samples loaded (**Figure 6.26**).

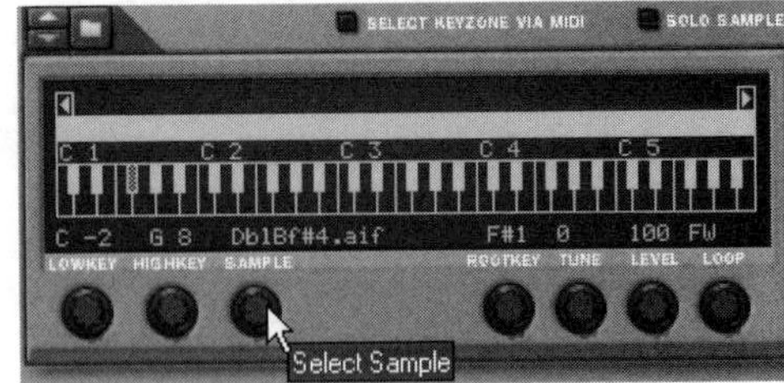

Figure 6.26 Use the Sample knob to verify that your samples loaded.

✔ Tip

- Each time a new sample is loaded, you should see its name at the bottom of the Key Map display. As you turn the Sample knob left, you'll scroll through all the samples loaded in the NN-19—this allows you to check that you haven't overwritten any samples during the loading process.

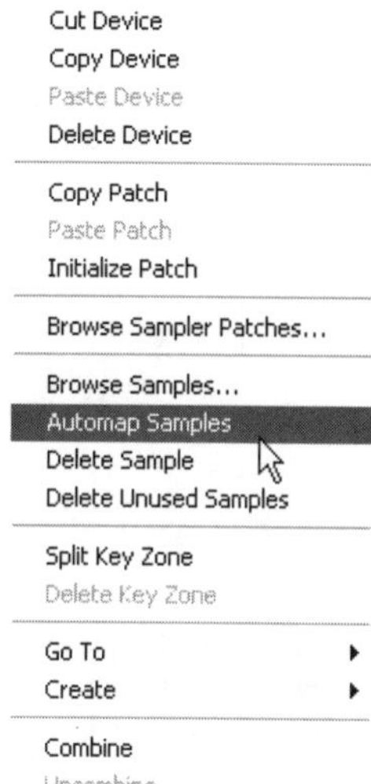

Figure 6.27 The Automap command sets key zones for all samples in memory.

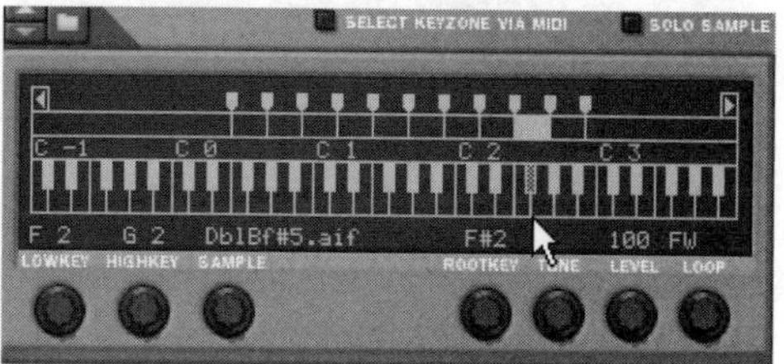

Figure 6.28 A correctly set root key sits centered below its key zone.

Figure 6.29 Automapped samples with no root key information get the default root key of C3.

Mapping Multiple Key Zones

To get all the samples to correspond to the same pitch scale, you'll next need to set key zones. Using Reason's Automap feature is the easiest way to do this.

To map zones automatically:

1. Select and load multiple samples, as you did in the preceding section.
2. Select Edit > Automap Samples (**Figure 6.27**). This assigns one key zone for each sample in memory.
3. Check that Reason has interpreted root keys correctly, by clicking key zones and looking for the shaded root key on the keyboard map at midpoint below the zone (**Figure 6.28**).

✔ Tips

- When a sample is missing root-key information, Reason will create key zones, but the root key is set to C3 by default (**Figure 6.29**).
- Use Automap any time you're reasonably sure your samples contain root-key information (for example, if you're using samples from the Factory and Orkester sound banks).

It's important to know how to manually map the keyboard, especially if you think you might want to load "unpedigreed" samples someday—or set up a performance patch with your own mapping scheme.

To map zones manually:

1. With unmapped samples loaded, click a key zone and add a new one by selecting Edit > Split Key Zone (**Figure 6.30**).
2. Select the new empty zone and drag the Sample knob until the desired sample name is displayed (**Figure 6.31**).

   The sample is assigned to the new key zone.
3. With the same zone selected, set the sample's root key using the Rootkey knob.
4. Repeat steps 1 through 3 for each sample.
5. Once you have more than two key zones, you can scroll over the keyboard ruler using the scroll arrows (**Figure 6.32**) in order to see keys not currently displayed.
6. If you need to adjust an existing key zone, you can use the Highkey and Lowkey knobs (**Figure 6.33**), or you can interactively drag the zone marker handles (**Figure 6.34**).

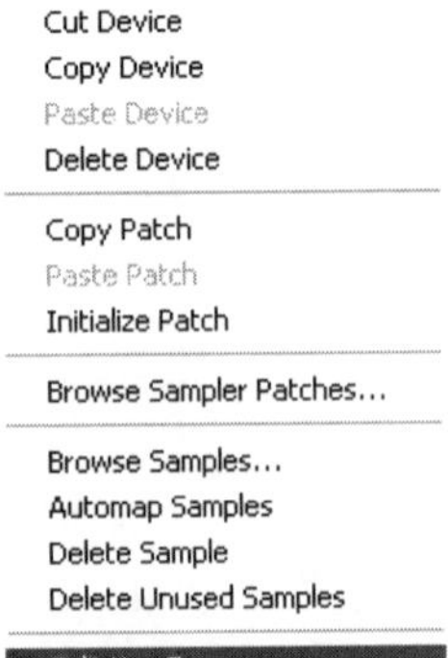

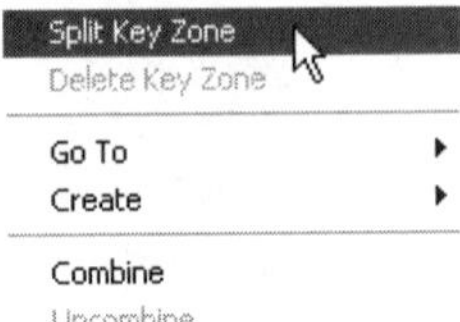

Figure 6.30 Use the Split Key Zone command when manually setting key zones.

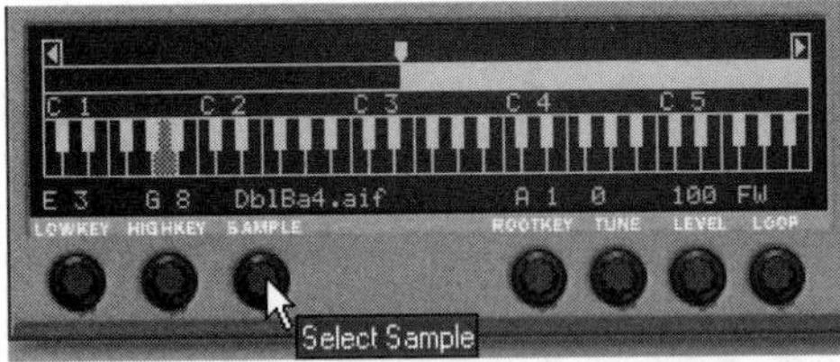

Figure 6.31 While a new key zone is selected, turn the Sample knob to assign a sample.

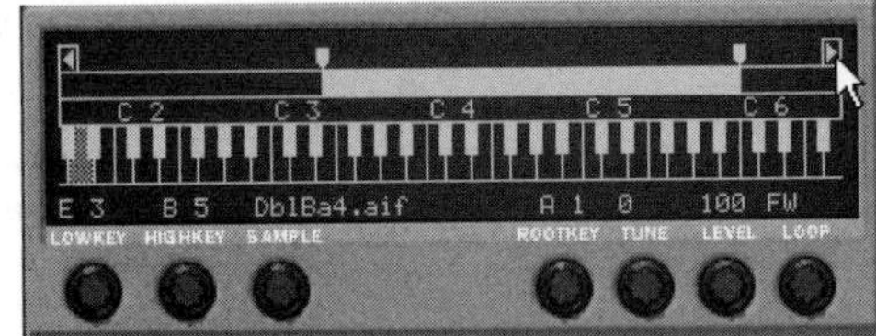

Figure 6.32 Use the scroll arrows to get to different parts of the keyboard ruler.

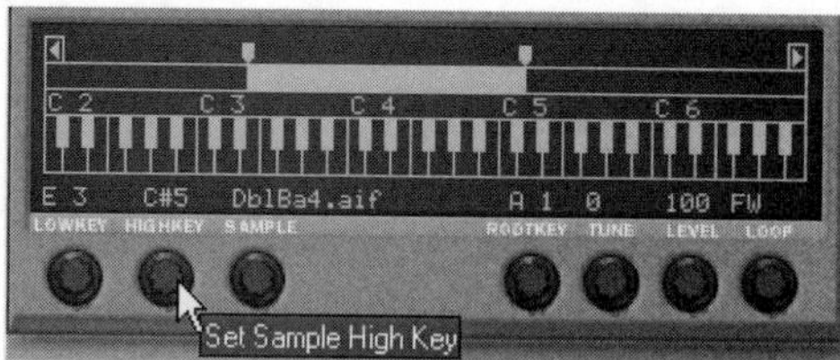

Figure 6.33 Use the Lowkey and Highkey knobs to adjust key zones...

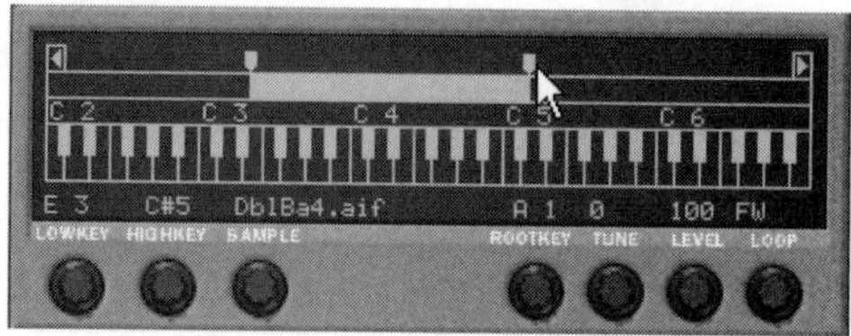

Figure 6.34 ...or use the handles to resize interactively.

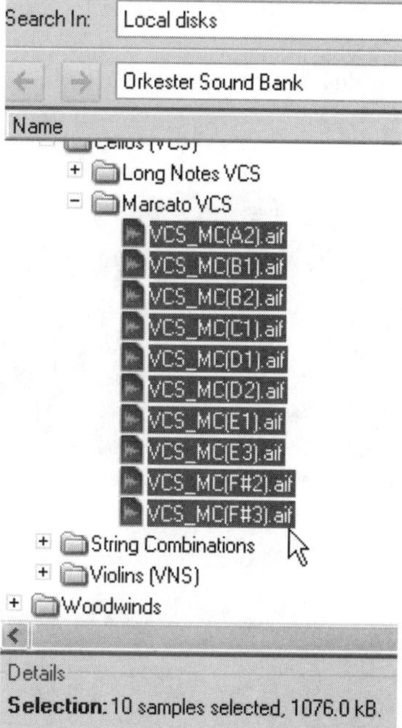

Figure 6.35 The Reason Factory and Orkester sound banks include a sample's pitch in its name.

✔ Tips

- Dividing the keyboard among various types of samples is handy for performance patches (for example, bass in the lower zone and a lead sound in the upper zone).
- When creating your own samples, include the root key in the sample name (F#5, C2, and so on) so that you can take your sample library with you to other studios and venues (**Figure 6.35**).

Using Unpitched Instruments

Most synths have *unpitched* drum or sound-effect patches that contain up to 128 unpitched samples. Reason's Factory Sound Bank doesn't have these for the NN-19—but making your own unpitched patch is simple, because *unpitched samples* typically need only play back at their recorded pitch.

To make an unpitched instrument:

1. Right-click the front panel of your NN-19 and select Initialize Patch from the context menu. The Sample field should read `** no sample **`, indicating you're in a blank sampler memory area.
2. Open the sample browser and navigate to the Reason Factory Sound Bank then `Redrum Kits/xclusive drums-sorted/01_BassDrums/BD1 1 OHSH.aif` (**Figure 6.36**).
3. Click Open. Now the sample map displays the loaded sample (**Figure 6.37**).
4. Turn the Sample knob back to blank memory so the next sample will not replace the current one (**Figure 6.38**).

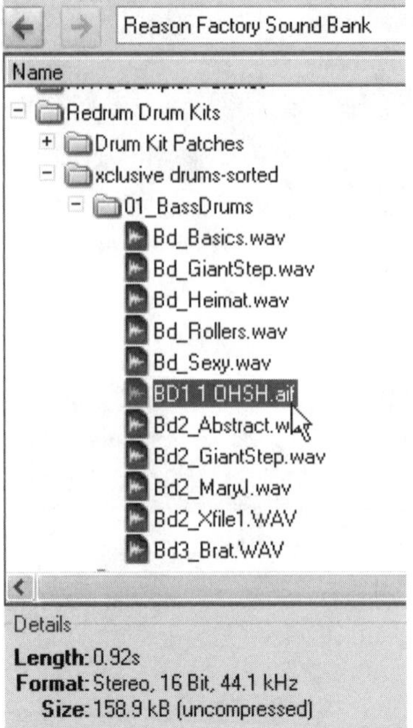

Figure 6.36 Load a bass drum sound from the xclusive drums-sorted folder into the NN-19.

Figure 6.37 The sample display field shows the most recently loaded sample.

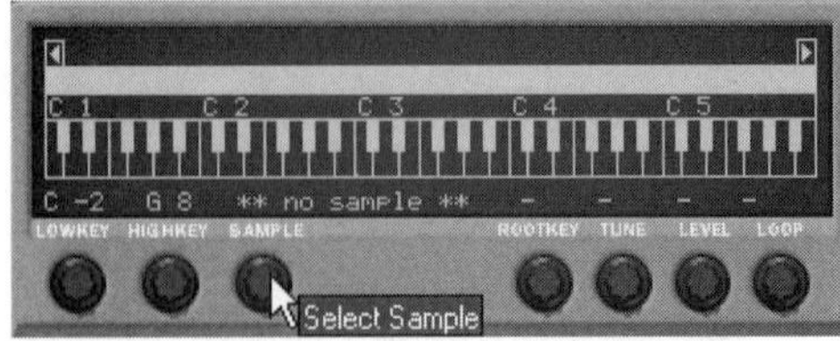

Figure 6.38 Before loading new samples, select the empty sample memory using the Sample knob.

Figure 6.39 Check the NN-19's sample map display to make sure it shows the most recently loaded sample.

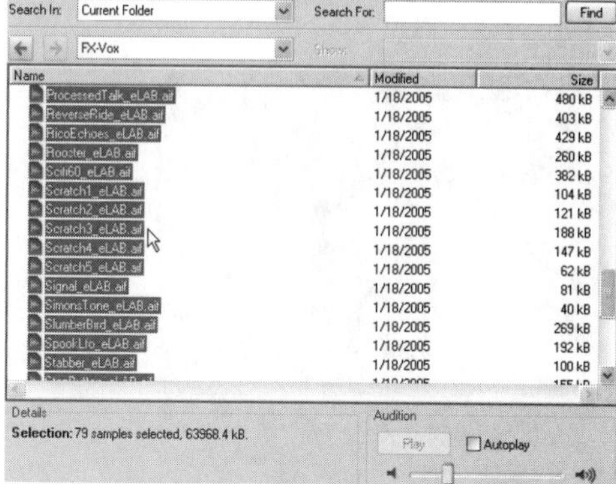

Figure 6.40 Select multiple samples to load them all into the NN-19 at once.

5. Load the next sample. In this example, I loaded `02_SnareDrums > Sd2_Abstract.wav` (**Figure 6.39**).
6. Repeat steps 4 and 5 until you're finished loading sounds.

   For this example, I loaded all the following from the `xclusive drums-sorted` folder:

   `/03_Rimshots/Rim1br.aif`

   `/04_Claps/Clp2_Tresor.wav`

   `/05_HiHats/HH1 2 RKTI.aif, /HH1V1 RKTI.aif, /HH1V11RKTI.aif`

   `/06_Cymbals/CYM1 10HSH.aif, /CYM1V10HSH.aif, /CYM1V20HSH.aif`
7. Open the sample browser to the Reason Factory Sound Bank, then `/Other Samples/ FX-Vox`.
8. Press Ctrl+A (Win) / Cmd+A (Mac) to select all the samples in the folder (**Figure 6.40**), and click Open to load them all at once.

   Expect a slight delay as these samples load.
9. Make sure nothing's been overwritten by scrolling through memory with the Sample knob.

✔ Tip

- If you overwrite a sample, just return to the blank memory area and reload it. Sample order won't affect a sample's key zone.

Mapping Unpitched Samples

When you load multiple samples into the NN-19, they're all assigned to the same root key, but no key zones are assigned. This means whatever key you press will trigger the currently selected sample, pitch-shifted as necessary.

With unpitched samples, the pitch-shifting may not seem like such a problem, but you still need to have separate keys triggering particular samples. So now let's set up the keyboard.

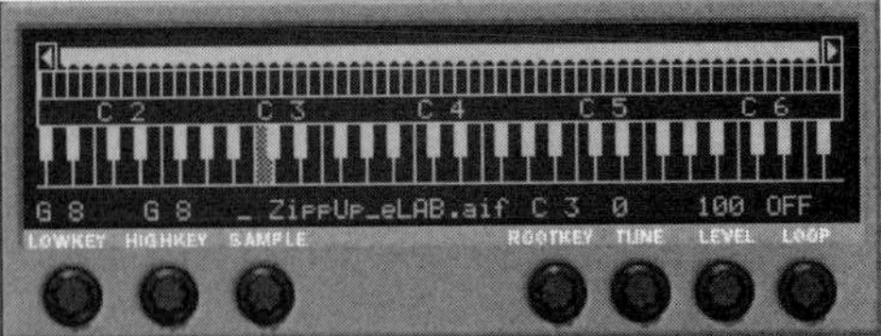

Figure 6.41 Automap samples to set up key zones quickly.

Figure 6.42 Disable the keyboard tracking feature so your samples all play back at their recorded pitches.

To set up unpitched key zones:

1. With unpitched samples loaded in your NN-19 (if you haven't done this yet, see the preceding section), select Edit > Automap Samples to set up key zones for all loaded samples (**Figure 6.41**).
2. Disable keyboard tracking in the Osc section (**Figure 6.42**).

   Now samples will play back at their recorded pitch, regardless of keyboard position.
3. Save your patch as `rhythm-SFX` in a location you'll remember, so we can come back to it.

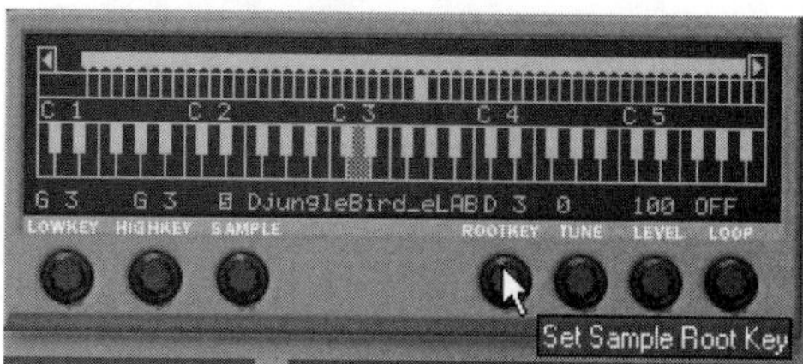

Figure 6.43 Set the root key of a sample by turning the Rootkey knob.

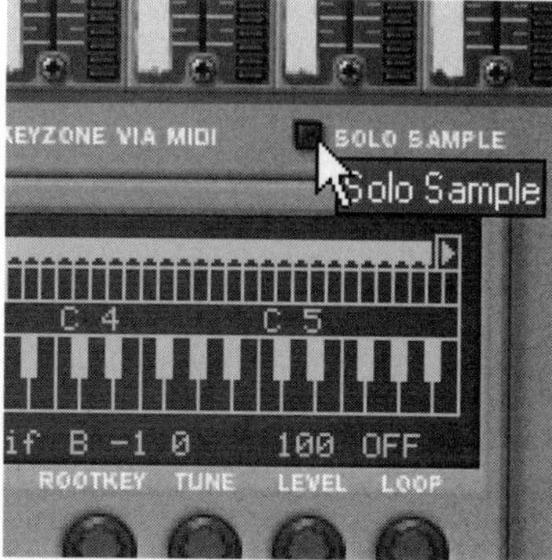

Figure 6.44 The Solo Sample button shuts off all but the selected sample. With keyboard tracking on, it lets you audition a sample at multiple pitches using the keyboard.

✔ Tips

- To alter a pitch with keyboard tracking off, select the sample and adjust the Rootkey knob to the left for lower pitch, or to the right for higher (**Figure 6.43**).
- To hear a ranged sample transposed to another tone, enable the Solo Sample button (**Figure 6.44**). Then audition using your master keyboard or by Alt-clicking (Win) / Opt-clicking (Mac) the sample map display keyboard.

Troubleshooting: Wrong Pitch

Pitch problems with unpitched samples can occur if you forget to turn keyboard tracking off. The symptom: low keys "squeak," and high keys "growl." Often the play speed is so out of range that there is little or no sound at all.

This occurs because Automap assigns unpitched samples a root key of C3 (in the middle of the keyboard), so they may be pitch-shifted on playback. To fix it, simply change the sample's root key.

You may want to leave key tracking on when, for example, you want to use the keyboard to transpose an unpitched sample; otherwise, though, it's not recommended.

Writing an Unpitched Track

Now it's time to write a rhythm track using the custom `rhythm-SFX` patch you made in the preceding section. Since our NN-19 patch has drum and sound effects, we'll be creating two Sequencer tracks (one for each type of sound) and using them both simultaneously to play one NN-19!

To set up two Sequencer tracks for one device:

1. Load the `rhythm-SFX` NN-19 patch you made in the last exercise.
2. In the Sequencer, switch to Edit mode and turn off the Key lane view by clicking the Show Key Lane button once (**Figure 6.45**).
3. Turn on the Drum lane view by clicking on the Show Drum Lane button (**Figure 6.46**). This will be your drum track.
4. Double-click the track name in the Sequencer device list, and rename it `Drum track` to avoid confusion.

   Next we'll set up the sound effects track.
5. Right-click the Sequencer window's device list and select Create Sequencer Track (**Figure 6.47**).

   This creates a new track, labeled New Track 1, with an empty device window (**Figure 6.48**).

Figure 6.45 You can hide the Key lane when it's open by clicking Show Key Lane.

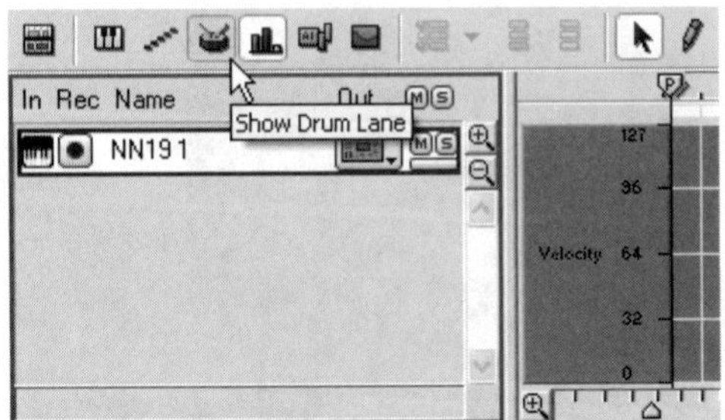

Figure 6.46 Use the Show Drum Lane button to see your track in drum view.

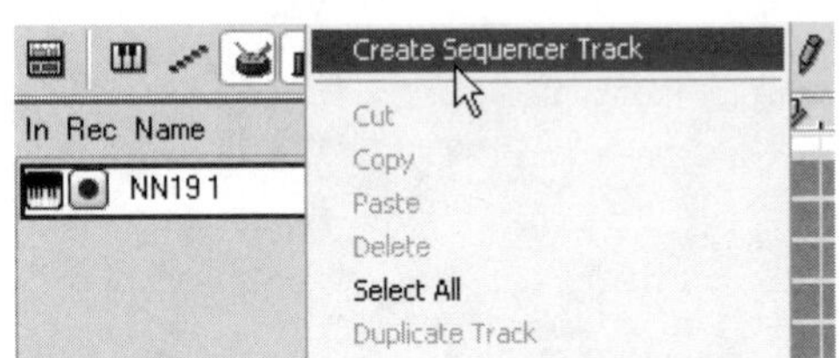

Figure 6.47 Create a new Sequencer track for your ambient sounds, so you can keep them grouped and mute or solo them separately.

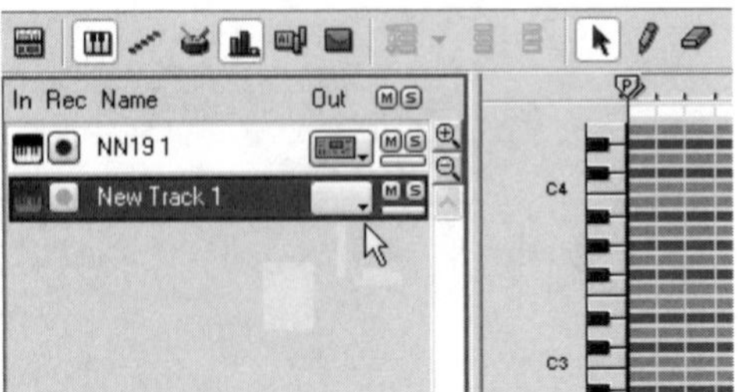

Figure 6.48 The new Sequencer track will not yet be assigned to a device.

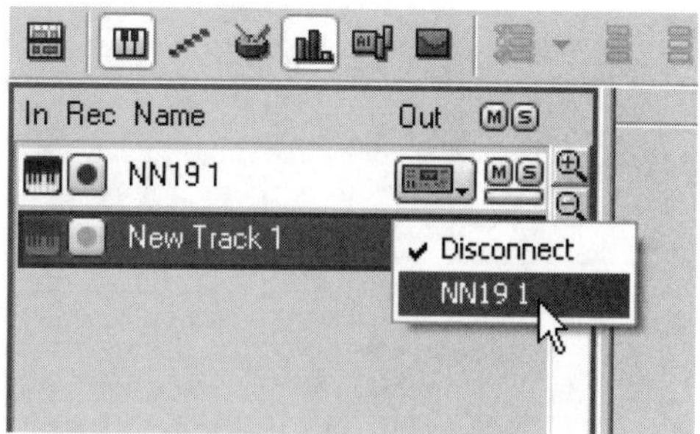

Figure 6.49 Assign a device using the pull-down menu.

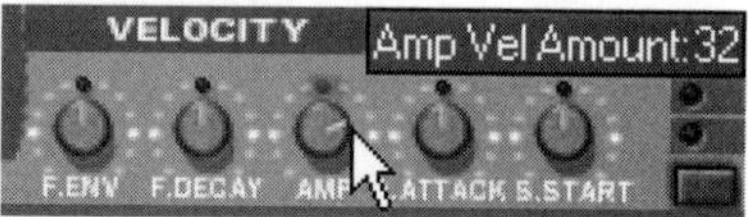

Figure 6.50 Increasing the Velocity Amp knob makes harder attacks play louder.

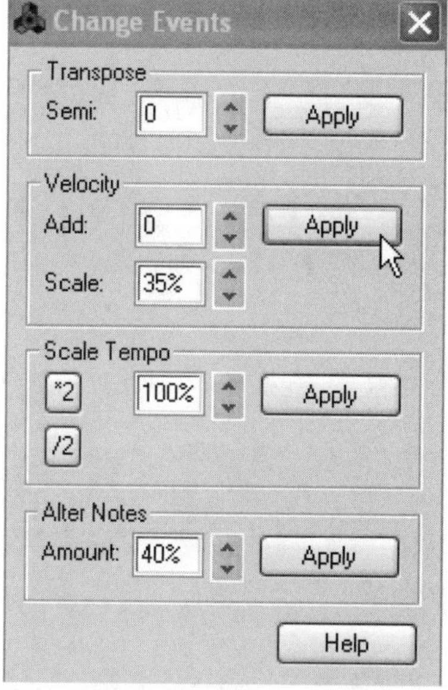

Figure 6.51 You can select and edit multiple notes with the Change Events menu. Here, velocity scaling is being used to lower some note velocities.

6. Click the arrow in the Out column of the device list to pop up a menu of Rack devices, and assign the new track to your NN-19 (**Figure 6.49**).
7. Double-click the name New Track 1 and rename it to SFX Track, but leave the track in default Key lane mode.
8. Save your patch and your song so that you can come back to them later.

✔ Tips

- For your drum parts, go to your NN-19 front panel and move the Velocity Amp knob to the right. This will make strong attacks play louder (**Figure 6.50**).
- To alter the velocity of individual notes, right-click the note and select Change Events > Velocity Scale > Apply (**Figure 6.51**). The Change Events menu also handles quantizing, transposition, tempo scaling, and note randomization for groups of notes.
- Scroll your drum track vertically so that the kick and snare drum sit just below the measure ruler, to help you keep track of where the beats and half-beats lie.

To write a sound effects track:

1. Arrange the windows so you can see both your NN-19 `sfx` track and the NN-19's front panel (**Figure 6.52**).
2. On the NN-19, click Select Keyzone Via MIDI to enable it (**Figure 6.53**).

   Now the NN-19 sample field will show you samples being triggered by the Sequencer in real time. This can help you learn the samples in your new patch while auditioning them in your track.
3. Using the keyboard ruler, audition some samples. As a sample plays, its name is displayed in the sample field on the NN-19 front panel (**Figure 6.54**).
4. To adjust the relative volume of samples, select the sample on the keyboard ruler and then adjust the Level knob on the NN-19 front panel (**Figure 6.55**).

✔ Tip

- In order to play their full duration, long-playing samples need to have long triggering notes.

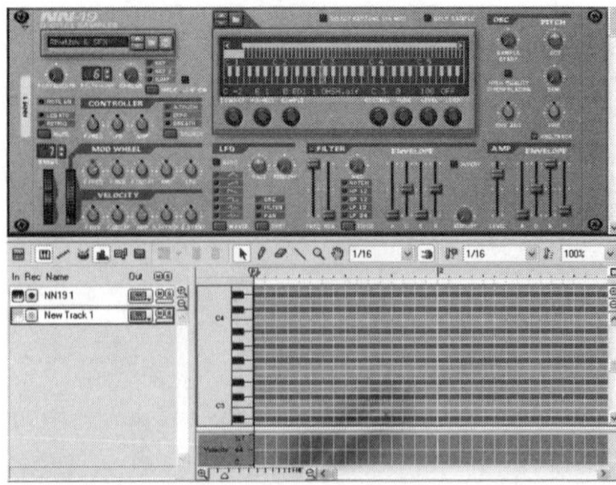

Figure 6.52 Scroll the Rack so your NN-19 sits directly above the Sequencer.

Figure 6.53 Select Keyzone Via MIDI tells the NN-19 to display samples as they play.

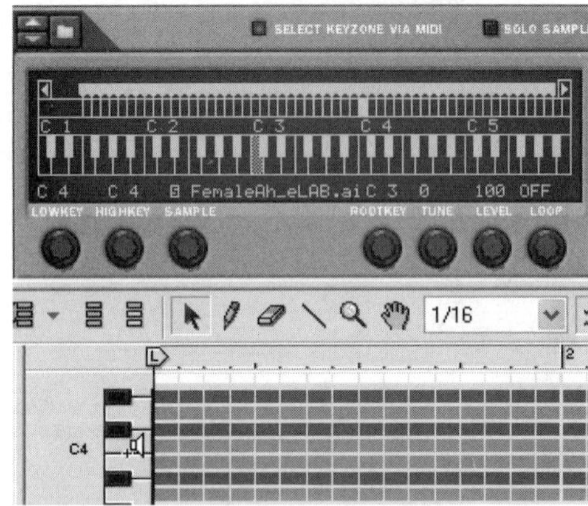

Figure 6.54 As a sample is auditioned in the Sequencer, it's shown in the NN-19 display.

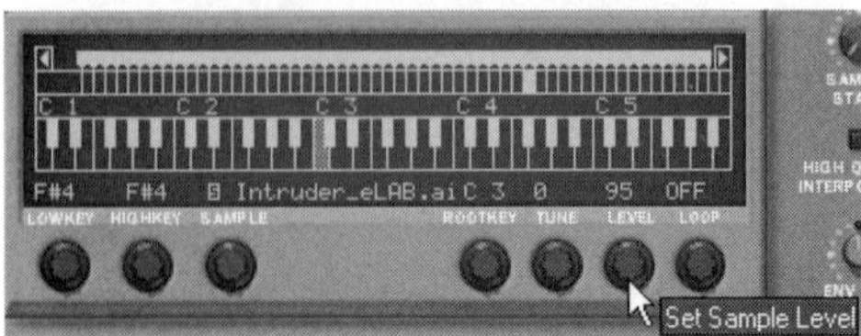

Figure 6.55 Adjust a sample's playback volume using the Level knob.

Figure 6.56 Select the ramp, or upward sawtooth LFO shape.

Figure 6.57 With Sync on, set the Rate to 4/4.

Figure 6.58 Set the LFO amount.

Using the NN-19 Controls

The NN-19 control sections (the filter, LFO, and envelopes) should look pretty familiar by now. They work just as they do on the SubTractor and Malström, but now you're using them on samples rather than generated sounds.

To warp pitch using the LFO:

1. Load the NN-19 song from the last exercise and start your loop.

   When you save a song, all patch modifications get saved, even if you haven't saved the patch separately.

2. Using the Wavef. button in the NN-19's LFO section, select the ramp (or upward sawtooth) waveform (**Figure 6.56**).

   The LFO destination should already be set to Osc, so the pitch will shift steadily upward.

3. Enable LFO Sync and set it to a rate of 4/4 (**Figure 6.57**). At this setting, the ramp in pitch caused by the LFO will last one measure.

4. Drag the Amount knob left and right to adjust the amount of increase and decrease to the effect (**Figure 6.58**).

Panning and Spread modes

Moving a sound between the left and right channels may be a simple trick, but it can sweeten headphones, and can buzz an audience if the club has good, wide left/right speaker separation.

You can do this with the LFO and have it affect the whole instrument, or you can distribute panning positions across the keyboard for your individual samples.

The NN-19 spread modes distribute panning positions among the samples in three ways:

- *Key* mode mimics the relative location of strings on a piano. The lower keys are at the left and move to the right as you move up the keyboard.
- *Key 2* mode is an eight-step (every half-octave) panning sequence that pans notes left to right.
- *Jump* mode switches successive notes between left and right as they are played.

To rotate panning using spread modes:

1. With your loop playing, change the LFO destination to Pan.
2. Set the Mode switch to Key 2 (**Figure 6.59**). This makes notes jump a half-octave per key as you move up the keyboard, and then repeat the cycle.
3. Set the Spread knob according to how much of the effect you want (**Figure 6.60**). Turning the knob hard right creates a full-left-to-full-right effect.

Figure 6.59 The spread modes offer three panning schemes.

Figure 6.60 The Spread knob determines how far left and right sample panning goes.

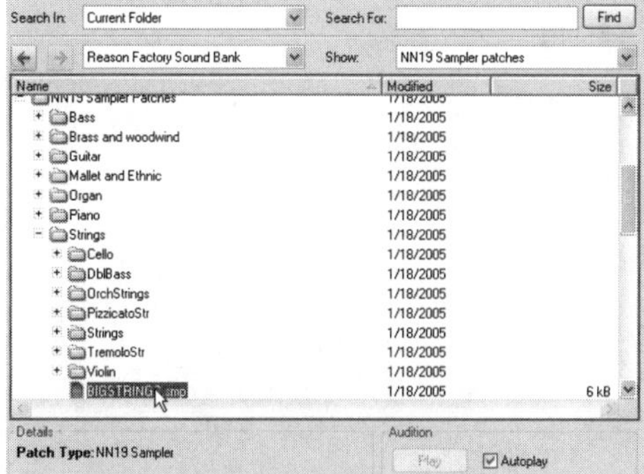

Figure 6.61 Load the BIGSTRINGS patch.

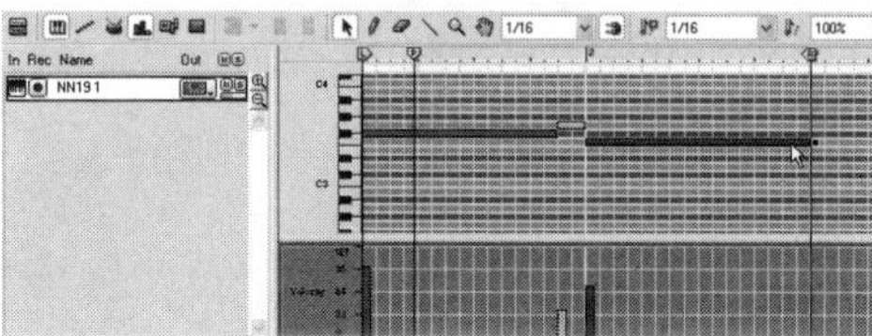

Figure 6.62 A basic melody for the BIGSTRINGS patch

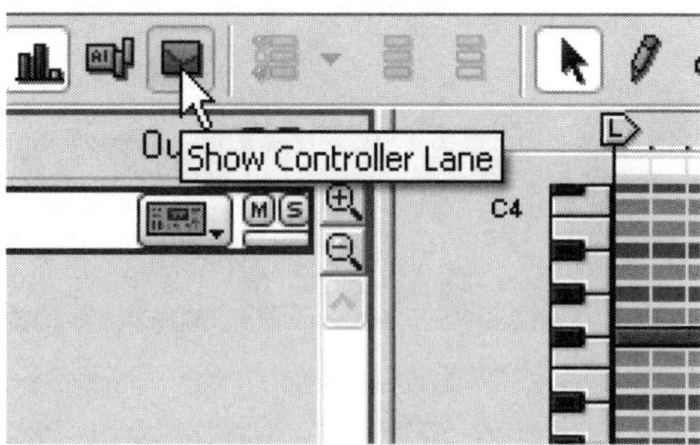

Figure 6.63 The Show Controller Lane button adds space in your Sequencer window to display knob movement or adjustable parameters for any device.

Controller Automation

One of the most powerful emulation tools at your disposal is *controller automation.* This means real-time, preset tweaking of control parameters such as volume, filters, envelopes, and LFOs.

Though you can record your knob movements, it's more reliable to draw them in your Sequencer track's *Controller lane.* The Controller lane gives you access to nearly every device parameter for all your Rack instruments. One typical use would be to create volume ebbs and swells to emulate the way a bowed string instrument gets louder and softer as it plays.

To emulate a string part using volume controllers:

1. Re-initialize your NN-19 and load the `BIGSTRINGS` patch from the `/NN19 Sampler Patches/Strings` folder of the Reason Factory Sound Bank (**Figure 6.61**).

2. In the Sequencer, map out a two-bar section using the loop markers, and input a sustained melody (**Figure 6.62**).

3. With your sustained loop playing, click the Show Controller Lane button (**Figure 6.63**) at the top of the Sequencer window. Space for Controller lanes will appear at the bottom of your Sequencer window.

continues on next page

Emulating "Real" Instruments

It takes work to make sampled instruments sound convincing. At worst, "passable" is usually possible—but the more versatile the instrument you're building, the more it will need coaxing with controllers and elaborate sample mapping.

In general, strings and brass are hostile to the sampling process, whereas piano and percussion instruments are more forgiving (though any pianist or a percussionist will tell you differently).

4. Now click the Controllers button (**Figure 6.64**) to pop up a list containing all the NN-19 controller parameters.
5. Select Master Volume from the list. A new blue Controller lane marked Master Level appears beneath the red Velocity lane (**Figure 6.65**).
6. Disable the Snap-to-Grid function so you can input smooth volume changes that are not quantized to the grid resolution value.
7. Use the Pencil or Line tool to draw in volume curves for the BIGSTRINGS instrument (**Figure 6.66**).

   Upward-moving curves will increase the instrument volume, and downward curves will decrease it.
8. Experiment to find volume variations that sound the most natural for your part.

✔ Tip

- Don't use too wide a volume range—real string instruments react to bow pressure and won't vary all the way from zero to maximum.

Figure 6.64 The Controllers button pops up a list of all the writable NN-19 parameters.

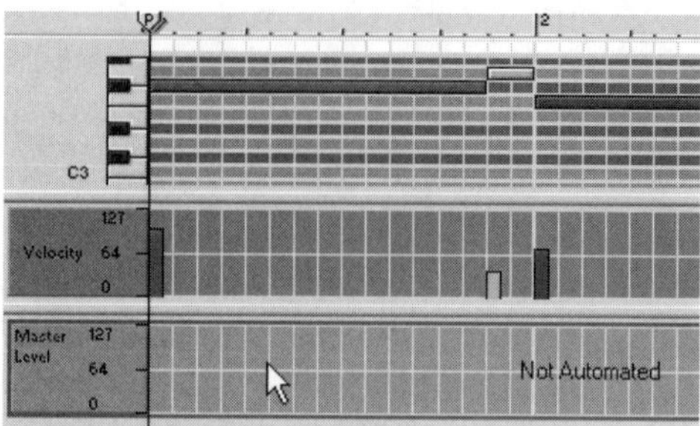

Figure 6.65 Add a master volume Controller lane in your Sequencer edit window.

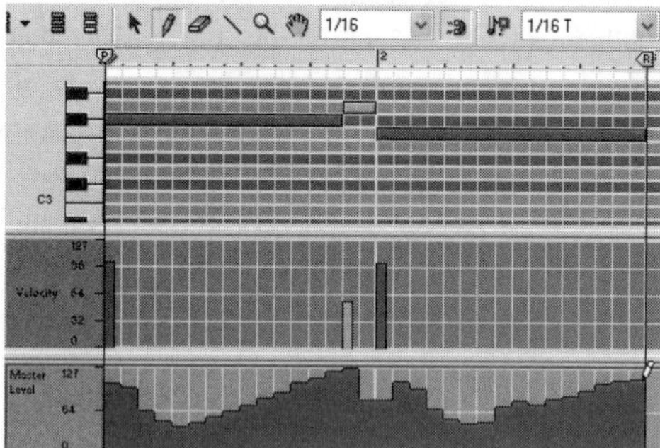

Snap-to-grid is on

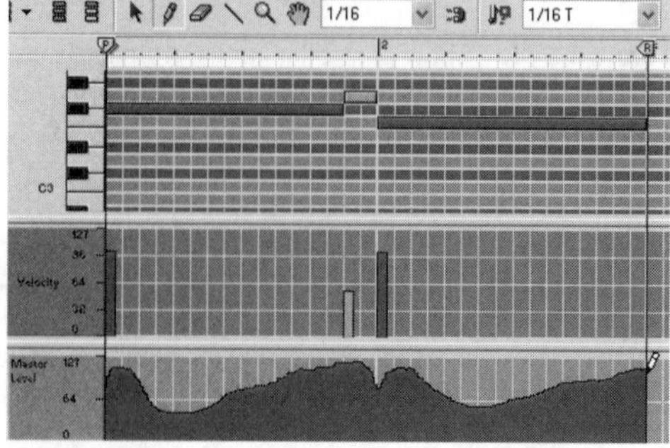

Snap-to-grid is off

Figure 6.66 With grid-snapping disabled, the master volume changes are smoother and more natural-sounding.

Figure 6.67 A default connection between an NN-XT and a 6:2 Line Mixer

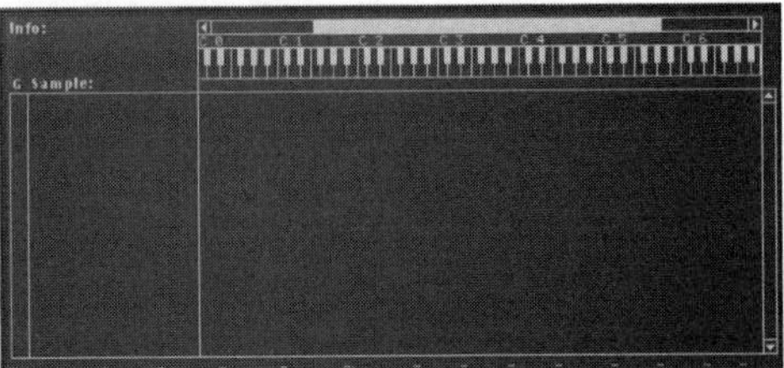

Figure 6.68 The NN-XT Advanced Sampler's Remote Editor works much like the NN-19's sample map.

The NN-XT Advanced Sampler

Unlike the NN-19, the NN-XT can assign more than one sample to a key. This allows you to switch among samples based on note velocity, so that different attack strengths trigger different sounds.

The NN-XT also adds more controls, and you can store different settings for each sample! This makes it possible to set up *crossfades* between samples, combine multiple patches into one, and even set up groups of samples in the same patch that behave differently. To top it all off, the NN-XT has *eight* stereo outputs.

To create an NN-XT sampler:

1. Select Create > NN-XT Advanced Sampler.
2. Press Tab, and check the back panel to make sure that the NN-XT's 1/L and 2/R outputs are connected to an open Mixer channel (**Figure 6.67**).
3. Return to the front panel view and click the right-pointing arrow at the bottom-left to unfold the Remote Editor panel (**Figure 6.68**).

Loading a patch or sample in the NN-XT is done exactly the same as in any other sampler, except that they show up in the Remote Editor instead of the main controls.

To audition and load a patch:

1. Play your loop and open the NN-XT's patch browser (**Figure 6.69**).
2. Go to the Reason Factory Sound Bank's `NN-XT Patches` folder and choose a sound (**Figure 6.70**).

   In the bottom-left corner of the browser you'll see the loading status of the selected patch (**Figure 6.71**). As soon as it's done loading, you'll hear your loop playing the new sound.

Figure 6.69 Load a patch in your NN-XT.

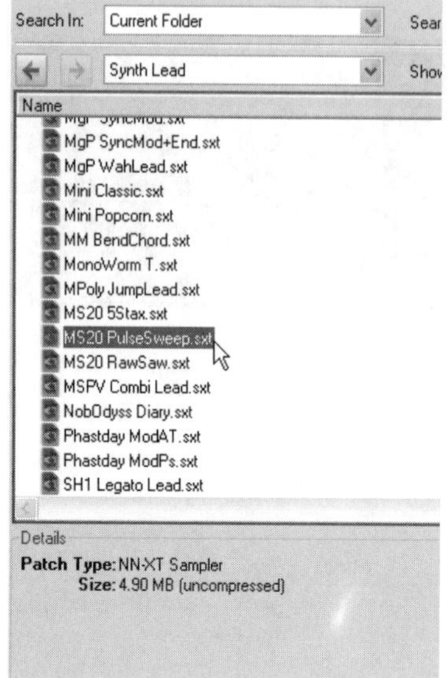

Figure 6.70 You can audition patches by playing a loop while using the browser.

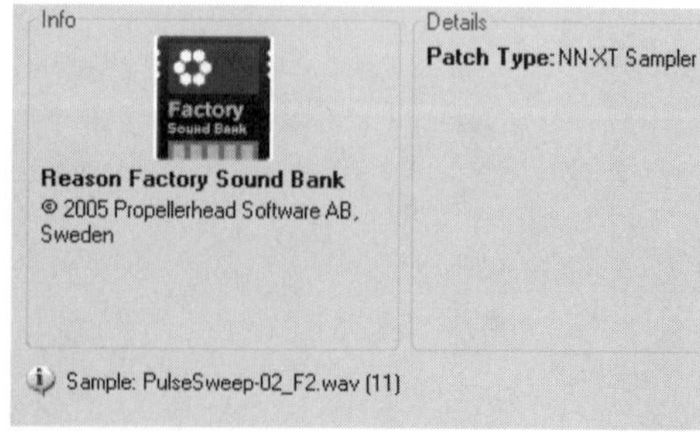

Figure 6.71 When loading a patch to audition, loading status is displayed at the bottom-left.

Figure 6.72 Load the NN-XT's A Grand Piano patch.

Figure 6.73 The NN-XT Remote Editor's sample map

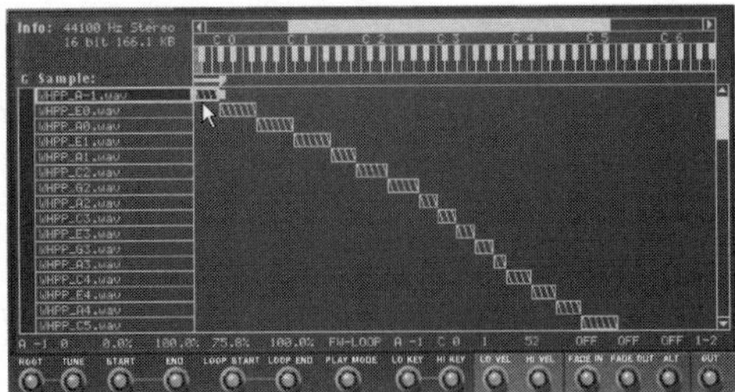

Figure 6.74 The NN-XT displays information about selected samples.

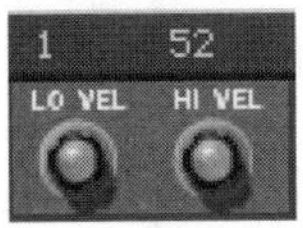

Figure 6.75 The Lo Vel and Hi Vel knobs set a sample's playable velocity range.

NN-XT Patch Anatomy

The easiest way to explain NN-XT patches is to show you what they can do. Let's load a piano patch in the NN-XT and compare it to the NN-19's `GRANDPIANO` patch.

To examine an NN-XT patch:

1. Using the NN-XT patch browser, load `NN-XT Sampler Patches/Piano/A Grand Piano.sxt` (**Figure 6.72**).
2. Open the Remote Editor to see the NN-XT sample map display (**Figure 6.73**).
3. Click a sample box in the Remote Editor. Across the bottom of the sample map display, you'll see information about that sample (**Figure 6.74**).

   Above the Lo Vel and Hi Vel knobs (**Figure 6.75**) is the velocity range at which this sample plays: from 1 to 52. This sample is only for very soft attacks.

continues on next page

4. Use the scroll bar on the right to scroll down until you see another sample at the same keyboard location (**Figure 6.76**).

   What may look like a whole separate patch is a second set of samples sharing the same key mapping.

5. Click the newly visible sample to see its velocity range information (**Figure 6.77**). With Lo Vel at 53 and Hi Vel at 89, this sample is for medium attacks.

6. Scroll down farther and you'll see that there are two more sets of samples, one with a velocity range from 90 to 109 and another with a range from 110 to 127.

7. Try playing the patch using your external keyboard, or input some notes with different velocities to hear how much more expressive this patch is than the NN-19 patch.

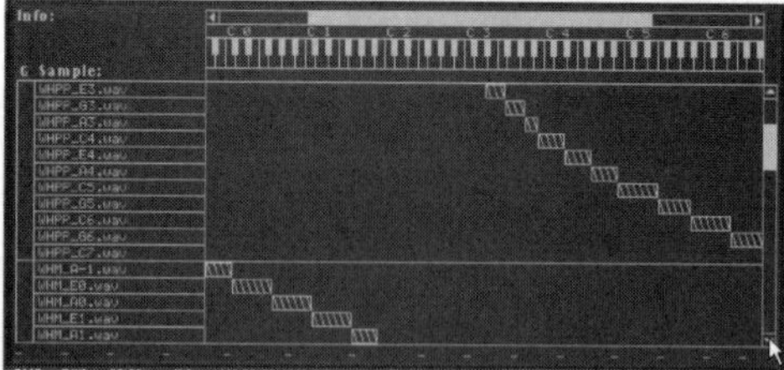

Figure 6.76 Scroll down the NN-XT sample map.

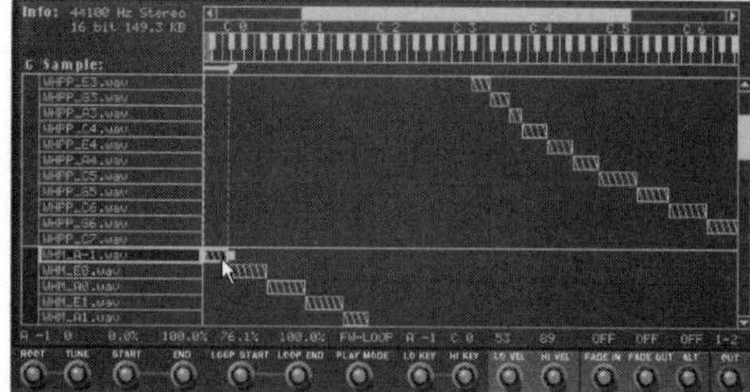

Figure 6.77 This sample has a different velocity range.

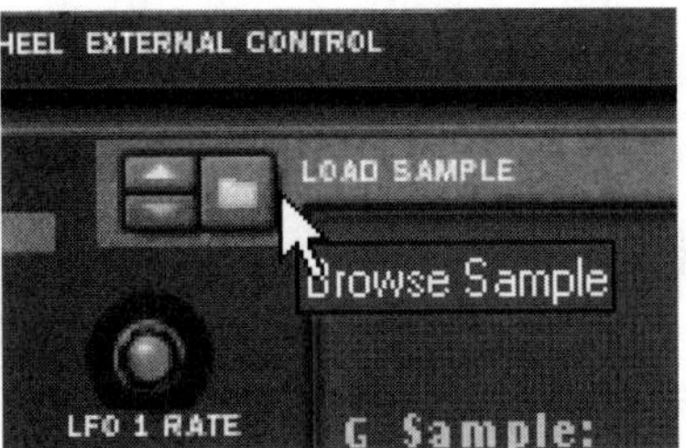

Figure 6.78 Browse samples for the NN-XT.

Figure 6.79 I selected all samples in the Chords-Phrases-Pads-Stabs directory.

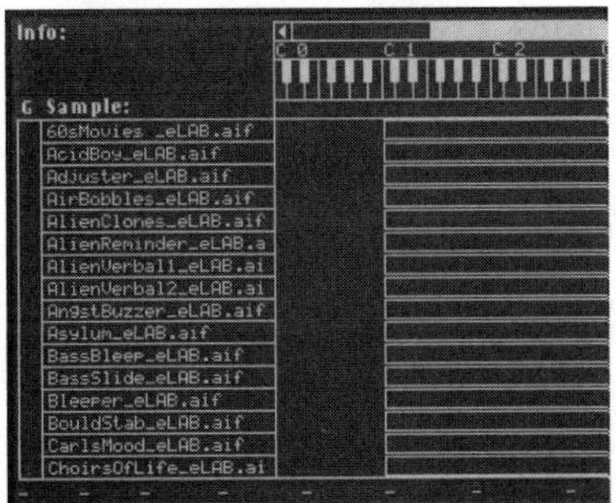

Figure 6.80 This is how the sample map looks after batch-loading samples.

Creating an NN-XT Instrument

You can create your own NN-XT patches using samples from the Factory Sound Bank. This means first loading samples using the patch browser.

To load samples:

1. Initialize the NN-XT patch (right-click and select Initialize Patch, or go to Edit > Initialize Patch).
2. In the Remote Editor, click the Browse Sample button (**Figure 6.78**).
3. Using the sample browser, navigate to the Reason Factory Sound Bank, then `Other Samples/Chords-Phrases-Pads-Stabs` and press Ctrl+A (Win) / Cmd+A (Mac) to select all samples in the directory (**Figure 6.79**).
4. Click Open. The entire directory of samples is now loaded into the NN-XT and visible in the Remote Editor display (**Figure 6.80**).

When loaded manually, NN-XT samples may need to have their root key set.

To detect root notes on multiple samples:

1. With multiple samples loaded in the Remote Editor, select all the samples by clicking in the G column (**Figure 6.81**).
2. Select Edit > Set Root Notes From Pitch Detection. A status window appears, indicating progress (**Figure 6.82**).
3. Click on a sample to see its root note highlighted on the keyboard ruler.

   Even though the key zones will look the same, the root keys for all the samples have been changed.

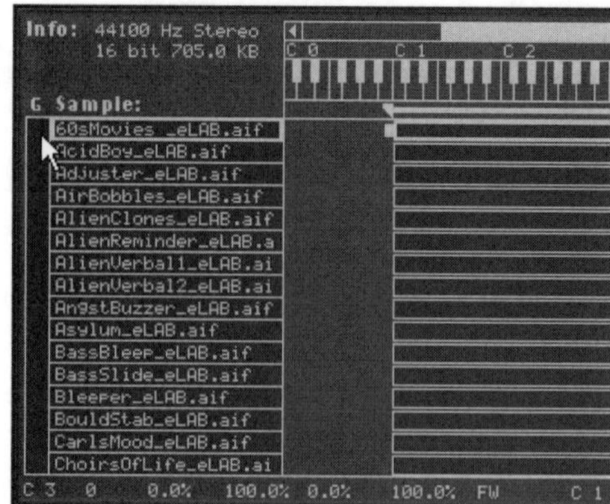

Figure 6.81 Samples loaded together are in the same group and can all be selected using the Group (G) column.

Figure 6.82 The Pitch Detection status window shows your progress.

NN-XT Sample Formats

Standard .wav files: Short for waveform audio format, WAV is a Microsoft/IBM format standard for storing audio on personal computers.*

Standard .aiff files: Co-developed by Apple and based on Electronic Arts' Interchange File Format, AIFF (audio interchange file format) is most commonly used on Macintosh systems.*

SoundFonts: A widely used format for storing instrument samples on PC sound cards developed by Creative Labs.

REX Slices: Reason's loop player format, developed by Steinberg. It uses slices of a sound to adjust tempo without affecting pitch.

* Source: http://en.wikipedia.org

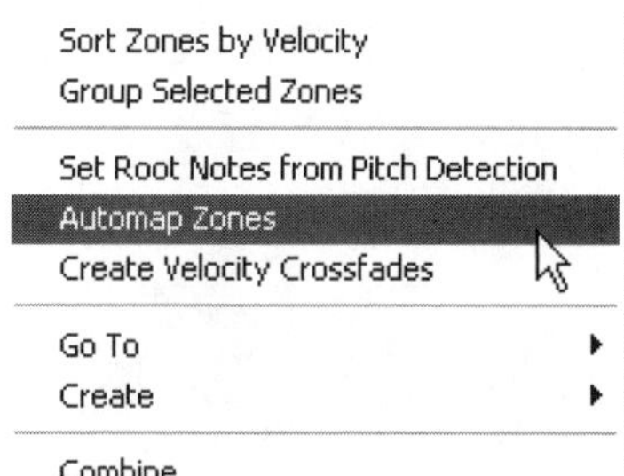

Figure 6.83 The NN-XT, too, uses the Automap command.

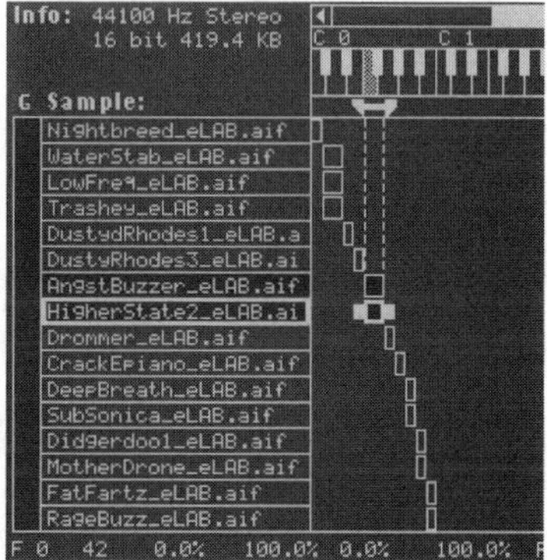

Figure 6.84 Automapped samples with the same root key will be assigned the same key zone.

Automapping samples' key zones works best when you have a set of samples that you know have different root keys. Automapping on the NN-XT works exactly the same as on the NN19.

To Automap samples' key zones:

- With a set of unmapped samples loaded, select Edit > Automap Zones (**Figure 6.83**).

  When samples share the same root note, Reason will map them to the same key (**Figure 6.84**).

Editing sample maps

Once a sample is loaded, you can edit it interactively by dragging it to a new key location, by lengthening its key zone, or by drag-selecting multiple samples. To assign multiple samples to the same key, you can use the Remote Editor to adjust this manually.

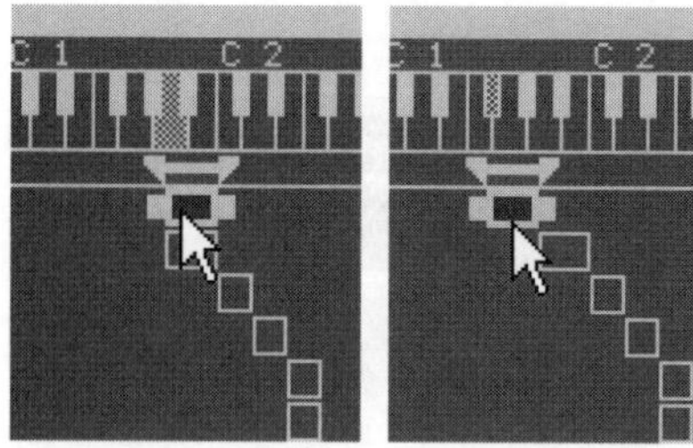

Figure 6.85 Key zones behave like objects and can be dragged around the keyboard ruler.

To edit key zones:

1. Select a sample in the NN-XT Remote Editor.
2. To adjust the key zone position, click and drag the zone box left or right. The root key setting will travel with it (**Figure 6.85**).
3. To adjust the zone's range, click and drag the handles on the sample box (**Figure 6.86**).
4. To adjust multiple sample ranges, click and drag the tab handles at the top of the display (**Figure 6.87**).

   The tab handles ignore selection status. They will drag all the samples with ranges beginning or ending at the handle position.

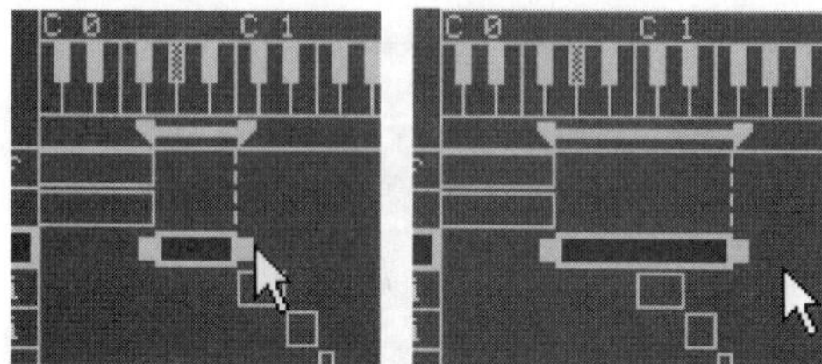

Figure 6.86 Zone handles allow you to adjust the length of a single key zone.

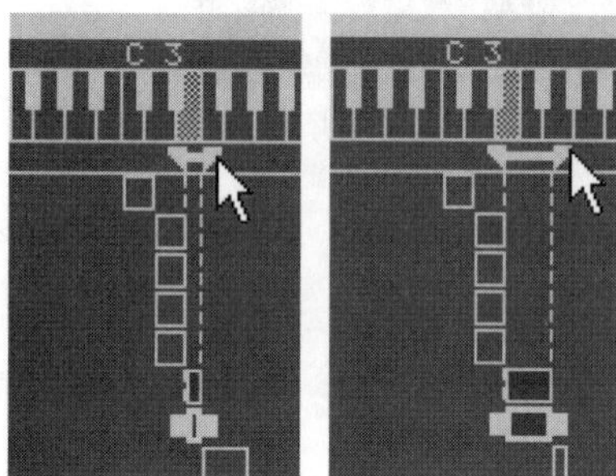

Figure 6.87 Tab handles ignore selection status, dragging whatever zone boundaries begin or end at the handle's position.

✔ Tips

- The tab handles adjust a sample's key range in relation to other samples. This means when a sample is stretched to a key area containing another sample, the stretched sample will "squeeze" out or "steal" range from the other one.
- If you're working with unpitched samples and want to set up one sample per key, you'll have to map each sample manually.

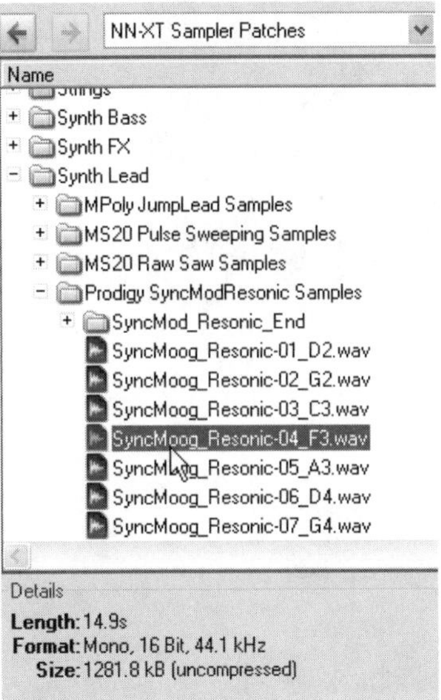

Figure 6.88 Load a synth lead sample from the Factory Sound Bank.

Figure 6.89 Set the root key to match the sample's recorded pitch.

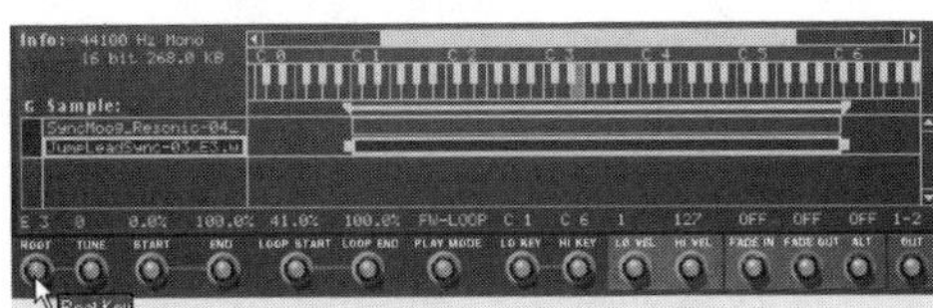

Figure 6.90 Set the second sample's root key.

Layering Samples

You can get two samples to play together by assigning them to the same key. We'll start with a single-sampled instrument in this example and add another sound to it.

To create a layered instrument:

1. Initialize your NN-XT patch.
2. Load your first sample using the Remote Editor's sample browser.

   In this example, I loaded `NN-XT Sampler Patches/Synth Lead/Prodigy SyncMod Resonic Samples/SyncMoog Resonic-04_F3.wav` (**Figure 6.88**).

   By default, the NN-XT will give the sample a five-octave range.
3. Set the root key of this sample to F3 using the Root Key knob (**Figure 6.89**). Without this step, you won't have a standard pitch reference when you add another sample!
4. Click on the sample map display to deselect the sample; then load a second sample, for example `/Synth Lead/MPoly Jump Lead Samples/JumpLeadSync-03_E3.wav`.
5. Select the new sample and set its root key to E3 (**Figure 6.90**). Now both samples should be playing the same pitch.

continues on next page

6. Tune the second sample to another interval using the Pitch/Semi knob (**Figure 6.91**).

7. Activate the Solo Sample button (**Figure 6.92**). This allows you to select a sample and use the keyboard ruler to hear it by itself.

8. Set the relative levels of the samples one at a time by selecting them and adjusting the Amp Envelope/Level knob (**Figure 6.93**).

9. Save your patch for the next exercise.

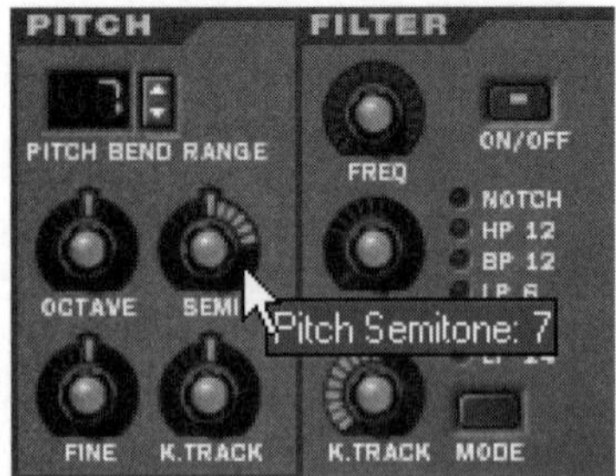

Figure 6.91 Transpose the second sample using the Pitch/Semi knob.

Figure 6.92 Activate the Solo Sample button.

Figure 6.93 Set sample volume by selecting the sample and then using the Amp Envelope level knob.

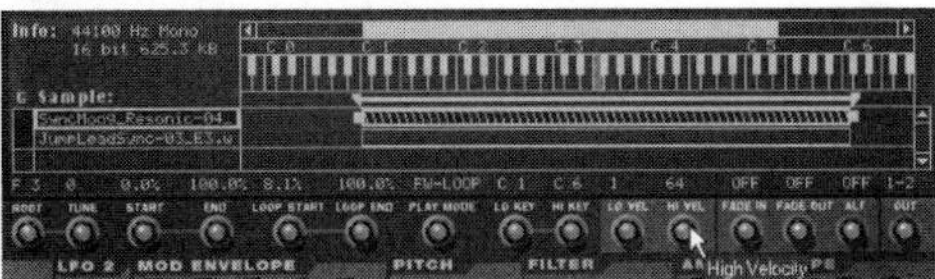

Figure 6.94 Set up a first velocity layer.

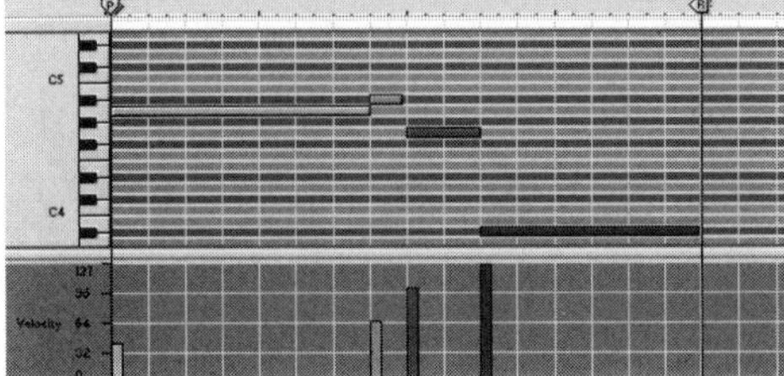

Figure 6.95 Use a track with velocity variations to test velocity layers.

Velocity range

The NN-XT can switch or fade between two samples with different velocity ranges.

To velocity-switch between samples:

1. With the layered patch from the last exercise still loaded, select the first sample and set the Lo Vel knob to 1 and the Hi Vel knob to 64 (**Figure 6.94**).

   The sample with partial velocity range will look striped in the NN-XT display.

2. Select the second sample and set its Lo Vel to 65 and Hi Vel to 127.

   If you set the Lo Vel of the second sample lower than the Hi Vel of the first, there will be overlap on shared velocities.

   If you set the Hi Vel of the second sample below 127, notes above that value will not sound!

3. Test your patch with hard and soft attacks on your external keyboard, or input some notes in your NN-XT track with velocity variations (**Figure 6.95**).

✔ Tip

- If you want, you can set up a track for testing switches and crossfades, and save it so you can use it on any instrument.

You can also use velocity to crossfade between samples in a layered patch—one sample fades in at a certain velocity as the other fades out.

To crossfade between two samples:

1. With your layered patch loaded, set the first sample's Lo Vel to 1 and its Hi Vel to 80.
2. Set the second sample's Lo Vel to 60 and the Hi Vel to 127 (**Figure 6.96**).

   The crossfade will occur where the velocity ranges overlap, between 60 and 80.
3. Once again, test with soft and hard attacks on your external keyboard or in your NN-XT Sequencer track.
4. To tune this effect, you may want to adjust the velocity overlap or the relative volumes of the samples.

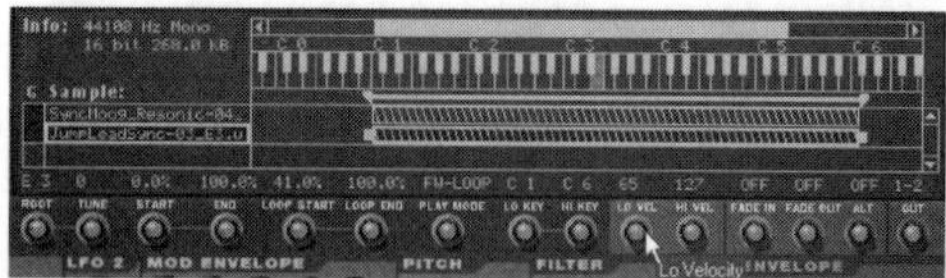

Figure 6.96 For a crossfade, set up the two velocity layers to overlap slightly.

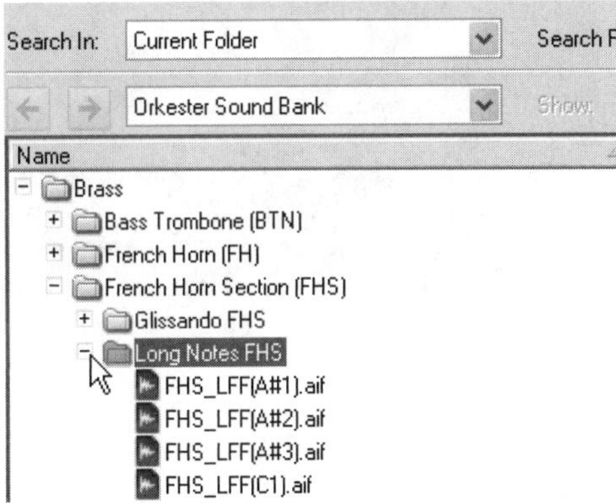

Figure 6.97 Unfold directories using the + icons in the 3.0 browser.

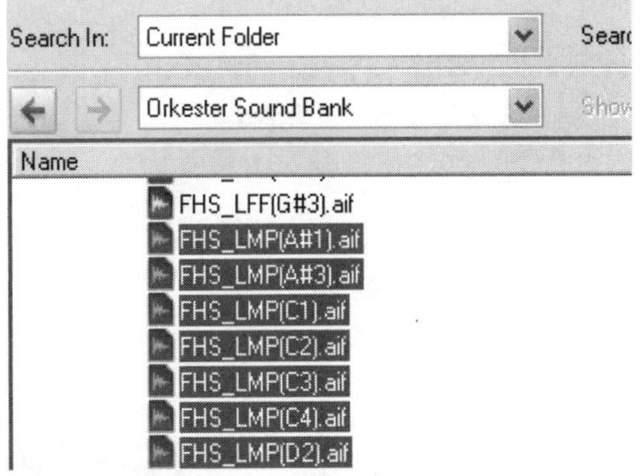

Figure 6.98 Load multiple pitched samples from the Orkester Sound Bank.

Figure 6.99 Use the G column to quickly select all samples in a group.

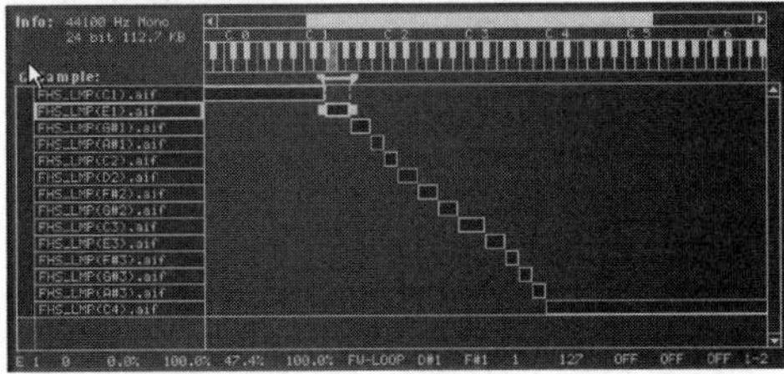

Figure 6.100 Automap the samples you loaded from the Orkester Sound Bank.

Setting Up Groups

The NN-XT will group samples that are loaded at the same time. Grouped samples can be selected using the G column in the Remote Editor. Once selected, certain parameters can be edited for the whole group in one step.

For this exercise, we'll set up a `French Horn Section` patch with multiple layers.

To create a group during loading:

1. Initialize the NN-XT patch.
2. Using the sample browser, go to the `Orkester Sound Bank/Brass/French Horn Section (FHS)` folder and click the + sign next to the `Long Notes` folder (**Figure 6.97**). This reveals the samples contained in this folder.
3. Select all the samples named `FHS_LMP` and load them (**Figure 6.98**).

   Samples loaded at the same time are automatically assigned to the same group. From now on, these samples can be easily selected together.
4. Select the whole sample group by clicking the G column in the Remote Editor (**Figure 6.99**).
5. Use Edit > Automap to set up key zones.

   Your samples should now all be spread across the keyboard (**Figure 6.100**).

Now let's load a second set of samples and assign them to a separate group.

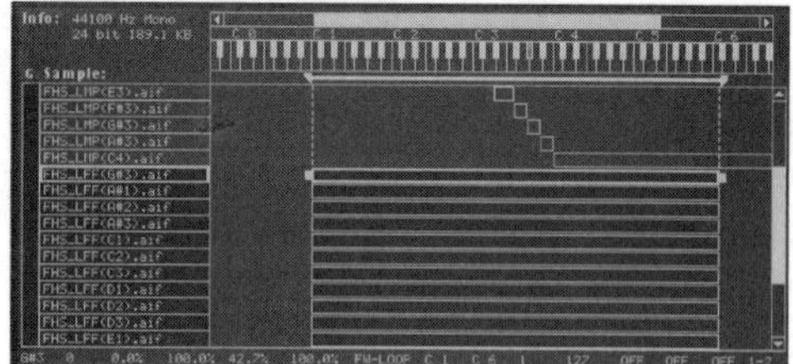

Figure 6.101 Load two sets of samples in the sample map.

To create a group manually:

1. Before loading more samples, first be sure all loaded samples are deselected by clicking on the sample map display. This prevents the next samples you load from overwriting the existing ones.
2. Using the sample browser, go to the Reason Factory Sound Bank `/Brass/French Horn Section (FHS)/Long Notes` and load all the samples that have `FHS_FF` in their name.

   The new set of unmapped samples now appears below the mapped samples you set up in the last exercise (**Figure 6.101**).
3. *Without* deselecting the newly loaded samples, right-click the sample map and select Group Selected Zones from the pop-up menu (**Figure 6.102**).

   You can now select each group separately using the G column. The new samples are now in their own group, and you'll see a horizontal group boundary between them and the samples above them (**Figure 6.103**).
4. With the new samples still selected, use the Edit > Automap command to set up key zones for them (**Figure 6.104**).
5. Save this patch as `French Horn Section` for later use.

Delete Zones
Select All Zones
Copy Parameters to Selected Zones

Sort Zones by Note
Sort Zones by Velocity
Group Selected Zones

Set Root Notes from Pitch Detection
Automap Zones
Create Velocity Crossfades

Go To ▸

Figure 6.102 Group selected samples manually from the context menu.

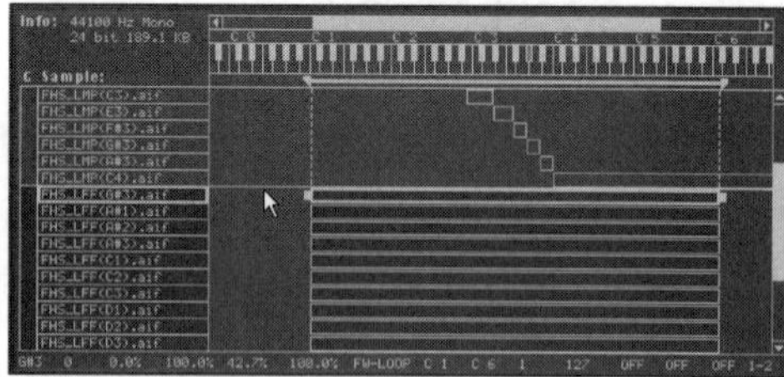

Figure 6.103 This sample map has two groups.

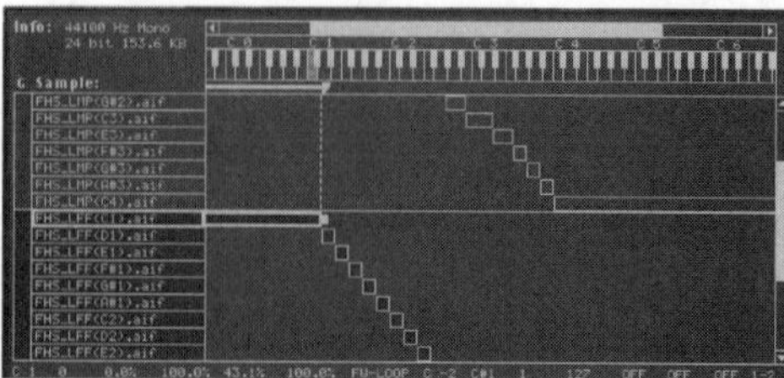

Figure 6.104 Automap the new group.

Figure 6.105 The group parameter knobs let you change settings for many samples at once.

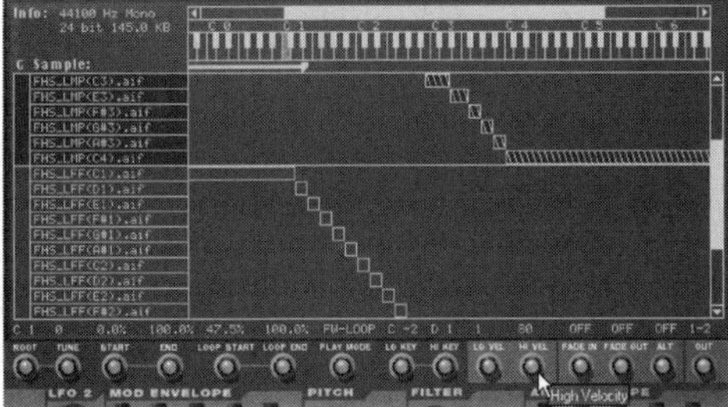

Figure 6.106 Striped samples have altered velocity zones.

The Group Parameter Knobs

Certain parameters can be set for an entire group of selected samples. These are the *group parameter knobs* located beneath the sample map on the right (**Figure 6.105**).

We'll use these to set up a velocity crossfade between the two sample groups that we created in the preceding section.

To set up a crossfade between groups:

1. With your `French Horn Section` patch from the preceding exercise loaded in your NN-XT, select the first group (`MF`) using the G column (we'll call this Group A).
2. Set the Hi Vel knob to 80 (**Figure 6.106**). Group A samples will now look striped and will play at softer velocities.
3. Set the Fade Out knob to 64. Group A samples will now begin to fade out at a velocity of 64 and will completely fade out by 80.
4. Select the second group (`FF`) using the G column (we'll call this Group B).
5. Set the Lo Vel knob to 64.
6. Set the Fade In knob to 64.

   Group B samples (`FF`) will start to fade in at the same velocity at which Group A samples start to fade out.
7. Test with soft and hard attacks to make sure the crossfade sounds the way you want it.
8. Tune the crossfade by shortening or lengthening the velocity overlap between groups. You may also want to adjust group volume using the Amp Envelope/Level knob.

Copying Samples Between Two NN-XTs

A fast way to layer another sound or add a group to a patch is to copy key zones and samples from one NN-XT to another.

In this example, we'll add a third layer to the `French Horn Section` patch: a set of short, staccato samples to use on the high note attacks.

To copy key zones from one NN-XT to another:

1. With the `French Horn Section` patch loaded in your NN-XT, create a second NN-XT device in your Rack.
2. Use the patch browser of the new NN-XT to load the patch Orkester Sound Bank `/NN-XT Sampler Patches/FHS Stacc alt`.
3. When all the samples are finished loading, they should appear as a new group, already selected (**Figure 6.107**). If the whole group isn't selected, click the G column.
4. Right-click the sample map and select Copy Zones from the context menu (**Figure 6.108**). The keyboard shortcut Ctrl+C (Win) / Cmd+C (Mac) works, too.
5. In the first NN-XT, click in the key map display. This activates the device and ensures that you don't overwrite any samples.
6. Paste the sample map to the first NN-XT by right-clicking the sample map and selecting Paste Zones from the context menu (**Figure 6.109**). Or you can use the keyboard shortcut Ctrl+V (Win)/ Cmd+V (Mac).

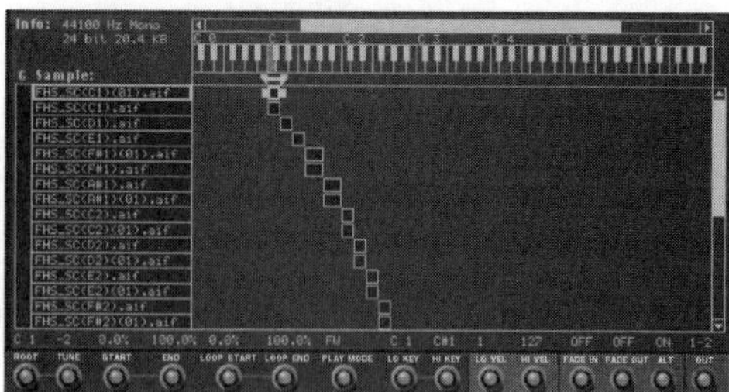

Figure 6.107 A patch loaded in a second NN-XT

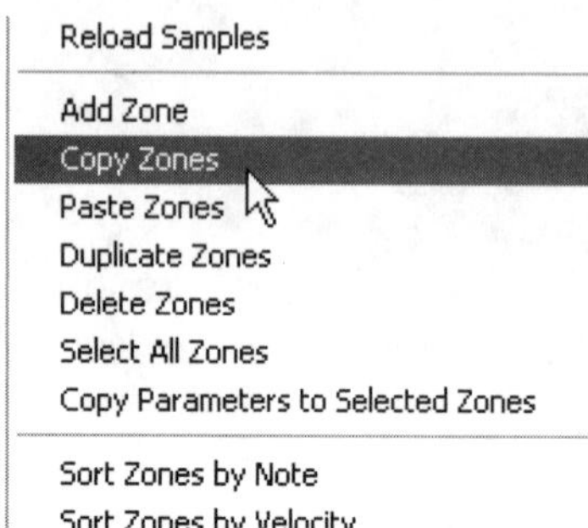

Figure 6.108 Copy the samples with the Copy Zones command...

Remove Samples
Reload Samples
Add Zone
Copy Zones
Paste Zones
Duplicate Zones
Delete Zones
Select All Zones
Copy Parameters to Selected Zones
Sort Zones by Note

Figure 6.109 ...and then paste them with the Paste Zones command.

Figure 6.110 A set of samples pasted from one NN-XT to another will retain all the zones and root keys.

Figure 6.111 When Alt is turned on, it switches between all group samples sharing a key zone.

You'll now see a third group of samples, which we'll call Group C, in your first NN-XT (**Figure 6.110**).

7. The newly pasted Group C (FHS_SC) should still be selected (if it's not, click the G column), so set its Lo Vel knob to 111.
8. Select group B (FHS_FF) in the G column and set the Hi Vel knob to 110.

   Now, at note velocities between 111 and 127, the staccato samples will play. In fact, the alternating samples in Group C work just as before!

✔ Tip

- Notice that the Staccato patch assigns more than one sample per key, but the samples are not striped. This is because both samples have full velocity ranges but are set to alternate anytime the note repeats. To set this up, select a group and turn the Alt group knob from Off to On (**Figure 6.111**).

Modifying NN-XT Parameters

The NN-XT's many controls function much the same as the familiar ones from other devices. Filters, envelopes, and LFOs work the same way, except that the NN-XT gives a greater amount of control, allowing you to set all the parameters for individual samples or groups of samples.

To adjust an individual sample:

1. Select the sample in the Remote Editor.
2. Adjust any of the sample parameter knobs located below the Remote Editor display (**Figure 6.112**).
3. Deselect the sample, and watch the adjusted parameter go blank or to the default value.
4. Again select the sample to check that the NN-XT has stored your new setting. This change will be stored when you save your patch.

To adjust multiple samples:

1. Select the desired samples in the Remote Editor (to select multiple samples, hold down Shift while clicking sample names).
2. Adjust any of the group parameter knobs (**Figure 6.113**).
3. Deselect the samples and then reselect to confirm that the changes you made are being remembered.

✔ Tip

- When creating large patches with many knob adjustments, it is strongly advised that you use groups whenever possible. This helps you to keep track of, check, and edit your settings quickly.

Figure 6.112 Sample parameter knobs

Figure 6.113 Group parameter knobs

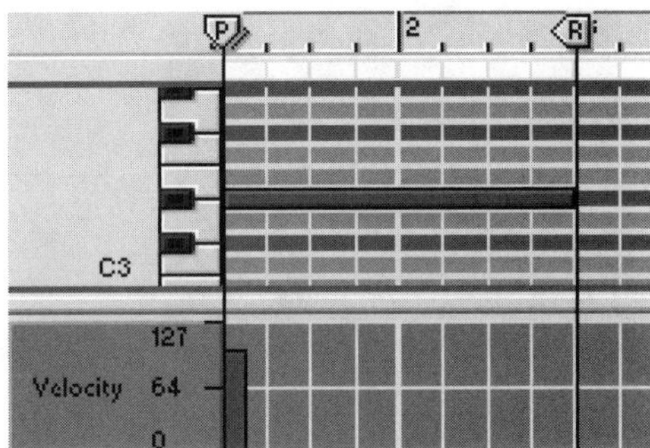

Figure 6.114 A two-bar sustained note for testing the FM Pad patch

Modulating samples

You may sometimes prefer a single-sample patch over a complex sound-mapping scheme as a way to use the sampler as a real-time sound processor.

The NN-XT's mod envelope allows you to create pitch and brightness variations over the course of a note. It can modulate pitch, filter, or both, and can modulate positively (increasing pitch or filter frequency) or negatively (decreasing pitch or filter frequency).

The NN-XT envelope ADSR controls (see Chapter 5) are knobs, and there's an additional hold stage that sets a length of time between the attack maximum and the decay stage. Hold settings include Off and a range from 0.3 milliseconds to 50.04 seconds.

Since the mod envelope's attack, hold, decay, and release stages have a wide range (0.3 milliseconds to 50.04 seconds), they can be used to make very fast adjustments to a short sound like a drum hit, or very slowly evolving (3.336 minutes, in fact) variations to a sustained pad or ambience.

To use the NN-XT mod envelope for pitch:

1. Load the Reason Factory Sound Bank `/NN-XT Sampler Patches/Pads/FM Pad` patch.
2. Create a two-bar loop in your Sequencer NN-XT track and input a sustained note (**Figure 6.114**).
3. In the Rack, select all the samples in the patch using the Edit > Select All Zones command, or by pressing Ctrl+A (Win)/ Cmd+A (Mac).

continues on next page

4. Turn the mod envelope's Pitch knob to the right (**Figure 6.115**). When you play your loop, you'll hear the sample's pitch ramp up, hold, decay, sustain, and ramp down as the envelope runs through its stages.

   The Pitch knob sets how far the pitch will travel through each envelope stage. Turning it to the right will cause the pitch to rise with the attack, ramp down to the sustain frequency, and then ramp down for the release. Turning it to the left will cause the pitch to fall with the attack, ramp up to the sustain frequency, and then ramp up for the release.

Figure 6.115 The NN-XT mod envelope Pitch knob sends the envelope to the oscillator section.

5. Adjust the attack knob to speed up and slow down the initial pitch change.
6. Adjust the decay knob to speed up or slow down how fast the pitch proceeds to the sustain frequency.
7. Adjust the sustain knob to set the frequency at which the pitch will rest while the note sustains.
8. Use the release knob to set the time that the pitch will take to ramp back to its starting frequency.

To use the mod envelope for brightness:

1. Load the Reason Factory Sound Bank `/NN-XT Sampler Patches/Pads/FM Pad` patch, if you haven't already, and create a two-bar loop with a sustained note in your Sequencer.
2. In your NN-XT, set the mod envelope Pitch knob back to the middle.
3. Since the mod envelope is an offset of your filter settings, make sure the NN-XT's Filter section is enabled (with the On/Off button) and your filter frequency (Freq knob) is tuned low enough so that positive filter movement by the mod envelope has the best effect.

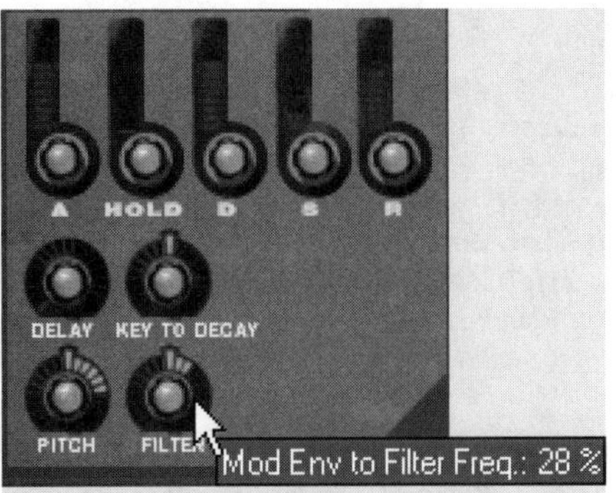

Figure 6.116 The mod envelope Filter knob only has an effect if the Filter section is active.

4. With your loop playing, turn the mod envelope Filter knob to the right. When you play your loop, you'll hear the brightness increase and decrease as the envelope runs through its stages (**Figure 6.116**).

5. Now set the filter frequency high, so that a negative mod envelope has an audible effect as it decreases.

6. Turn the mod envelope Filter knob to the left, and you'll hear the brightness decrease and increase as the envelope runs through its stages.

7. Adjust the mod envelope attack to speed up and slow down the initial change in brightness.

8. Adjust the decay to speed up or slow down the filter frequency's progression to the sustain setting.

9. Adjust the sustain stage to set the frequency at which the filter will rest while the note sustains.

10. Adjust the release stage to set the time the filter will take to return to its starting frequency.

✔ Tip

- At maximum, just one envelope stage set high can easily "gobble up" your note duration, so pay attention to the value indicators to stay inside your note duration.

Advanced Maps: Reverse Drums

For our most advanced exercise in this chapter, we're going to set up a forward/reverse drum kit capable of simulating turntable effects and abstract techno beats.

This will involve grouping the samples to edit one set of parameters, then changing the grouping to edit another set of parameters. Don't worry—we'll take it in easy stages. First we'll get the samples loaded and set up the key zones.

To map samples for a reverse drum patch:

1. Load some kick, snare, hat, cymbal, and percussion samples into the NN-XT from the `xclusive drums-sorted` subdirectories in your Factory Sound Bank. For example, I loaded the following:

   `01_BassDrums / Bd1Dub.aif`

   `02_SnareDrums / Sd2_Brat.wav`

   `05_HiHats / Hh1_sht3.aif`

   `06_Cymbals / CYM1V20HSH.aif`

   `07_Percussion-Hi / Cb_Cheese.wav`

2. Click in the G column to select all your samples.
3. Drag the left and right tab handles towards the center key until all the key zones are one key wide (**Figure 6.117**).
4. Assign the samples to different keys by dragging them one at a time (**Figure 6.118**). The root key values will stay with the samples.

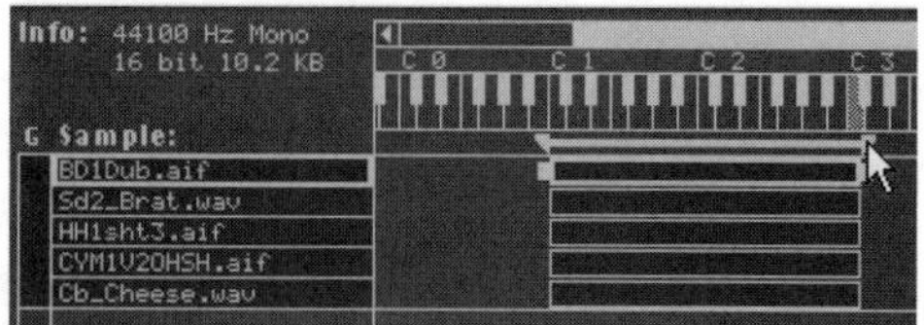

Figure 6.117 Drag tab handles to center all the key zones one key wide.

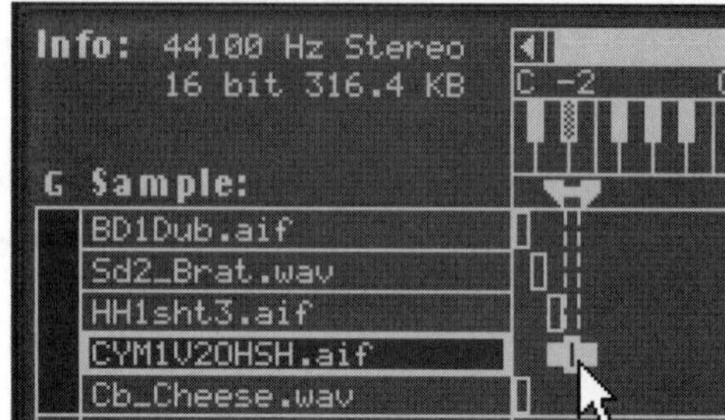

Figure 6.118 Drag individual notes to their own key zones.

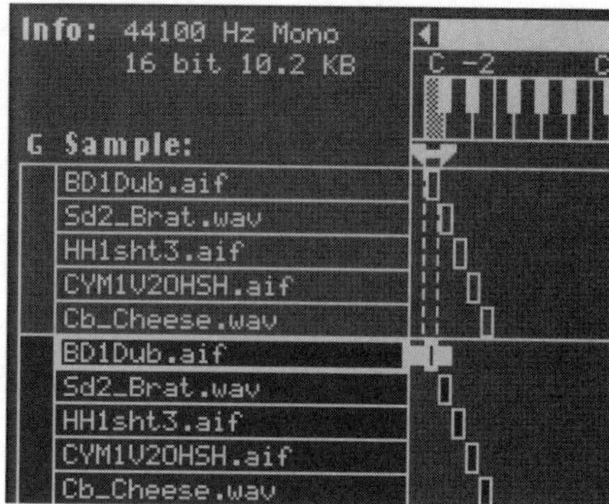

Figure 6.119 Duplicate the sample group.

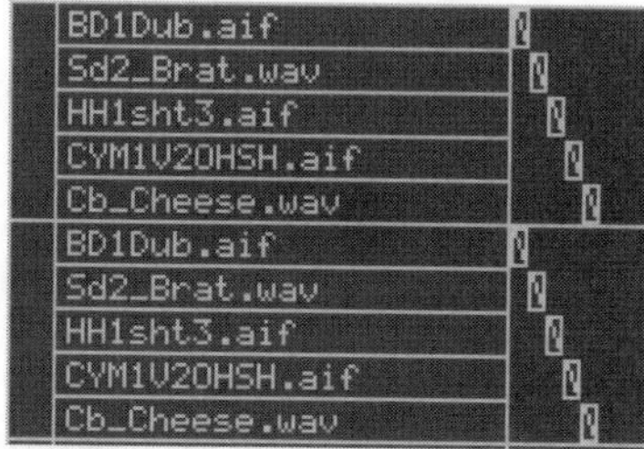

Figure 6.120 Alter the groups' velocity zones, and the samples become striped.

5. Click in the G column and copy the key zones, using either the Edit menu or the context menu.

   You're going to paste these into your NN-XT and set them to play backward.

6. Deselect all samples, and execute the Paste Zones command or Ctrl+V (Win)/ Cmd+V (Mac). Reason automatically assigns the duplicate samples to their own group (**Figure 6.119**).

7. Select the group of copied samples and set the Lo Vel knob to 120. These will be the reverse sounds, triggered at higher note velocity.

8. Now select the group of original samples, and set the Hi Vel knob to 119. Both groups of samples now appear striped (**Figure 6.120**).

Now we'll set the sample parameters. We want all the copied samples to play backward and skip the tails.

To set samples to play in reverse:

1. Select each copied sample and set its Play Mode knob to BW (**Figure 6.121**).

   Since Play Mode is not a group parameter, you'll need to do this for each sample individually.

2. To skip the sample tails, set the End knob for each sample to a small percentage, such as 12% for closed hi-hats and shakers, or 6% for kick drums, ambient snares, and open hi-hats (**Figure 6.122**).

   For faster tempos such as 150–180 bpm, try lowering the percentages even more, to 4–10%.

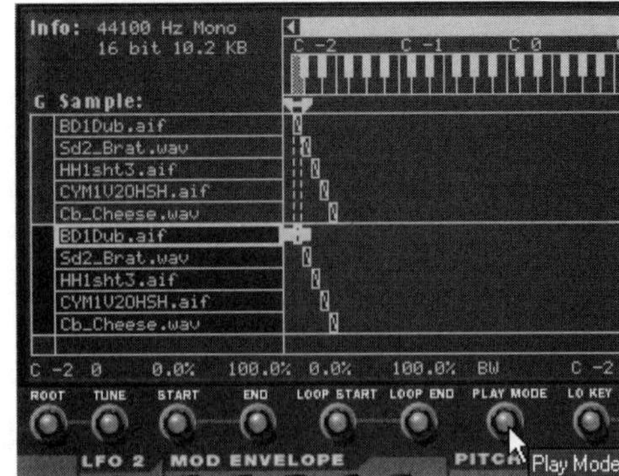

Figure 6.121 Set samples to play backward using the Play Mode knob.

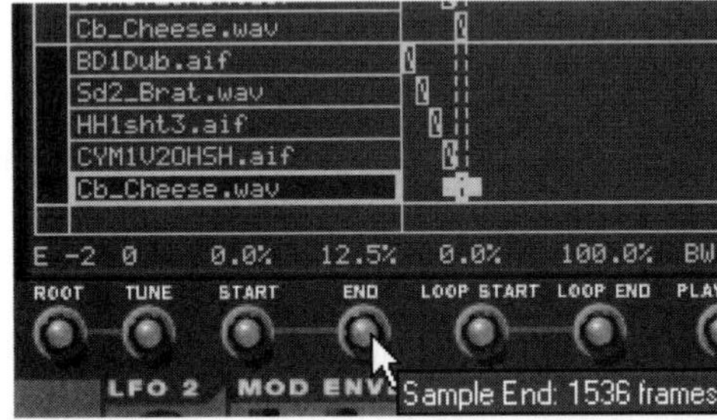

Figure 6.122 Changing the End percentage makes forward samples end closer to the start, and reverse samples start closer to the end!

Reverse Logic: Things to Keep in Mind

With reverse drum samples, you want to stay close to the loud "suck" at the end of the sample. The NN-XT's End knob allows you to do this.

In BW (backward) play mode, the End knob controls the attack. Unfortunately, End is not a group knob, so you'll have to set it once for every reverse sample in your kit.

End settings are based on percentages of the total sample length. The shorter the sound, the larger the percentage you're likely to use.

For fast tempos you'll need to lower the End percentage setting even more!

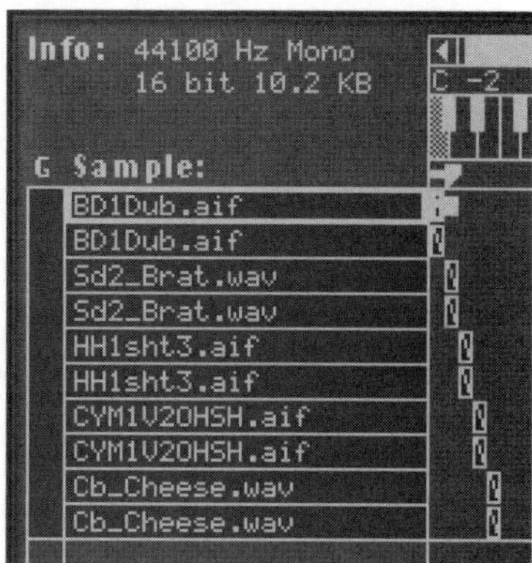

Figure 6.123 Arrange key zone pairs together using the Sort Zones By Note command.

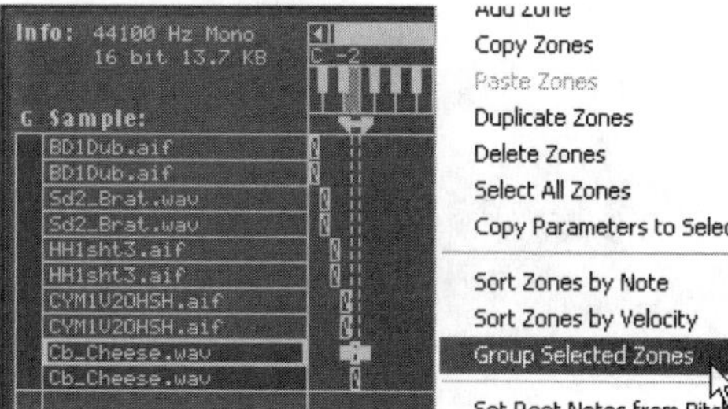

Figure 6.124 If you want to retain the order in which the samples are displayed in the sample map, start grouping them at the bottom.

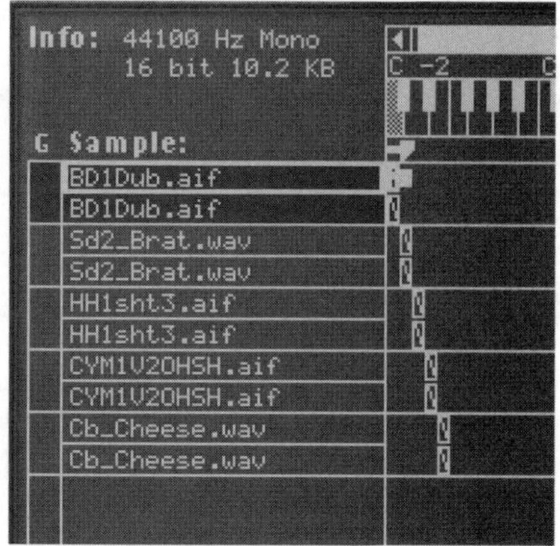

Figure 6.125 The key zone pairs are now grouped.

Now it's time to regroup the samples and make final edits so you can use this patch in your own tracks.

To set up groups of key pairs:

1. Select all samples with Ctrl+A (Win) / Cmd+A (Mac) and go to Edit > Group Selected Zones. This puts all the samples back in one big group, so we can sort them more easily.
2. With all samples selected, right-click the sample map and choose Sort Zones By Note. This arranges sample key zone pairs together (**Figure 6.123**).
3. Select the bottom two samples (`Cb_Cheese` in my example), and make the sample pair a new group using Edit > Group Selected Zones (**Figure 6.124**).

   Starting at the bottom keeps your samples in their current display order.
4. Continue up the sample map, grouping each sample pair (**Figure 6.125**).

To set up and tune group articulation:

1. Select all samples and adjust the Key Poly counter to 1 (**Figure 6.126**). This keeps the velocity zone pairs from overlapping, which is important for the backward effect to sound tight.
2. Alt-click to audition each `BW` sample and fine-tune its End knob settings.
3. Create a Sequencer track that includes notes with high enough velocity (at least 111) to trigger the reverse samples (**Figure 6.127**).
4. Play the loop and adjust the reverse sample's End knob as necessary.
5. Drag the notes up so that they play the next `BW` and `FW` pair, and adjust the End setting; repeat for each pair.
6. To make harder notes play louder, select all the samples and set the Level knob in the Velocity section to a positive value.

✔ Tips

- You can set up a "reverse" velocity range for the backwards notes by selecting them and setting the Velocity section Level knob to the left (**Figure 6.128**). This is more effective when the samples have a wide velocity range.
- Velocity settings will vary based on the samples you are using.

Figure 6.126 Use a Key Poly setting of 1 to keep samples from overlapping other samples in the same group.

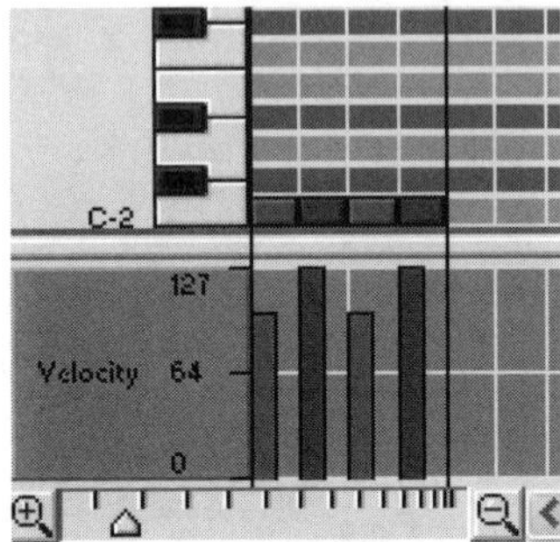

Figure 6.127 You can use a very simple Sequencer track to test the strong and weak velocity zones in the current patch.

Figure 6.128 To give the reverse samples an inverse velocity response, you can set the Velocity Level switch to a negative number.

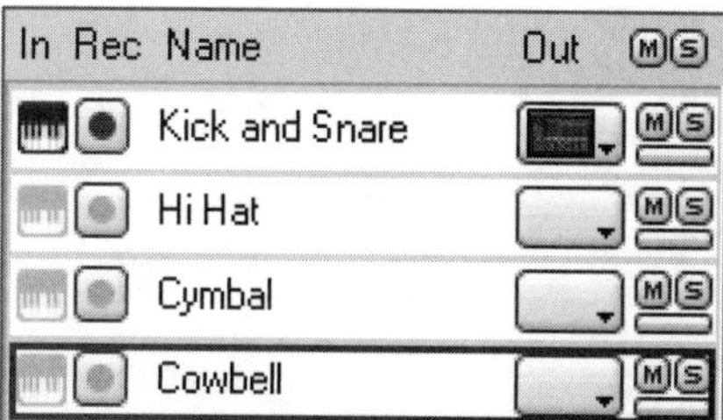

Figure 6.129 Create separate Sequencer tracks for different drum sounds to help you focus on one at a time.

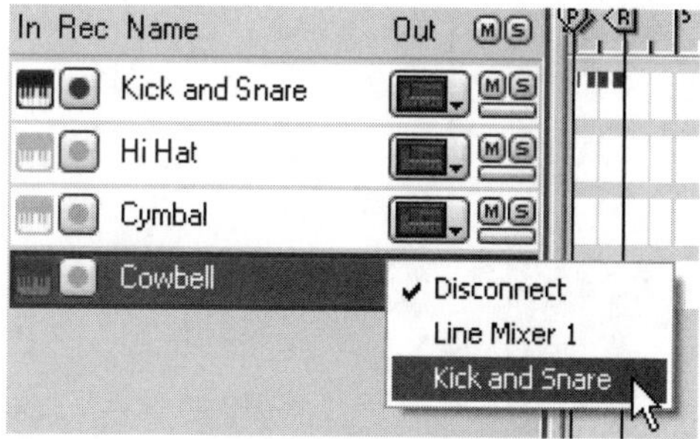

Figure 6.130 Assign all new tracks to the NN-XT.

Let's take a moment to set up a Sequencer track for each drum we're going to use. Manipulating this velocity-sensitive reverse kit will be tricky enough without having them all in the same track. With separate tracks for each drum, we can use the Mute and Solo buttons to better focus on each drum.

To set up separate tracks for drums:

1. In your Sequencer, use the Edit > Create Sequencer Track command once for each drum pair in your patch.
2. Double-click the track name, and rename it for the sound you'll write in it (**Figure 6.129**).

   I created one track for the kick and snare together, since it's harder to write them separately.
3. Use each name's Out column pull-down menu to assign each track to the same NN-XT device (**Figure 6.130**).

   The NN-XT will already be listed for the original track created at the same time as the device. Go ahead and select it for each new track—it won't affect the other track names.

To write a reverse part:

1. In the Sequencer, drag the separator up so that your Velocity lane stretches to a resolution at which the reverse velocity zone is visible (**Figure 6.131**).
2. Write a kick-and-snare pattern, using one or two hits at high velocity to trigger reverse samples (**Figure 6.132**).
3. Do the same for the hi-hat, cymbal, and cowbell tracks (**Figure 6.133**).

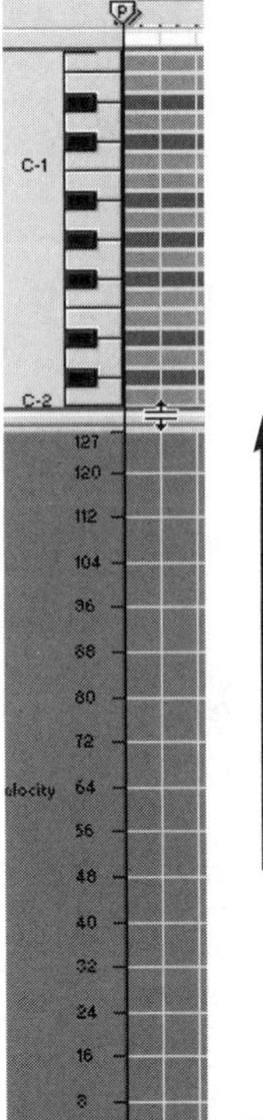

Figure 6.131 Drag the separator bar to resize the Velocity lane.

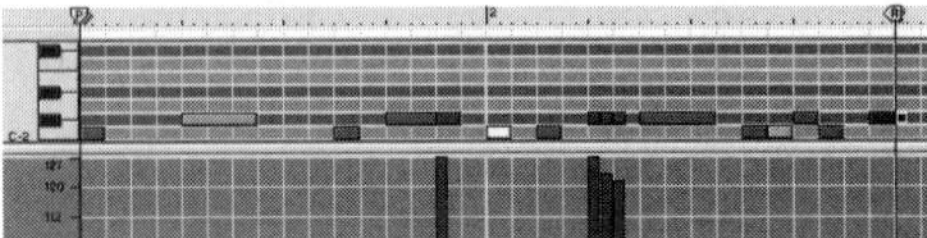

Figure 6.132 A kick-and-snare part with high and medium velocity will trigger forward and reverse hits.

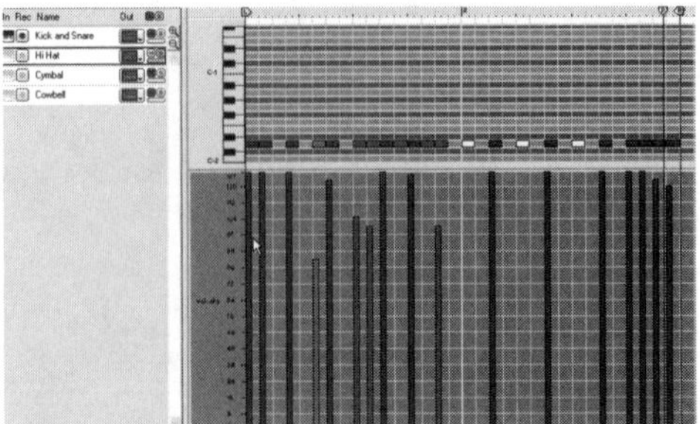

Figure 6.133 I used the Solo and Mute buttons to isolate the hi-hat part here.

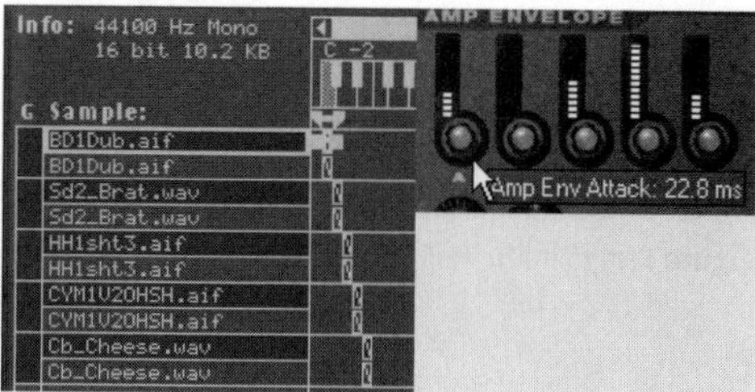

Figure 6.134 A slightly increased attack value in the amp envelope will help smooth out the first bytes of a sample.

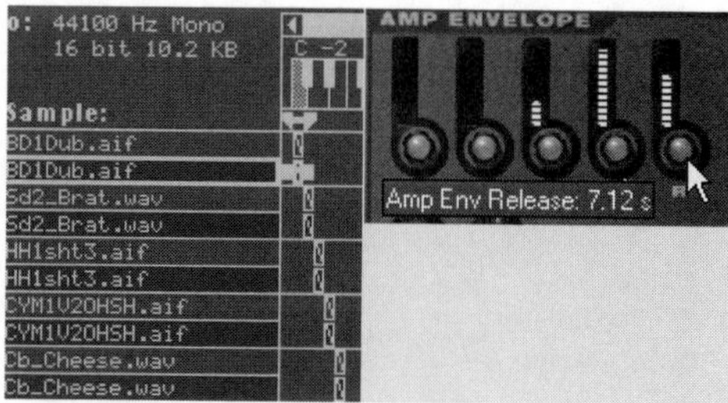

Figure 6.135 With groups all set to one voice, there's no downside to using a long amp release for the forward samples.

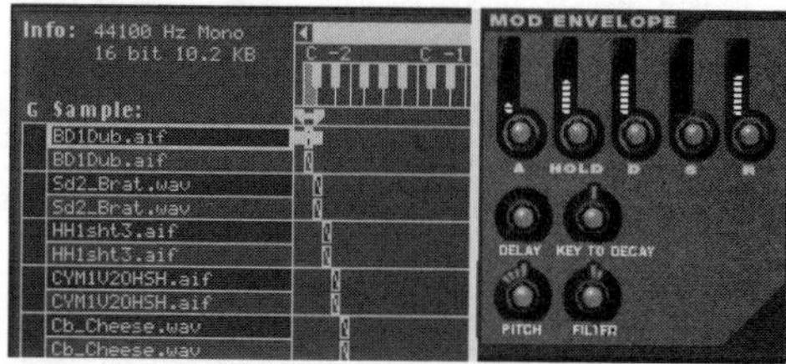

Figure 6.136 Use the mod envelope to pitch-shift the reverse samples down and increase brightness, for an exaggerated "reverse" effect.

To tune a reverse part:

1. With your loop playing, go to the NN-XT Remote Editor.
2. Optimize the amp envelope for the backwards notes by pushing the attack stage slightly above zero and setting a short decay (**Figure 6.134**).

   Since the backwards samples are set to start playing midway or farther into their fade-ins, this will smooth out any clicks and artifacts.
3. Optimize the amp envelope for the forward notes by setting the decay and sustain stages higher (**Figure 6.135**).
4. Select the reverse samples and try a positive or negative Pitch and/or Filter value on the mod envelope to accentuate the reverse effect (**Figure 6.136**).

✔ Tip

- Make note of any parameter adjustments that create interesting effects! You can always automate real-time changes to that parameter in the Controller lane of your NN-XT tracks to make them evolve in interesting ways.

The Dr. Rex Loop Player

The Dr. Rex is a special kind of sampler that plays back loops and sequences. It is designed to adjust music or beat loops to song tempo using special samples called *slice files.*

Slice (`.rx2`) files are complete music and rhythm loops chopped up and reassembled, so that the slices can be spread farther apart for slower tempos or pushed closer together for faster tempos—without altering pitch.

To create a Dr. Rex Loop Player:

1. If you're starting with an empty Rack, select Edit > Create > Mixer.
2. Select Edit > Create > Dr. Rex Loop Player. This creates an empty loop player and connects it to an open channel on your Mixer (**Figure 6.137**).

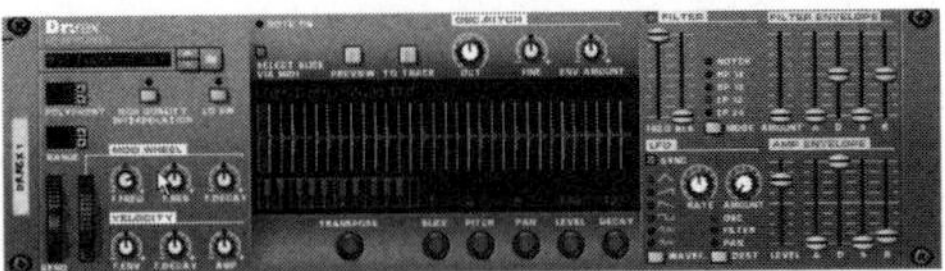

Figure 6.137 The Dr. Rex Loop Player

Figure 6.138 Click the Browse Loop button to find slice files in the Factory Sound Bank.

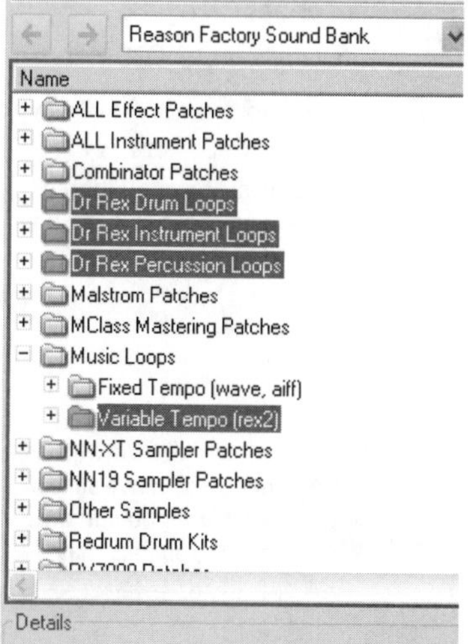

Figure 6.139 Several factory folders contain slice files for your loop player.

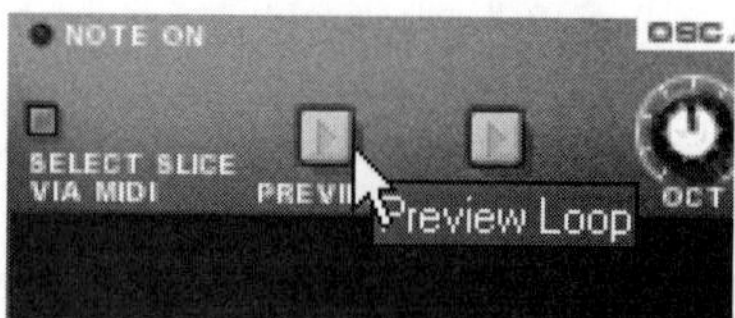

Figure 6.140 The Preview button plays the current slice.

Now we'll browse loops, load one, and hear how the Dr. Rex automatically adjusts the tempo.

To load and audition Rex files:

1. Click the Browse Loop button to open up the 3.0 browser (**Figure 6.138**). The Factory Sound Bank has a variety of folders that contain loops, or slice files (**Figure 6.139**).
2. Check the browser's Autoplay box, and click on a loop to audition it.
3. When you find a loop you like, click OK to load it.
4. With a loop loaded, click the Preview button on the front panel of the Dr. Rex Loop Player (**Figure 6.140**).

continues on next page

5. Use the arrow buttons or right-click in the slice file display to surf the other loops in the same directory (**Figure 6.141**).
6. Click the Select Slice Via Midi button to watch the loop player move through the slice file as it plays back (**Figure 6.142**).

✔ Tips

- You can encode your own Rex files using a Propellerheads program called ReCycle (see Appendix A).
- The Dr. Rex has a 92-slice limit per loop. Some commercial `.rx2` libraries may exceed 92 slices. If that happens, you'll see a warning message when you try to load the file into your Dr. Rex (**Figure 6.143**).

Figure 6.141 Use the arrow buttons to scroll through other loops, or right-click the loop name to pop up a menu of all loops in the current directory.

Figure 6.142 When Select Slice Via MIDI is enabled, active slices are highlighted in the display as they play.

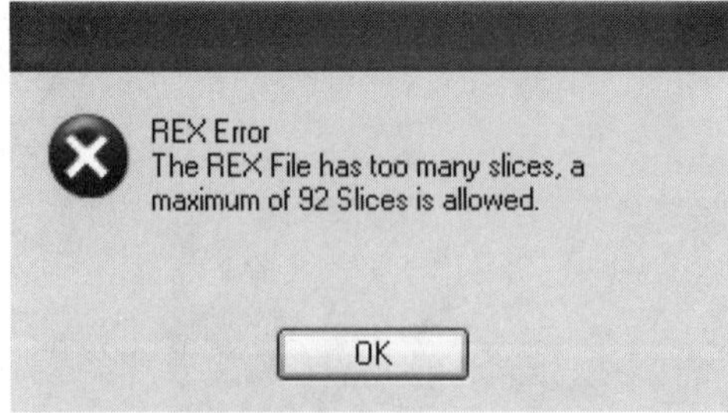

Figure 6.143 The Dr. Rex has a 92-slice limit. If your file goes over, you'll see this message when you try to load it.

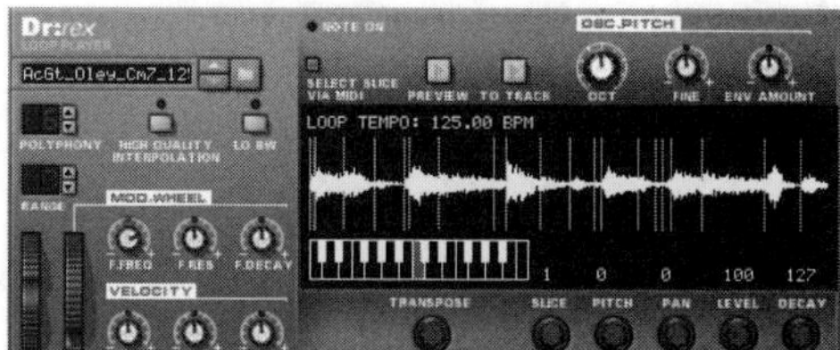

Figure 6.144 Load a slice file of an acoustic-guitar rhythm part.

Dr. Rex Dance Guitar

Because every loop is different, the best way to get a feel for the loop player's controls is to try it out. In this example, we'll take a rhythm guitar loop and turn it into a repeating dance figure.

To load a loop:

1. In the transport bar at the bottom of the Sequencer, set your song tempo to 140.
2. Go to the Dr. Rex in your Rack, and click the Browse Loop button.
3. In the loop browser, load the loop Reason Factory Sound Bank `/Dr Rex Instrument Loops/Guitar Loops/Ac Guitar Strum 125 bpm/AcGt_Oley_Cm7_125.rx2` (**Figure 6.144**).

   Since the loop is recorded at a slower tempo (125 bpm) the slices will be slightly longer than needed, giving us some decay to work with.
4. Click the Preview button.

   For a rhythm guitar part, the tempo right now is a bit fast. But we're going to turn it into a dance loop, so this is about right.

The amp envelope works by the slice, so it shapes notes the way most amp envelopes do. But since slices usually pass quickly and don't often extend very far beyond an attack, the attack and decay stages have more effect than sustain and release.

Figure 6.145 Set the amp envelope.

To set the amp envelope and filter:

1. With the guitar loop loaded in your Dr. Rex and with Preview enabled, set the amp envelope attack to 27. This gives each slice a softer attack.
2. Set the amp decay stage to 60 and the sustain to 0 (**Figure 6.145**). This has the effect of tightening up the loop by creating space between the slices.
3. Turn on the Filter section, and set the Res fader to 50.
4. Set the filter frequency to 0 (**Figure 6.146**). This temporarily shuts off all sound, but don't worry—we're going to open the filter using the filter envelope.
5. Set the filter envelope Amount fader to 112, the attack to 12, the decay to 56, the sustain to 30, and the release to 0 (**Figure 6.147**). These settings turn the soft, sparse guitar part into a dance guitar line.

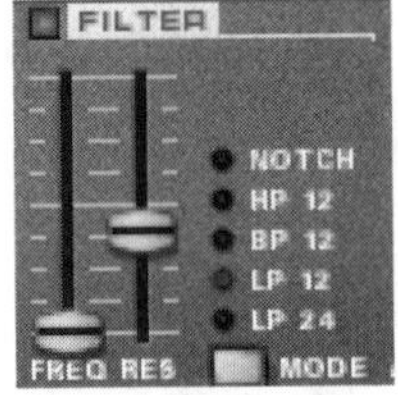

Figure 6.146 Set the filter (don't worry that you don't hear anything).

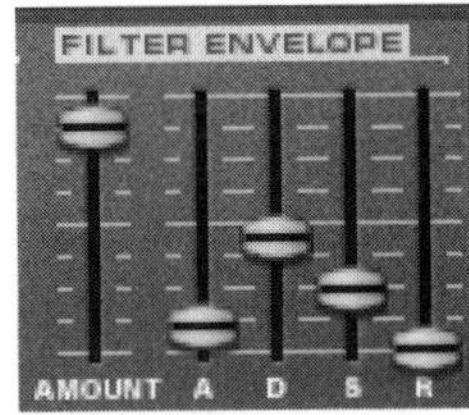

Figure 6.147 Set the filter envelope.

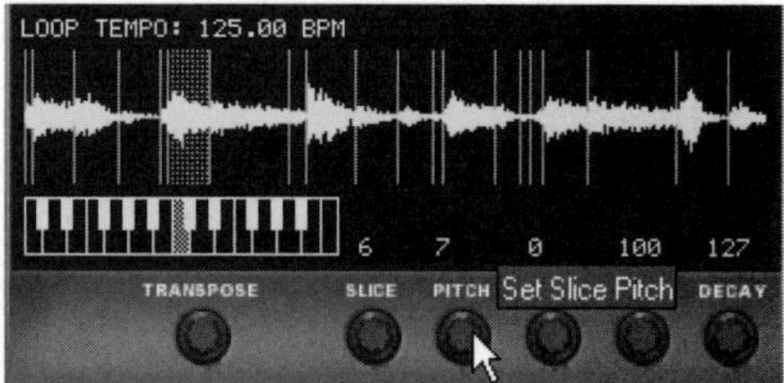

Figure 6.148 Transpose the pitch of a single slice.

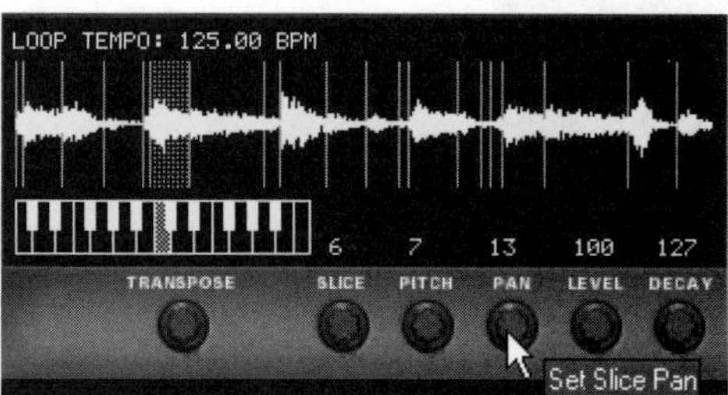

Figure 6.149 Setting the pan for an individual slice overrides LFO panning.

Unlike with other samples, you can adjust individual portions of a slice file. This gives you a great deal of creative freedom without even having to write a note! Now let's try adjusting the slices.

To adjust the slice settings:

1. With the `AcGt_Oley_Cm7_125bpm` loop still previewing, turn the Slice knob to 6. This determines the slice of the loop that you'll alter.
2. Hold down Ctrl (Win) / Cmd (Mac) to get the fine adjustment mode, and turn the Pitch knob to 7 (**Figure 6.148**). This raises the pitch of Slice 6 a perfect fifth.
3. Now turn the Pan knob to 13 (**Figure 6.149**). This separates the adjusted slice from the others in the stereo field. It also fixes Slice 6's panning position for when we apply the LFO to panning in the next exercise.

Now we'll set up a nice panning rotation that will highlight this sound and emphasize the slice we altered in the last exercise.

Figure 6.150 Set the LFO to modulate panning.

To modulate panning using the LFO:

1. With the `AcGt_Oley_Cm7_125bpm` loop still previewing, set the LFO destination to Pan (**Figure 6.150**).
2. With Sync enabled, set the LFO rate to 4/4 and the Amount to 127. This causes all the other slices in the loop to rotate between the left and right stereo fields, with only Slice 7 remaining fixed.
3. Set the Wavef. switch to triangle so that the sound pans smoothly from side to side (**Figure 6.151**).

   The upward sawtooth waveform will pan smoothly from left to right and then jump hard left.

   The downward sawtooth will pan smoothly from right to left and then jump hard right.

   The square waveform will ping-pong from left to right (try increasing the Rate knob to 1/8 or 3/8 for standard ping-pong pan).

   The square noise setting will randomly jump panning positions at the selected rate.

   The soft noise waveform will randomly pan from one position to the next, smoothly, at the selected rate.

Figure 6.151 Use the triangle LFO waveform for a smooth modulation curve.

✔ Tip

- Panning effects work more predictably for mono loops!

Figure 6.152 Set up the Mod wheel for a muted version of the sound.

The Mod wheel in Dr. Rex can add some drama. Let's set it for a more muted sound, which can be used to fade the loop into a song.

To fade with the Mod wheel:

1. Set the Mod wheel's F.Freq knob to –26, the F.Res knob to 18, and the F.Decay knob to 45 (**Figure 6.152**).
2. Move the Mod wheel to 127. This causes the filter to close, the resonance to increase, and the synthetic-sounding filter envelope effect to decrease.
3. Now slowly move the Mod wheel back to 0 while previewing the loop, to hear the effect.

   Slowly fading from a muted to a bright sound is a common dance music technique.

Finally, we'll add a beat loop to our dance guitar.

To load a beat loop:

1. Create a second Dr. Rex player.
2. Load the Reason Factory Sound Bank `/Dr Rex Drum Loops/House/Hse46_Houseback_130_Griffin.rx2` loop.
3. Click Preview.

Bouncing a Loop

Now you can bounce these loops to a Sequencer track. After this is done, the loop player's controls will still affect the sound. Working inside a track lets you change the slice sequence, edit slice velocities, and input Controller lane data.

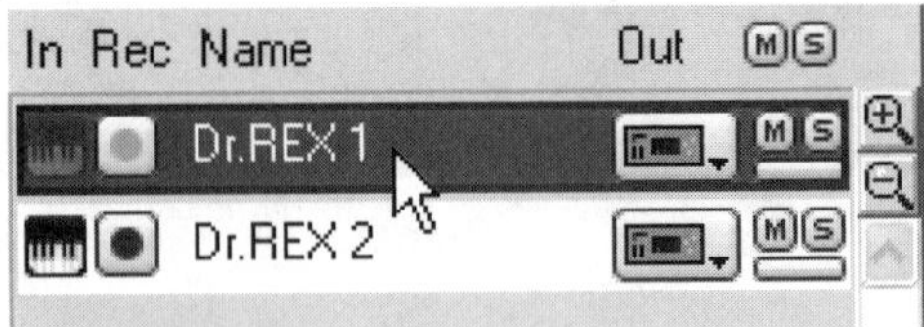

Figure 6.153 Select a track to bounce a loop to.

To bounce your loops to tracks:

1. Go to the Sequencer window and select the Dr. Rex 1 device track (**Figure 6.153**). This tells Reason which track you're going to send the notes to.

Figure 6.154 Bounce a loop to the Sequencer using the To Track button.

2. Go to your first loop player and click the To Track button (**Figure 6.154**).

   This creates a set of notes in your Sequencer track that repeats throughout your loop. The notes will be surrounded by a box. This is a *Sequencer group*, and it allows you to move the whole loop as one object in your Arrange window (**Figure 6.155**).

Figure 6.155 Slice files are given a Sequencer group when bounced. This lets you move them around without changing their relative position.

3. Go to your Dr. Rex 1 Sequencer track and click the Edit mode button to see what the loop notes look like.

   When a loop is bounced to a track, Reason's Sequencer opens up the Rex lane, which arranges slices on a grid. Notes are arranged left to right, bottom to top, starting at Slice #1 (**Figure 6.156**).

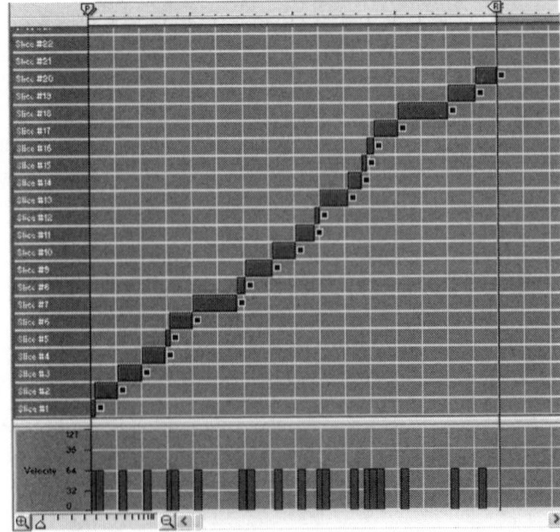
Figure 6.156 The Rex lane shows all the slices.

BOUNCING A LOOP

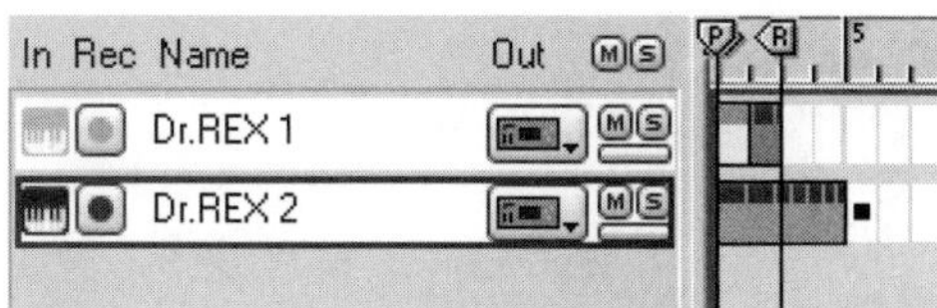

Figure 6.157 When a loop is longer than the current song loop, Reason bounces one complete length.

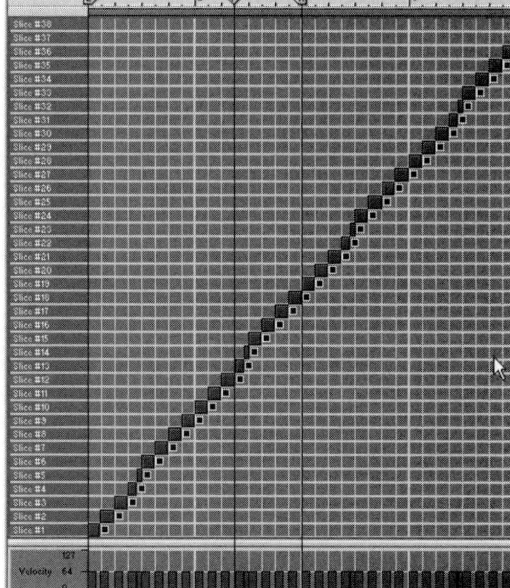

Figure 6.158 A loop player beat bounced to a Sequencer track

4. Select the Dr. Rex 2 track device in the Sequencer.
5. Go to the second Dr. Rex Rack device, and click the To Track button.

   If the Rex loop is longer than your Sequencer loop, the loop player will bounce one full sequence, or enough notes to play through the whole loop once (**Figure 6.157**).
6. Go to your Dr. Rex 2 Sequencer track and click Edit mode to see what the loop notes look like (**Figure 6.158**).
7. Press play to hear both loops playing together.

Modulating a Bounced Loop

Now we're going to make some adjustments to the beat loop in the second loop player.

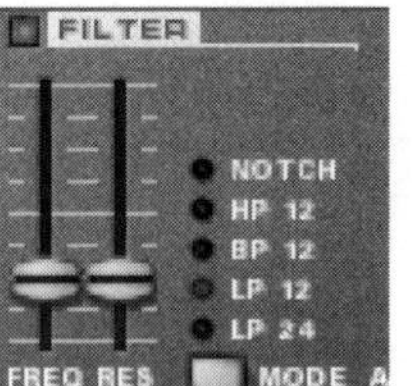

Figure 6.159 Set the filter for your space beat.

Figure 6.160 Set the filter envelope for your space beat.

To use the filter envelope on a beat:

1. With your two Dr. Rex loops bounced to the Sequencer (done in the preceding section), set up your Sequencer loop points to the playback length you want. Press play.
2. Go to the front panel of the second loop player. Push the filter envelope Res fader to about 1/4 and set the Freq fader to about 1/4 (**Figure 6.159**).

   Dropping the Freq fader gives the filter envelope room to move. Boosting the resonance will provide the "spacey" effect. (Use lower resonance values if you want less of this effect.)
3. Set the decay stage to about 41 and the Amount fader to 127 (**Figure 6.160**).

   Low decay values keep the envelope tight and percussive.

✔ Tips

- Just as in the SubTractor, the Dr. Rex filter and pitch envelopes are trumped by the amp envelope. In other words, if the amp envelope is tightened up with low fader positions, the other envelopes won't have much effect, since the amp envelope will be muting much of the sound.
- By default, the Dr. Rex Loop Player does not respond to velocity with volume changes. To set this up, you'll need to go to the Velocity section and turn the Amp knob to the right to get a standard velocity-to-volume effect.

Figure 6.161 The oscillator Env Amount knob turns the filter envelope into a pitch shifter.

The filter envelope can be used to control pitch by increasing or decreasing (*inverted envelope)* the Osc. Pitch section's Env Amount knob.

Even when the filter is disabled, the envelope controls still work for pitch. Leaving the Env Amount knob at 12 o'clock (to zero) turns the pitch feature off.

To use the pitch envelope:

1. Turn off the Filter section so that we can better hear the pitch effect.
2. Turn the Osc. Pitch/Env Amount knob left to –4, to activate the pitch envelope (**Figure 6.161**). This Env Amount setting creates an inverted pitch envelope—meaning that the pitch will move farther down as the envelope faders go higher.
3. Increase the filter envelope decay stage to move the pitch farther, or turn the Osc. Pitch/Env Amount knob higher to increase the overall effect.

Rearranging Slices in Your Sequencer

After they're bounced to a track, many Rex loops can be rearranged in the Sequencer. This allows you to use the Dr. Rex like a drum machine.

To scramble slices in a track:

1. Go to your Dr. Rex 2 Sequencer track and adjust the window to look at one set of loop notes.
2. Using the slice ruler or master keyboard, audition various slices until you find some that are good-sounding hits (**Figure 6.162**).
3. With a good kick, snare, or hi-hat hit, you can create a fill or a new beat (**Figure 6.163**).
4. Save this song—we'll use it in the next section!

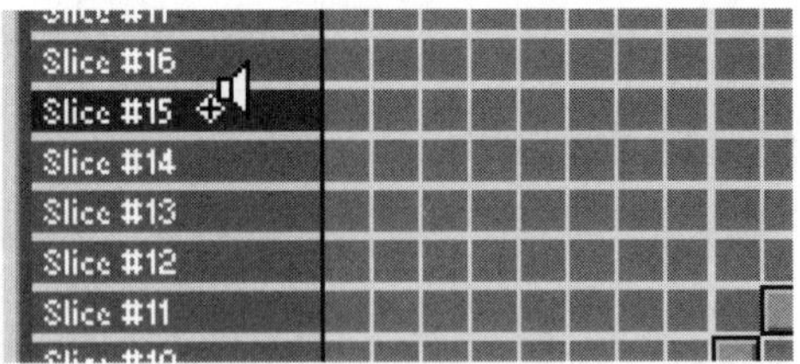

Figure 6.162 Audition slices in the Rex lane using the slice ruler.

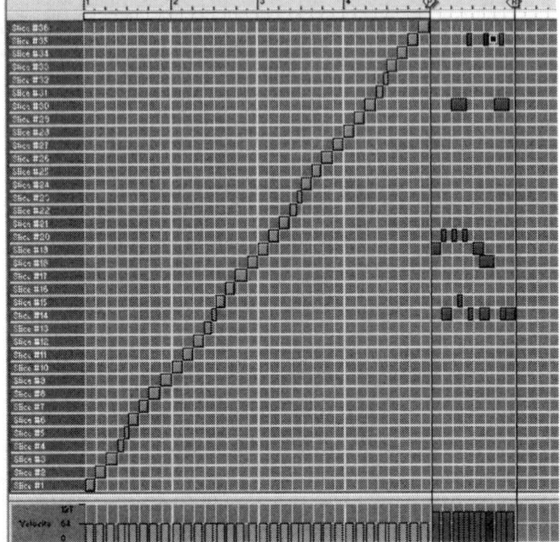
Figure 6.163 A set of scrambled slices can provide quick variety to a loop for a break or turnaround.

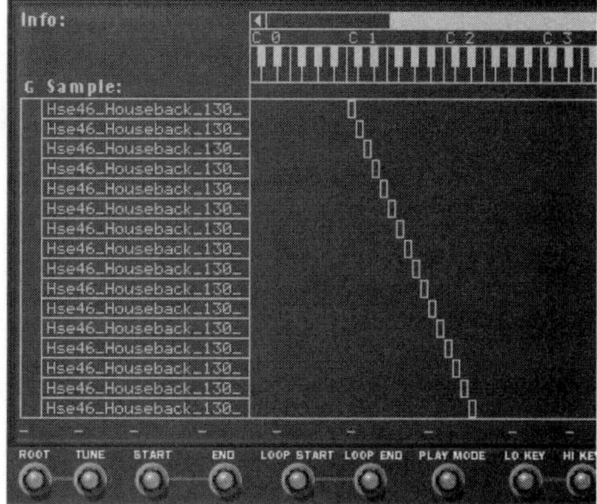
Figure 6.164 Load a slice file into an NN-XT sampler.

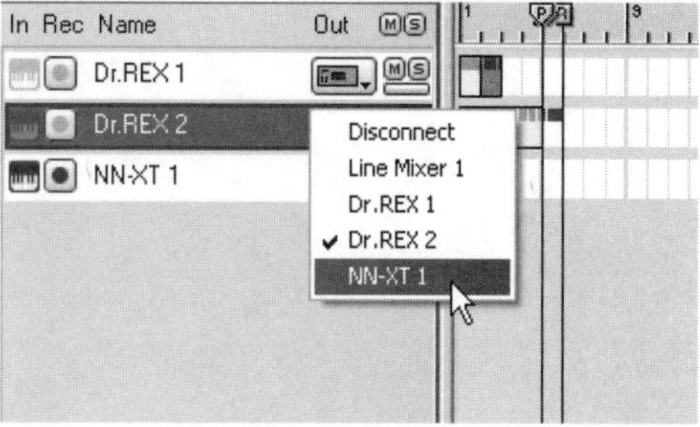

Figure 6.165 Assign a loop player track to an NN-XT.

Slice Files and the NN-XT

The NN-XT, too, can be used as a loop player for Rex files, and can save any changes you make as custom patches. The NN-XT creates key zones automatically when a slice file gets loaded. This makes it easy to layer slice files in groups, play slices backward, or apply filter and control settings.

To turn a slice (Rex) file into an NN-XT track:

1. With your loop player song from the preceding section still open, select Create > NN-XT Advanced Sampler.
2. Make sure your sampler is hooked to an open Mixer channel, and open the patch browser.
3. Once again load the patch Reason Factory Sound Bank `/Dr Rex Drum Loops/House/Hse46_Houseback_130_Griffin.rx2`.
4. Open up the Remote Editor to see each slice loaded as a separate sample with its key zone automatically assigned (**Figure 6.164**).
5. Go to the Dr. Rex 2 track in the Sequencer, and change the device to the NN-XT 1 instrument, using the Out column pop-up menu (**Figure 6.165**).

   With the NN-XT playing the loop, you gain the ability to use various control settings and outputs for each sample, to play slice files backward, and to save your changes as a sampler patch!

7

PATTERNING

Reason has two devices that can sequence notes directly from the Rack: the Matrix and Redrum *pattern sequencers.* Reason's pattern sequencers allow you to write short patterns and store them in banks easily selected on the front panel.

Pattern sequencers write and store notes in a way that is well suited for live performance. If you are a DJ or electronic music performer, you may prefer pattern sequencers over computer sequencers because they are more flexible to adjust and tweak in real time.

The Redrum Pattern Sequencer

The Redrum pattern sequencer (**Figure 7.1**) is built around 16 note trigger buttons that work on one drum channel at a time. Think of these as a series of notes moving left to right, like a track display for the selected drum sound (**Figure 7.2**). Just click the note buttons to toggle them on and off.

Figure 7.1 The Redrum pattern sequencer

Figure 7.2 The note buttons represent a 16-note series moving left to right. By default these notes are off (gray). Click the note buttons to activate them.

To write a one-bar pattern using the Redrum sequencer:

1. Create a Redrum, hook it up to a Mixer, and load it with sounds.

   If you don't remember how to do this, review Chapter 4.

2. Click Enable Pattern Section and then the Run button to start the Redrum sequencer (**Figure 7.3**).

   This won't produce sounds until you activate the note buttons.

3. Click the Select button in a drum channel to begin writing a pattern for it.

4. Set the Dynamic switch to either Hard, Medium, or Soft (**Figure 7.4**), and input the notes you want your drum channel to play (**Figure 7.5**).

5. Switch to another drum channel and repeat steps 3 and 4 (**Figure 7.6**).

Figure 7.3 The Enable Pattern Section button must be active to use the Redrum sequencer, and the Run button must be active to begin playing.

Figure 7.4 Use the Dynamic switch to set how hard or soft you want a note to play, before clicking the note button.

Figure 7.5 A one-bar part with the kick drum (Channel 1) selected. (Attack strengths are indicated on the buttons by H=hard, M=medium, and S=soft.)

Figure 7.6 A one-bar open hi-hat pattern for Channel 9.

Figure 7.7 The Steps counter sets the length of your pattern.

Figurer 7.8 For longer patterns (17–64 notes), use the Edit Steps switch to advance the note button display to the next section of the pattern.

To write a longer pattern using the Redrum sequencer:

1. Adjust the Steps counter to the number of notes you want in your pattern (**Figure 7.7**).

   The maximum step range is 64, or four measures.

2. Program notes one channel at a time as before. Then use the Edit Steps switch to advance forward another 16 notes (**Figure 7.8**).

3. Use the Resolution knob to change the note value of the note buttons. By moving the knob to the right (1/16T–1/128), you can "zoom" in on faster note values, and by moving the Resolution knob to the left (1/8T–1/2), you can "zoom" out.

✔ Tip

- Avoid confusion in longer patterns! Write the entire pattern length for each drum sound *before* selecting the next channel.

The Pattern Bank

You can program an entire drum track on the pattern sequencer if you know how to manage more than one pattern using the pattern bank buttons. Up to 32 patterns can be called up by using a combination of a bank button (A through D) and a pattern number button (1 through 8).

Each time you create a Redrum instrument, you start with an empty pattern bank and begin writing at pattern A1. To write additional patterns, you change to another bank setting.

To write additional patterns:

1. Start a new (empty) pattern, by clicking a different pattern button (1 through 8).
2. Start writing, or copy an existing pattern to a new location by using Edit > Copy or Ctrl+C (Win) / Cmd+C (Mac) in your old pattern. Then select a new pattern (1 through 8), and select Edit > Paste or Ctrl+V (Win) / Cmd+V (Mac) in the new location.
3. To write and store more than eight patterns, move to an empty bank (buttons A through D) and start saving again.

✔ Tip

- Use adjacent pattern locations (A1, A2, A3, A4, B1, B2, etc.) for patterns that will play consecutively. As your patterns multiply, this arrangement will help you keep track of them. During playback, Reason will finish playing the currently selected pattern and then switch to the next one you select.

Figure 7.9 The Flam enable button and Flam amount knob create two staggered notes instead of one.

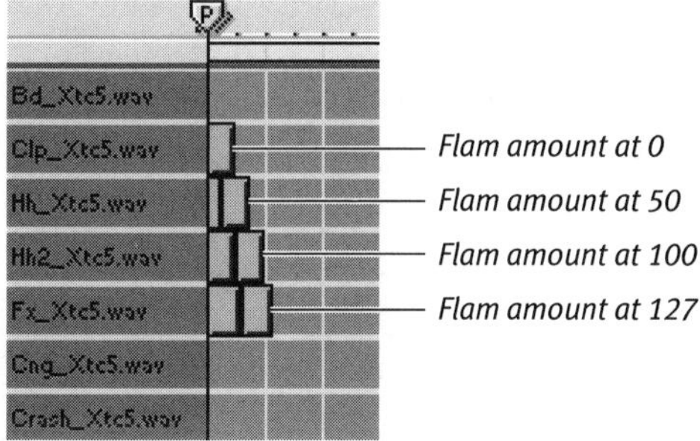

Figure 7.10 What the Redrum's flam section does, as seen in the Sequencer's Edit view

The Redrum *flam* controls create two staggered hits instead of one, and can be used on any note.

To use flam:

1. With your pattern running and the desired drum channel selected, click the Flam enable button (**Figure 7.9**) and click a note key.
2. Adjust the Flam amount knob to control how far apart your flam hits are "staggered" (**Figure 7.10**).

   0 = simultaneous hit/flam off

   127 = maximum separation
3. To decrease the time interval of the flam, turn the Flam knob to the left.

Since pattern length is set by the Steps counter value (1–64), changing the resolution will decrease the maximum beat length of your pattern (in measures) and shrink the work area represented by the note buttons.

For example, at a resolution setting of 1/32 with the Steps counter set at maximum (64), the pattern length can be no more than two measures, or 64 thirty-second notes.

At the maximum resolution of 1/128, the maximum step length of your pattern is still 64, but the musical length of your pattern has decreased to a fraction of a measure.

To increase resolution for a complex beat or a fill:

1. Move the Resolution knob to 1/32.

   The 16 note buttons now control a 16-note series of thirty-second notes. This gives you twice the resolution but shrinks the work area to half a measure.
2. Input notes as you did before, keeping in mind that if you want to continue to input sixteenth notes, you'll need to leave an inactive button between your notes.

The Resolution knob can be decreased, too, if you want to write longer, simpler patterns.

To increase pattern length:

- Turn the Resolution knob to the left to the setting you want.

  For an eight-bar pattern, you'll need to have the Resolution knob at 1/8, and the Steps counter set to 64.

  For a 16-bar pattern, the resolution knob must be at 1/4 or slower, and the Steps counter set to 64.

To use multiple Redrums in a live performance:

1. Use a Redrum set at low resolution with long patterns for infrequent hits. (Remember, you can also load nondrum sounds such as vocal yells, sound effects, and musical samples in your drum channels!)
2. Set another Redrum just for the basic kick-and-snare sounds.
3. Use a third Redrum to store shorter, more complex hi-hat patterns at a higher resolution, such as 1/16 or 1/32.
4. Devote a fourth Redrum to frantic or high-resolution drum fills, note frenzies, and so on.

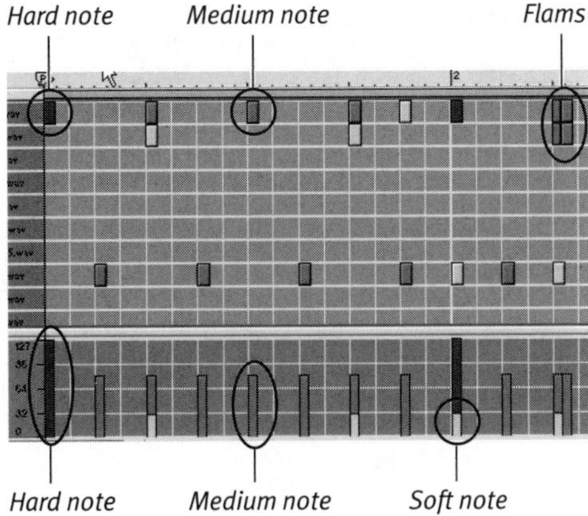

Figure 7.11 Reason's main Sequencer showing a track that originated from the Redrum's pattern sequencer

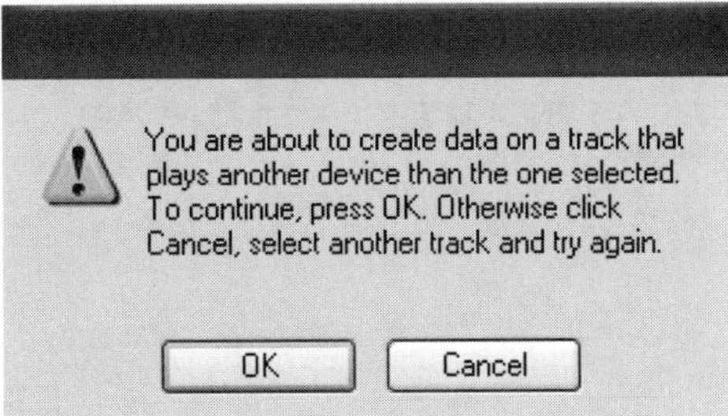

You are about to create data on a track that plays another device than the one selected. To continue, press OK. Otherwise click Cancel, select another track and try again.
OK
Cancel

Figure 7.12 A track association reminder will pop up anytime you are dumping a pattern to a device other than the one for which it was written.

Figure 7.13 The Pattern Lane button allows you to automate pattern switching.

It's easy to transfer a pattern from the pattern sequencer to a track in the main Sequencer for more controlled editing.

To dump a Redrum pattern to a Sequencer track:

1. In the main Sequencer, select the track you want to dump to.
2. Select the pattern in the Redrum that you want to dump.
3. Use the Edit > Copy Pattern To Track command.
4. Go to the Redrum track in your main Sequencer and make whatever adjustments you want (**Figure 7.11**).

✔ Tip

- You can dump your Redrum pattern to a different instrument, but Reason will check with you to make sure (**Figure 7.12**).

You can also fill up the pattern banks on the Redrum and then create a track in Reason's main Sequencer that just switches patterns for you.

To automate pattern switching:

1. Go to the desired Redrum track and click the Pattern Lane button (**Figure 7.13**).
2. Set the Snap-to-Grid function to the maximum value that makes sense.

   Set your grid to the lowest resolution you can—fine resolutions are a nuisance during pattern drawing because they make it easy to mess up the timing!

continues on next page

3. Use the arrow button in the upper-left corner of the pattern lane to select the pattern you want to activate in your track (**Figure 7.14**).
4. Use the Pencil tool to input a "pattern start" point in your track, and drag to the right until you reach the end of the track section where you want it to play. The pattern will continue playing until you either turn it off (switch to an empty pattern) or switch to another pattern (**Figure 7.15**).

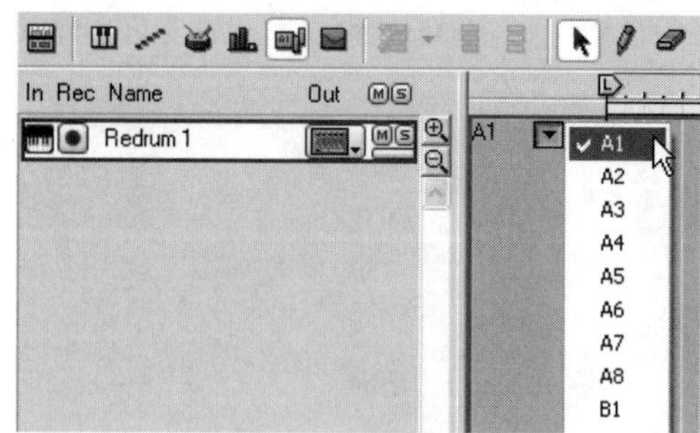

Figure 7.14 Click the arrow next to the pattern lane to choose a pattern for writing to a track.

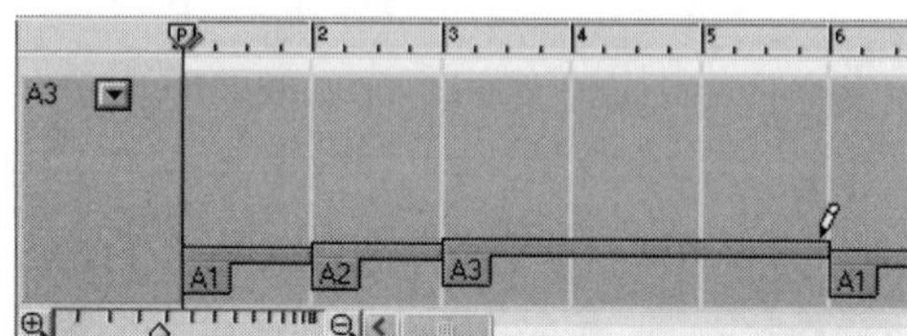

Figure 7.15 This Sequencer track displays pattern changes.

✔ Tips

- Editing and changing the durations of pattern automation objects is more challenging than working with controllers. The Erase tool doesn't work on these objects, and the only way to overwrite pattern data is to select a new pattern number and overwrite.
- Sometimes it is faster to use the Undo command, Ctrl+Z (Win) / Cmd+Z (Mac), when you "overshoot" or make manual errors when drawing pattern automation.
- To delete all pattern information, use the Edit > Clear Automation command.

Figure 7.16 The Matrix Pattern Sequencer, front panel

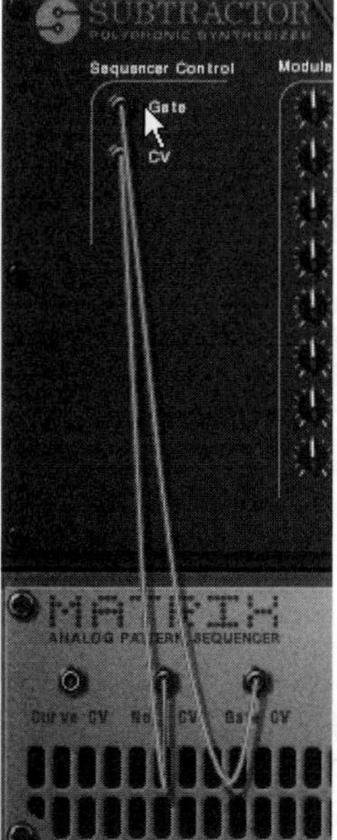

Figure 7.17 The Matrix back panel: To begin playing, the Note and Gate CV outputs must be connected to the CV inputs of an instrument.

The Matrix Pattern Sequencer

Reason's other Rack sequencer, the Matrix, can play patterns and store them for any Reason device, including effects and Mixer parameters such as channel volume and pan.

To play, the Matrix must first be connected to a Reason instrument. Let's set one up and introduce you to CV control signals.

To connect the Matrix:

1. Create the instrument you want to sequence (say, a SubTractor synth). Hook it to an open Mixer channel and then create a Matrix (**Figure 7.16**).

   Reason automatically cables the Matrix to the last selected instrument.

2. From the back panel, the Matrix's Note CV output should be connected to your instrument's CV input, and the Matrix's Gate CV output should be connected to a Gate input (**Figure 7.17**). If this is not the case, go ahead and connect these manually by clicking and dragging from output to input.

   The Note CV output says what pitch to play; the Gate CV output says how loud to play and whether to attack or to slur into the next note.

The Matrix plays notes constantly as long as it is on. For the Matrix, Off just means zero volume. Technically, you don't write notes on the Matrix—you turn notes up. Let's start by turning up the stream of steady notes that the Matrix is always playing.

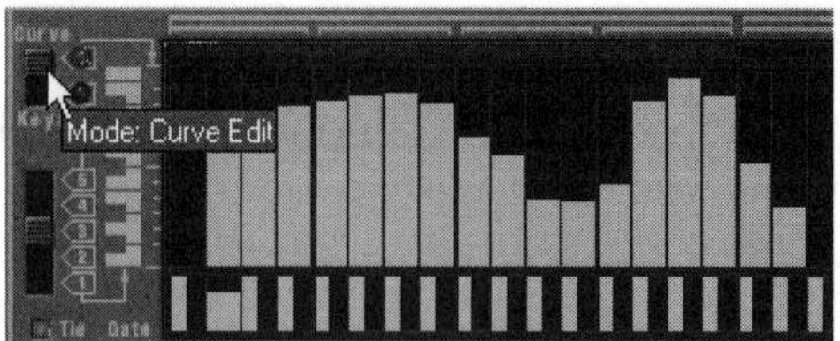

Figure 7.18 The Matrix's Curve mode display

To sound notes on the Matrix:

1. On the front panel, the Matrix's Step counter and Resolution controls are exactly like those on the Redrum pattern sequencer. Use them now to set the length and note value of your pattern.
2. Click the Run button to start the Matrix (you won't hear any sound just yet).
3. Now, using the mouse as you would in the Sequencer, draw greater-than-zero gate values in the black Gate display at the bottom of the Matrix.
4. Then use the mouse to draw in some note strengths greater than zero above the gate values (**Figure 7.18**).
5. Hold down the Shift key to draw a straight line, and leave Gate values at zero to make a rest.

   You should now be hearing a repeating tone for every Gate value you changed.
6. Click the Tie enable button, and draw in the Gate window to create *sustains*—a sustained note is any note that's followed directly by a tied gate, represented by a wide vertical line (**Figure 7.19**).
7. Now click anywhere in the note display to change note pitches. Remember, only notes with visible gate values will sound.
8. The Matrix note display has a range of one octave. Use the Octave switch (**Figure 7.20**) to choose another of the Matrix's five octaves.

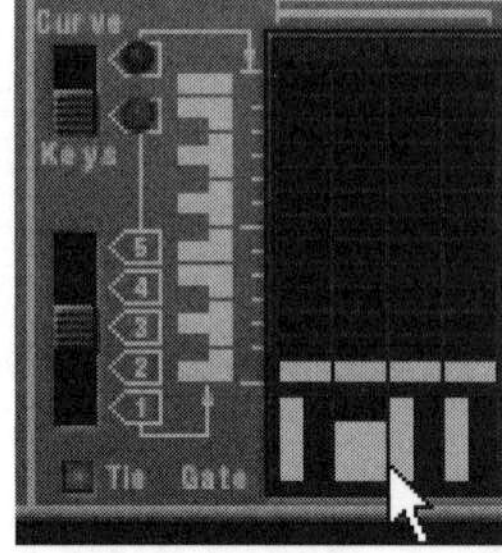
Figure 7.19 The Tie enable button allows you to input tie gates after a note to create a sustain.

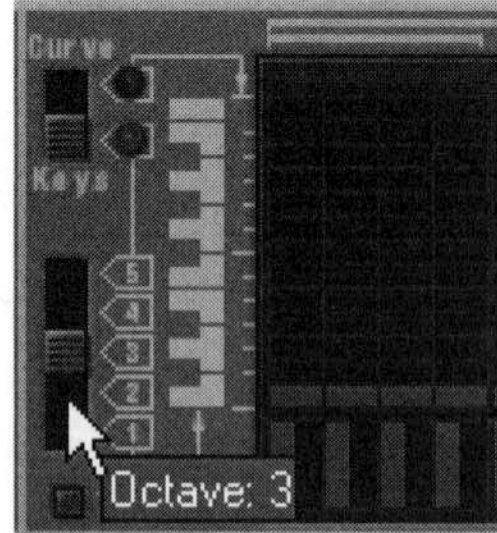

Figure 7.20 The Matrix's Octave switch expands the pitch range to five octaves. By default, it is set to the middle range, or 3 (the equivalent of C3).

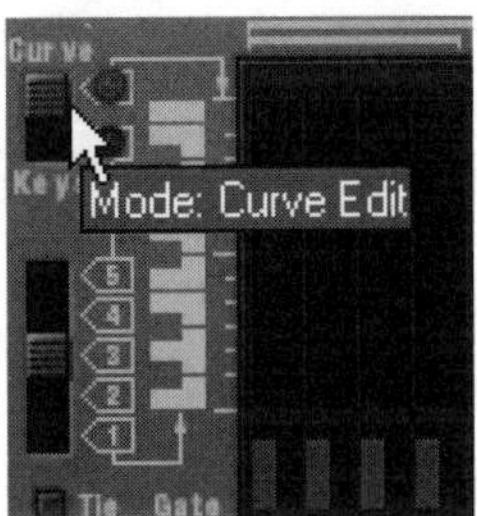

Figure 7.21 Activate the Curve mode of the Matrix.

Figure 7.22 CV sensitivity knobs increase or decrease the effect of CV signals.

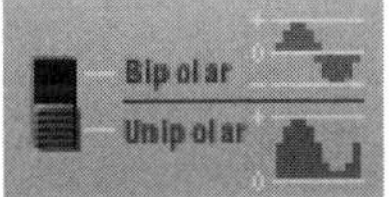

Figure 7.23 The Unipolar/Bipolar curve polarity switch

The Curve is a step-increment parameter controller, meaning it changes at the rate of the current note value. For accenting brightness on a sequence of notes, the Curve can't be beat. However, for smooth knob movements, the Controller lane is better because you can turn off the grid to facilitate smooth changes.

To sequence an instrument parameter using Curve:

1. Use the Curve/Keys switch to activate Curve mode in the Matrix (**Figure 7.21**).
2. Press Tab, and on the back panel, connect the Curve CV output of the Matrix to the Modulation CV input of any instrument parameter you want to control, such as Filter 1 Freq or the Mod wheel (**Figure 7.22**).
3. Still on the Matrix's back panel, choose a curve polarity (**Figure 7.23**).

   Unipolar moves away and toward a base starting point. This is good for parameters such as volume or resonance that usually go in one direction.

   The other mode, Bipolar, moves up and down above and below a middle point. It's good for adjusting parameters with positive and negative capacity, such as panning or velocity sensitivity.
4. Press Tab again and return to the Matrix front panel.
5. Use the mouse to draw a curve in the Matrix display. (Hold down Shift to draw a straight line.)
6. You may need to go to the back panel of the instrument you're modulating and adjust the CV sensitivity knob for the effect you want.
7. Play your track to hear the effect.

If you use Reason in live performances, you'll be happy to know there are a number of fast operations you can perform on patterns from the Edit menu that are not possible with Reason's main Sequencer (**Figure 7.24**).

To use Matrix Edit commands:

1. Slightly alter a pattern by right-clicking on the Matrix and selecting Alter Pattern. (This can be a great way to vary and store a new pattern quickly.)
2. You can also completely scramble the note, Gate and Curve settings using the Randomize Pattern command.
3. To nudge the timing of the pattern, use the Shift Pattern Left and Shift Pattern Right commands.
4. To nudge the pitch of the pattern up and down a half step, use the Shift Pattern Up and Shift Pattern Down commands.

   This is a great real-time transposition tool for performances.

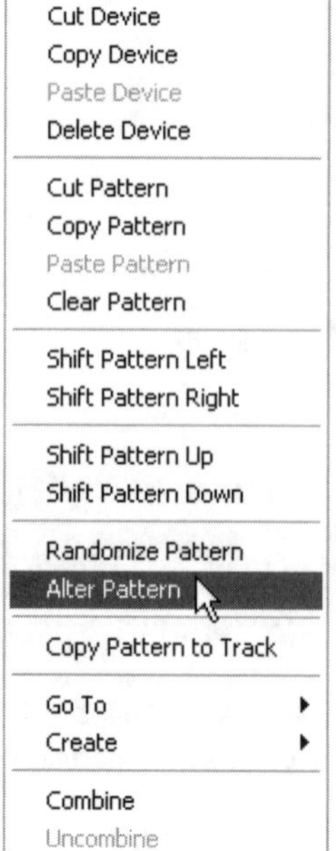

Figure 7.24 Right-click the front panel of the Matrix to quickly change, shift, or even scramble your pattern.

8

EFFECTS

Chances are you've had at least some experience using effects. If not, get ready for some fun.

Reason's effects sound processors can animate your instruments in many ways: They can add realism or incongruity, enhance or reduce quality, distance sounds or bring them to the fore, and even distort or add speech effects.

It's a good idea to get your tracks sounding their best without effects first, especially if you plan on using a lot of tracks. Effects that sound great with a few tracks can become a burden as you add more.

However, this is not always possible. Sometimes you'll choose to build a song around a particular effect. This does not have to be a problem—just keep in mind that you may need fewer (or sparser) parts as a result.

Adding Echo

Echo and reverberation are two kinds of indirect, reflected sound. What's the difference? *Echoes* bounce back across long distances, whereas closer sounds *reverberate* with our surroundings to create room ambience.

Since echo is generally a discrete reflection and less complicated than reverb, we'll start there. Reason has one effect that strictly handles echo, or delay: the DDL-1 Digital Delay Line.

The DDL-1 Digital Delay Line

The DDL-1 is an easy-to-use echo effect. It simply copies the sound coming in, then repeats it. You set the repeat rate, number of repetitions, and volume.

To use the DDL-1 as an insert effect:

1. With an instrument such as a SubTractor selected, choose Create > DDL-1 Digital Delay Line.

   The DDL-1 will appear in your Rack (**Figure 8.1**).

2. Press Tab to go to the back panel, and you'll see that Reason has cabled the DDL-1 between the SubTractor and the Mixer. The SubTractor's mono audio output is plugged into the DDL-1's left (mono) audio input, and both DDL-1 audio outputs are now running out to the SubTractor's Mixer channel (**Figure 8.2**).

   An effect that sits between the instrument and the Mixer is called an *insert effect*.

3. On the front panel, turn the DDL-1 Dry/Wet knob left to about 26 for a starting mix between the incoming sound and the repeated signal (**Figure 8.3**).

   The *wet* sound is the effect, in this case the echo; the *dry* sound is the original signal, in this case, the SubTractor.

Figure 8.1 The DDL-1 Digital Delay Line, shown here front and back, creates an echo.

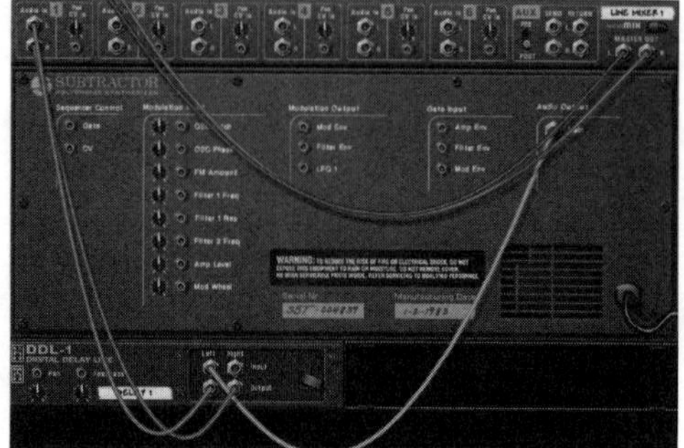

Figure 8.2 A DDL-1 delay is used here as an insert effect between a SubTractor and a Mixer.

Figure 8.3 A Dry/Wet knob setting of 26 will keep your dry signal in the forefront.

Step units

Milliseconds

Figure 8.4 The Unit switch can be set to tempo-based steps or milliseconds (in MS mode the Step Length button has no effect).

4. Play your SubTractor to hear the results.

   By default, the delay is tempo-synchronized and timed well for most situations.

5. To alter the settings, use the Unit switch to tell the DDL-1 what type of time increment you want to use (**Figure 8.4**).

   Your choices are *MS* (milliseconds) or *Steps* (tempo subdivisions).

6. Now set the delay interval.

   In MS mode input a time value using the counter keys (the range is 1–2,000 milliseconds, or 2 seconds).

   In Steps mode, choose a step length of either 1/16 (sixteenth notes) or 1/8T (eighth-note triplets), then specify how many steps using the step counter.

7. Set how long you want each echo to repeat using the Feedback knob (the range is 0 = 1 repeat to 127 = infinite repeat).

8. Use the Pan knob if you want the delay signal to go out the left or right channel.

   The Pan knob doesn't affect the dry signal, which will still go equally out the left and right channels.

✔ Tips

- When switching between modes, Reason simply translates the current step timing between steps and milliseconds. This behavior is useful if you want to slightly offset a step setting in MS mode.
- The default step unit value of 3 and a step length of 16 ("dotted eighth" time interval) is a great starting delay time for most parts—it adds a sense of "feel" to the timing, yet "stays out of the way" of the dry signal. The equivalent for a shuffle (triplet) feel is to set the unit value to 3 and step length to 1/8T.
- Repeat times that fall "on the beat" (such as a 4-unit, 16-length setting) may sound less like delay and more like a repeating line.

Even though the DDL-1 is a mono delay (meaning it sends out the same delay signal through both the left and right outputs), you can pan it for a stereo effect.

To get a ping-pong delay using pan automation:

1. With a DDL-1 set up as an insert effect, as in the previous task, press Tab to see the back panel.
2. From the back panel, cable the LFO 1 Modulation output of the SubTractor to the Pan CV input on the DDL-1 (**Figure 8.5**).

   This sends a fluctuating waveform to the DDL-1's panning control.
3. On the DDL-1's back panel, locate the CV sensitivity knob (below the Pan CV input) and turn it all the way to the right (**Figure 8.6**).

   This ensures that the waveform controlling the pan will have the width to pan hard left to right.
4. Return to the front panel, and on the SubTractor, enable the LFO 1 Sync switch and set the tempo you want for your delay to go left and right.

✔ Tip

- The SubTractor LFO runs even when it's not modulating anything, so it's a great control source for panning. And the LFO shape gives you different choices on how to move the delay left to right. For example, the triangle shape will move the pan position smoothly from one side to another. A square shape will toggle panning from side to side. The random shapes will place the pan varying degrees to the left and right at random.

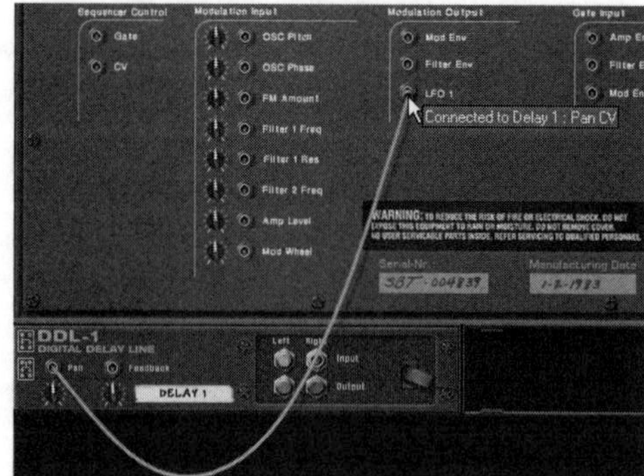

Figure 8.5 Use a SubTractor LFO to modulate delay panning.

Figure 8.6 Set the DDL-1 Pan sensitivity knob to maximum to pan hard left and hard right.

Figure 8.7 A Spider Audio Merger/Splitter combines audio signals on the left side and splits them on the right.

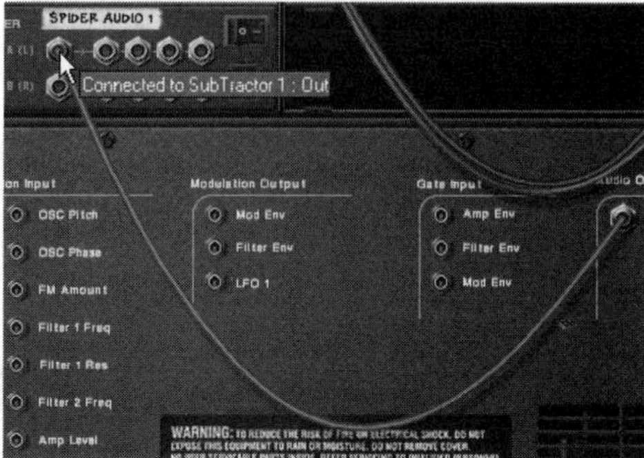

Figure 8.8 Split the SubTractor output between two DDL-1s.

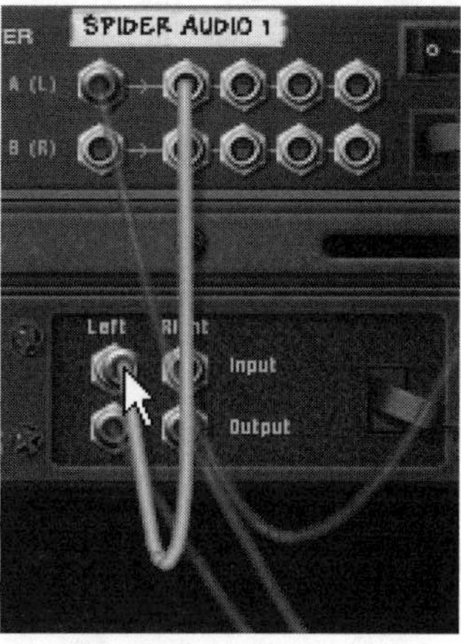

Figure 8.9 Send a SubTractor output from the splitter to the first DDL-1.

Using two DDL-1 units and a signal splitter, you can pan the delay signal and have the dry signal coming out both channels equally.

To echo in stereo with an audio splitter and two DDL-1 delays:

1. With a DDL-1 set up as an insert effect, hold down the Shift key to disable auto-cabling and create a second DDL-1.
2. Select Create > Spider Audio Merger and Splitter.

   This will create a new device that joins audio signals on the left side and splits them on the right (**Figure 8.7**).
3. Press Tab to go to the back panel, and cable the SubTractor's main output to the left input at the right (splitter) side of the Spider patch bay (**Figure 8.8**).

   This will allow you to send the mono SubTractor signal to two destinations.
4. Now take one of the left Spider outputs and run it to the left input of the first DDL-1 (**Figure 8.9**).

continues on next page

5. Then take a second left Spider output and run it to the left input of the second DDL-1 (**Figure 8.10**).
6. Cable each DDL-1 stereo output pair to its own Mixer channel.
7. Return to the front panel, and in the Mixer pan one DDL-1 channel hard left and the other hard right.
8. Make sure both your DDL-1s are set to the same Dry/Wet setting; otherwise, your dry signal won't come out both left and right sides (**Figure 8.11**).
9. Now set the DDL-1 units to different delay times. For example, set one to 3 steps at 1/16 and the other to 6 steps at 1/16 (**Figure 8.12**).

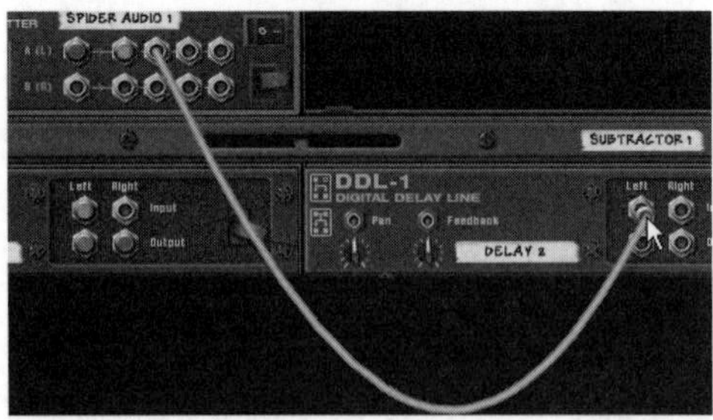

Figure 8.10 Send a SubTractor output from the splitter to the other DDL-1.

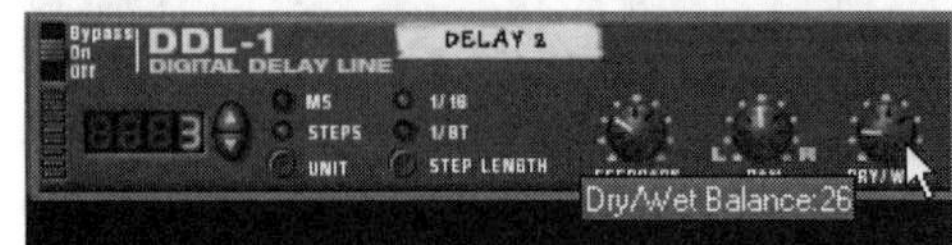

Figure 8.11 Set both DDL-1s to the same Wet/Dry knob setting.

Figure 8.12 Set the two DDL-1s to different step numbers.

Adding Reverberation

Although reverb is also just reflected sound, it is more complicated than echo since it may consist of many reflections off many surfaces returning quickly, depending on the size and shape of the room.

The RV-7 Digital Reverb

Reason has two devices designed to handle complex echoes that simulate room ambience: the RV-7 Digital Reverb and the RV7000 Advanced Reverb. The RV-7 is the easiest to configure, since it uses room simulation presets and just a few controls, so we'll start there.

What Is Reverb?

Direct sound travels the shortest possible course to our ears and reaches us first. Soon after comes reflected sound, or reverberation, carrying with it all sorts of information about the shape, size, and nature of our surroundings. This is what's known as the "sound of a room."

With our eyes closed we can still sense much about the space we're in. Your brain knows that odd-shaped or multifaceted spaces reflect more intricately, larger spaces take longer to reflect, and porous surfaces absorb brightness rejected by harder surfaces.

Always use a bit less reverb than you think you need. Whether you use reverb because it sounds cool or to simulate a room type, a final audition space is going to add one more reverb stage to your mix. Also, headphones are actually *more* likely to lead to overuse because they are reverb free and may tempt you to overcompensate.

Before your final mixdown, ask yourself whether your mix still has definition or has become "muddy." The reflected sound should enhance, not overpower, your tracks.

To test the RV-7 Digital Reverb:

1. With a SubTractor selected, choose Create > RV-7 Digital Reverb.

   This will insert an RV-7 reverb effect (**Figure 8.13**).

2. Write a short test loop for the SubTractor, either in the Sequencer or using a Matrix Pattern Sequencer, and start it playing.

   Leave some rests between notes—your reverb will thank you (**Figure 8.14**).

3. On the RV-7, scroll through the presets ("algorithms") using the arrow keys (**Figure 8.15**).

Figure 8.13 Add an RV-7 Digital Reverb to your Rack (front and back panels shown here).

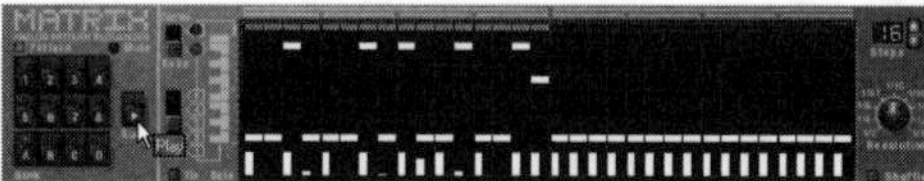

Figure 8.14 Make sure your test loop has room for the RV-7 to do its thing.

You can fine-tune the effects of a preset using the RV-7's Decay and Size knobs. Decay is just a sustain knob; it doesn't affect quality or timing. The Size setting determines how long it takes the dry signal to bounce off the virtual walls of the preset room type.

Figure 8.15 The reverb type selection arrows let you scroll through the presets.

To adjust reverb Size and Decay:

1. With an RV-7 inserted, turn the Decay knob hard left.

   This allows you to focus on the Size parameter.

2. With your loop playing, adjust the Size knob (**Figure 8.16**).

   At the minimum Size setting, the reverb will nearly match the primary sound, overlaying it for a phase effect. As you increase the Size setting, the delay between the original signal and the reverb effect will become audible. A slightly higher Size setting sounds like a tiled bathroom. At high settings, it sounds more like an echo.

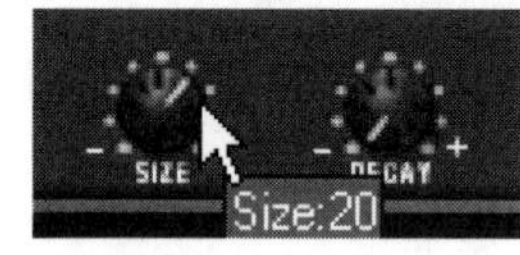

Figure 8.16 The Size knob is a good place to start tweaking your reverb sound.

Table 8.1

RV7 Algorithms	
Hall	A large room with a long decay
Large Hall	Concert hall/maximum room size
Hall 2	Similar in size but brighter than Hall
Large Room	A typical large room
Medium Room	A typical medium-sized room
Small Room	A small room such as a studio booth
Gated	Reverb with a forced decay "cutoff"
Low Density	A "courser" reverb (discernible echoes)
Stereo Echoes	A medium-length ping-pong delay (sharper quality)
Pan Room	A ping-pong delay with reverb added to the delay (softer quality)

Figure 8.17 The Bypass switch is a fast way to mute the reverb.

3. Now change the Decay knob to lengthen the reverb.

   A long decay on a small Size setting turns a tiled bathroom into a deep, tiled well.

4. Use the Damp knob to filter out high frequencies, especially with brighter voices. These can sound too harsh with bright reverb settings.

✔ Tips

- Try to avoid fixing one problem by adjusting a parameter somewhere else. It's a bit like asking a well-behaved student to talk less to compensate for the loudmouth in the back. For example, use the Dry/Wet knob to control reverb volume. Though raising the Damp knob may sound the same, it leaves low frequencies lurking about your mix that could come back to haunt you later.
- Don't adjust more than you have to. Use the Bypass switch to mute reverb (**Figure 8.17**) whenever possible; it doesn't affect your settings and is faster.
- Long decays work better on fewer tracks.

Creating a Master Effect

If you want to use reverb on more than one instrument, you don't have to insert an RV-7 for each one. Reason will also let you set up a *master effect*, which is cabled to the Mixer so it can be used for any instrument in the Rack.

To use an RV-7 Digital Reverb on multiple instruments:

1. Select a Mixer in your Rack and choose Create > RV7 Digital Reverb.

   Reason will automatically cable the RV-7 left audio input to the first available Mixer Aux channel send (**Figure 8.18**).

2. Cable the RV-7 audio outputs to the left and right Aux channel returns.

   All the Mixer channels can now feed into the Aux channel as little or as much signal as you want using the channel Aux Send knobs.

3. On the RV-7, turn the Dry/Wet knob all the way to the right.

   Your dry signal is in the Mixer channel, so you don't need it in your effect.

4. In the Mixer, simply turn the Aux knob on any channel to feed signal to the master effect (**Figure 8.19**).

5. Play your track to hear the reverb.

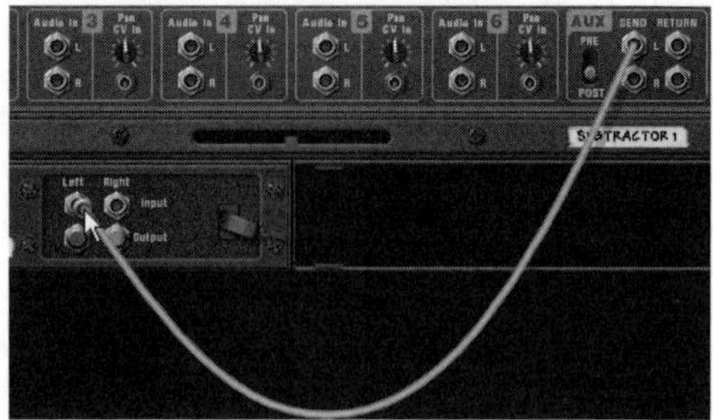

Figure 8.18 The RV-7 is connected as a master effect here, so it can work on any instrument connected to the Mixer.

Figure 8.19 Feed a master effect in the Mixer using your instrument's Aux Send knob.

Figure 8.20 The RV7000, shown here front and back with cables hidden, operates in stereo.

Figure 8.21 Use the RV7000 Browse Patch button to audition a patch.

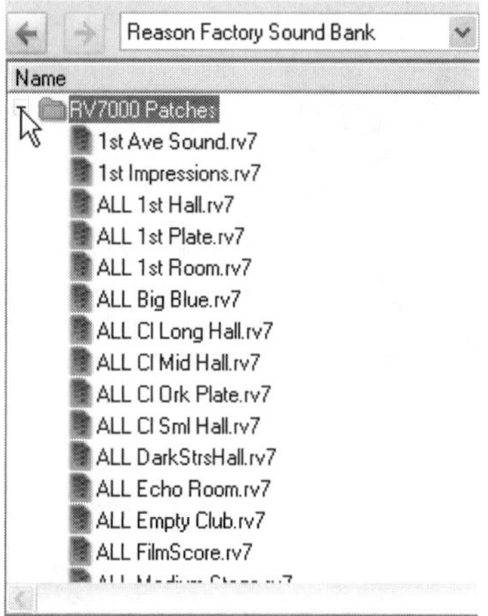

Figure 8.22 Choose a sound from the Factory Sound Bank's folder of RV7000 patches.

The RV7000 Advanced Reverb

The RV7000 (or RV7K) uses the same principles as the RV-7 but operates in stereo, comes with more presets, gives you greater control, and allows you to save your changes as a custom patch.

To use the basic RV7000 controls:

1. Select the Mixer and choose Create > RV7000 Advanced Reverb to set up an RV7000 master effect (**Figure 8.20**).
2. Play an instrument track and use the Aux knob in the instrument's Mixer channel to feed the effect.

   The RV7K init patch provides a good basic reverb sound if you want to start right in.
3. With your loop playing, use the RV7K's Browse Patch button (**Figure 8.21**) to audition a patch from the Factory Sound Bank `RV7000 Patches` folder (**Figure 8.22**).
4. Use the Hi EQ knob to boost the treble of the reverb sound.
5. Use the HF Damp knob to filter out high frequencies, just like on the RV-7.

Now that you know how to use the RV7000 as a preset patch reverb, it's time to open up the advanced reverb controls. From now on you'll have a display screen to help you "see" what each control does.

Figure 8.23 The RV7000 Remote Programmer gives you access to advanced controls.

To select a reverb algorithm:

1. With an RV7K set up as a master effect, as in the previous exercise, click the Remote Programmer arrow on the front panel to access the RV7K's advanced controls (**Figure 8.23**).
2. Turn up the Aux knob on your instrument's Mixer channel, and set up a test loop with a couple of notes at the beginning. Be sure to leave space for the RV7K's reverb to breathe (**Figure 8.24**).
3. Play your loop, and on the RV7K Remote Programmer, turn the Algorithm knob to the type of reverb you want (**Figure 8.25**).

   In addition to the algorithms available in the RV-7, the RV7K offers some new reverb types:
   - **Arena** (a very big room)
   - **Spring** (mechanical spring reverb)
   - **Plate** (classic metal plate reverb)
   - **Multi Tap** (a step-programmable echo)
   - **Reverse** (a backward reverb that fades into the original signal)

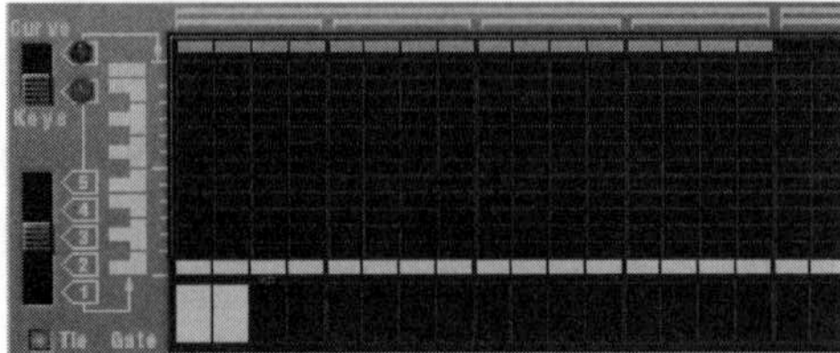

Figure 8.24 Write a basic one-note reverb test pattern.

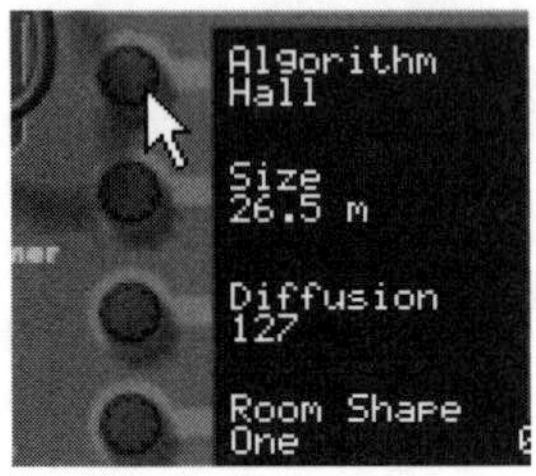

Figure 8.25 Turn the Algorithm knob to change the reverb type.

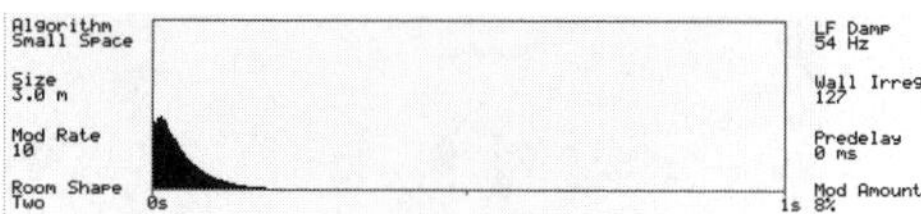

Figure 8.26 In the Remote Programmer, set the Algorithm knob to Small Space.

Exploring Reverb Types

There are many different types of reverb, and although each has a basic characteristic effect on sound, the final result depends a lot on the dry signal. Perhaps the easiest way to learn what to expect is to try out the different types on a fairly simple instrument, such as the SubTractor we'll use for these exercises.

Each type of reverb uses its own sound model and set of parameter knobs. As we move through the reverb types, we'll skip those parameters that we've already covered unless it makes sense to adjust them sequentially with other controls.

Small Space reverb

We'll start with the *Small Space* reverb. This is a lot like the Small Room algorithm in the RV-7, but you can adjust it more precisely in the RV7K.

To adjust the Small Space algorithm:

1. With a Mixer and a SubTractor in your Rack, select the Mixer and choose Create > RV7000 Advanced Reverb to make it a master effect.
2. In the Sequencer or using a Matrix, write a simple test loop with a couple of notes at the beginning and plenty of space for reverb.
3. With your loop playing, open the RV7K's Remote Programmer and set the Algorithm knob to Small Space (**Figure 8.26**).

continues on next page

4. Use the Size knob to set the room size (the range is 0.9 meters to 9.7 meters). Notice how the display changes as the knob moves.

   Like on the RV-7, Size is your most powerful reverb quality knob—it affects all the other parameters.

5. Use the Mod Rate and Mod Amount knobs to pitch-modulate the reverb sound.

   Reverb modulation creates a synthetic *shimmer*, or noise effect, at high Amount settings.

6. Use the Room Shape knob to pick the more subtle reverb characteristics.

7. Use the LF Damp knob to cut out deep frequencies by specifying the frequency at which lows fade out (the range is 20 Hz to 1,000 Hz).

8. Set the Wall Irreg (wall irregularity) knob to move progressively from 0, a basic opposing-wall model with a clear sonic backlash, to 127, a very complex and diffuse room containing many walls and angles.

9. Turn the Predelay knob to increase or decrease the time lapse between the input signal and the reverb.

   Long predelays can make a reverb more dramatic and the input signal sound more distant.

✔ Tip

- Sometimes predelay adjustments can help direct the "meat and potatoes" of your reverb sound into a rest or other space in your mix; this can impact whether you'll want to use the effect as song tracks multiply.

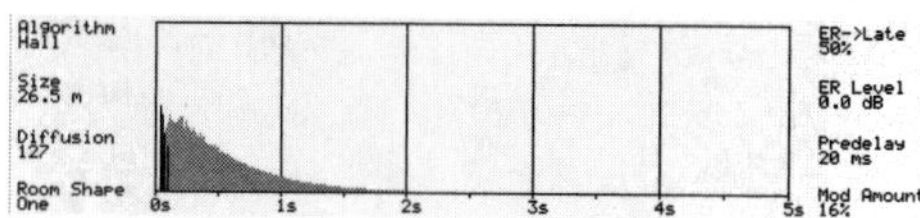

Figure 8.27 The Room and Hall reverb control knobs are the same.

Room and Hall reverbs

You've already heard *Room* and *Hall* reverb types, but the RV7K gives you some additional ways to adjust them.

To adjust the Room or Hall algorithm:

1. In the RV7K Remote Programmer, select the Room or Hall algorithm (**Figure 8.27**).
2. Set the Diffusion knob to a low setting if you want to hear the distinct reflection events, or set it high if you want a smoother, more blended reverb.
3. Use the ER->Late knob to specify what percentage of the reverb occurs early. Low knob values place more reflections at the reverb tail, and can lead to some interesting results.
4. If you want to amplify or de-emphasize the early reflection effect, turn the ER Level knob up or down to change the ER volume.

Arena reverb

Arenas reflect sound off larger structures over wider distances, creating large time discrepancies from multiple positions. The *Arena* algorithm addresses this divergence by generating three separate reverbs—one for left, one for right, and one in the center (mono)—and allowing you to mix them manually.

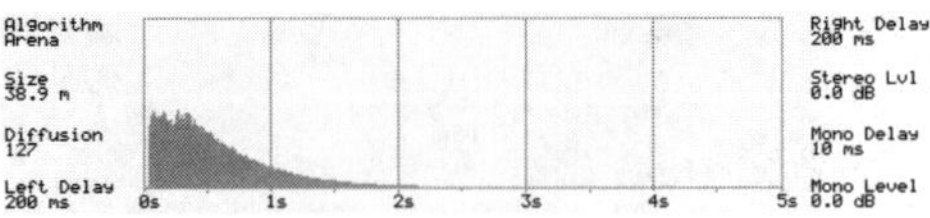

Figure 8.28 The Arena algorithm generates three separate reverbs and allows you to mix them manually using these control knobs.

To adjust the Arena algorithm:

1. With your loop playing, set the Algorithm knob in the RV7K Remote Programmer to Arena (**Figure 8.28**).
2. Set the Size and Diffusion knobs as preferred.
3. Now set the predelay time for the left and right reverb signals using the left and right delay knobs, respectively.
4. Adjust the volume level of the left and right reverb signals together by using the Stereo Level knob.
5. Set the predelay time and level for the center (mono) reverb using the Mono Delay and Mono Level knobs, respectively.

Calculating Point of Origin

Basic stereo reverbs are not true 3D, because they only allow you to place an object left to right, with the dry signal acting as the point of origin (POO). The POO is always dry or, geographically speaking, "close."

For close sounds, adding a center signal allows you to simulate four POOs: the dry sound, and the reflected left, right, and center sounds.

For distant POO, eliminate the dry sound altogether—this means using the Pre-fader function of the Mixer's Aux 4 channel or using the RV7000 as an insert effect.

In this case the *shortest* predelay time and the loudest signal represent the POO, while the other two reverb signals decrease in predelay time and volume in order of proximity.

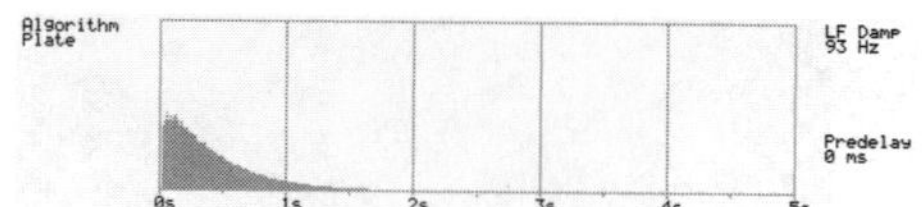
Figure 8.29 The Plate algorithm has few control knobs.

Plate and Spring reverbs

Reason has two reverb types that simulate simulators: the *Plate* and *Spring* reverbs. Both are metal resonators used to emulate sound reflection in early recordings.

The Plate algorithm is well suited for vocals or other instruments that sit in the front of a mix, because its rich decay and expansive tone fill lots of space (**Figure 8.29**). It works especially well on high-profile parts in songs with just a few tracks.

Plates don't create discrete reflections, but they sound uniquely warm. Most of the "magic" is in the algorithm itself: The Decay knob functions like a "plate size" knob and the only other knobs are LF Damp and Predelay. You already know those parameters, so we'll continue on to the Spring reverb.

Spring reverbs were known as the "traveling man's plates" because they could be mounted in a portable cabinet. They create distinctive pulses as they resonate, and they ring a bit. This ringing is called *dispersion*.

Sims Squared

The Plate and Spring reverb types both simulate simulators, but what are they exactly? In the case of a Spring reverb, an actual spring is inserted into an audio path and loaded into a chamber to block out external noise. Sound travels through the spring coils, imitating sound reflection with economy of space and cost.

Plate reverbs use the same principle except that instead of a spring a large metal plate is used as a resonator. The plate is typically suspended from a frame and mounted inside a sound-proofed wall. Electronic pickups or *contact mics* are attached to the plate to transmit sound back out to the studio.

Plate reverbs are still popular because of their high-fidelity resonance quality. They can be recognized in the vintage vocal tracks of the 1950s and '60s, especially styles like country and Motown that used lots of reverb.

To adjust the Spring algorithm:

1. With your loop playing, set the RV7K Remote Programmer's Algorithm knob to Spring (**Figure 8.30**).
2. To better hear (and see on your display) what the model does, set the Disp Amount knob to 0%.
3. Adjust the spring's "size" using the Length parameter. Though longer lengths will reverberate longer, this is different from the Decay sustain. Think of Length as how fast sound goes through the spring.
4. Both the Disp knobs stand for "dispersion," or the "spring ring." Turn the Disp Amount knob to 100% so you can hear the other dispersion control better.
5. Now use the Disp Freq knob to set the spring's dispersion tone.

   The knob sets a center frequency between 741 Hz and 7,470 Hz.

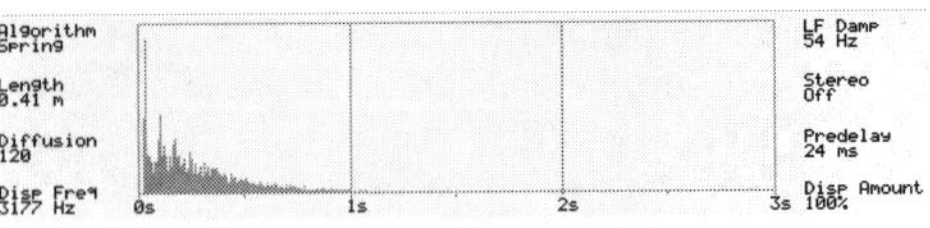

Figure 8.30 In the Remote Programmer, set the Algorithm knob to Spring.

How Spring Length and Diffusion Interact

At long spring lengths, the reverb pattern takes place slowly for pulsing (high-diffusion), tremolo (medium-diffusion), or delay (low-diffusion) effect results.

At short lengths, these "pulses" remain but are too rapid to distinguish, sounding like a small, bright room.

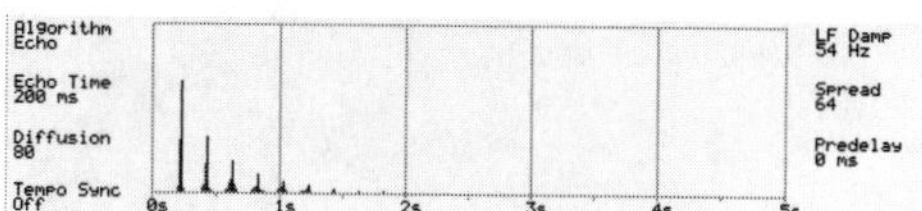

Figure 8.31 Set the Algorithm knob to Echo.

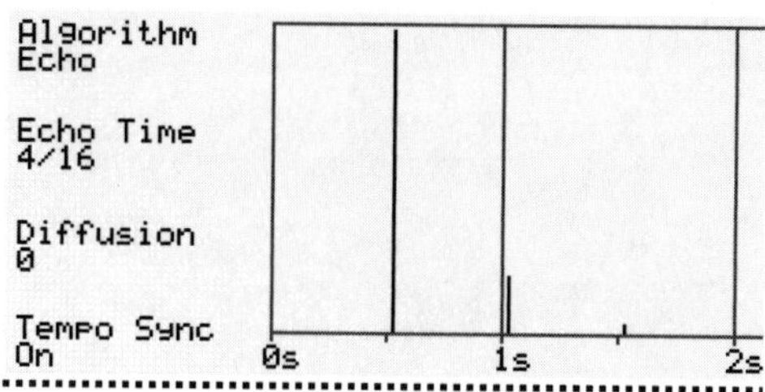

Figure 8.32 Set the Diffusion parameter to 0 for the Echo algorithm.

Echo

As you may remember from the beginning of this chapter, the DDL-1 produces a simple echo effect. However, using the RV7K gives you stereo echo, as well as much finer control.

To use the RV7K for echo:

1. With your loop playing, set the RV7K Remote Programmer's Algorithm knob to Echo (**Figure 8.31**).
2. Set the Diffusion parameter to 0.

   This will give you "pure" repeat of the dry signal, appearing as vertical lines diminishing to the right across your display (**Figure 8.32**).
3. Turn the Tempo Sync knob to On if you want to synchronize the delay time to your song tempo.
4. Adjust the Echo Time parameter to a tempo subdivision such as 3/16 or pick a millisecond time value if you want to keep Tempo Sync off.
5. Set the LF Damp knob high if you don't want low frequencies in your delay; set the knob low if you do (the range is 20 Hz to 1,000 Hz).
6. To add reverb to your echo, boost the Diffusion knob and watch the display. Technically this knob "blurs" the echo, allowing you to hear reflections around the various echo points.
7. Turn the Spread knob to further spread out or "blur" the reverb away from the echo points, and watch the display. At maximum diffusion and spread the echo is no longer an echo, but more like the Spring reverb with a longer pulse timing range.

Multi Tap echo

The most versatile (and complicated) echo is the RV7K *Multi Tap* step-programmable echo. You can program up to four repeats; set a time interval, pan position, and level for each; and pick a rate at which the whole set repeats as the Decay knob is moved up and down.

Multi Tap can do anything that a regular echo does and much more, but trying to get "standard" results can be frustrating if you don't know your way around.

To use Multi Tap echo for a standard panning delay:

1. With your loop playing, set the RV7K Remote Programmer's Algorithm knob to Multi Tap (**Figure 8.33**).
2. Turn the Diffusion knob to 0.

   I recommend keeping the diffusion at 0 so the echoes are clear.
3. Set the Tempo Sync knob to On.
4. To adjust the first tap, turn the Edit Select knob to Tap 1.
5. Set the time interval for Tap 1 to 3/16 using the Tap Delay knob (the Sync range is 1/16 to 12/8T).
6. Set the Tap Level knob to around 6.0 dB.
7. Set the Tap Pan to –64, or hard left.

   In this example, each successive tap will pan progressively to the right.
8. To adjust Tap 2, turn the Edit Select knob to Tap 2 and repeat steps 5–7, using the following values: Delay: 6/16, Level: 4.0 dB, Pan: 63.
9. Adjust Tap 3 with these values: Delay: 9/16, Level: 2.0 dB, Pan: –32.

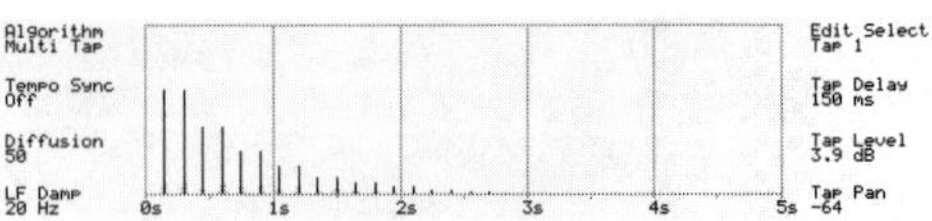

Figure 8.33 Multi Tap is the most versatile (and complicated) echo algorithm.

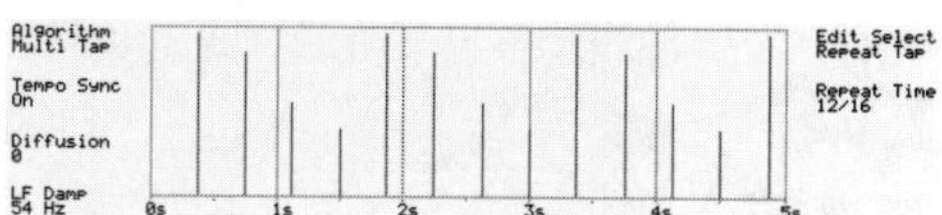

Figure 8.34 This standard Multi Tap echo has a repeat time of 12/16.

10. Adjust Tap 4 with these values: Delay: 12/16, Level: 1.0 dB, Pan: 32.

    You should now hear a typical echo with regular, decrescendoing repeats that move back and forth.

11. Now turn the Edit Select knob all the way right to the Repeat Tap function to set the repeat interval for all four taps.

12. For a regular repeat interval, set the Repeat Time value to 12/16.

    This tells the repeat function that 12/16 is the last tap in the set and to repeat at the next interval.

    The graphic display should show a regular repeat interval for the tap set (**Figure 8.34**).

Diffusion and Multi Tap

The Diffusion parameter works differently on Multi Tap, blurring the echoes progressively as the tap set repeats.

The higher the Diffusion knob setting, the faster the effect progresses. A nice use of this feature is to set the main RV7K Decay knob high so the tap set repeats many times.

A medium Diffusion setting will increase gradually for a "riding into the distance" effect, blurring and dissipating the echoes as the taps fade out.

There is a trade-off between many repeats and diffusion, however. High Diffusion settings decrease the tap volume overall. Boost the Diffusion knob when the Decay knob is high to see the effect (**Figure 8.35**).

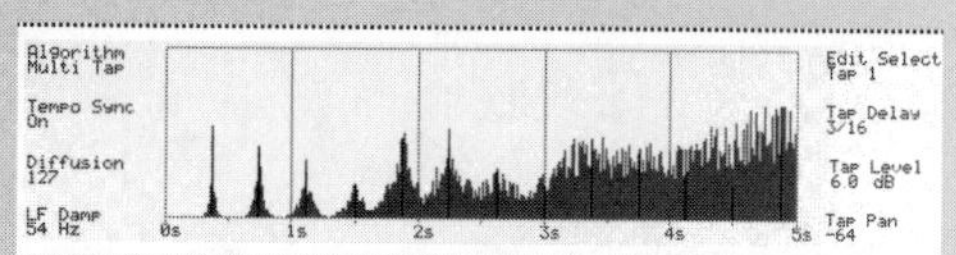

Figure 8.35 In Multi Tap mode, diffusion increases progressively.

Reverse reverb

The *Reverse* algorithm (**Figure 8.36**) plays reverb backward followed by a forward copy of the original sound. For maximum drama, use it with no dry signal, either as an insert effect or through an Aux channel that has a Pre-fader function.

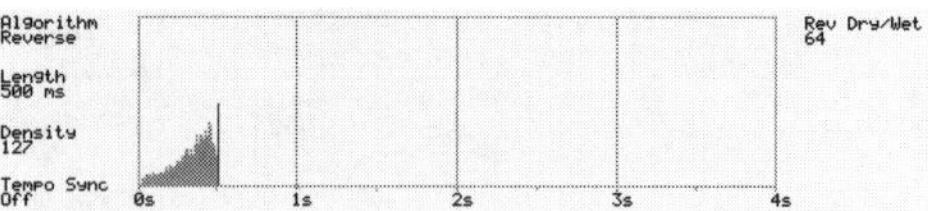

Figure 8.36 The Reverse reverb algorithm plays reverb backward followed by a forward copy of the original sound.

Both the Line Mixer and the 14:2 can be set up to feed a channel to an effect even when the channel fader is at 0. Here's how to set this up.

To use Reverse reverb as a master effect:

1. Set up your instruments, write a test loop, and press play.
2. Select your Mixer and create an RV7K.
3. On the back panel, connect the RV7K to the Aux 4 inputs of a 14:2 Mixer (**Figure 8.37**).

   or

   Connect the RV7K to the Aux channel of a Line Mixer (**Figure 8.38**).

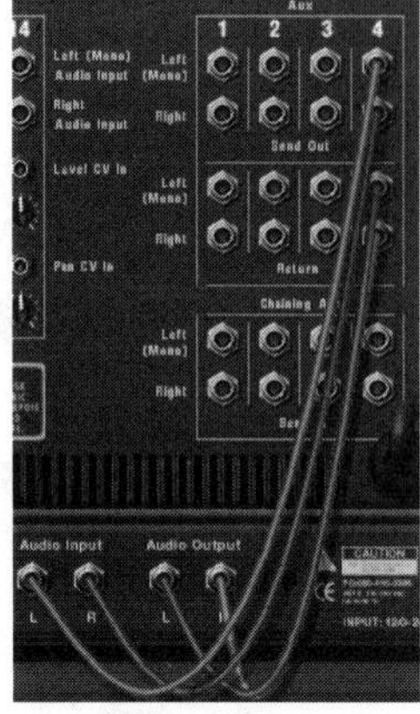

Figure 8.37 Here the RV7K is connected to the Aux 4 channel of a 14:2 Mixer.

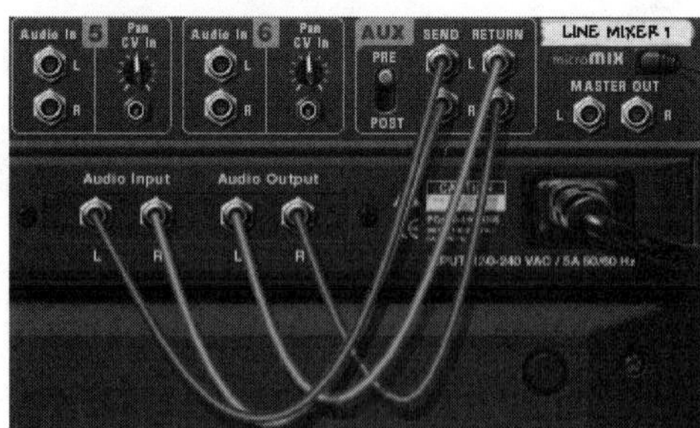

Figure 8.38 Here the RV7K is connected to the Aux of a Line Mixer 6:2 with the Pre-fader function enabled.

Figure 8.39 Activate the 14:2 Mixer's Pre-fader button on the appropriate channel.

Figure 8.40 Turn the Aux 4 Send knob to the maximum value.

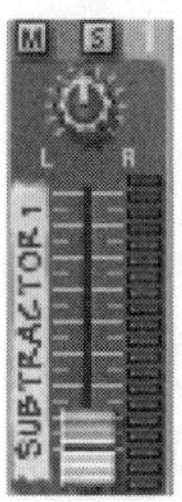

Figure 8.41 With Pre-fader settings active, you can turn your channel fader to 0 and the Aux sends will still send sound.

Figure 8.42 Turn the Dry/Wet knob all the way to the right to return only the effect.

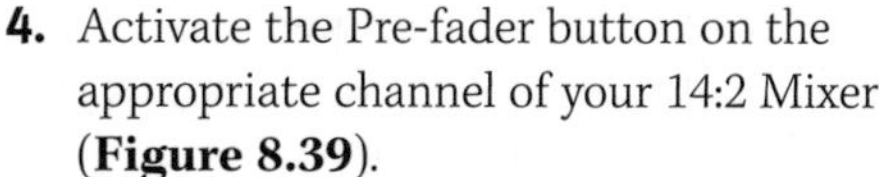

4. Activate the Pre-fader button on the appropriate channel of your 14:2 Mixer (**Figure 8.39**).

   or

   Activate the Pre setting on your Line Mixer's back panel and turn the Aux 4 Send knob all the way to the right (**Figure 8.40**).

5. Drag the channel level fader for your instrument all the way down to 0 (**Figure 8.41**).

6. On the RV7K front panel, turn the Dry/Wet knob all the way to the right (**Figure 8.42**) and select the Reverse algorithm on the Remote Programmer.

continues on next page

7. Use the Length knob to specify the length of time between your initial signal and the Reverse reverb effect (values vary according to whether Tempo Sync is on or off).
8. Use the front panel Decay knob to set whether or not you want the Reverse reverb to fade in.

   Fade-ins don't happen when your Decay setting exceeds the Length setting because the Reverse reverb can't fade in before its beginning! Instead, the fade-in levels out as the decay increases (**Figure 8.43**).
9. Use the Remote Programmer Density knob to control whether the reverb sounds like ambience (high density) or discrete reflections or echoes (low density).

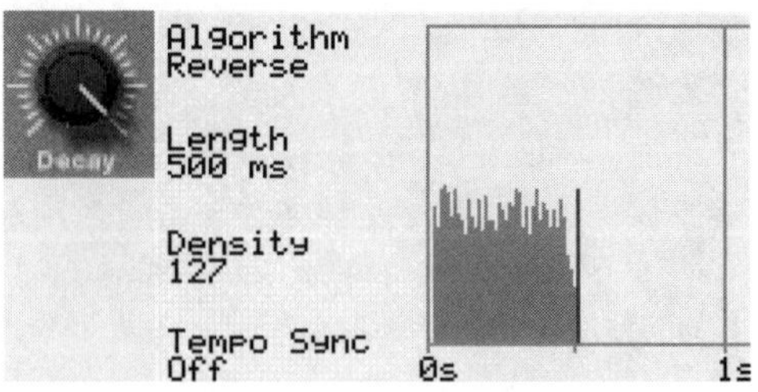

Figure 8.43 With Reverse reverb, if the decay exceeds the Length setting, there is no fade-in.

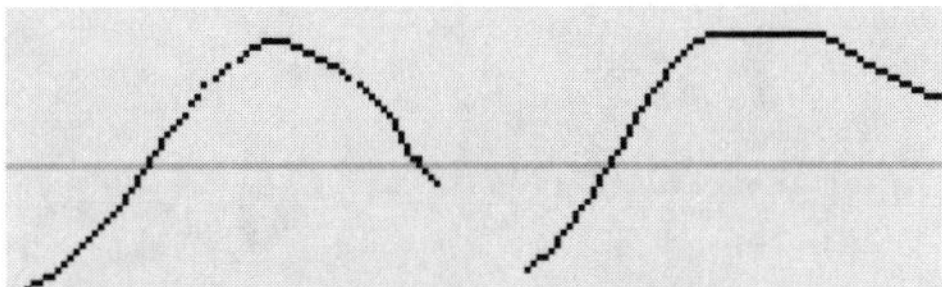

Figure 8.44 The left signal is at maximum and the right is clipping above maximum.

Adding Distortion

Reason gives you many ways to amplify and distort your tracks, but there are really only two kinds of distortion: intentional and unintentional.

Distortion occurs when a sound level exceeds the capacity of the line transmitting it. When this happens, its waveform peaks "clip," or level off, because they can't go any higher (**Figure 8.44**).

Unintentional clipping is never a good thing. Your level indicators will show red when your signal level exceeds the maximum.

Controlled distortion typically involves two volume controls that work together. The first (usually called the "gain") boosts the level internally and the second ("master" volume) controls the output separately.

The D-11 Foldback Distortion

The D-11 is a shaping tool that works on clipping. The Amount knob boosts the signal and the Foldback knob dulls or sharpens the clipping angle, directly affecting how harsh (sharp) or smooth (rounded) the distortion is.

Distorted signals seldom benefit from a dry/wet mix. For this reason distortion is primarily used either as an insert effect or with Pre-fader sends.

To create a D-11 insert effect:

1. With the instrument of your choice selected, choose Create > D-11 Foldback Distortion to insert a D-11 (**Figure 8.45**).

   Look at the back panel to make sure your instrument output is connected to the D-11 input and that the D-11 output is connected to your Mixer (**Figure 8.46**).
2. With your track playing, turn the Amount knob on the D-11 to the right to set how much distortion you want.
3. Turn the Foldback knob to the right to add more harsh harmonics to your distortion, and turn it to the left to mellow the effect.

✔ Tip

- In the middle position the Foldback knob is "neutral," or does not shape the distortion. (Clipping will still occur when the level meter is at maximum.)

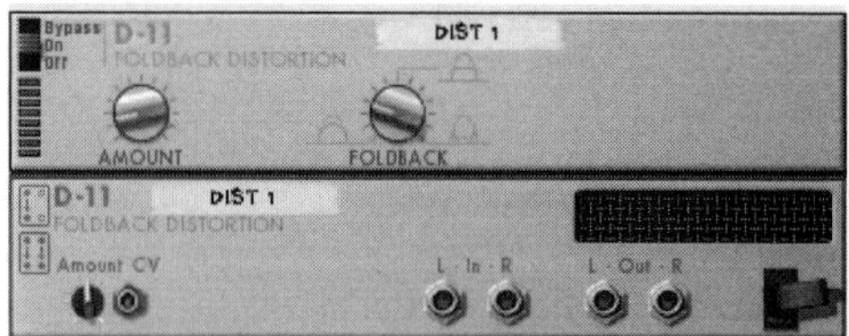

Figure 8.45 Create a D-11 Foldback Distortion (shown here, front and back) as an insert effect.

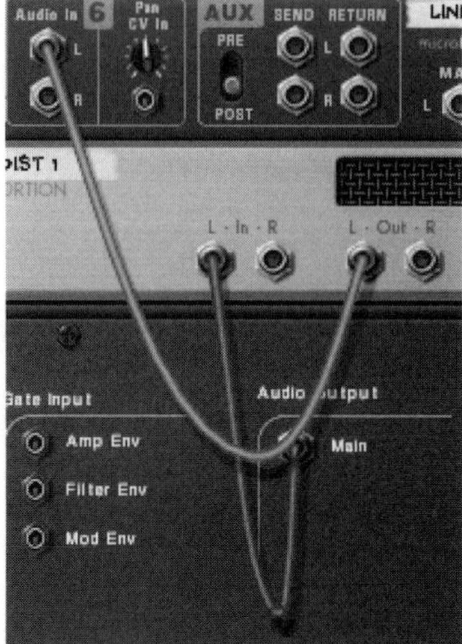

Figure 8.46 This D-11 is connected as a mono insert effect.

Adding Distortion

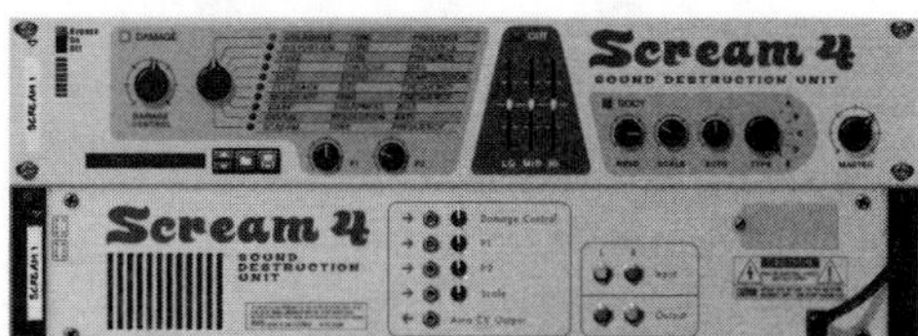

Figure 8.47 The Scream 4 Sound Destruction Unit (shown here, front and back) is a good distortion effect.

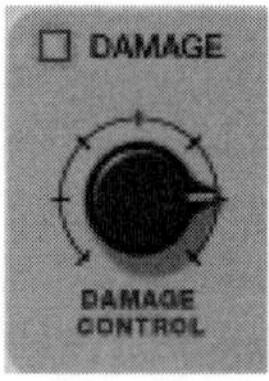

Figure 8.48 The Damage Control knob determines how much gain goes into the distortion model.

Figure 8.49 The P1 (parameter 1) knob controls different things for different models. For the Overdrive model it controls tone.

The Scream 4 Sound Destruction Unit

The Scream 4 uses acoustic models to emulate many different types of distortion. Like the RV7000, its adjustable parameters change according to what model is selected.

Analog models

First let's look at the three analog distortion models: *Overdrive, Distortion,* and *Fuzz.* They sound different but have identical parameters.

To use the Scream 4 analog model:

1. With the instrument of your choice selected, choose Create > Scream 4 Distortion to insert a Scream 4 (**Figure 8.47**).
2. With your track playing, turn the Damage Control knob clockwise to hear the Scream's default setting of Overdrive distortion (**Figure 8.48**).

   The Damage Control knob, like the D-11 Amount knob, boosts the level of the incoming signal. It doesn't affect the character of the distortion, only how much distortion occurs.
3. To adjust Overdrive *tone,* turn the P1 knob left (darker) or right (brighter) (**Figure 8.49**).

continues on next page

4. Adjust the Overdrive *presence* using the P2 knob.

   Presence is a pre-distortion tone control that affects midrange. It affects the tone (more presence means brighter), but it also affects the character of the distortion. High presence is harsher, and sometimes punchier.

5. Use the Damage Type knob to pick from the other two analog distortion models:

   Distortion is denser and more severe in the high frequency range than Overdrive.

   Fuzz is more severe in response to the Damage Control knob than the Distortion knob.

Tube model

The Scream 4 also models the distortion produced by vacuum tubes, such as you would find in a guitar amplifier.

Tubes clip in a distinctive way: They let in less sound as they fill up. This variable sensitivity to incoming sound adds a small amount of compression to clipping, for a mellower distortion.

To adjust the Tube damage type:

1. With your loop playing and a Scream 4 inserted, set the Damage Type knob to Tube.
2. Use the P1 knob to adjust tube contour, which sounds like a subtle high-pass filter. Think of *contour* as a frequency response curve that the P1 knob shifts up and down.
3. Use the P2 knob to adjust the tube bias. *Bias* involves a tube's "resting" state, or how its response to signals gets focused. The P2 knob will subtly alter the character and harmonic content of the distortion—the middle P2 setting is like a 20/20 focus.

Tape model

The Scream 4 Tape damage type models the way that recording tape saturates. Like the Tube model, it adds compression, accepting less sound when more sound is coming in.

To adjust the Tape damage type:

1. With your loop playing and a Scream 4 inserted, set the Damage Type knob to Tape.
2. Use the P1 knob to adjust the tape speed.

   Remember that with tape, the faster the tape speed, the more particles per second available and the higher the resolution (i.e., more high frequencies).
3. Use the *P2* knob to adjust the amount of compression.

   In this case, *compression* refers to soft clipping, characteristic of how tape responds to an overloaded signal.

Compression vs. Distortion

Distortion is a raw excess of capacity that clips sharply, adding harsh harmonics. Compression uses a gate with a fade-in (attack) and fade-out (release) that sets a maximum shelf and regulates how sound levels impact it. Thus clipping is minimized and unruly peaks keep a rounder shape.

Compressors can also boost low-level sounds by increasing the overall signal level without spilling over the top. (For an explanation of Reason's MClass Compressor, see Chapter 11, "Mastering.")

Beware of overcompressing a signal. A signal that is so loud that most of its peaks have to be gated will lose its louds and softs. Instead what you'll hear is the gate opening and closing with no apparent relation to the pulses in the music, as if someone's messing with the volume knob.

Judiciously used, compression can help you hear as much sound as possible in the most situations, both emphasizing low-level sound that would otherwise be buried in a mix (expanding) and making sure the loudest peaks don't get pushed too high in the process (limiting).

Feedback model

Feedback simulates a feedback loop, such as when a microphone is placed next to a speaker playing the microphone signal back to itself. As the signal gets amplified more signal plays back—eventually building to a sustained, wailing noise pattern.

The parameters won't make much sense unless you are feeding a signal into your Scream 4 and can listen to the effects, so be sure you have at least a test loop set up.

To adjust the Feedback damage type:

1. With your loop playing and a Scream 4 inserted, set the Damage Type knob to Feedback.
2. The P1 (size) knob adjusts the timing between the source signal and the signal feeding back; the results will be unpredictable, so you'll have to experiment.
3. Use the P2 (frequency) knob to control the center frequency, or wailing tone of the effect.

Modulate model

Modulate is another unpredictable effect that will require some experimenting to get a feel for. This distortion model filters and compresses the incoming signal, and then applies it to the original for some ringing distortion effects.

To adjust the Modulate damage type:

1. With your loop playing and a Scream 4 inserted, set the Damage Type knob to Modulate.
2. Use the P1 (ring) knob to adjust the effect's filter resonance.
3. Use the P2 (frequency) knob to adjust the filter's frequency. High P2 values will make the sound harsher and more piercing.

Warp model

The Warp model copies the signal, distorts it, and then combines it with the original. This causes the original signal and the distorted signal to cancel each other out, emphasizing the distorted effect and the resulting overtones.

To adjust the Warp damage type:

1. With your loop playing and a Scream 4 inserted, set the Damage Type knob to Warp.
2. Increase the P1 (sharpness) knob to get more overtones for a harsher sound, and decrease it for a softer effect.
3. Increasing the P2 (bias) knob will phase out the cancellation effect, allowing more of the fundamental (input) sounds to remain.

Digital model

The Digital damage type models lo-fi digital gear, producing a "dirty" or "vintage" sound (depending on your perspective).

To adjust the Digital damage type:

1. With your loop playing and a Scream 4 inserted, set the Damage Type knob to Digital.
2. In Digital mode, the Damage Control knob determines how much of the dry signal is re-sampled. If you want to affect all of the incoming signal using this model, set the Damage Control knob to maximum.
3. Use the P1 (bit) knob to reduce bit depth, or "crush" the dynamic range. The full right position leaves the bit rate of the signal alone; full left gives you "1-bit," or no dynamic range at all, just on or off.
4. Use the P2 (rate) knob to set how much sample rate reduction you want. Sample rate affects high-frequency response. The lower the sample rate, the lower the highest frequency. The full right position leaves the sample rate alone.

Scream model

The Scream model adds a resonant filter to a fuzz-like distortion. Like the Feedback model, this effect can be used for distortion that has a prominent tonal, wailing quality to it.

To adjust the Scream damage type:

1. With your loop playing and a Scream 4 inserted, set the Damage Type knob to Scream.
2. Increase or decrease the P1 (tone) knob to brighten or deaden the tone.
3. Use the P2 (frequency) knob to set the frequency for the high-resonance filter.

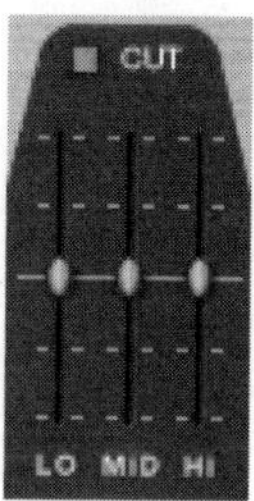

Figure 8.50 The Cut section equalizer lets you boost or lower low, mid, and high frequencies.

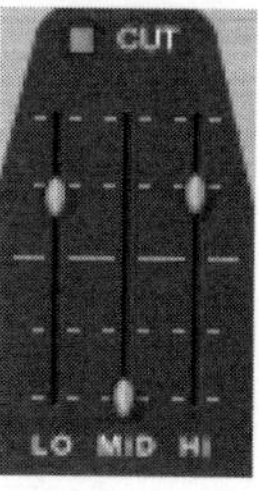

Figure 8.51 This EQ setting produces a heavy-sounding guitar.

Using the Other Scream 4 Controls

The Scream 4 has a three-band EQ, called the Cut section (**Figure 8.50**), which can drastically boost or lower low, mid, and high frequencies.

Warning: The Cut section has an 18 dB range, so take care not to blow out your speakers, headphones, or ears when boosting these faders!

To use the Cut section:

1. With your loop playing and a Scream 4 inserted, click the Cut On/Off button to activate the EQ.
2. Drop or boost the Lo, Mid, and Hi faders to taste.

✔ Tips

- By default these faders are set at neutral (halfway) and have no effect.
- Use a V shape to emulate a dark, Black Sabbath type of guitar sound (**Figure 8.51**).

Body section

The Scream 4 Body section allows you to further shape the tone of the distortion through a combination of filters, modeling, envelopes, and cabinet simulation. Think of the Body section as creating a resonating enclosure around the sound, and the controls will make more sense as we explore them.

Figure 8.52 The Body section lets you further shape the tone of the distortion.

To use the Body section for resonant filtering:

1. With your track playing and a Scream 4 inserted, click the Body On/Off button to turn on the Body section (**Figure 8.52**).
2. Turn the Reso, Scale, and Auto knobs hard left so you can test them one at a time.
3. Boost the Reso knob to resonate the Body section's filter.

   When the other knobs are set to the left, the Reso knob will have a subtle effect.
4. Now turn the Scale knob slowly from left to right.

   Though at first the Scale knob may seem like a frequency knob, it "shrinks" the enclosure model as you turn the knob clockwise—the smaller the enclosure, the higher the resonant frequency.
5. Move the Auto knob to the right.

   The Auto knob controls the Scream 4's envelope follower, a gate that opens and closes with the volume of an incoming sound. This shape is then applied to a filter for an "auto-wah" effect.
6. The Type knob gives you five different enclosure shapes to choose from. Try out the different settings and you'll hear how this control can be used for speaker-cabinet simulation.

More About Auto and Scale

The Scale knob affects the sound of the envelope follower. When the Scale knob is set low (large), the envelope follower shifts in the low-frequency range and the effect is subtle. As the Scale value increases and the body size shrinks, the filter shifts up in frequency, creating more of a classic, acid-bass-line type of filter shift. Slightly higher Scale settings will push the Auto filter into the vocal range, creating interesting "talk box" effects. At the highest Scale setting the Auto filter shifts more quickly, and becomes more of an attack effect.

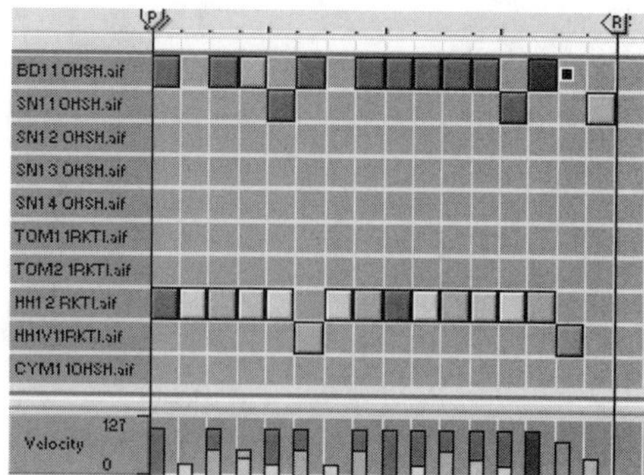

Figure 8.53 This short drum loop will be used to drive the Scream 4 envelope follower.

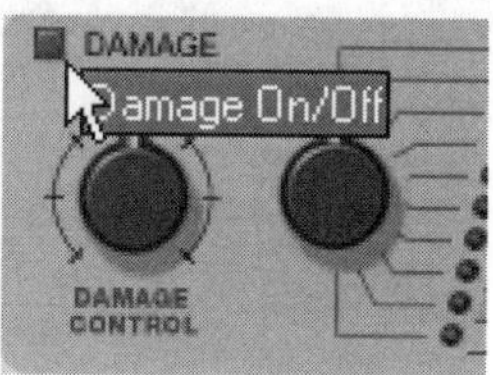

Figure 8.54 Disabling the Damage section won't affect the envelope follower.

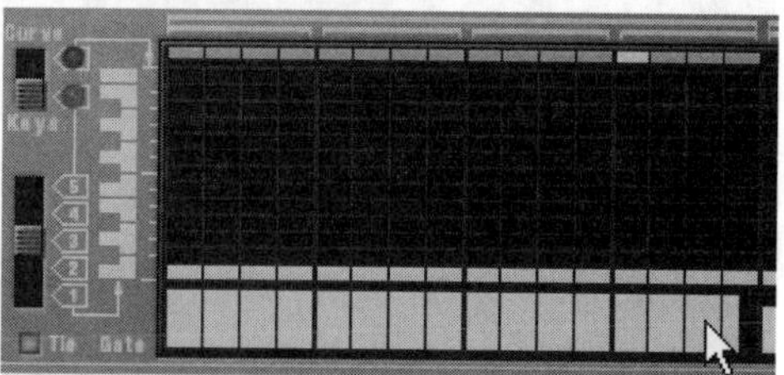

Figure 8.55 This Matrix plays a one-bar sustained-note loop (the Tie function is enabled).

The Auto CV output

You can also use the Scream 4 Auto filter CV output like an amp envelope signal, to control another Scream parameter or another device.

To use the Auto CV output:

1. Create a Redrum drum machine and load the patch `/Redrum Drum Kits/Rock Kits/Groovemasters Rock Kit 1` from the Factory Sound Bank.
2. Write a one-bar drum loop (**Figure 8.53**).
3. Select the Redrum and create a Scream 4.

   Reason will insert the Scream 4 between the Redrum and the Mixer.
4. Click the Damage On/Off button to disable the Damage section of the Scream 4 (**Figure 8.54**). We're just using the envelope follower for this exercise.
5. Create a SubTractor synth and load the Factory Sound Bank patch `/SubTractor patches/Bass/Dodger Bass`.
6. Select the SubTractor and create a Matrix Pattern Sequencer.

   This will auto-route the Matrix to control the SubTractor.
7. Write a one-bar sustained-note loop on the Matrix (**Figure 8.55**).

continues on next page

8. From the back panel, run a cable from the Scream 4 Auto CV output to the SubTractor's Filter 1 Freq modulation input (**Figure 8.56**).

9. Adjust the SubTractor's Filter 1 Freq CV knob (**Figure 8.57**).

   You should now hear the SubTractor part pulsing along with the drums.

10. Try muting the drum track in your Mixer to focus in on the bass sound.

11. Now try optimizing the SubTractor controls to tune this effect with these settings:

    On the front panel, set Filter 1 frequency to 16 and resonance to 74. Set Filter Envelope amount to 0. On the back panel, set the Filter 1 Freq CV knob to 16–22.

To modulate the drums:

1. Turn on the Scream 4 Body section.

   You will hear a phase effect as the type (cabinet simulator) kicks in.

2. Set the Type knob to B.

3. Set the Reso knob to maximum and the Scale knob to 42.

4. Set the Auto knob to 81 (**Figure 8.58**).

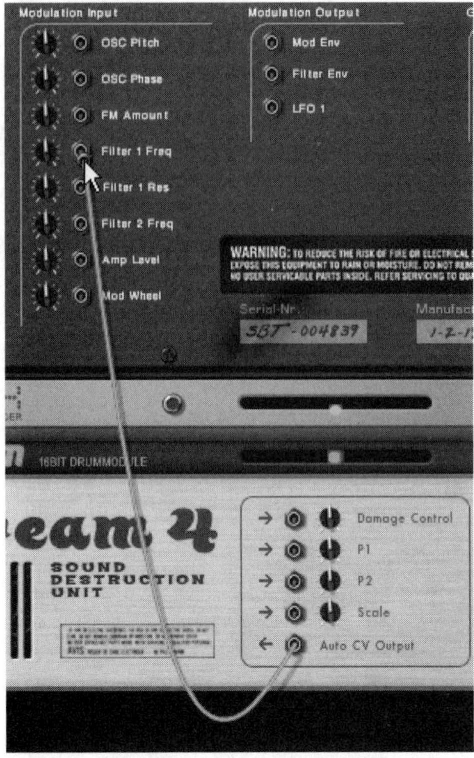

Figure 8.56 The Scream 4 Auto CV output will now control the filter 1 frequency of the SubTractor.

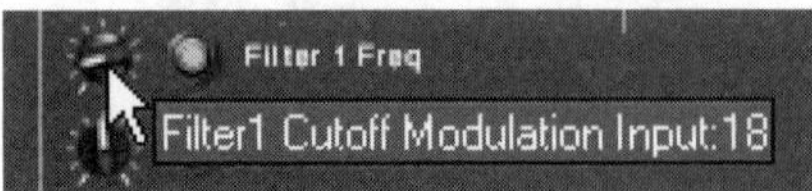

Figure 8.57 Optimize the current SubTractor patch for the incoming control signal using the CV sensitivity knob.

Figure 8.58 Use these Body settings for drum modulation.

Phase Effects

Reason has three phase effects: the CF-101 Chorus/Flanger, the UN-16 Unison, and the PH-90 Phaser. All three generate various interference patterns by copying an incoming signal, changing its timing or pitch, and then mixing it back with the original signal.

What is phasing?

Phasing gets its name from the concept of identical signals playing back at slightly different times or tunings.

This effect can happen unintentionally if you're not careful. For example, when microphones are placed at different distances from the same source, sound takes longer to travel to one than the other, and the time difference creates interference at the mixing console. When this happens, the sounds are said to be "out of phase" because of timing.

An example of pitch phasing is when two instrumentalists are tuning against each other and a rapid beating cycle, or wave, starts to occur. As the tones get closer in pitch, the beat slows down. These sounds are "out of phase" as well, but the phasing difference is due to the wavelength (pitch) of the sounds, not the timing.

Used deliberately (and with care) timing and pitch phasing can add stereo width to a mono sound, depth to a thin one, or "shimmer" to a voice in a mix. At higher settings drastic filter effects can be created.

The CF-101 Chorus/Flanger

The CF-101 delays a sound copy before mixing it back with the original, and can also pitch-modulate the delay using an LFO.

This double method of phasing is probably the most effective for sounds that don't have lots of harmonic content, such as electronic keyboards, clean guitars, or drums.

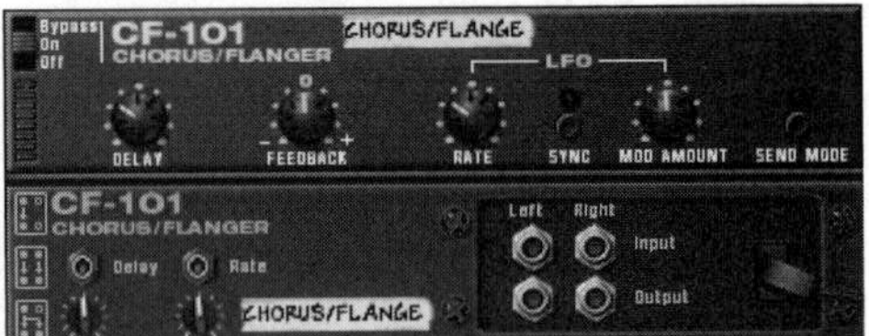

Figure 8.59 The CF-101 Chorus/Flanger delays a sound copy before mixing it back with the original.

To use the CF-101 Chorus/Flanger as an insert effect:

1. Select an instrument in your Rack and choose Create > CF-101 Chorus/Flanger to insert a CF-101 (**Figure 8.59**).
2. Check to make sure Send mode is disabled on the CF-101.

   Send mode is only for master effects—it does not output the original sound, only the processed copy.
3. To focus on the timing, first turn the Mod Amount knob all the way to the left (off) to disable the LFO (**Figure 8.60**).
4. With your track playing, use the Delay knob to lengthen (right) or shorten (left) the timing phase used for the effect.
5. Turn the Feedback knob to the right to increase the phasing.

   The Feedback control magnifies the timing effect by sending the processed sound copy back into the original signal. The farther it's turned, the more processed signal feeds back, and the more drastic the effect.
6. Now engage the LFO by turning the LFO Mod Amount knob to the right.
7. Adjust the rate of pitch modulation using the LFO Rate knob.
8. Use the Sync button to set the LFO rate in tempo increments.

Figure 8.60 Disable the CF-101 LFO.

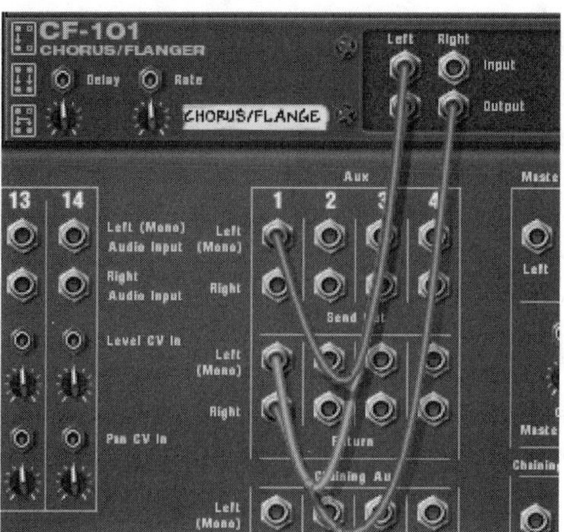

Figure 8.61 We'll set the CF-101 as a master effect.

Figure 8.62 Enable Send mode when using the CF-101 as a master effect.

Figure 8.63 For master effects, use the Aux Send for processed sound and the channel fader for dry sound.

With the CF-101 as a master effect, all the controls work the same. But as with any other effect, the initial setup is a little different.

To use the CF-101 as a master effect:

1. With your Mixer selected, choose Create > CF-101 Chorus/Flanger, then check your back panel to make sure the CF-101 is connected to an open Aux channel on your Mixer (**Figure 8.61**).
2. Check your front panel; if the Send Mode indicator is not lit, click the Send Mode button to activate it now (**Figure 8.62**).
3. Mix the dry signal using your Mixer channel, and the wet signal using your Mixer channel Aux Send knob (**Figure 8.63**).
4. When you have a good strong effects level, set your CF-101 knobs accordingly.

The PH-90 Phaser

The PH-90 is a phase shifter, or timing effect. It notch-filters using cancellation between the incoming and delayed signals, then allows you to modulate the notch frequencies using an LFO. In sonic terms, this allows you to create very drastic tonal sweeps and control the rate.

The PH-90 gives you additional controls that make it more versatile than a typical phase shifter. However, these controls can be tricky to work with if you're shooting for the familiar effect used on old recordings.

We'll start by disabling the more advanced controls so we can focus on the primary filter controls.

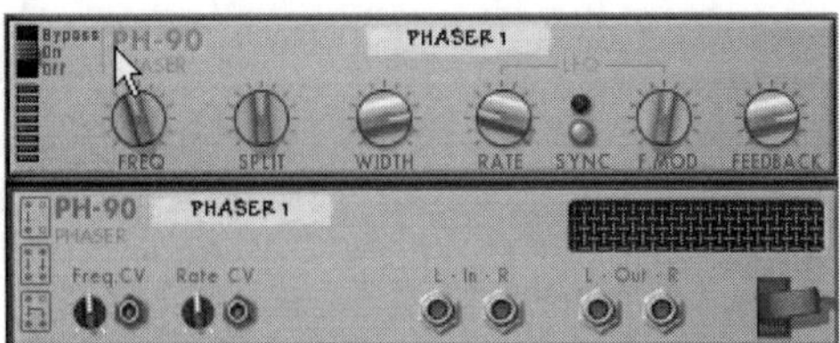

Figure 8.64 The PH-90 Phaser (shown here front and back) provides additional controls that make it more versatile than a typical phase shifter.

To use the PH-90 Phaser filter:

1. Select an instrument in your Rack and choose Create > PH-90 Phaser to insert a PH-90 (**Figure 8.64**).
2. Play your track and disable the LFO by setting the F.Mod knob left to 0 (**Figure 8.65**).
3. Next, set the Split knob to 0 (**Figure 8.66**).
   The Split knob changes the character of the filter. For simplicity's sake, we don't want to add this yet.
4. Set the Feedback knob off (left).
   Later you can use the Feedback knob to magnify your settings.
5. Set the Width knob to maximum (right).
   Low Width values barely filter any sound, and won't sound like much without the other controls (**Figure 8.67**).
6. Make the notch "shimmer" by moving the Freq knob left and right, manually sweeping the filter's frequency.

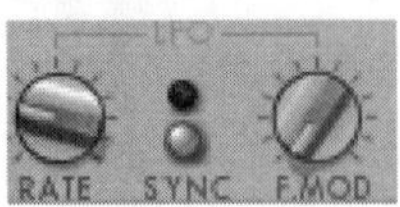

Figure 8.65 Set the F.Mod knob to 0 to disable the LFO.

Figure 8.66 Disable Split by turning the knob all the way to the right.

Figure 8.67 The Width knob adjusts the notch-filter width (higher values are more audible).

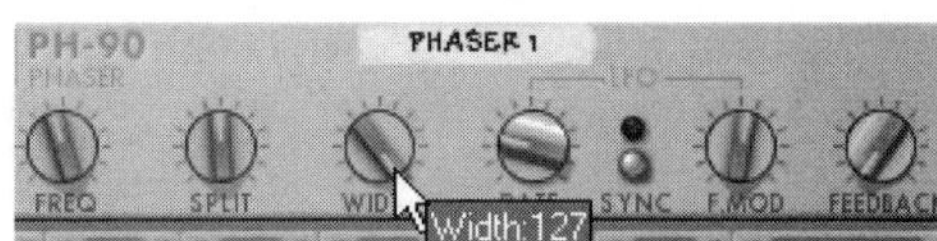

Figure 8.68 Set up the main controls for classic phase shifting.

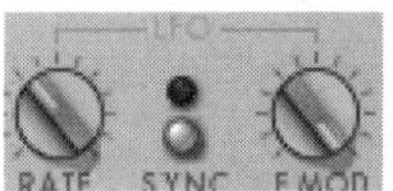

Figure 8.69 Also set up the LFO for classic phase shifting.

For a classic phase-shifting effect, let's activate the LFO and use it to move the Freq knob for us.

To use the PH-90 for classic phase shifting:

1. With a PH-90 inserted and your loop playing, set the Split knob midway.
2. Turn the Feedback knob all the way down to 0, and set Width to maximum (**Figure 8.68**).
3. Set the F.Mod knob to maximum and the Rate knob to about 48 (**Figure 8.69**).

   This will cause the filter frequency to move slowly up and down the spectrum for an automated (subtle) shimmer effect.
4. Now turn the Feedback knob to the right to magnify the effect.

   As on the CF-101, the PH-90 Feedback knob internally sends filtered sound back into the input, increasing the phasing effect.
5. Now increase the distance between the notch filters by turning up the Split knob.

   When the Split knob is off, the filters are spaced regularly for a straight notch-filter sound. However, when the feedback is turned up, the Split knob magnifies the feedback interference.
6. Now that you've established a solid phasing effect, you can adjust the Width knob to change the character of the sound.
7. Use the Sync button to set the Rate knob in tempo-based increments.

✔ Tip

- For a stereo effect, try this technique with a mono source, like a SubTractor, connected to the PH-90's left audio input. Make sure that both the left and right outputs of the PH-90 are connected to your Mixer.

The UN-16 Unison

The UN-16 is a delay and tuning phase effect that copies, delays, and detunes multiple voices, then spreads them about the stereo field. It sounds great with very little fussing.

With a mono signal going in and stereo outputs, the UN-16 will add stereo width to a mono sound. When stereo inputs/outputs are used, it can "thicken" a stereo sound with an effect similar to chorus.

Figure 8.70 The UN-16 Unison copies, delays, and detunes multiple voices, then spreads them about the stereo field.

To use the UN-16 to add stereo width to a mono source:

1. Use the Create > UN-16 Unison command with an instrument selected for an insert effect or with your Mixer selected for a master effect (**Figure 8.70**).
2. Play your track and adjust the number of voices using the Voice Count button (**Figure 8.71**).
3. Use the Detune knob to set how much detuning you want (**Figure 8.72**).

   More detuning results in a thicker sound between all the voices.
4. Adjust the Dry/Wet knob to mix the dry signal with the added detuned voices.

   If you are using the UN-16 as a send effect through your Mixer's Aux channels, set the Dry/Wet knob to maximum (right), since your Mixer channel's Aux Send will handle the dry/wet mix for you.

Figure 8.71 The Voice Count button sets how many copies of the incoming signal will be made.

Figure 8.72 The Detune knob thickens the effect.

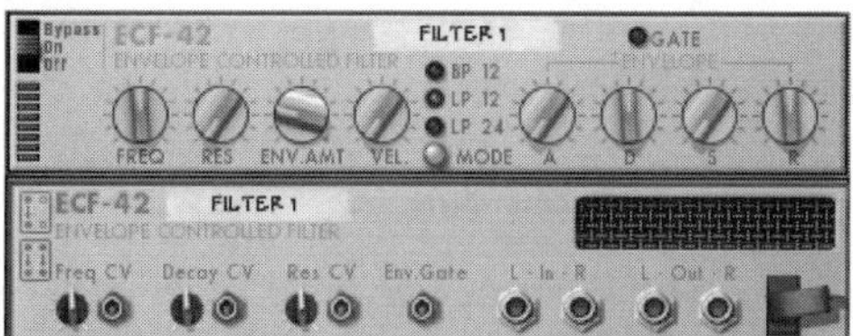

Figure 8.73 We'll use the ECF-42 Envelope Controlled Filter as a straight resonant filter.

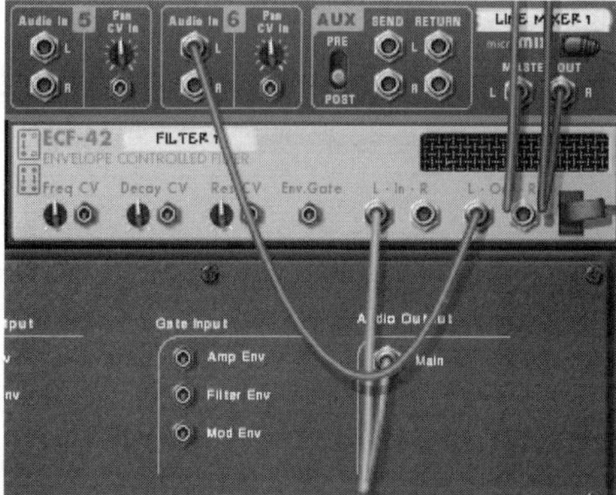

Figure 8.74 With the ECF-42 used as a mono effect, only the left inputs and outputs are used.

EQ Effects

By now you're familiar with the idea of frequency filters and how emphasizing different frequencies changes and shapes an instrument's tone.

Like filters, equalizers are powerful tools to keep tracks sounding their best and place them properly alongside others in a mix. You can make EQs resonate just like filters or use them as very sensitive tone controls.

Equalizers are used as insert effects, since they "fix" a dry signal to begin with, and mixing a dry and an equalized signal will produce unintentional phasing.

The ECF-42 Envelope Controlled Filter

The first EQ effect we'll look at is, in fact, a filter. The ECF-42 is designed to provide the kind of responsive filtering that the SubTractor's filter module allows, but is available to any instrument that is connected to it.

The simplest way to use it is to connect it to an audio source and use it as an insert filter effect. When cabled with audio inputs and outputs only, the gate, velocity, and envelope amount controls will have no effect, and the ECF-42 will act as a regular filter.

To use the ECF-42 as a straight resonant filter:

1. Select the instrument you want to use as a signal source and choose Create > ECF-42 Envelope Controlled Filter (**Figure 8.73**).

   If you're hooking up a mono source like a SubTractor synth, only the left inputs and outputs will be used (**Figure 8.74**).

continues on next page

2. Use the ECF-42 Res knob to add resonance.
3. Use the Freq knob to set the filter frequency.

Now for the "envelope-controlled" part. To use the filter's envelope generator, you'll need to supply a gate CV signal to the ECF-42's Gate CV input.

In this example we'll use one Matrix to play a SubTractor and another to play the ECF-42. The result is one pattern for the instrument, and a second pattern for the filter.

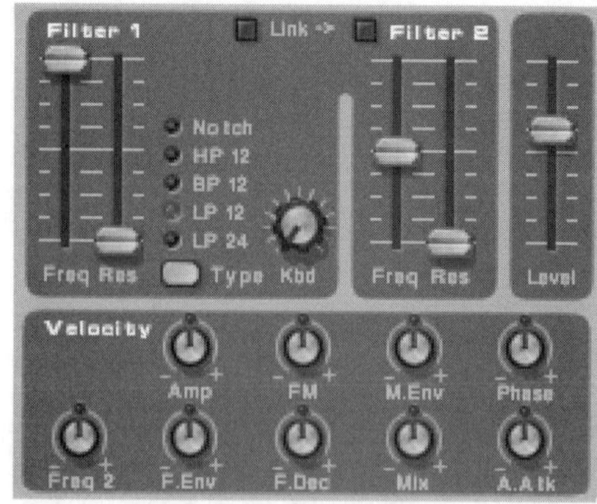

Figure 8.75 Set up the SubTractor so it produces no filter activity.

To set up two pattern sequencers:

1. Create a SubTractor synth.
2. Set the Filter 1 Freq fader to maximum and set both the F.Env and F.Dec velocity knobs to the middle (**Figure 8.75**).

   This is so we don't have any filter activity from the SubTractor.
3. Select the SubTractor and create a Matrix Pattern Sequencer.

   This will automatically connect the Note outputs and Gate CV of the Matrix to Gate and CV inputs of a SubTractor (**Figure 8.76**).

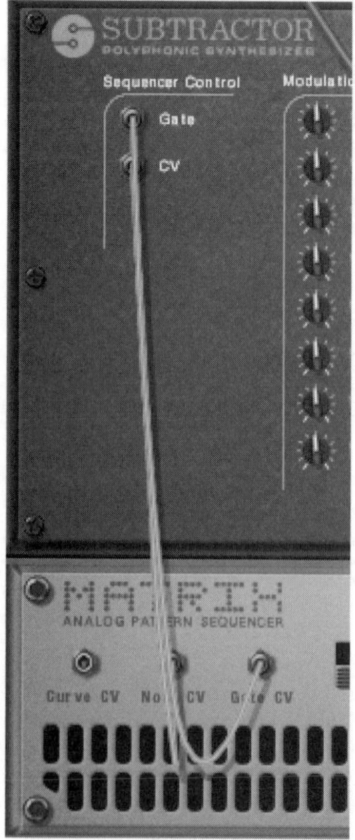

Figure 8.76 Connect a Matrix to the SubTractor.

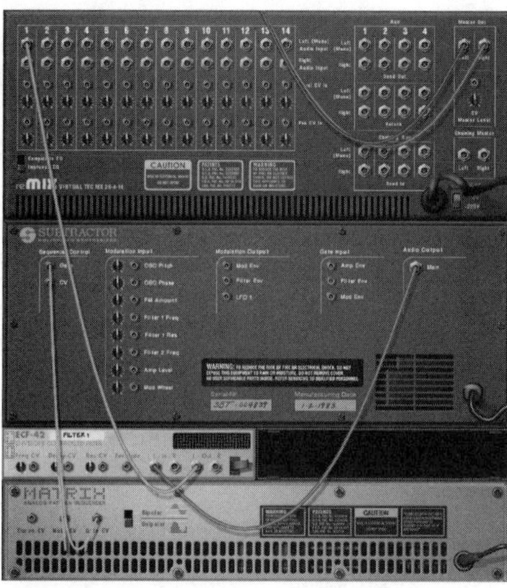
Figure 8.77 Set up an ECF-42 as an insert effect.

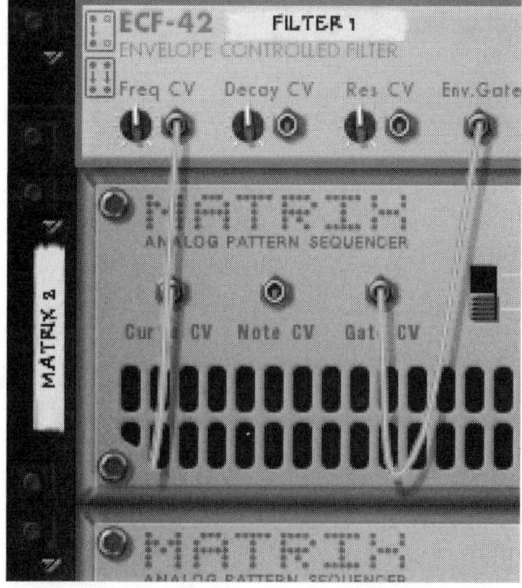

Figure 8.78 Connect a second Matrix to the ECF-42.

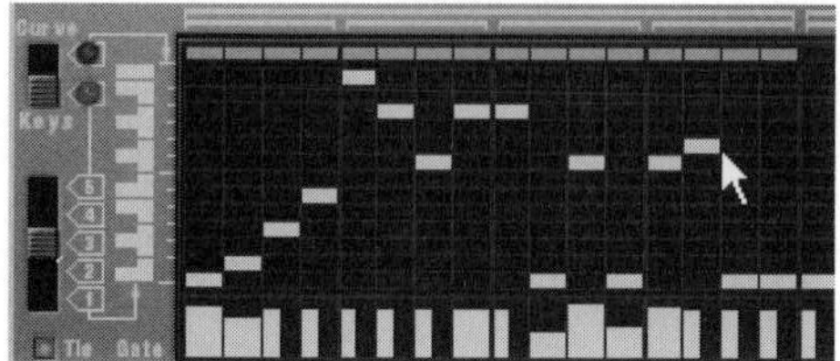
Figure 8.79 Create a Matrix bass loop for the SubTractor.

4. With the SubTractor selected, create an ECF-42.

   Reason will insert the ECF-42 between the SubTractor and the Mixer (**Figure 8.77**).

5. Select the ECF-42 and create a second Matrix.

   Reason will route the Gate CV output of the new Matrix to the Env Gate CV input of the ECF-42 (**Figure 8.78**). Once a gate signal is patched to the ECF-42, you'll have extra controls, which function just like the velocity sensitivity controls of the SubTractor.

6. In the Matrix controlling the SubTractor write a short bass loop (**Figure 8.79**).

To control the ECF-42 with Matrix velocity:

1. Draw velocity variations in the Gate lane of the second Matrix (**Figure 8.80**) and click Run.

   Higher gate values will make the sound brighter.

2. Turn the ECF-42 Freq knob all the way to the left (**Figure 8.81**).

   Starting the filter at a closed position gives the Matrix room to open it up.

3. To begin filter motion, turn the ECF-42 Vel knob to the right (**Figure 8.82**).

   The ECF-42 will start varying the brightness of the SubTractor. The Vel knob determines how far the filter will open in response to velocity increases.

4. Boost the ECF-42 Res knob for the desired amount of resonance.

5. Continue to balance the Freq and Vel knobs until you have the desired sound.

   Low Vel settings mean that the filter is moving less, so higher Freq settings may be necessary.

   High Vel settings move the filter more—a lower Freq setting can create a mute effect, which makes the high-velocity notes more striking.

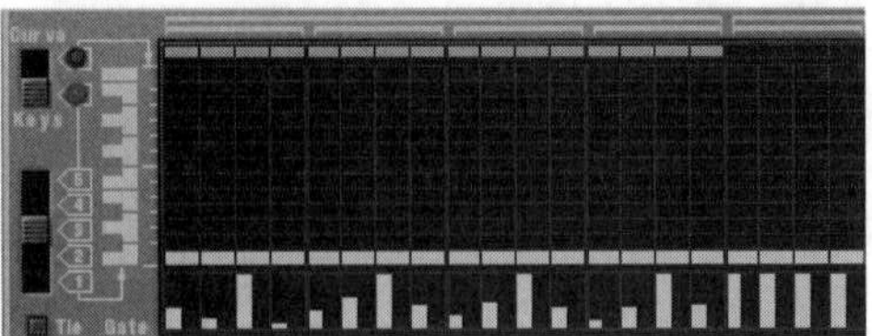

Figure 8.80 A gate track in the Matrix will drive the ECF-42 filter.

Figure 8.81 Turning the ECF-42 Freq knob to the left leaves room for the Matrix to open the filter with high velocities.

Figure 8.82 To start motion, turn the ECF-42 Vel knob to the right.

Figure 8.83 Turn the Env.Amt knob to about halfway.

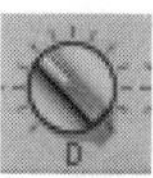

Figure 8.84 Short envelope decays can sound "bubbly."

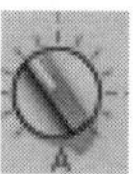

Figure 8.85 Boost the A (attack) knob for a rapid fade-in.

Now we'll use these settings to move the envelope.

To control the ECF-42 envelope:

1. With your Matrix devices running, boost the ECF-42 Env.Amt knob to about halfway (**Figure 8.83**).
2. Now try decreasing the envelope D knob to about 44 (**Figure 8.84**).

   This will shorten the decay and make the SubTractor line sound as if it's bubbling.
3. Try boosting the A knob to fade in high frequencies during note attacks (**Figure 8.85**).
4. Turn the A knob hard left (off) and the D knob left to about 32, then start increasing the S knob.

   Unless A and D are set very low, the S knob has little effect on rapid notes.

✔ Tip

- For a quick refresher on ADSR and filters, see the "Filter Envelope" section of Chapter 5, "Building a Song."

Now let's set a pattern in a Sequencer track and control the ECF-42 that way.

To control the ECF-42 from a sequencer track:

1. Continuing with the setup from the previous task, delete the second Matrix.

   This will mute the sound temporarily.
2. In your Sequencer, choose Create > Sequencer Track.
3. Assign your new Sequencer track to the ECF-42 (**Figure 8.86**).
4. Switch to Edit mode and input a series of notes (**Figure 8.87**).

   This is a gate track, so there's no need to write melodies.

✔ Tip

- You can also control any CV input on the ECF-42 from the Sequencer track's Controller lane (**Figure 8.88**), or from another device by patching CV outputs from it to any of the ECF-42's CV inputs.

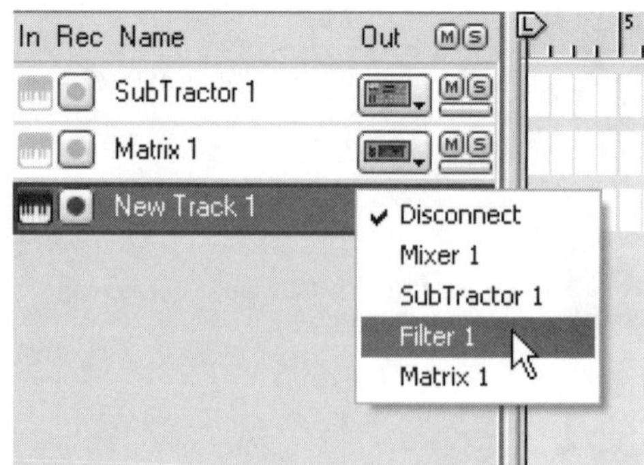

Figure 8.86 Assign a new Sequencer track to control the ECF-42.

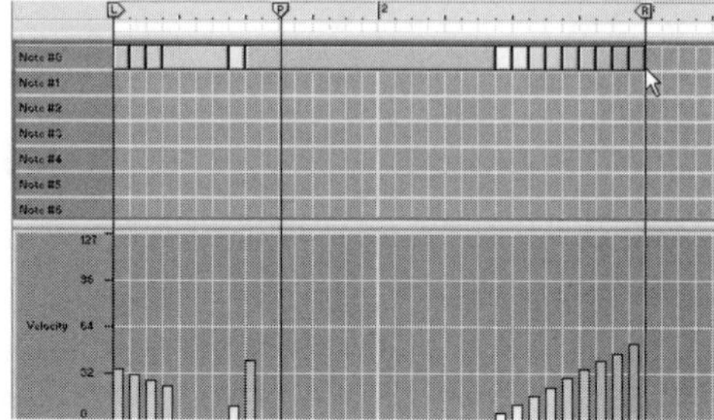

Figure 8.87 This series of notes is designed to drive the ECF-42 gate.

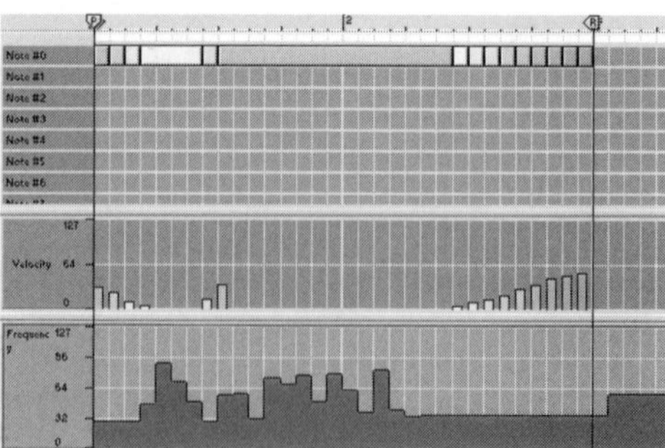

Figure 8.88 Control the ECF-42 frequency using the Controller lane.

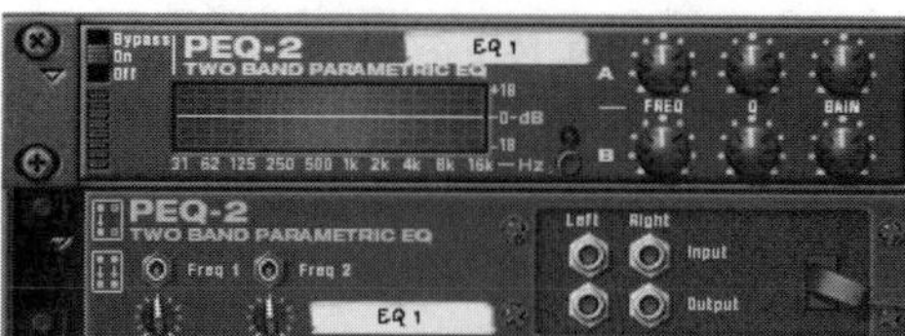

Figure 8.89 We'll use the PEQ-2 equalizer (shown here front and back) as a tone control.

Figure 8.90 The Gain knob lowers or raises the frequency, as shown in the display.

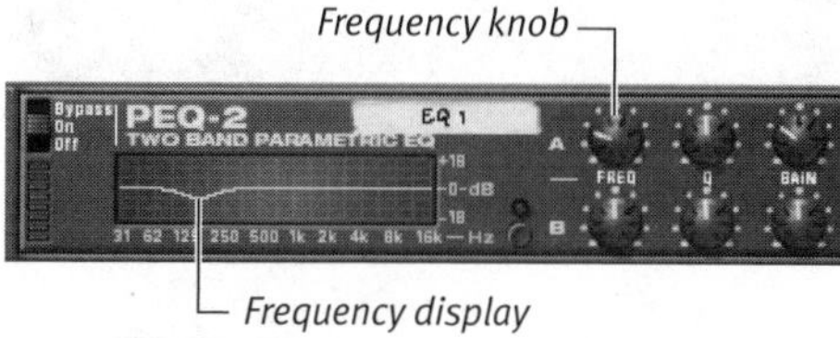

Figure 8.91 The display ruler marks frequency values as the Freq A knob moves.

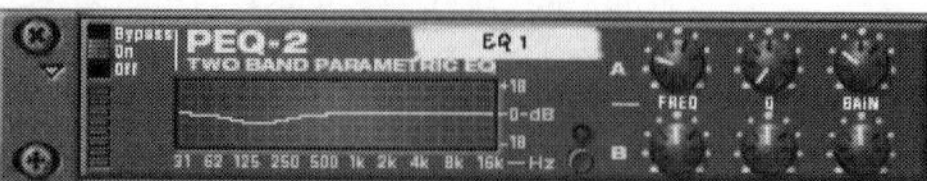

Figure 8.92 The Q knob narrows and widens the selected band.

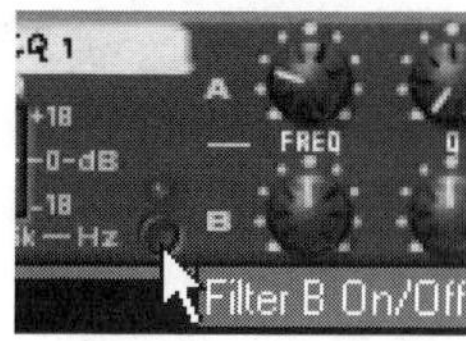

Figure 8.93 Click the Filter B On/Off button for a second tone control.

The PEQ-2 Two Band Parametric EQ

Unlike graphic equalizers, which assign levers to frequency bands, parametric EQs are adjustable. They can be set to any frequency and bandwidth.

Say you want to eliminate noise at a specific frequency. A graphic EQ won't work, but a parametric EQ can be set to the exact frequency required, and narrowed to avoid filtering out sounds you want to keep.

This adjustability makes Reason's PEQ-2 EQ more useful than it might seem at first.

To use the PEQ-2 as a tone control:

1. Insert an EQ by selecting your instrument and choosing Create > PEQ-2 Two Band Parametric EQ (**Figure 8.89**).
2. With your track playing, increase or decrease the EQ A Gain knob to lower or raise the current EQ setting (**Figure 8.90**).
3. Move the Freq A knob until it is affecting the frequency you want to cut or boost.

   Watch the display for the actual frequency value selected (**Figure 8.91**).
4. Use the Q knob to widen (left) or narrow (right) the frequency area you want to adjust (**Figure 8.92**).
5. Click the Filter B On/Off button to activate a second tone control (**Figure 8.93**).
6. Tune the second band using the same controls as in steps 2–4.

✔ Tip

- When very narrow Q values are used with high gain, the effect is basically that of a resonant filter, where a particular harmonic becomes audible. When very narrow Q values are used with low gain to cut the signal drastically, the result is that of a notch filter.

The BV512 Vocoder

As we shall see, the BV512 Digital Vocoder is a great voice synthesizer. But first and foremost it is an equalizer (and a very fancy one, at that).

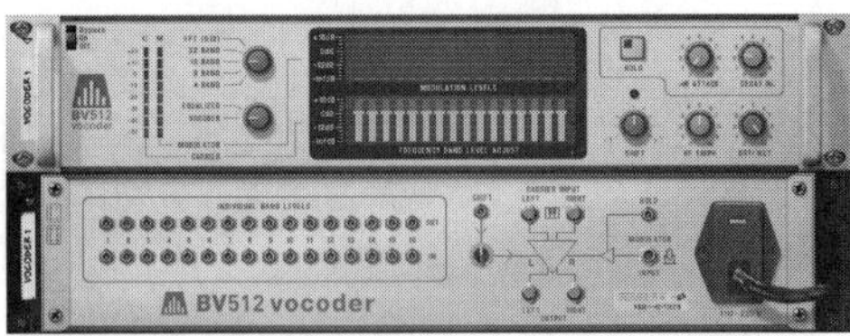

Figure 8.94 The BV512 Vocoder (shown here front and back) is both a great voice synthesizer and a great graphic equalizer.

To set up a BV512 as a graphic EQ:

1. Insert an EQ by selecting an instrument or effect and choosing Create > BV512 Digital Vocoder (**Figure 8.94**).
2. Check the back panel to make sure that the input signal you want to equalize is going to the left/right carrier inputs and that the left/right outputs are going to your Mixer (**Figure 8.95**).
3. Set the Vocoder/Equalizer knob to Equalizer.
4. Use the Band Count knob to choose whether you want 4, 8, 16, or 32 equalization bands (**Figure 8.96**).

   The FFT (512), or 512-band mode, does not work in EQ mode.
5. Play your track and drag the yellow faders in the Frequency Band Level Adjust section to shape the tone (**Figure 8.97**).
6. Use the Shift knob to shift the EQ settings up or down the frequency spectrum (**Figure 8.98**).

   This is a fast way to check (or find better) settings.

Figure 8.95 Insert a BV512 to use as a graphic equalizer.

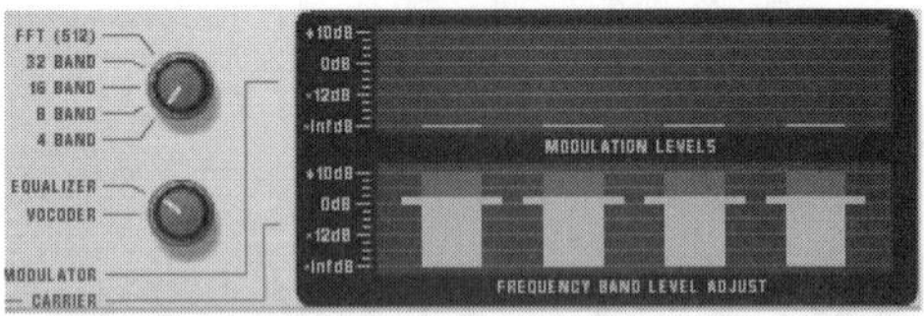

Figure 8.96 You can select 4, 8, 16, or 32 bands in Equalizer mode.

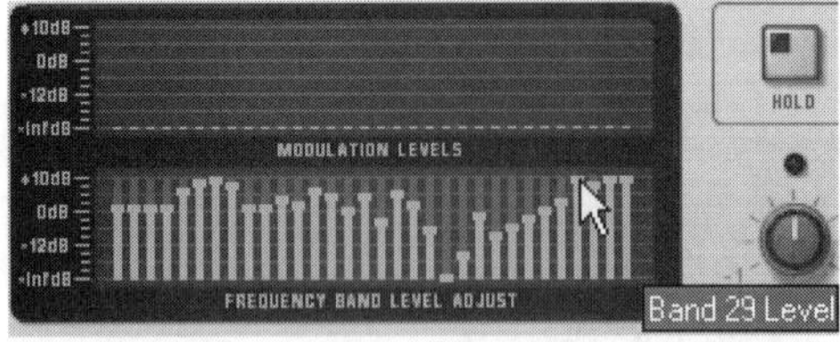

Figure 8.97 Click at a point above a fader or drag the fader handle up and down to adjust EQ on that band.

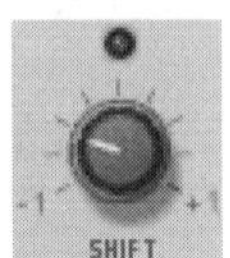

Figure 8.98 The Shift knob functions like a focus knob in Equalizer mode.

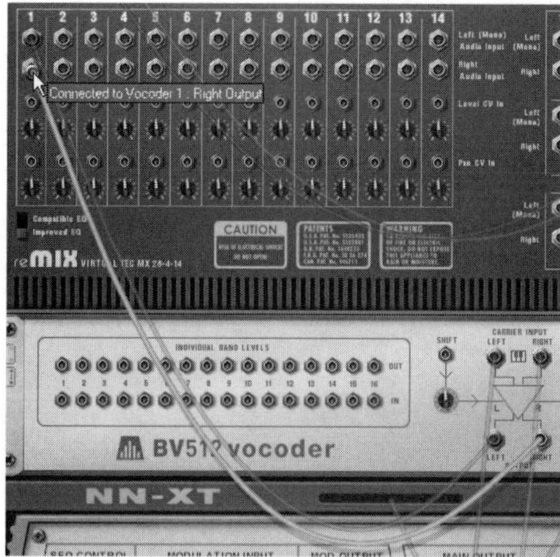

Figure 8.99 For vocoding, the BV512 should be cabled to an open Mixer channel.

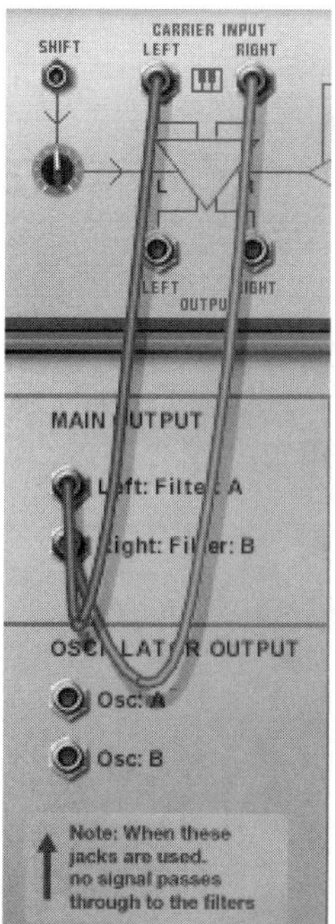

Figure 8.100 Cable a Malström to the carrier inputs of the BV512.

Vocoding

Vocoder devices were the first human speech synthesizers. Responsible for the familiar "talking" keyboard or "robotic voice" effect, they sound like an instrument chord or note that can "speak" vowels and consonants. Simply put, the vocoder is an EQ that analyzes the frequency signature of one sound (speech) and transfers it onto another (the note or chord).

To use the BV512 as a "classic vocoder," you'll need to find some speech samples to use in a musical context, or record some of your own.

It's easy to find speech samples on the Internet. (Try typing "speech samples" in your favorite search engine and see what comes up.) Linguists frequently post sound clips of speech dialects on their Web pages—try searching for some of these. Just make sure you aren't violating any copyrights!

As a simple example, we'll load an NN-XT with a speech sample from the Factory Sound Bank and pick a Malström sound to carry its imprint.

To set up a vocoder patch:

1. Create a BV512 (if you haven't already).
2. Make sure the BV512's left and right outputs are cabled to an open Mixer channel (**Figure 8.99**).
3. Select the BV512 and create a Malström to play the musical part.

   Reason will auto-route the Malström's outputs to the left and right Carrier inputs of the BV512 (**Figure 8.100**).

continues on next page

4. Holding the Shift key, create an NN-XT and plug its left output into the Modulator input of the BV512 (**Figure 8.101**).

5. In the NN-XT Remote Editor, click the Browse Sample button and from the Factory Sound Bank load the sample `/Other Samples/FX-Vox/MessageSpot_eLAB.aif`.

   This is a long speech sample, but it will do fine for our example.

6. In the Malström, load a bright-sounding patch or pick bright oscillator waveforms to use for the music track (**Figure 8.102**). I used VocoderSwirl and Xaphoon.

✔ Tip

- To imprint speech on a music track, the vocoder needs a lot of high-frequency content. The Malström is a very bright synth, perfect for the task.

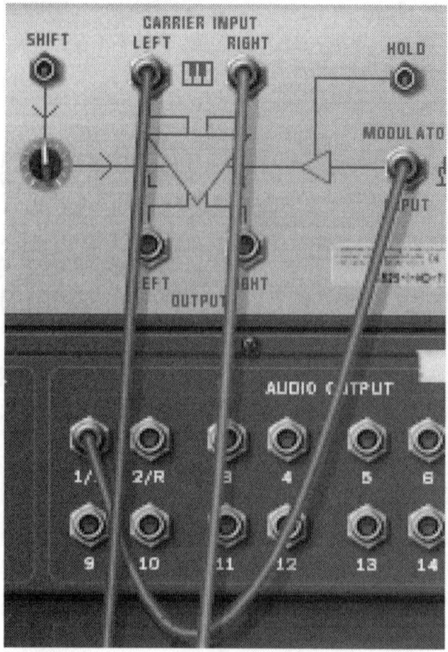

Figure 8.101 Connect the NN-XT to the Modulator input of the BV512.

Figure 8.102 Set your Malström oscillators to play bright-sounding waveforms.

Figure 8.103 Set MIDI bus A to control an instrument from your master keyboard.

Figure 8.104 Select a device on the MIDI channel that matches your master keyboard.

Figure 8.105 With MIDI bus B selected, you can control a second instrument from your master keyboard's MIDI channel.

In order to get your vocoder setup to make sound, you'll need to play both the NN-XT and the Malström at the same time. This is easiest if you're using a master keyboard. You can tell your interface that you want it to play both devices.

To vocode using a master keyboard:

1. Go to your Reason hardware interface and click the A Bus Select button (**Figure 8.103**).
2. Click the arrow key on the MIDI channel display matching your keyboard setting (it's usually Channel 1) and select the NN-XT from the pull-down menu (**Figure 8.104**).
3. Now click the B Bus Select button and set your keyboard's MIDI channel display to the Malström (**Figure 8.105**).

How Does Vocoding Work?

Just as the Auto filter of the Scream 4 superimposes the envelope of one sound onto another, the vocoder transfers the "tone" envelope of one sound onto another.

As you can imagine, a tone envelope complex enough to transmit speech must track many moving frequencies. To track them all, the vocoder splits the sound it's copying (the *modulator*) into multiple bands, then tracks how these different bands go up and down over time. The result is a frequency map, or *tonal signature*, of the original sound.

It takes more than a few EQ faders to mimic the human voice, so the BV512 must track as many as 512 frequency bands in real time for enough resolution to emulate vocal patterns. As the EQ bands "replay" their movements while the second signal (the *carrier*) is playing, the first sound has been successfully superimposed on the first!

If you're using a mouse, you'll need to set up at least one Sequencer track to trigger the Malström. Then you can use the NN-XT audition function to test your sound manually.

To vocode using the Sequencer:

1. Set the BV512 to Equalizer mode (**Figure 8.106**).

   This will allow you to hear the Malström while you write a short part.

2. Go to the Malström's Sequencer track and write the music part you want it to play (**Figure 8.107**).

   A simple part is usually enough to hear the effect.

3. Set the BV512 back to Vocoder mode.

4. With your loop playing, go to the NN-XT Sequencer track and audition notes to hear the effect.

In most cases, you'll need to tune both the Malström and the NN-XT to get the kind of effect you want. Here are some ways to optimize your vocoder setup for speech emulation.

To optimize your vocoder setup:

1. Set the BV512 HF Emph knob to maximum to optimize your NN-XT signal (**Figure 8.108**).

2. Try increasing the amp release for both your NN-XT and Malström oscillators (**Figure 8.109**).

   The `MessageSpot_eLAB.aif` sample is long, so it will benefit from longer release values.

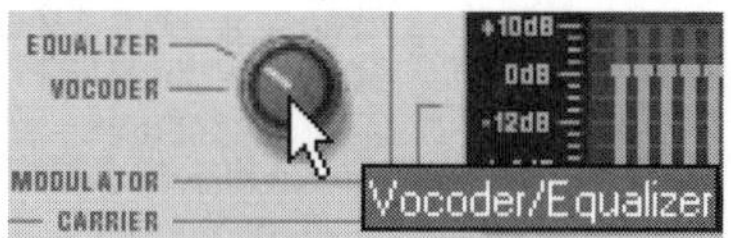

Figure 8.106 Set the BV512 temporarily to Equalizer mode while you adjust the carrier sound.

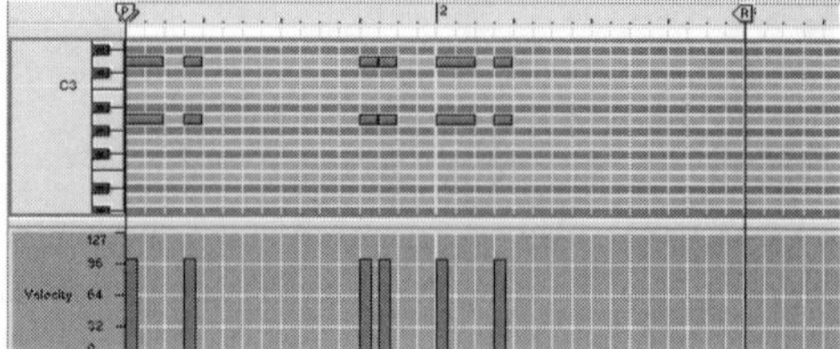

Figure 8.107 Write a carrier part for the Malström to play.

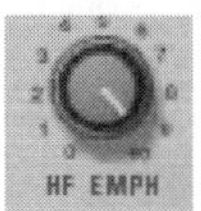

Figure 8.108 The HF Emph knob boosts modulator (NN-XT) high frequencies that the vocoder needs to simulate speech.

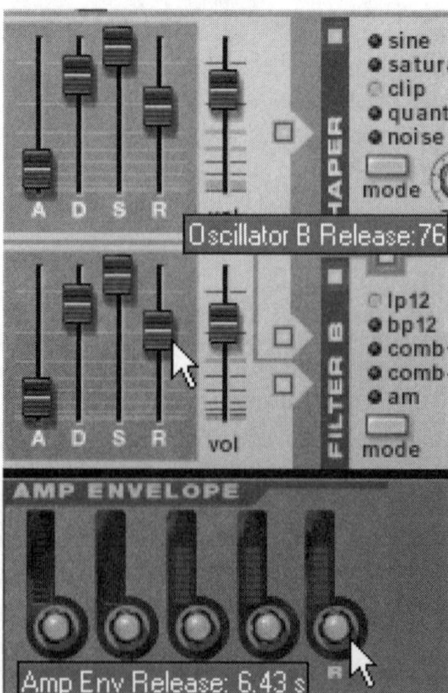

Figure 8.109 Set high amp releases for both instruments to allow more of the speech sample to play (or use sustained notes in your Sequencer).

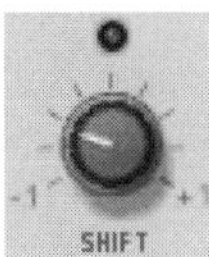

Figure 8.110 When pitch-shifting a speech sample downward, you can compensate for lower modulator formants by boosting the BV512 Shift knob.

Figure 8.111 Eliminate voice overlap on your NN-XT by setting the Key Poly count to 1; this can also help clarify speech simulation.

Figure 8.112 The sample start velocity control can "scramble" a speech sample for an interesting effect, especially with longer speech samples.

3. Playing lower notes in your NN-XT (or turning the Octave knob in the NN-XT pitch section to the left) may also help clarify speech fragments if they need more time to "develop."

   Detuning your speech sample will lower the quality of the speech sample as well, which you do simply by turning the BV512 Shift knob to the right (**Figure 8.110**).

4. Drop the polyphony for the NN-XT to 1 by selecting the sample in the Remote Editor and decreasing the Key Poly to 1 (**Figure 8.111**).

5. Try boosting the NN-XT S.Start (sample start) velocity knob (**Figure 8.112**).

   This will make notes with harder velocity play back farther into the sample, and is a good effect for long speech samples.

6. Optimize your carrier signal by making it brighter. Use the Malström filters, boost the oscillator Shift knob, or run the oscillator through the Shaper if needed.

The BV512's envelope controls can be useful as a focus (use short attack and decay) or a blur (use longer attack and decay) tool.

To use the BV512 envelope controls:

1. Make sure that you are fairly happy with your vocoder setup at this point (envelope controls can improve things, but they won't fix a bad patch).
2. Use the Attack knob to slow down the EQ signature pattern at the beginning (**Figure 8.113**). This can help out speech samples that have attacks you want to emphasize.
3. Use the Decay knob to slow down the rate at which the EQ faders drop at the end (**Figure 8.114**).
4. Click the Hold button to freeze the EQ signature at its present point until disabled (**Figure 8.102**).

✔ Tip

- The Hold button is very useful as an automated effect triggered from your Sequencer's Controller lane.

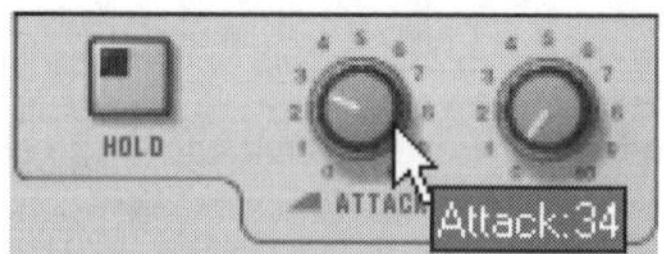

Figure 8.113 Using the BV512 Attack knob can blur a fast speech sample or clarify a slow one.

Figure 8.114 The BV512 Decay knob can sustain a speech sample or blur the release.

Figure 8.115 The Hold button freezes the EQ signature until it is clicked again.

VOCODING

CABLING SETUPS

Now that you've become familiar with instruments, audio and CV signals, and effects, it's time to start experimenting with back-panel configurations of your own.

More complex setups can be harder to manage. With window space always limited, even a few devices can use up much of your Rack if you are using effects processors, multiple outputs, and pattern players. This can lead to some confusion as you move on to new instruments.

In this chapter, we'll look at some more ambitious Rack setups, and learn how to minimize the confusion as your devices proliferate.

Introducing the Combinator

New in version 3.0 of Reason, the Combinator can take any Rack setup—including combinations of instruments, effects, Mixers, and internal connections—and put them into just one rack device (**Figure 9.1** and **Figure 9.2**). This can then be saved as a *Combi* patch, loaded and saved just like an instrument sound.

The Combinator is ideal for storing templates of frequently used setups, creating and saving chains of effects, or cordoning off Rack setups that share the same purpose.

Let's try running all 10 channel outputs of a Redrum to their own Mixer channel. This gives us many more ways to augment the sound of each drum.

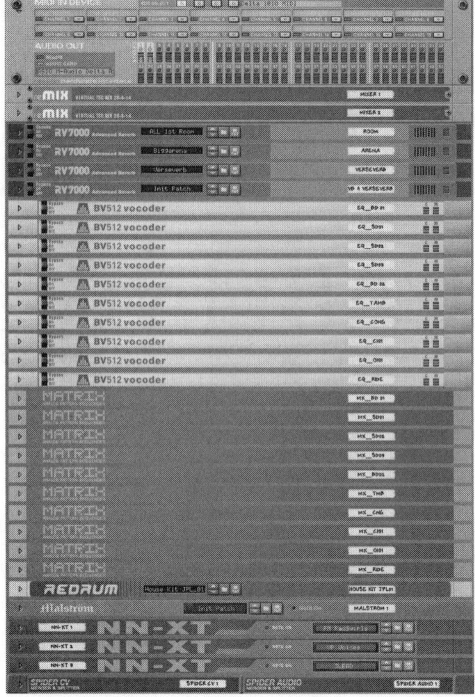

Figure 9.1 The Combinator turns a complex Rack setup like this...

Figure 9.2 ...into this compact setup.

Figure 9.3 Start with a basic 10-channel drum setup.

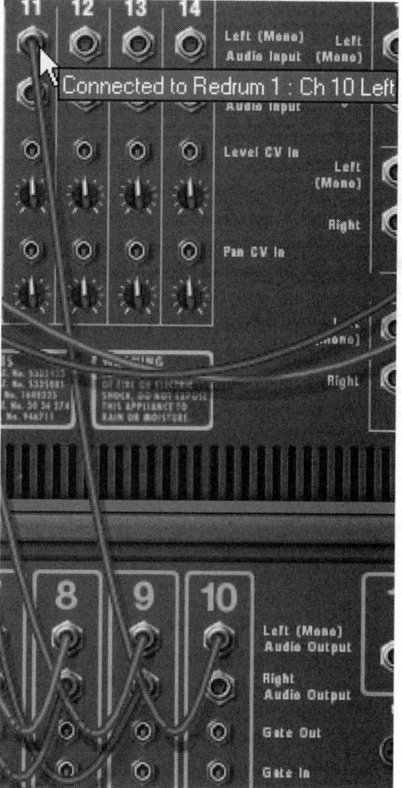

Figure 9.4 Disable auto-routing when connecting channels containing mono sounds.

To create a basic 10-output drum setup:

1. In an empty Rack, create a 14:2 Mixer.
2. Press Shift and create a Redrum.
   This will bypass auto-routing.
3. From the back panel, cable each drum channel audio output to a separate 14:2 Mixer channel (**Figure 9.3**).

✔ Tip

- By default Reason connects both the left and right drum channel outputs to each Mixer channel. If you're sure you want to use mono samples, you can press the Shift key while dragging the cables to disable auto-routing (**Figure 9.4**).

Now save yourself future setup time and embed this Rack configuration into a Combinator device that can be easily loaded as a patch. There is no downside to doing this, since you can still edit this setup however you want.

To combine a setup:

1. Holding the Shift key, select all the Rack devices you want to save as a Combi setup.
2. Select Edit > Combine or right-click and select Combine from the context menu (**Figure 9.5**).

   Your setup is turned into a Combinator (**Figure 9.6**).
3. Go to the front panel to view your setup as a Combinator (**Figure 9.7**).

   You may need to scroll up the Rack window to see the Combinator front panel.

Figure 9.5 Combine your devices.

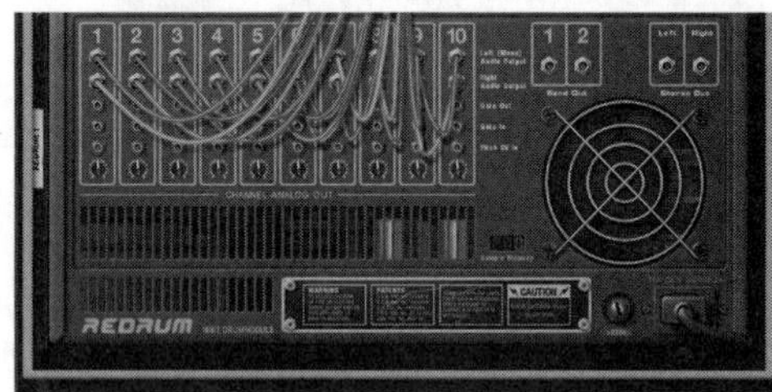

Figure 9.6 On the back panel you should see that a gray Combinator frame now encases your setup.

Figure 9.7 This is the front view of a combined 10-channel drum setup in a Combinator device.

INTRODUCING THE COMBINATOR

Figure 9.8 Use the Combinator Show/Hide Devices button to further expand or minimize.

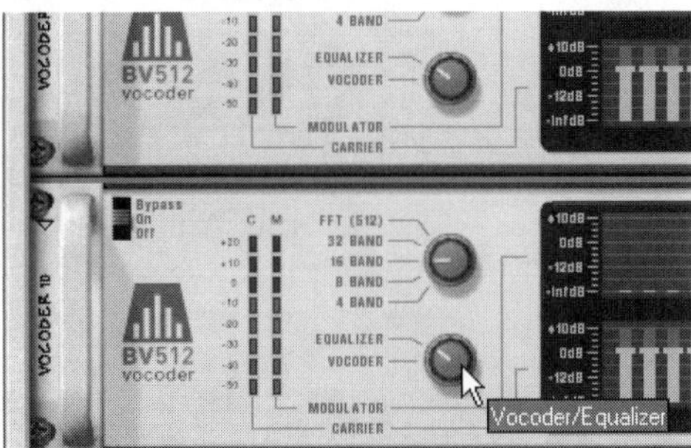

Figure 9.9 You won't hear any sound unless you set the BV512 units to Equalizer mode.

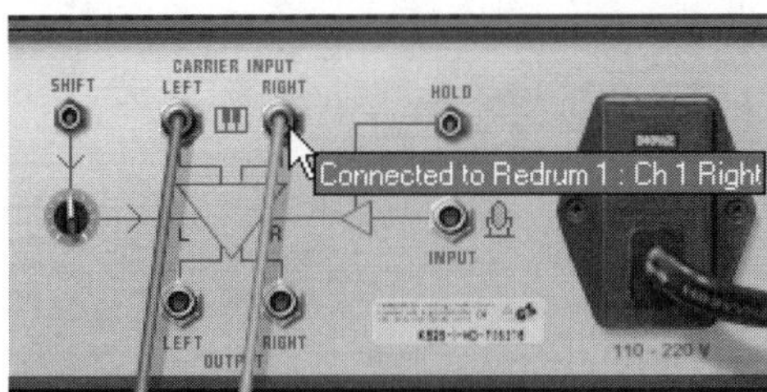

Figure 9.10 Switch the Redrum cables from Mixer channel inputs to BV512 inputs to set up the equalizers as insert effects.

In the next example, we'll continue with the 10-channel drum setup, and insert a BV512 equalizer for each separate drum channel. This will involve some repetitive tasks, but you'll only have to perform this procedure once—then you can save it as a new patch and use it from now on.

To add more devices to a combined setup:

1. If your Combinator is folded, unfold it and click the Show Devices button (**Figure 9.8**).
2. Click inside the Combinator device area.
3. Hold Shift and (one by one) create 10 BV512 devices.
4. From the front panel, set each BV512 unit to Equalizer (**Figure 9.9**).

   This may seem tedious, but at least you only have to do it once!
5. From the back panel, switch the Redrum's first Mixer channel input cables to the first BV512 inputs (**Figure 9.10**).

continues on next page

6. Cable the first BV512 outputs to the first Mixer channel inputs (**Figure 9.11**).
7. Minimize the finished BV512 so you don't have to scroll your Rack view as you continue.

   Reason will help you track your connections visually by color-coding the cables. Once they are passing through an effect, the cables will turn green.
8. Repeat steps 5 through 7 for each BV512, cabling all 10 drum outputs through a BV512 (**Figure 9.12**).

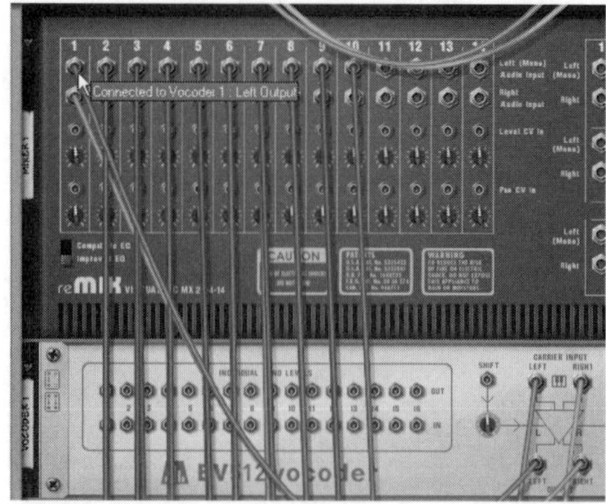

Figure 9.11 Cable the BV512 outputs to the Mixer channel inputs.

Figure 9.12 All 10 drum channels are now running through their own equalizers.

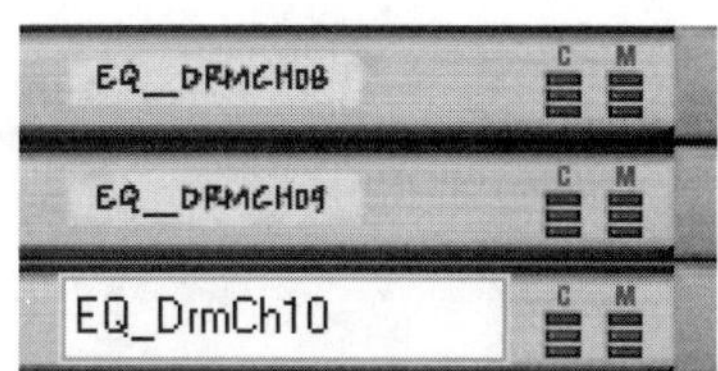

Figure 9.13 To avoid confusion, keep your device names short but descriptive.

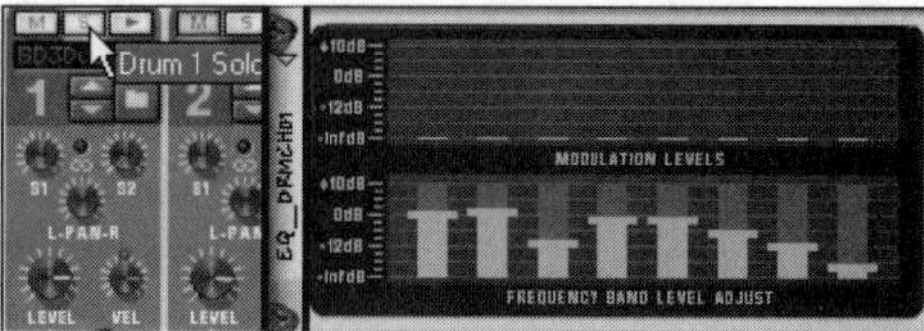

Figure 9.14 Solo each Redrum channel and adjust its EQ.

9. In the Rack, click the name of each BV512 device and give it a new, descriptive name (for example, "EQ_DrmCh01") so that you can tell what each device is connected to at a glance (**Figure 9.13**).

10. Now go to the Redrum, solo each drum in turn, and adjust its EQ until you like the sound of the kit (**Figure 9.14**).

✔ Tip

- When renaming devices, keep the names short so they won't truncate in Reason's pull-down menus.

Now is a good time to save or rename the patch.

To save a Combinator patch:

1. On the Combinator front panel, click the Save Patch button (**Figure 9.15**).
2. In the Save dialog box, select a destination for your patch (**Figure 9.16**).
3. Name your patch and click Save (**Figure 9.17**).

   Your new patch name should now appear in the Combinator display screen (**Figure 9.18**).

Figure 9.15 The Save Patch button saves the entire Combinator setup.

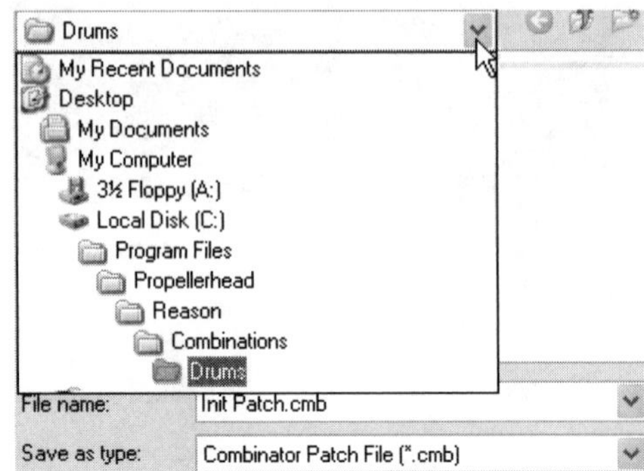

Figure 9.16 Save your custom patches where you can easily find them later.

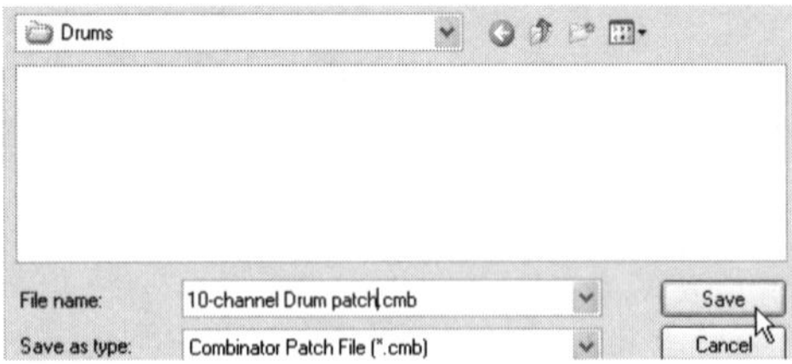

Figure 9.17 Name and save your patch.

Figure 9.18 The Combinator patch display should now show the new patch name.

Figure 9.19 Create multiple instruments and quickly set them up to play together using a Combinator.

Figure 9.20 Combined instruments can be controlled together from the Sequencer.

Creating Multi-Instruments

You can also use a Combinator to quickly set up multiple instruments to play together from one Sequencer track.

To quickly set up a multi-instrument track:

1. Create a Mixer, select it, and create the instruments you want to use together (**Figure 9.19**).
2. Select the Mixer and the instruments and use the Edit > Combine command to create a new Combinator device.
3. Go to the Combinator's Sequencer track and start writing your part (**Figure 9.20**).

You can also sequence a multi-instrument using a Matrix Pattern Sequencer.

To sequence a Combinator using a Matrix:

1. Create a Mixer, instruments, and any other devices you want to combine.
2. Select the devices you want to combine and use the Edit > Combine command.
3. With the Combinator selected, create a Matrix in your Rack.

   This will automatically cable the Matrix Gate CV outputs to the Combinator Gate CV inputs (**Figure 9.21**).
4. Write a pattern in the Matrix to sequence your instruments (**Figure 9.22**).

✔ Tip

- When the Combinator is being controlled by a Matrix, it will ignore note messages from Reason's main Sequencer.

Figure 9.21 Select the Combinator and create a Matrix.

Figure 9.22 Click Run on the Matrix to hear your full multi-instrument setup.

Figure 9.23 Click the Show Programmer button.

Figure 9.24 The Combinator programmer display gives you finer control over combined devices.

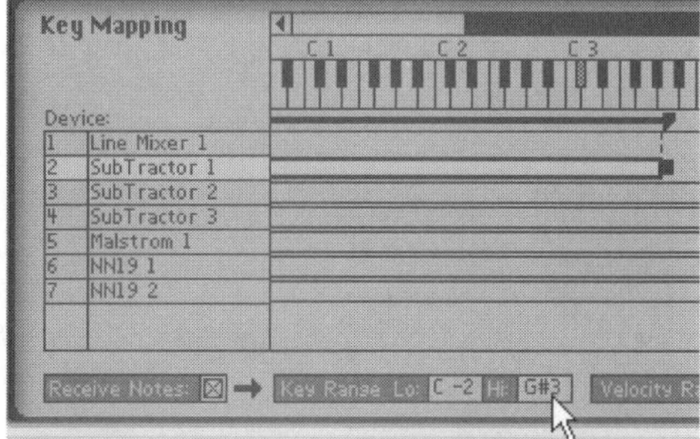

Figure 9.25 The High and Low Key Range controls allow you to limit which notes will trigger instruments.

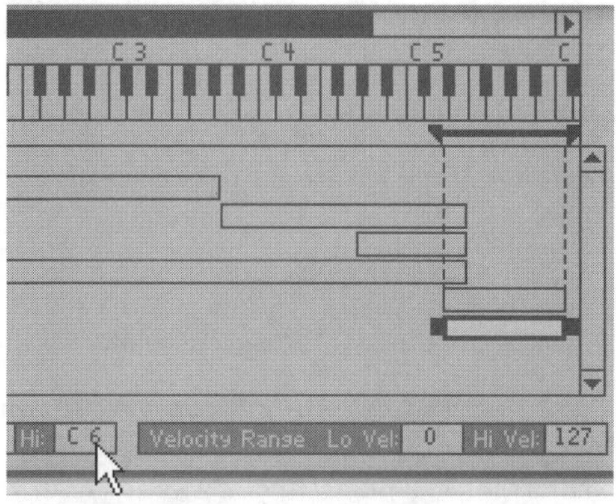

Figure 9.26 This multi-instrument keyboard setup shows the key range handles.

To spread multiple Combi instruments across the keyboard:

1. On the Combinator front panel click the Show Programmer button (**Figure 9.23**).

   This will bring up the Combinator program display (**Figure 9.24**).

2. Select the device you want to map in the left column, and click and drag the Key Range/Hi box to increase or decrease the upper end of the key range (**Figure 9.25**).

3. Drag the Key Range/Lo box to increase or decrease the low end of the key range.

   Tab handles similar to those on the NN-XT Remote Editor will appear, showing the new key range of the selected instrument (**Figure 9.26**).

4. Repeat steps 2 and 3 for the other instruments.

Modulation routing

The Combinator programmer's Modulation Routing section lets you specify how you want the front-panel knobs to affect the various instruments.

To set up modulation routing:

1. Select a device in the left column of the Combinator programmer window (**Figure 9.27**).
2. In the Modulation Routing section on the far right, select a knob in the Source column, then click the Target column next to it (**Figure 9.28**).
3. Choose a parameter to control from the pop-up list (**Figure 9.29**).
4. Set the Min and Max values for the knob (**Figure 9.30**).

   The Rotary knobs can select any value within their set range. The Min setting is when the knob is turned hard left, the Max is when the knob is turned hard right (**Figure 9.31**).

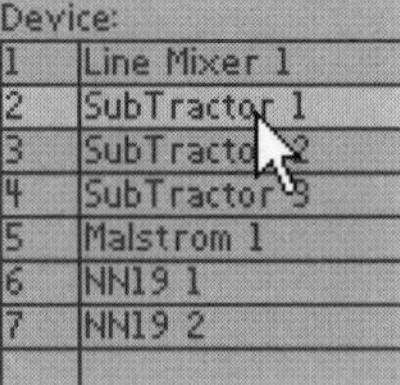

Figure 9.27 Select a device in the Combinator programmer window.

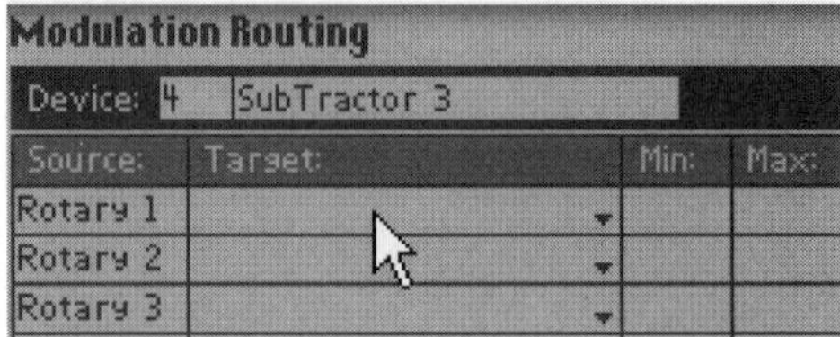

Figure 9.28 Select a Combinator Rotary knob to control the device.

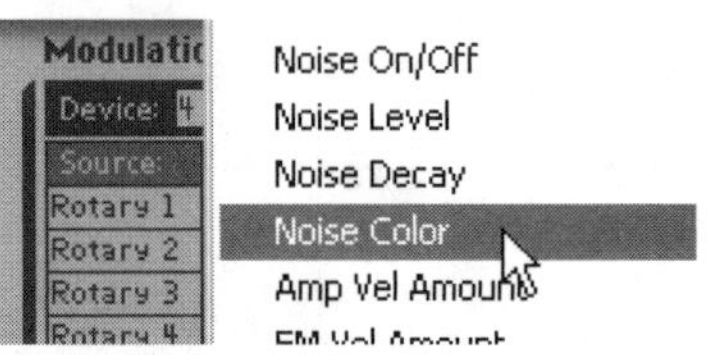

Figure 9.29 Select a Target parameter for the knob.

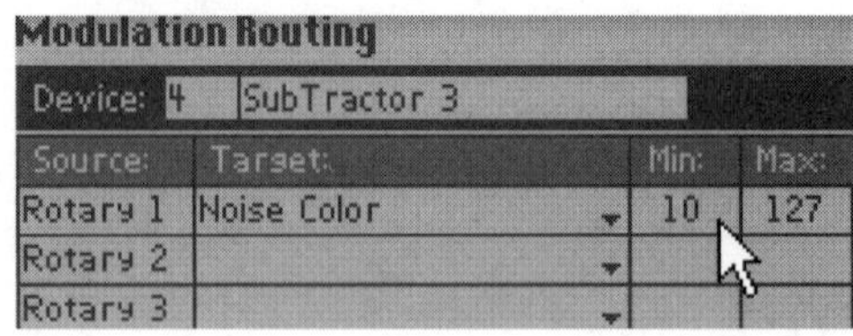

Figure 9.30 Set the Min and Max range of the knob.

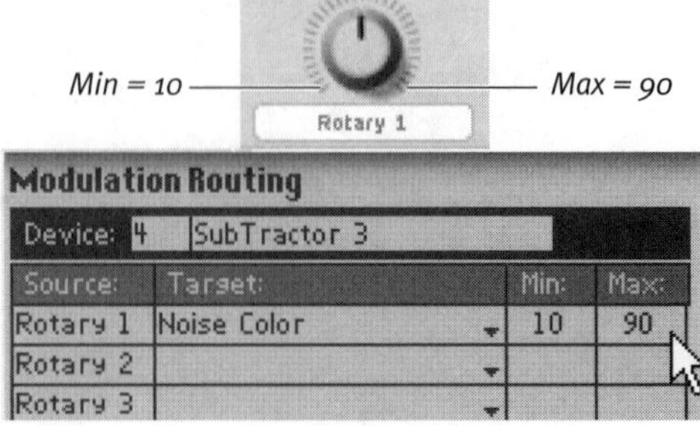

Figure 9.31 The range of a Rotary knob goes from hard left to hard right. The range for buttons is simply On/Off.

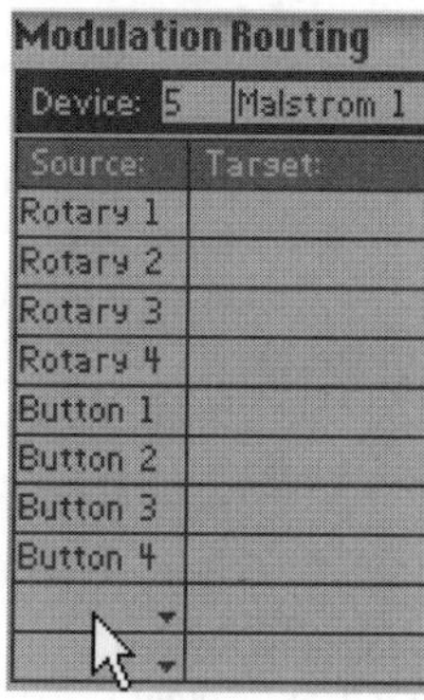

Figure 9.32 The Modulation Routing section gives you two blank spaces to use.

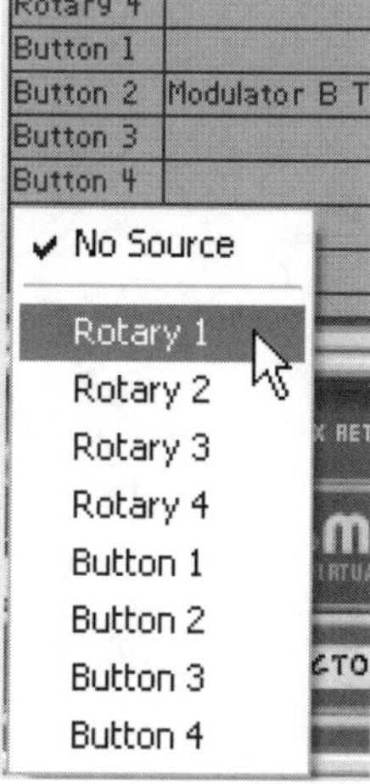

Figure 9.33 Click in the Source column to select a Rotary knob or Button.

Modulation Routing

Device: 5 Malstrom 1

Source:	Target:	Min:	Max:
Rotary 1	Oscillator B Index	0	127
Rotary 2			
Rotary 3			
Rotary 4			
Button 1			
Button 2	Oscillator A On/Off	0	1
Button 3			
Button 4			
Button 2	Filter B On/Off	0	1
Rotary 1	Oscillator A Index	0	127

Figure 9.34 Using the blank spaces, you can assign more than one parameter to a single Rotary knob or Button.

5. In the Source column, select a button to control, and choose a Target parameter from the pop-up list.

   The Min and Max values for buttons toggle between On and Off.

6. You can assign two additional parameters using the blank Source rows at the bottom of the Modulation Routing section (**Figure 9.32**). Just click the blank Source field and choose a knob or button from the pop-up list (**Figure 9.33**), then select a Target parameter for each.

   This feature allows you to assign a button to more than one parameter on a single device (**Figure 9.34**).

7. Repeat steps 1 through 6 for each device you wish to control using the Combinator front panel.

continues on next page

✔ Tips

- You can set knobs to move a parameter in any direction you want. For instance, you can use a Rotary knob to crossfade between two Mixer channels by setting one channel to a Min/Max of 0/127 and another channel to a Min/Max of 127/0 for the same knob.
- Like other Reason parameters, the Combinator knobs and buttons can be automated in the Combinator Sequencer track Controller lane (**Figure 9.35**).

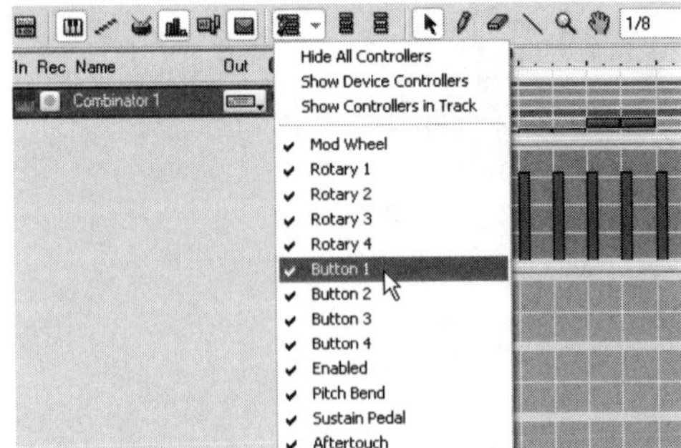

Figure 9.35 Controller lane automation works the same in Combinator tracks as it does for other instruments.

Figure 9.36 Connect an RV7000 as an insert effect for Channel 1 of the Redrum.

Using Gated Reverb

Gates help manage reverb so that you can get a "big" drum sound, but the reverb decays don't hang around in the background of your mix muddying things up.

This strategy demands one reverb per drum, set up as an insert effect. This arrangement allows you to tune each reverb for a particular drum sound and volume.

Let's create a Combinator patch to handle this setup and save it so you can quickly load it when you need it.

To set up reverb for a drum channel:

1. Create a 14:2 Mixer.
2. Hold Shift and create a Redrum, then load a standard kit like the Factory Sound Bank's `Groovemasters Rock Kit 1` patch.
3. Hold Shift and create an RV7000 reverb.
4. Cable the Channel 1 audio outputs from the Redrum to the RV7000 audio inputs, and the RV7000 outputs to an open Mixer channel (**Figure 9.36**).

   This adds a reverb insert effect for drum Channel 1.

First we'll adjust the reverb settings, tightening up late reflection and predelay.

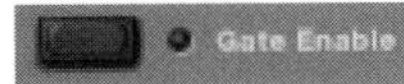

Figure 9.37 Click the RV7000 Gate Enable button.

To tighten reverb before gating:

1. If the RV7000 Gate Enable light is on, click the Gate Enable button to disable it while we adjust the reverb (**Figure 9.37**).
2. Open the RV7K Remote Programmer, set the Edit Mode switch to Reverb, and select the Room algorithm.
3. Set the ER–>Late parameter to 0%.

   This concentrates the reflections nearer the source sound (**Figure 9.38**).

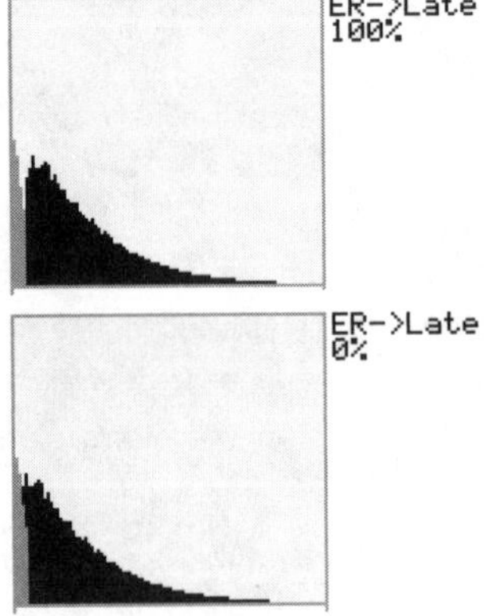

Figure 9.38 Setting the ER–>Late parameter to 0% concentrates more reflections at the beginning stage.

4. Set the ER level. Early reflections carry a brighter "imprint" of the source sound, but are masked when the dry signal is louder.

   For "wet" reverbs, an ER level above 0.0 dB adds a crisp reverb attack (**Figure 9.39**).

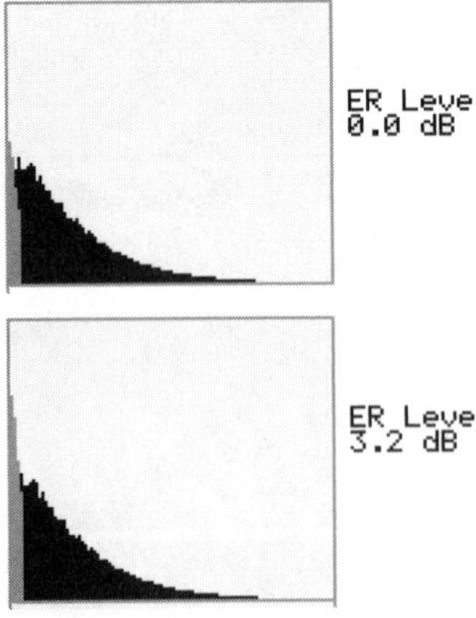

Figure 9.39 Set the early reflection level to 3.2 dB.

5. Set the Predelay parameter to 0 ms.

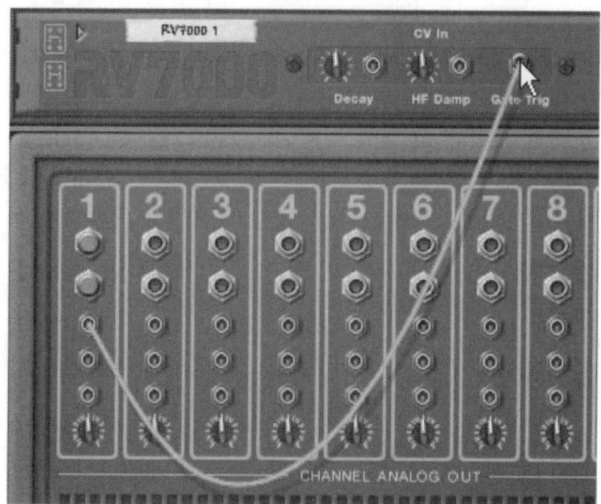

Figure 9.40 Connect a drum Gate CV output to the Gate Trig CV input of an RV7000.

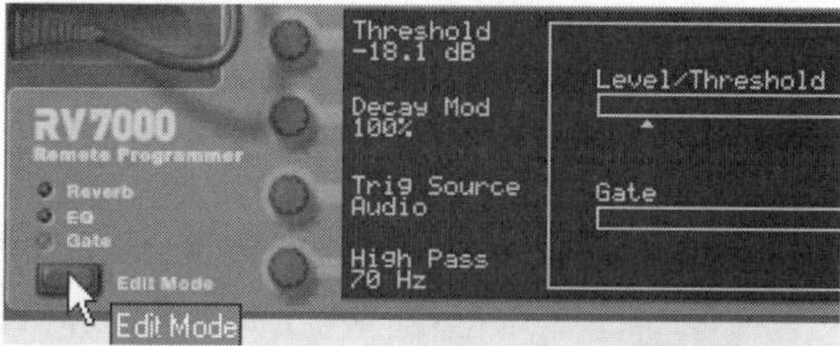

Figure 9.41 Set the Remote Programmer to Gate mode.

Figure 9.42 Drag-copy a Rack device.

The fastest way to set up a gate is to use the Gate Out CV signal from the drum channel. CV gate signals are on/off in type, and the length is determined by note duration.

To use a MIDI/CV triggered gate:

1. From the back panel, connect the Redrum Channel 1 Gate CV output to the Gate Trig CV input on the RV7000 (**Figure 9.40**).
2. On the Redrum, select a drum channel, program some notes on the Redrum Sequencer track, and press play.
3. Click the Gate Enable button on the RV7K front panel.
4. Open the RV7K Remote Programmer and set the Edit Mode to Gate (**Figure 9.41**).
5. To trigger reverb using the CV gate signal, turn the Trig Source knob to MIDI/CV.

   On MIDI/CV setting, all drum notes will trigger the reverb and the Threshold and Hold parameters have no effect.
6. Set the Release knob to time how fast the gate closes (the range is 100–4,110 ms).

With basic settings taken care of, you can quickly duplicate the RV7K for the other drums.

To drag-drop duplicate:

1. While pressing Ctrl (Win)/Cmd (Mac), grab the left margin of the RV7000 front panel and drag up or down.

   As you drag, a box with a (+) sign will appear below your cursor and a transparent image of the selected device will follow your cursor as it moves (**Figure 9.42**).

continues on next page

2. When a red Rack destination bar appears, release the mouse.

   You should see a duplicate RVK at the new location. This device will have the same settings as the one you copied, regardless of whether you saved the original as a patch.

3. Connect the audio outputs from the drum on Channel 2 to the inputs of the new reverb and the audio outputs from the reverb to the next open Mixer channel.

4. Connect the Gate CV output from the drum on Channel 2 to the Gate Trig CV input of the RV7K.

   You don't have to scroll up and down the Rack to do this—sometimes it's faster to click a cable output and select a destination from the pop-up list (**Figure 9.43**).

5. Repeat steps 1 through 4 for each drum channel you want to gate (**Figure 9.44**).

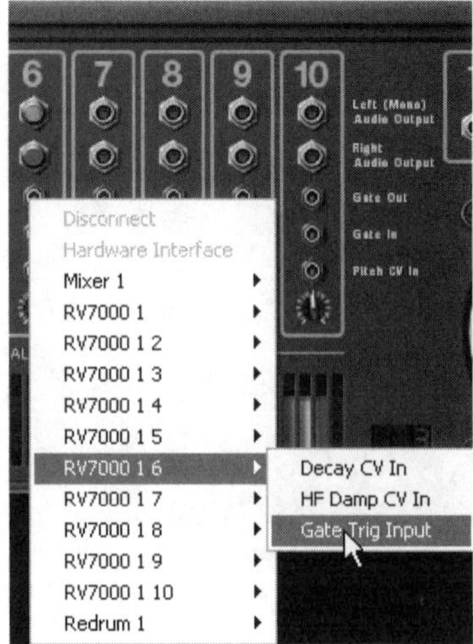

Figure 9.43 The cable pop-up list saves you scrolling up and down extensive Rack setups.

Figure 9.44 This 10-channel gated reverb setup is now complete.

Figure 9.45 Change the Edit mode to Gate.

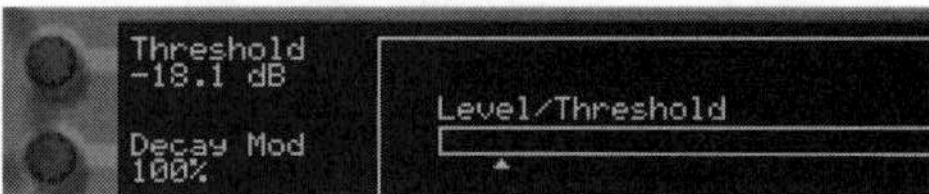

Figure 9.46 With Trig Source set to Audio, you can tune the threshold so that only loud notes trigger the gate.

Setting up audio-triggered gates

MIDI/CV mode perfectly gates all drum notes played on a channel. However, if you want control over the gate timing and envelope, use the RV7000 Audio gate trigger mode instead.

To set an audio-triggered gate:

1. On the RV7000, set the Edit Mode to Gate (**Figure 9.45**).
2. In the Remote Programmer set the Trig Source knob to Audio.
3. Play your Redrum pattern and set the Threshold knob to the volume level at which the audio signal will trigger the gate (**Figure 9.46**).

   In Audio mode it is possible to tune the gate threshold so that softer notes don't trigger it but louder ones do.
4. Adjust Decay Mod, which mutes residual reverb across repeated notes by speeding up the reverb decay while the gate is closed (100% is fastest).

continues on next page

5. Use the Attack knob to set how long the gate takes to open after it is triggered.

   Note that with high Decay Mod settings, attack times longer than note lengths will mute the reverb.

6. Use the Hold knob to set how quickly the gate closes again after the attack.

   Since the gate follows the volume curve of the incoming sound (like the envelope follower on the Scream 4), louder incoming sounds push the gate higher, so it takes longer to drop down again.

7. Use the High Pass knob to fine-tune gate timings on very fast gates. This setting filters trigger response to low frequencies: Anything below the displayed frequency won't trigger the gate.

   Though it may sound like a tone control, it's really a timing effect. Since high frequencies happen faster, an HF-calibrated gate will "shut down" before low frequencies develop. At high settings the result is a faster, brighter-sounding reverb.

8. Set the release the same way you would in MIDI/CV trigger mode.

✔ Tip

- When attack, hold, and release are slow, the High Pass setting has little or no effect.

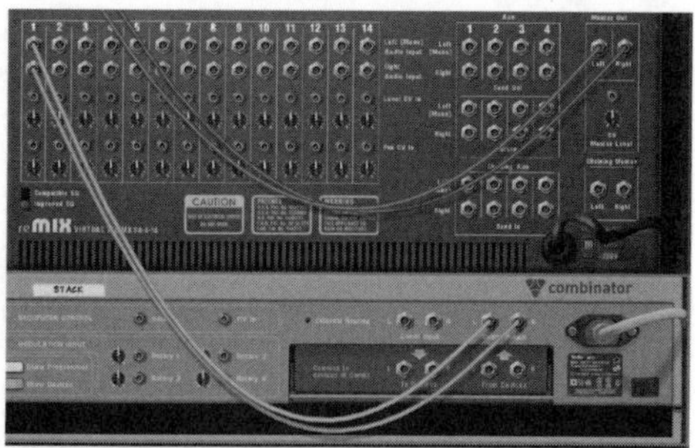

Figure 9.47 Auto-route the outputs of the new Combinator into an open Mixer channel.

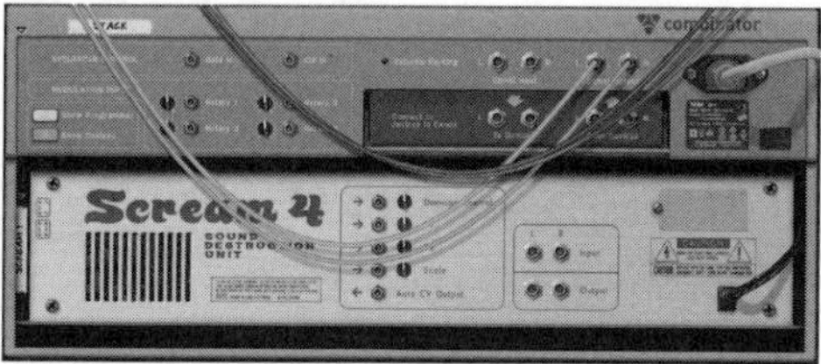

Figure 9.48 Create a Scream 4 inside the Combinator.

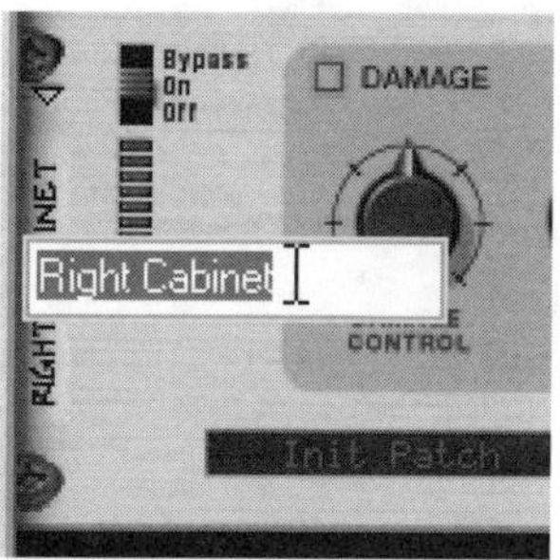

Figure 9.49 Label the Scream 4 devices according to their stage in the sound process.

Chaining Effects

Using effects together can yield combinations of effects that you come back to again and again.

Stereo amplifier stack

Here's a chain of effects that simulates a large stage amplifier for an instrument of your choice.

It uses two Scream 4 Damage sections for amplification and two Scream 4 Body sections to simulate left and right speaker cabinets.

To cable the effects:

1. With a Mixer selected, create a Combinator and label it "Stack."

   This will automatically route the outputs of the Combinator into an open Mixer channel (**Figure 9.47**).

2. Click in the Combinator device area, hold Shift and create a Scream 4 (**Figure 9.48**).

3. Hold Ctrl (Win)/Cmd (Mac) and drag-copy three more Scream 4s in the Combinator device area.

4. Label the Scream 4 units "Pre-Amp," "Main Amp," "Left Cabinet," and "Right Cabinet" (**Figure 9.49**).

continues on next page

5. From the back panel, cable the left and right Combinator To Devices audio outputs to the left and right audio inputs of the Scream 4 Pre-Amp (**Figure 9.50**).
6. Run the Scream 4 Pre-Amp audio outputs to the Scream 4 Main Amp audio inputs (**Figure 9.51**).
7. Hold Shift and run the Scream 4 Main Amp left audio output to the Scream 4 Left Cabinet left audio input (**Figure 9.52**).
8. Hold Shift and run the Scream 4 Main Amp right output to the Scream 4 Right Cabinet left audio input (**Figure 9.53**).
9. Cable the Scream 4 Left Cabinet left audio output to the Combinator From Devices left audio input and the Scream 4 Right Cabinet left audio output to the Combinator From Devices right audio input (**Figure 9.54**).
10. Click the Combinator Save Patch button and save your setup as `Amp Stack`.

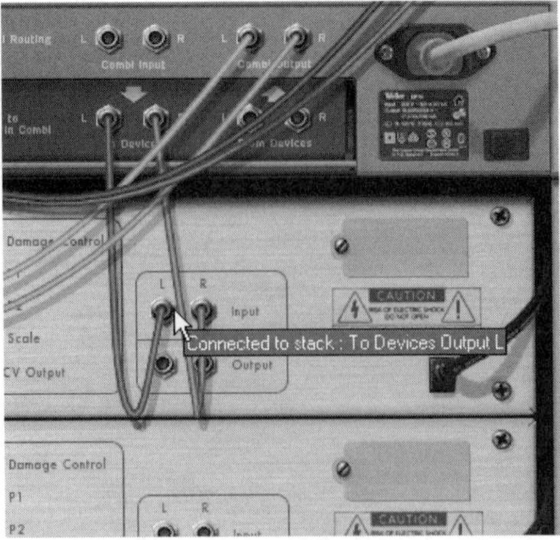

Figure 9.50 Create a basic audio path in the Combinator.

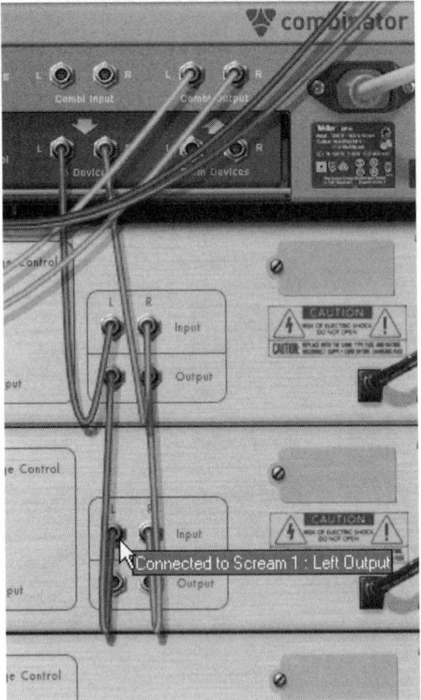

Figure 9.51 Chain the distortion stages in stereo.

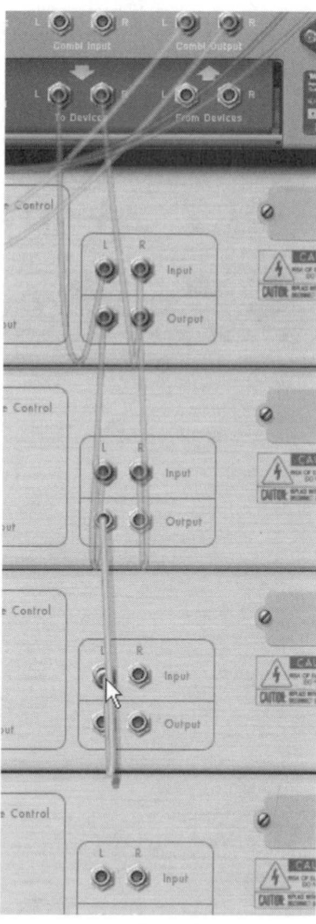

Figure 9.52 Split the left signal for the left cabinet body.

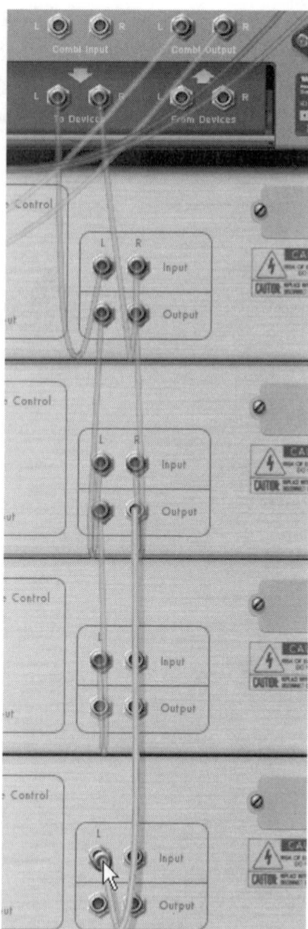

Figure 9.53 Split the right signal for the right cabinet body.

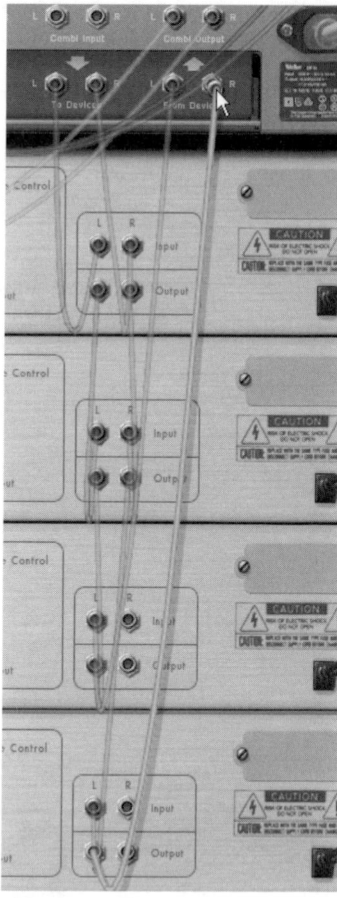

Figure 9.54 Complete the effects chain by returning the audio signal back to the Combinator.

Now that your amp stack is set up, you can run any instrument through it.

To connect an instrument:

1. With your Combinator Amp Stack patch loaded, hold Shift and create the instrument you want to amplify.
2. Plug the instrument's audio outputs into the Combinator External Routing Combi input jacks (**Figure 9.55**).

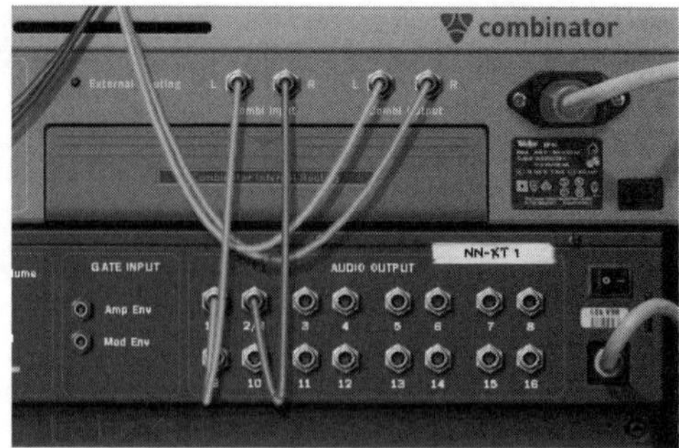

Figure 9.55 Run an external instrument into the Combinator.

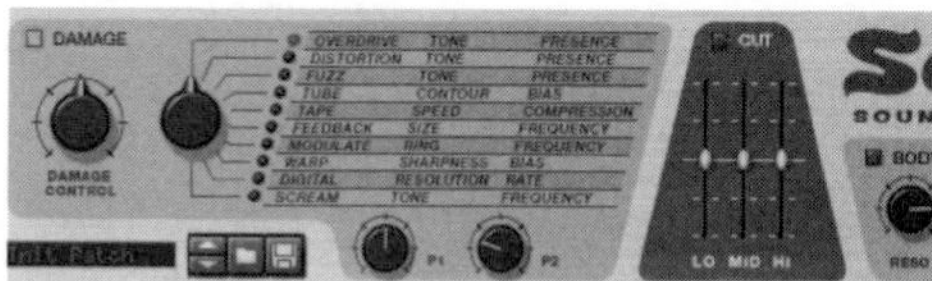

Figure 9.56 Disable the Cut and Body sections for the distortion stage, leaving Damage only.

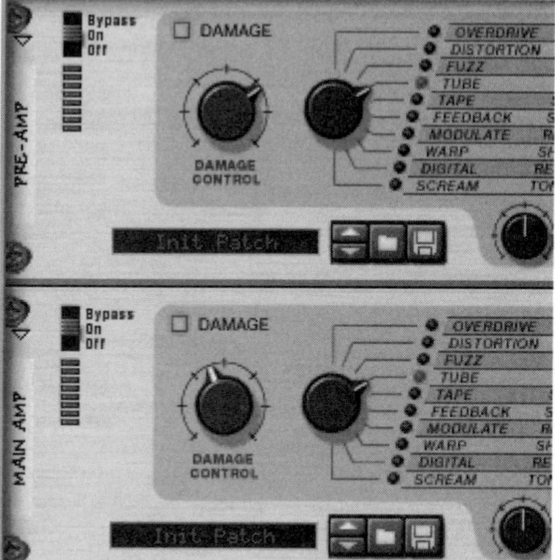

Figure 9.57 Choose an analog damage type for the Main Amp and Pre-Amp.

Figure 9.58 Choose different cabinets for the left and right sides.

To configure the settings:

1. Enable the Damage section of the Pre-Amp and Main Amp Screams and make sure that the Cut and Body sections are disabled (**Figure 9.56**).
2. Choose analog damage types like Overdrive, Distortion, or Tube for the Pre-Amp and Main Amp distortions (**Figure 9.57**).
3. Set the Pre-Amp Damage Control at about 75 percent and the Master knob around halfway. Otherwise, unintended signal level distortion could carry over into the Main Amp stage.
4. Set the Main Amp Damage Control knob slightly lower than the Pre-Amp stage and use the P1 and P2 parameter knobs as your primary tone controls.
5. Enable the Left Cabinet and Right Cabinet Body sections and disable the Damage and Cut sections for both.
6. Choose a small resonant body type (A or B) for the Left Cabinet Scream and a large resonant body type (D or E) for the Right Cabinet Scream (**Figure 9.58**).

✔ Tip

- Though you can adjust the Auto, Scale, and Reso knobs on the Left and Right Cabinet effects for additional tonal effects, they aren't necessary for straight amplifier simulation.

10 Arranging and Mixing

When you are reasonably satisfied that you have all the instruments and parts you need to finish your song, it's probably a good time to step back and listen to what you've created so far. Take a moment to ask yourself if you like the way your song is put together and the way it progresses from beginning to end.

When you start thinking about how you want all your parts to fit together, it's time to start arranging—making decisions and reconciling what you set out to do with where your song seems to be going.

Once your song is arranged, you can begin mixing—adjusting parameters of each part so that they better complement one another. Then you will master your final stereo mix and burn your polished song to a CD or save it as an audio file.

Grouping Sections

By now you may have just a few tracks or many. You may have a simple setup or lots of controller tracks and pattern switching going on. Either way, this is a good time to start organizing your Sequencer tracks by grouping them into chunks that can be moved around and duplicated in the Arrange window.

Grouping lets you take segments of a track and turn them into self-contained objects that can be easily moved and edited. It also minimizes the risk of leaving "orphaned" notes and controller data behind when you move sections from one place to another.

To group a section of a track:

1. In your Sequencer, choose the track and section you want to group together and set your grid to the best value to select it.

   When working with large sections or tracks with controller or pattern data, use the Arrange window—Reason will then automatically select all controller data when you make a selection.

2. Drag-select the track section or notes you want to group using the arrow tool (**Figure 10.1**).

3. Use the Edit > Group command to create a new group.

   Your grouped data will now appear as a colored box in the Arrange window (**Figure 10.2**).

4. You can quickly check your group in Edit mode by double-clicking it in the Arrange window.

   Do this before moving or editing your group, just in case you missed controller or pattern data crossing from one section to the next. That way, you know the group is "safe," or self-contained (**Figure 10.3**).

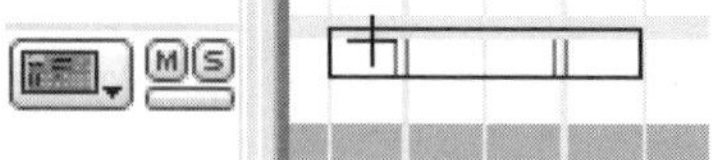

Figure 10.1 Even though the blue Controller lane is not being selected, all controller data are gathered into the group anyway.

Figure 10.2 A grouped section of a track shows up as a colored box.

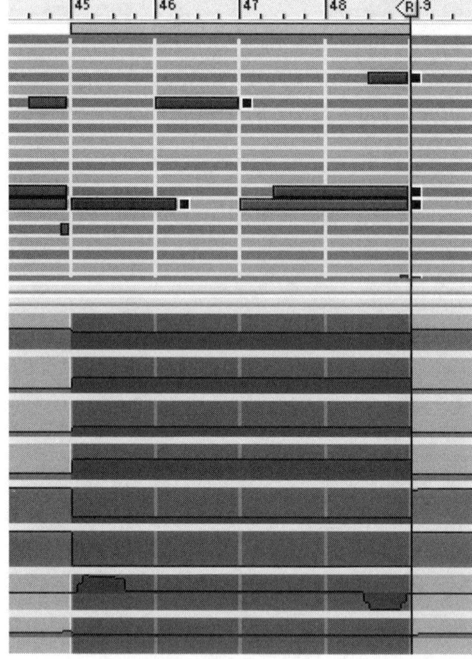

Figure 10.3 Though this track has a lot of controller data, the group is self-contained because the controller changes don't cross the measure boundaries.

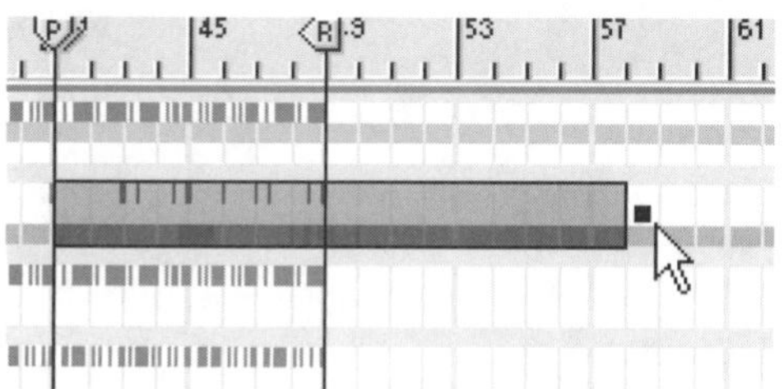

Figure 10.4 Groups display length handles when selected.

Editing Groups

Groups can be drag-copied, moved, and length-adjusted in the Arrange window.

To move a group:

1. Click any group box in the Arrange window to select it.
2. Drag the selected box to a new location.

✔ Tip

- By default, the Arrange window is conveniently set to a one-bar grid value. If you want finer control, change the grid value before moving your group.

To duplicate a group:

1. Select the group(s) you wish to duplicate.
2. Hold Ctrl (Win)/Cmd (Mac) and drag the group to a new location.

   The original group will remain where it was, and a new group will be copied to the new location.

To lengthen or shorten a group:

1. Select the group(s) you wish to edit.

   The selected group will darken and a length handle will appear to the right of the group (**Figure 10.4**).
2. Click and hold the mouse on the length handle and drag left to shorten the group and right to lengthen it.

   Lengthening and shortening a group has no effect on the MIDI data inside or outside the group; it merely changes what's included in the group.

To ungroup:

1. Select the group(s) you wish to edit.
2. Choose the Edit > Ungroup command.
   MIDI data inside and outside the group are not affected by the Ungroup function.

Editing multiple groups

Selecting, moving, or editing multiple groups simultaneously works best if your group boundaries follow your song sections.

You may find that a simple arrangement doesn't require much more than duplicating song sections to fill out a predetermined song length.

To move multiple groups:

1. Shift-select the groups you want to move.
2. Click and drag the groups to a new location and release the mouse.

✔ Tip

- You can also duplicate and adjust the length of multiple groups after Shift-selecting them.

Mixing

When you feel your arrangement is solid, the next step is to add Sequencer tracks to control your Mixers.

The goal of mixing may seem simple enough: Make your music sound as good as possible in the maximum number of playback situations. But mixing is far from simple, and there is no rulebook for certain success.

Balancing equalization, volume, panning position, and the amount and type of effects for one track can be a juggling act in itself, but shaping these elements so that a multi-track project forms a cohesive whole is an art that requires great ears, skill, experience, and intuition.

Though this chapter won't make you an expert mixer, it will give you some technical and organizational methods to start you on your way.

Keep in Mind While Mixing

- Listen carefully and critically.
- Know the quirks of your studio and address them if necessary.
- Try to realistically assess the potential and weakness of the material.
- Stay organized to manage many tracks.
- Keep maximum control with the fewest faders.
- Be inquisitive so you can identify problems and ask the right questions.
- Be flexible and imaginative when solving problems.
- Have patience! Leave plenty of time for your mixing.
- Be thorough. Test your mix on many different playback systems and be prepared to make changes.

Chaining Mixers in Parallel

The first stage of mixing is to set up the Mixers you'll need for the project so that you can manage your instruments and effects tracks.

When you fill up a Mixer, the quickest way to add another instrument is to create a second Mixer and join it to the first by *chaining* inputs.

Chained Mixers use the existing Mixer's auxiliary channels and master outputs, so chaining is just like adding more channels to your mixing board. Better still, you can chain together as many Mixers as you want!

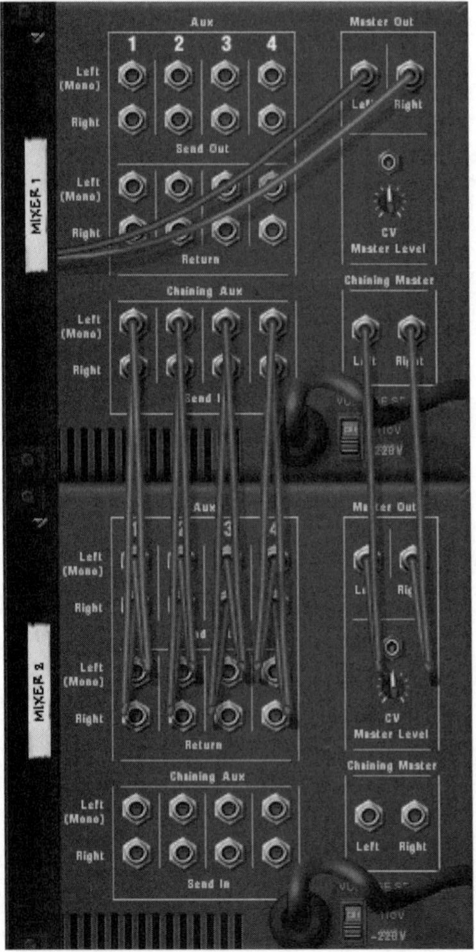

Figure 10.5 The Aux and Master chaining outputs allow one Mixer to extend the channels of another.

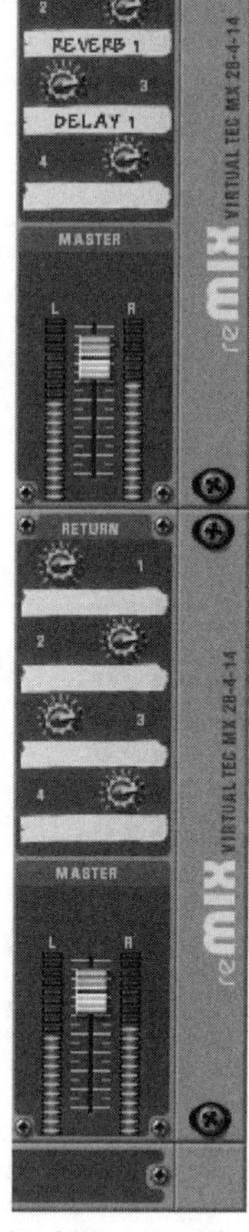

Figure 10.6 A chained Mixer uses the auxiliary channels of the Mixer it is connected to.

To chain a Mixer:

1. Select the Mixer you want to expand and use the Create > Mixer 14:2 or Create > Line Mixer 6:2 command.

   Reason will automatically connect the aux send and master outputs of the new Mixer to the auxiliary and master chaining inputs of the existing one (**Figure 10.5**). Note that the Aux return knobs on a chained Mixer are bypassed and have no effect (**Figure 10.6**).

2. Select the new Mixer and create the next instrument to continue writing tracks.

3. Turn up the auxiliary send knob on your new instrument and hear the signal in the effects mix in the first Mixer.

Submixing

The second task of mixing is to keep track of the various instruments, effects, and Mixer channels you have created. As your parallel setup expands, controlling it will require more and more separate adjustments. If you are using three or more chained Mixers and are still adding tracks, you should consider *submixing* instead.

Submixing means merging any number of channels into a single channel somewhere else. It allows you to handle relative balance on one Mixer and then have a second Mixer channel adjust the group. It also enables you to use more master effects and balance more tracks with fewer controls.

You can turn any Mixer into a submix by routing its audio outputs to a single channel on another Mixer (**Figure 10.7**). Chained Mixers function the same way (**Figure 10.8**).

To set up a master Mixer:

1. Hold down the Shift key and create a new Mixer or drag-copy your existing one.
2. Label the new Mixer `Master`.
3. Go to the back panel and re-cable the master outputs of the old Mixer to a channel input of the new one.
4. Cable the master outputs of the master Mixer to your hardware interface.

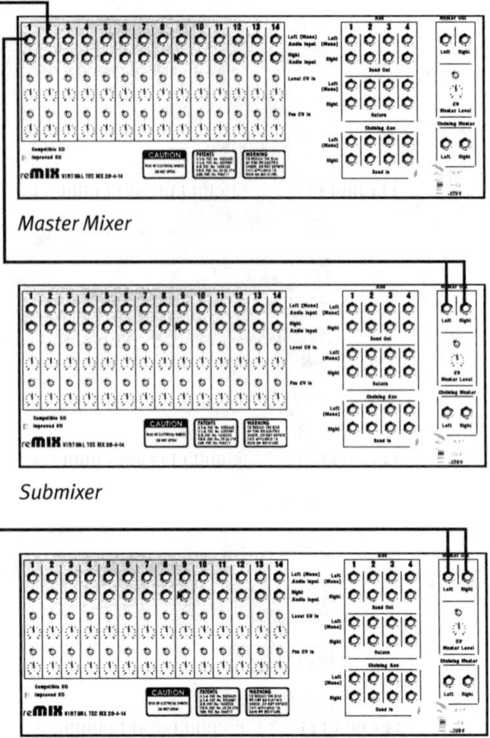

Figure 10.7 Submixing is a mixing hierarchy that allows you to adjust individual channels and also have master control over a project.

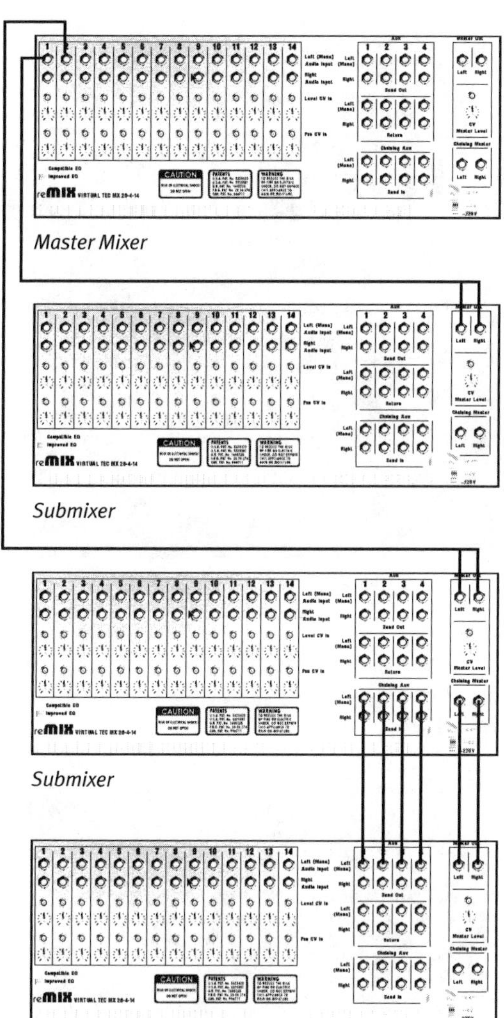

Figure 10.8 You can submix a Mixer chain.

Organizing your submix

Planning in advance what instruments should share a Mixer can save you time. Here are some guidelines for what to submix.

Multi-output devices: Dedicating an entire Mixer to one instrument is common when using all the outputs of a Redrum or NN-XT sampler.

Instruments sharing master effects: You may want to submix an entire Mixer chain if all the instruments use the same master effects.

Ensembles/parts at the same song location: You may choose to submix instrument ensembles or parts in a particular section of the song.

Similar volume changes: Any time you find yourself adjusting the volume of particular tracks together, consider submixing them so you can do it with one fader.

Like instruments: You may want to group all rhythm instruments together, for example Redrums, Dr. Rex Loop Players, and percussion samplers.

Submixing with a Combinator

Nesting a complex setup away into one tidy, "spaghetti-free" space in your Rack is more than just a convenience for big projects.

When even a well-organized submix strategy becomes slow to navigate, converting submixes to Combinator patches will add another layer of organization to your project.

To combine a submix:

1. Select all the instruments, Mixers, and effects in a particular submix and choose Edit > Combine (**Figure 10.9**).

   The Combinator will not change the submix inputs and outputs.

2. Assign the rotary knobs and buttons to device parameters (**Figure 10.10**).
3. Name the Combinator device as you want it to appear in the master Mixer.
4. Save the patch, and from now on you can load this setup into any song.

Figure 10.9 This Combinator is holding an orchestral submix.

Figure 10.10 In this Combinator, rotary knobs are assigned to orchestral instrument group channels.

Figure 10.11 Create a Mixer inside a Combinator if you know your project will be complicated.

If you know you're going to be scoring a large project with lots of instruments, you can organize your instruments into combinations from the start.

To start a project inside a Combinator:

1. In an empty Rack, create a 6:2 or 14:2 Mixer to use as your master Mixer.
2. With your Mixer selected, create a new Combinator.

   Reason will connect the Combinator to the master Mixer automatically.
3. Click in the Combinator device area and create another Mixer to use for the instruments that you'll create inside the Combinator (**Figure 10.11**).
4. Start creating instruments and writing your tracks.

Setting Signal Levels

Once your project is organized enough to manage, it's time to set your levels. Mixing means raising some levels and lowering others. Because of this, set your Mixer channels to unity gain (see sidebar, "Unity Gain"), or 100, before you start mixing.

If your song's volume is going to increase down the line, or you are using a lot of distortion effects in your tracks, you might even want to set your initial levels lower still, to about 75–80.

Maintaining headroom

This unused gain is sometimes referred to as *headroom*, and it is both a protection measure and a tool for you as you mix your music.

Headroom makes sudden sound spikes less likely to distort and leaves space to bring a solo instrument to the forefront when you want to.

To add headroom to a Mixer's settings:

1. First set your Mixer's master faders to unity gain by Ctrl-clicking (Win)/Cmd-clicking (Mac) the fader.

   This is especially important for chained Mixers, because the master outputs of a chained Mixer control the master levels for Mixers down the chain.

2. Choose how much headroom you think you need for your song, and set your Mixer's channel faders at unity gain or below it.
3. Use the same settings for all submixes and Mixer chains in your setup.

Unity Gain

Reason's Mixers have a range from 0 to 127. When a fader is set at 100, it is said to be at *unity gain*, meaning it isn't boosting or lowering a signal level.

Use fader values below or at unity gain unless you need to alter a signal's level in some way. You will preserve your chosen amount of headroom, keep your mixing levels from varying too much, and make it so you only have to look at automated data when making an adjustment or fixing a level that's gotten too high.

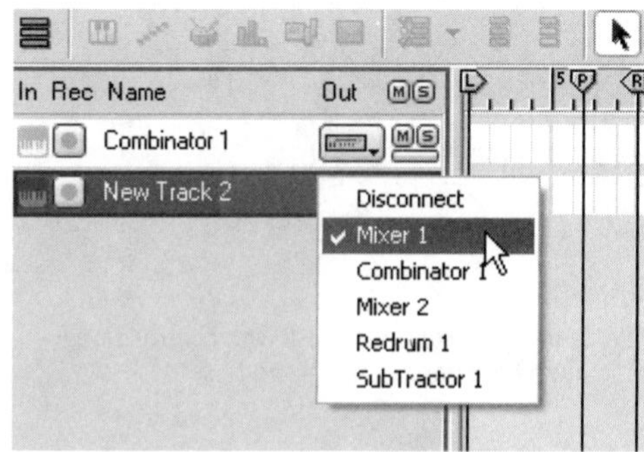

Figure 10.12 Set up a Sequencer track to record Mixer movements.

Figure 10.13 Record-enable a Mixer track.

Automating a Mix

Now that you've set your initial levels, it's finally time to start mixing.

All of Reason's Mixer controls can be recorded or automated just like Reason's instruments. In cases where you want to make just a few adjustments, the easiest method is to set up a single Sequencer track to record all your Mixer movements.

To set up your Sequencer to record mix moves:

1. In the Sequencer, select Edit > Create Sequencer Track and assign the new track to the Mixer device you want to control (**Figure 10.12**).
2. Record-enable the track by clicking the keyboard icon in the device In column.

   A red circle will appear next to the icon indicating that the Mixer track is ready to record (**Figure 10.13**).
3. If you want to record knob and fader movements from an external keyboard or control surface, you will also need to select the Mixer on Reason's hardware interface on the appropriate MIDI channel.

To start recording a mix:

1. Click record to enter Record mode.
2. Click play to record and begin moving the controls.

   In Arrange view, a blue strip will appear in the track, indicating that controller information is now being recorded. Dark blue patches indicate controller data (**Figure 10.14**).
3. When you are done, press stop.
4. Open the Mixer track in Edit mode to see the controller data (**Figure 10.15**).

   In the Rack, the Mixer front-panel controls with automation data will be outlined in green (**Figure 10.16**).

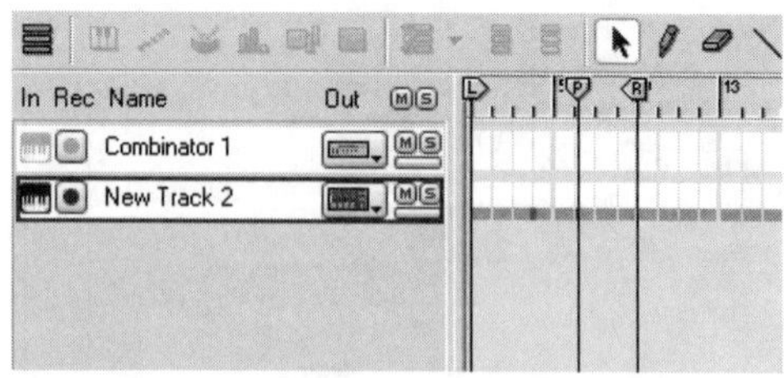

Figure 10.14 A Sequencer track with control data displays a blue bar in Arrange mode.

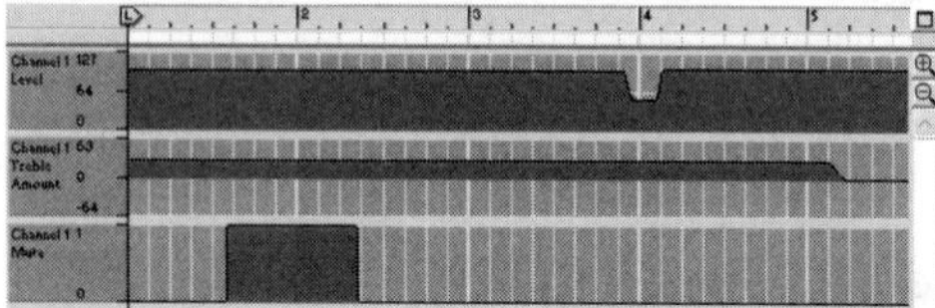

Figure 10.15 Mixer control information recorded from the Rack can be fine-tuned in Sequencer Edit mode.

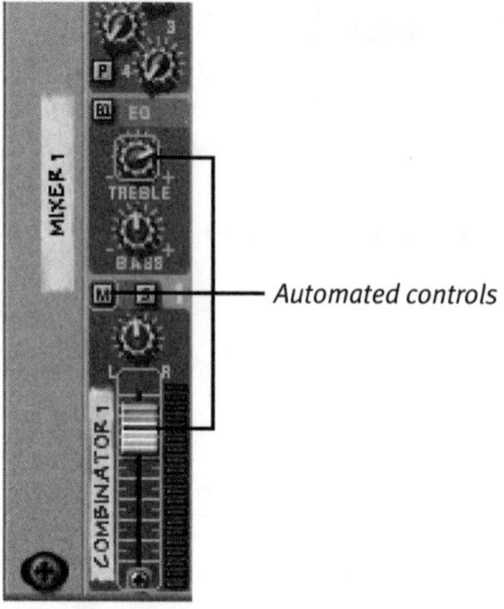

Figure 10.16 Mixer controls with automation have green outlines in the Rack.

Automating a master Mixer

If you organize your project well, with luck your final mix won't involve much more than moving the levels of a few tracks up and down over the length of the song, and maybe triggering a Mute or Solo button for some of the channels.

In cases like this, a typical final mix can be managed in one Sequencer track assigned to your master Mixer.

To manage a master Mixer track:

1. Record-enable the Sequencer track assigned to your Mixer.
2. Set your loop length for the part of the song you wish to record.
3. Set your record mode to Replace or Overdub.
4. Click the Record button to enter standby mode.
5. Hit play to begin recording.
6. Make your Mixer adjustments, and press stop when you are done.
7. Open your track in Edit mode and play it back. Make fine adjustments to your Controller lanes if desired.

Controlling one device with many Sequencer tracks

If you plan on automating many different Mixer parameters in your Sequencer, consider using different Sequencer tracks for different controls. This allows you to edit and mute the control changes for each Sequencer track independently.

It also helps keep your automated tracks organized by minimizing the number of blue lanes to manage in each track (**Figure 10.17** and **Figure 10.18**).

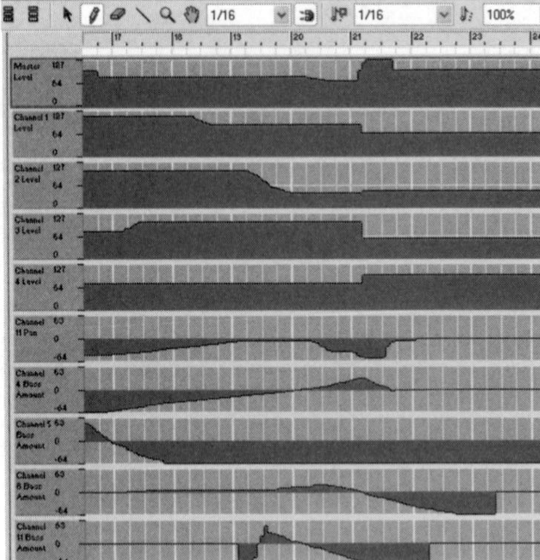

Figure 10.17 If a Mixer track contains many different kinds of controls, consider breaking it up into several tracks and sorting them by control type.

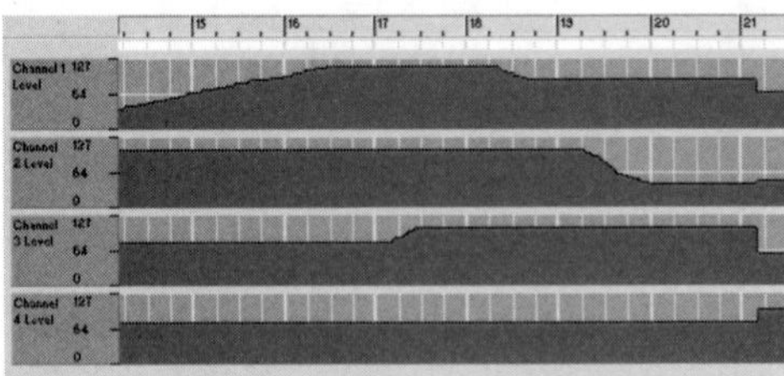

Figure 10.18 This Mixer track is dedicated just to making level adjustments and is much easier to edit.

Figure 10.19 You can assign more than one Sequencer track to a single Mixer device.

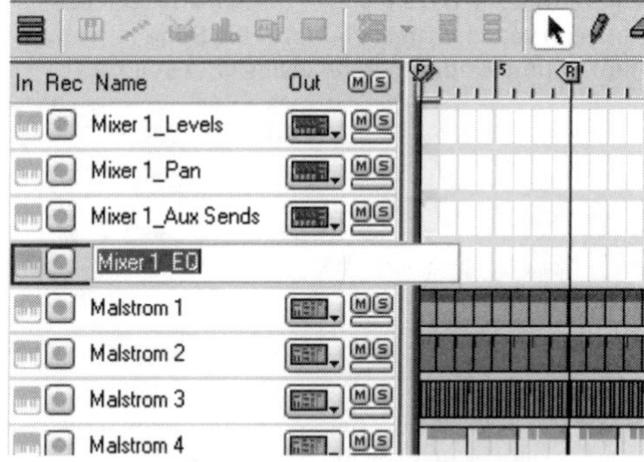

Figure 10.20 Give your Sequencer tracks new, descriptive names to avoid confusion.

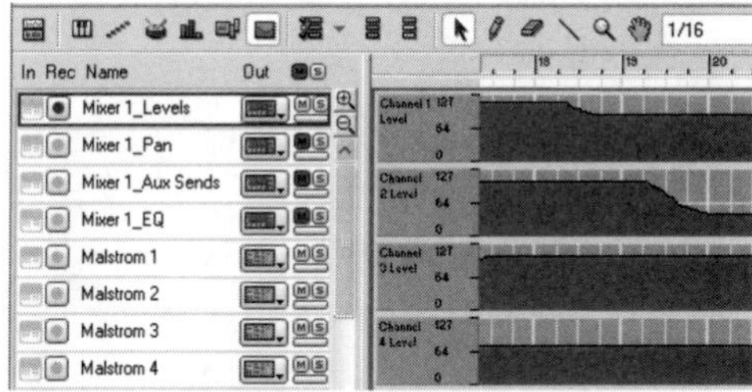

Figure 10.21 The track Mute buttons work on controller data just as they do on notes. Simply click Mute to bypass the controller changes.

To set up multiple control tracks:

1. In your Sequencer, select Edit > Create Sequencer Track for each Mixer control you want to record (**Figure 10.19**).
2. Assign the new Sequencer tracks to your master Mixer and rename each track: for example, `Mixer 1_pan`, `Mixer 1_level`, `Mixer 1_auxsend` (**Figure 10.20**).
3. Record-enable the new track, click record then play, and move the desired parameter.

   Reason 3.0 can record on multiple tracks simultaneously, so make sure you have record-enabled only one track.
4. You can focus on each control track individually during playback by muting the other control tracks (**Figure 10.21**).

✔ Tip

- Try not to mix controllers between tracks when using this method, or you may get "orphan" controller data that is hard to find later.

Saving multiple mixes

Once you feel you are getting close to the mix you want, start saving each mix as a separate song. These can all be burned to CD and tested on many different systems.

It is also a good idea to take descriptive notes when saving each mix, while it is fresh in your mind. That way, when you return to it later, you'll know exactly what was unique about the mix—what elements you were focusing on, correcting, or altering.

To add and save mixing notes with a song:

1. Press Ctrl+I (Win)/Cmd+I (Mac) to open the Song Information window.
2. Type in the relevant information (**Figure 10.22**).
3. Save the song with a descriptive name so you can tell it from other versions.

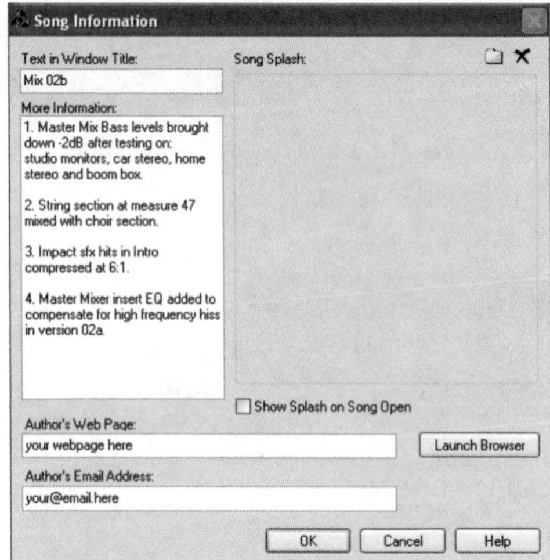

Figure 10.22 To track mix information and changes between versions, make notes in the Song Information window before saving your song.

Rack Remixing with the Combinator

If you expect to do a lot of alternate versions or remixes of a song, it makes sense to combine your effects setups and even to track with pattern devices inside a Combinator.

To trigger all combined pattern devices:

- Toggle the Run All Pattern Devices button on the Combinator front panel to start and stop playback.

  Even though you can't typically save Redrum or Matrix pattern banks, you can save them inside a Combinator patch.

You can also turn on and off all effects inside a Combinator.

To toggle all combined effects on and off:

- Toggle the Bypass All Effects button on the Combinator to turn effects off and on.

Enhancing a combination

It is also more effective to use a Combinator to enhance an existing setup. Since Combinator patches preserve controller data and many other settings, you can change your mix by simply changing patches.

In this example, we'll set up a basic drum kit, then enhance it with extra bass. We'll do this by creating a second version that uses the gate signal from the kick drum to trigger a low-frequency sine wave.

To add kick emphasis using a synth:

1. Create a Mixer and a Redrum device inside a Combinator (**Figure 10.23**).
2. Using the Redrum patch browser, load the Factory Sound Bank patch `Redrum Drum Kits/Techno Kits/Techno Kit 01.drp` (**Figure 10.24**).

Figure 10.23 Create a Mixer and Redrum inside a Combinator.

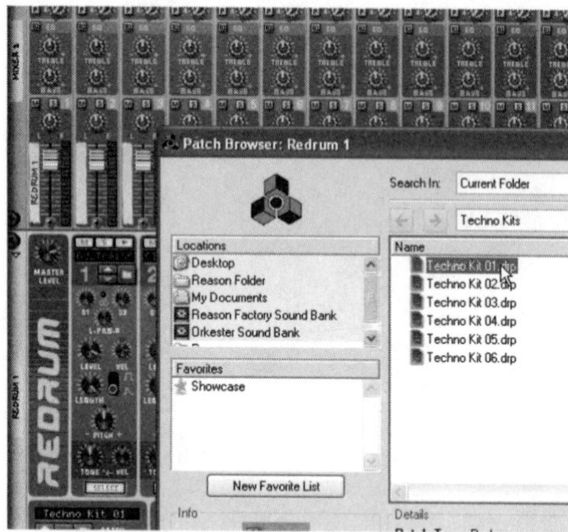

Figure 10.24 Pick a Redrum patch.

Figure 10.25 A standard multi-out drum setup can be used inside a Combinator and saved as a patch.

Figure 10.26 Connect a drum channel Gate CV output to a SubTractor to trigger a low-frequency sound (the note CV signal is not needed to make a single tone).

3. Cable each drum channel to a separate Mixer channel (**Figure 10.25**).
4. Program a basic drum pattern and save the setup as a Combinator patch named `Beat 01_simple`.
5. Click the Mixer in the Combinator device area and create a SubTractor synth.
6. Connect the drum channel CV gate output to the SubTractor gate in CV input (**Figure 10.26**).

   Every time the kick drum on the Redrum plays, the SubTractor synth will play a note, too.

continues on next page

7. Set oscillator 1 of the SubTractor to Sine, or waveform 3, and tune it to an Oct setting of 1 (**Figure 10.27**).
8. Boost the amp envelope decay, sustain, and release faders on the SubTractor to 127, 121, and 58, respectively (**Figure 10.28**).

   Now the SubTractor's oscillator will play a low-frequency tone, adding bass emphasis to the kick drum.

Now it is a simple matter to switch from the plain drum beat to the version with extra bass.

Figure 10.27 Set the SubTractor oscillator for a low-frequency sine wave.

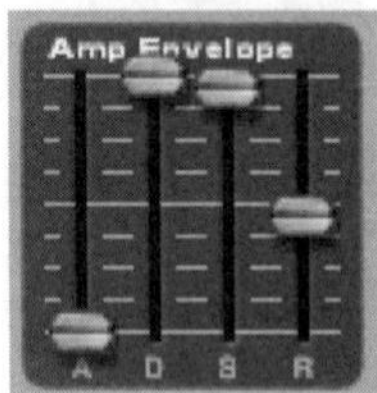

Figure 10.28 Set the SubTractor amp faders to enhance the drum.

To switch between the simple and enhanced patches:

1. Save the enhanced Combinator patch as `Beat 01_sine` in the same directory as the `Beat 01_simple` patch.
2. Use the arrow keys on the Combinator patch browser to switch between the two setups.

The Combinator modulation routing opens up new possibilities for using devices together. Using the `Beat 01_simple` patch, we can assign a rotary knob to select patterns from the Redrum's pattern bank.

Figure 10.29 The Combinator's Show Programmer button gives you access to programmable parameters.

To select patterns with a Combinator rotary knob:

1. Click the Show Programmer button on the Combinator front panel (**Figure 10.29**).
2. In the programmer window, select the Redrum in the Device column.
3. In the Modulation Routing section, click the Target field next to Rotary 1 and choose Selected Pattern from the pop-up list of Redrum parameters (**Figure 10.30**).
4. Double-click the Name field under the Rotary 1 knob and type in `Pattern select`.

   Now the Rotary 1 knob will change patterns on the Redrum's pattern sequencer during playback.

Figure 10.30 Set up the Combinator Rotary 1 knob to change the Redrum pattern bank.

Figure 10.31 Export Song as Audio File saves your entire song as an audio file so you can burn it to CD.

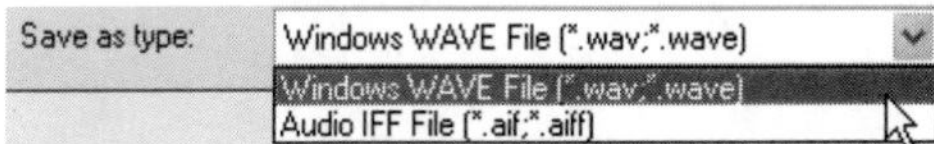

Figure 10.32 Choose whether you want to save your audio file as .aiff (more common for Mac) or .wav (more common for Windows).

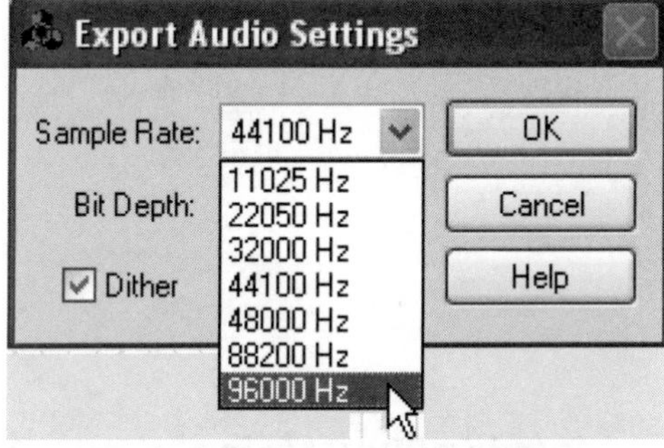

Figure 10.33 Exporting at the highest rate is fine if you want to import back into Reason, but for CD, pick 44,100 Hz.

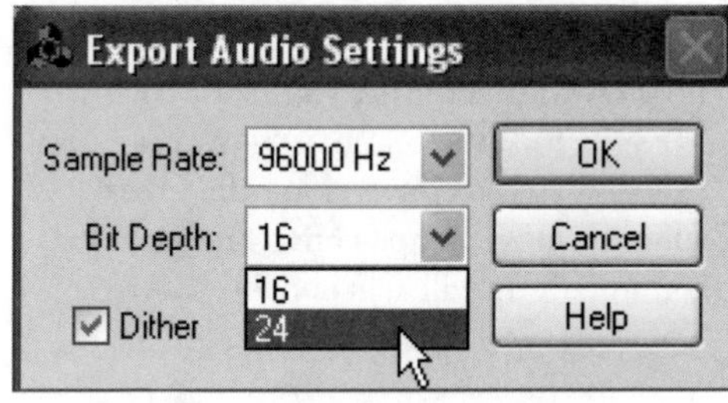

Figure 10.34 Pick a bit depth—use 16 for CDs.

Exporting Audio

When you are ready to burn a CD of your song, you will first need to "bounce" or save your song as an audio file.

To export your song as an audio file:

1. Select File > Export Song as Audio File and choose a save location (**Figure 10.31**).
2. Choose either WAV or AIFF file format for your audio file (**Figure 10.32**).
3. Choose a sample rate (11,025 Hz to 96,000 Hz) for your audio file (**Figure 10.33**).

   Files destined for audio CDs need to be saved at 44,100 Hz. Choose this option if you don't have a program that can convert sample rates.
4. Choose a bit depth of 16 or 24 for your file (**Figure 10.34**).

   For CD, choose 16. For archiving or bringing back into Reason as a sample, use 24 for the best quality.

✔ Tips

- If you have a sound editing program like Sound Forge or Peak, save your song at the highest rate your sound system supports—that way, you'll have a top-quality archive. When you're ready to burn a CD, use your editing program to convert the sample/bit rates to 44,100/16.
- Though most CD software can handle WAV and AIFF formats, WAV is a more common Windows format and AIFF is more common for Macintosh.

If you want to create a loop to use as a sample in Reason or to burn a short version of your song on CD, use the Export Loop command instead.

To export your loop as an audio file:

1. Select File > Export Loop as Audio File.
2. Choose a location and file format for your audio file (see the previous task for details).

   The Export Audio window will show you how much of your loop remains to be saved (**Figure 10.35**).

Figure 10.35 The Export Audio status bar shows your file's progress.

Burning CDs/Making MP3s

Once your audio file is exported, you should be able to use any CD burning software application to create an audio CD of your song.

If you want to convert your song to an MP3 file for Internet sharing, you can probably find a conversion utility that suits you at www.mp3-converter.com. Most sound editors will also convert to MP3. Try www.synthzone.com/digaudio.htm for some ideas.

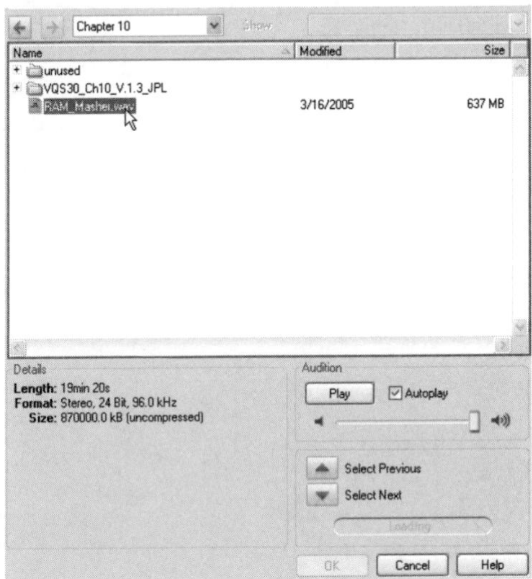

Figure 10.36 Loading a long audio file into one of Reason's samplers is possible, if you have enough RAM to do it.

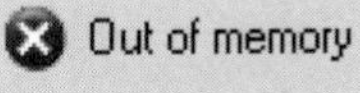

Figure 10.37 Reason will let you know if a file is too large to load.

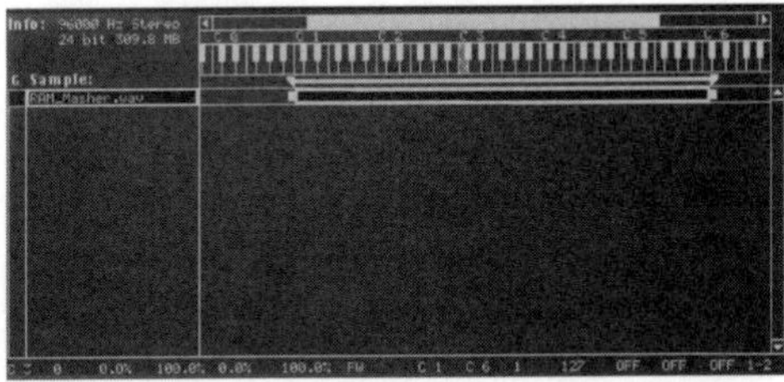

Figure 10.38 This sampler patch is loaded with a long audio file.

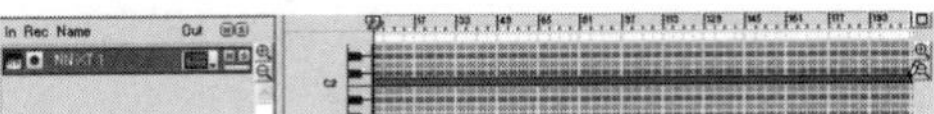

Figure 10.39 You can use a Sequencer track to trigger a long sample, giving you a limited capability to play audio tracks within your song.

Importing Audio

To manipulate a saved loop sample in one of Reason's sampling instruments, just import the audio file back into your project.

To import audio for use in Reason:

1. Create an NN-XT sampler in your Rack.
2. Open the Remote Editor and click Browse Sample.
3. Navigate to your exported sound file and select it to load it into your sampler (**Figure 10.36**).

   If your computer doesn't have enough spare RAM or processing power to handle the sample, Reason will display an "Out of memory" message in the lower-left corner of the browser window (**Figure 10.37**).
4. Once the file is loaded into your sampler (**Figure 10.38**), you can use a sustained note in the sampler's Sequencer track to trigger the sample (**Figure 10.39**).

11

MASTERING

Reason's MClass tools make it possible for you to *master* your music. "Mastering" originally meant creating the master copy or master recording—the final version that gets duplicated and mass-produced. Today, it means getting music ready for any form of distribution, and with so many digital processing tools available, that can be accomplished through a variety of processes.

For our purposes, it means adjusting the final equalization, dynamics, and output level of your song so it will stand up to other professional recordings. Generally, the goals of mastering are to

- Correct equalization imbalances.
- Reign in tone and loudness variations between tracks.
- Repair pops, clicks, and hums that could impact airplay.
- "Fatten" anemic or "smooth out" harsh-sounding digital recordings.

Although the actual process depends on your own song, this chapter will teach you what to listen for and introduce you to Reason's tools for outputting a CD master that will be acceptable at any duplication plant.

Before You Start Mastering

The most important mastering tool of all is your own ears, so the first order of business is to give your ears as clear a picture as possible.

Don't try to master your music after a long day of mixing has given you a case of sonic fatigue. If possible, don't listen to a work for a couple of days before you start mastering it. That way, when you start mastering you are coming at your work with a fresh set of ears.

Also, think about the sound you're going for and try to find some recordings that represent it well. If you aren't sure, listen to some recordings you love in similar styles to your song.

If possible, find more than one comparison recording so you get a broader target range. Sound variations between comparison recordings are helpful because they keep the reference point general (and more attainable) as you master.

Always check your mix carefully one last time before you start mastering. Ideally, you should listen to every instrument soloed in your song from beginning to end. For a big project, you should at least check your major submixes, instrument groups, and tracks with lots of controller data.

Check your setup

No matter how good your ears are, they won't help you if your monitoring setup can't faithfully reproduce the sound coming out of Reason. Studio monitors are designed for this purpose, and though some are better than others, this is the best (and most expensive) way to go.

Home stereo speakers and receivers are far from ideal, because they usually enhance frequency response and brands vary widely in how they do it. If you have to use stereo equipment, keep all controls off or at the middle setting.

Do everything you can to minimize interference from inside and outside your sound system. Check your signal integrity from the time it leaves the Reason hardware interface until it comes out the monitors. Any signal alteration will mask the sound you want to polish, making mastering difficult or impossible.

✔ Tip

- Don't master with headphones. The left and right sides of your music don't ever meet or interact, so headphones cannot give you an accurate idea of how your music is going to sound on stereos, PAs, radio, and so on.

Check Your System

- Check your computer's sound system, and make sure that all drivers are up-to-date and any system enhancements like equalizers, tone controls, and bass boosts are *off*.
- Check your console settings to make sure that all hardware effects you don't intend to use are set to bypass and that equalization, level, and panning knobs are set to neutral positions.
- Turn off your receiver loudness controls, effects, and surround decoders, and set all tone controls midway so you don't boost or cut frequencies.
- Check your speakers: Any knobs or boost controls (often located under the grill screen) should be at minimum or neutral settings; the speakers should sit on a solid surface, equidistant from your point of reference, and away from anything that may rattle, as well as resonating objects like pianos or cases.
- Minimize outside noise (especially constant hums from refrigerators, computers, etc.) by closing doors and windows or turning off extraneous equipment when possible.

Adding an MClass Mastering Suite

Reason 3.0 introduces four new mastering effects, which can be used separately or loaded together by creating an MClass Mastering Suite Combi.

Loading the devices together is recommended when you're starting out, since it chains the effects together in the right order and contains useful parameter routings for the rotary knobs and buttons. And since it's really a special type of Combinator, the master controls will already look familiar.

Figure 11.1 An MClass Mastering Suite sits at the end of the signal chain, between the Mixer and the audio interface.

To create an MClass Mastering Suite:

1. Open the song you want to master.
2. Select the hardware interface and choose Create > MClass Mastering Suite Combi.

   This will insert your tools at the very end of the signal chain between the final mixed output of your song and the hardware interface (**Figure 11.1**).
3. In the devices area of the Mastering Combinator, find the MClass Maximizer at the bottom and set the Bypass switch in its upper-left corner to Bypass.
4. Set the MClass Compressor and MClass Stereo Imager to Bypass, but leave the MClass Equalizer set to On, as we'll explore that in the next section.

Figure 11.2 Enable the MClass Equalizer.

Figure 11.3 The Lo Shelf band affects everything below the Freq setting.

Figure 11.4 The Hi Shelf band affects everything above the Freq setting.

Using the MClass Equalizer

The MClass EQ sits first in the signal path to correct frequency spikes or imbalances that would otherwise "top" your compressor/limiters later in the chain. The controls are designed for fine compensation, correction, or enhancement of frequency areas that are thin or oversaturated. The curve in the display window shows the effect of all except the Lo Cut button.

To adjust the MClass Equalizer:

1. With your song playing and an MClass Mastering Suite loaded, set the MClass Equalizer Bypass switch to On (**Figure 11.2**).
2. In the MClass EQ, use the five enable buttons to select frequency bands for adjustment. Enable the Lo Cut band if you want to protect against subsonic sound.
3. In an enabled frequency band, use the Freq knob to adjust the EQ frequency.

   In the Lo Shelf band, all frequencies below the Freq setting will be affected (**Figure 11.3**).

   In the Hi Shelf band, all frequencies above the Freq setting will be affected (**Figure 11.4**).

continues on next page

4. Turn the Gain knob right to boost a frequency and left to cut.
5. Turn the Q knob right to sharpen the curve and left to make it more gradual.

   As the Q value increases, a slight dip at the cutoff frequency occurs for positive gain, and a slight boost occurs for negative gain (**Figure 11.5**). This helps accentuate a boost or cut, allowing you to sharpen slight EQ adjustments to make them more audible.

✔ Tip

- If you need to boost or cut more than 6 dB, you may have a problem that is better fixed in the mix.

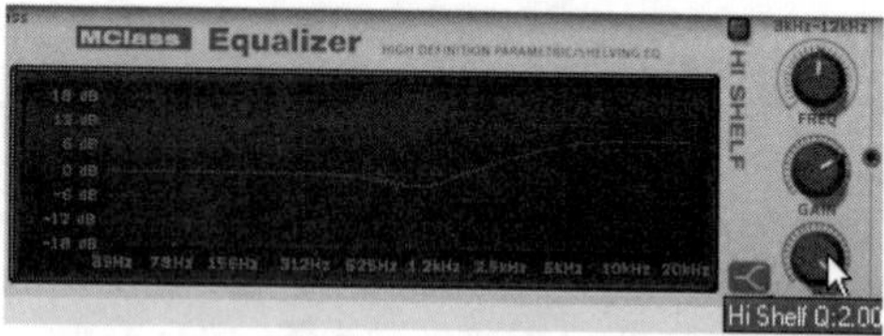

Figure 11.5 The Q value creates an opposite dip when set high.

Cut the Quake

Unless your song is mixed for a specific subwoofer, there's no reason to pass subsonics through the mastering stage.

Subsonic waveforms are long compared to frequencies in the audible range. High-gain subsonics can trigger and hold open a compressor gate, making it unresponsive in the audible range when you need it.

The Lo Cut button won't register on your graphic display, but it's there nonetheless, cutting off subsonic frequencies (below 30 Hz) that can wreak havoc with speakers.

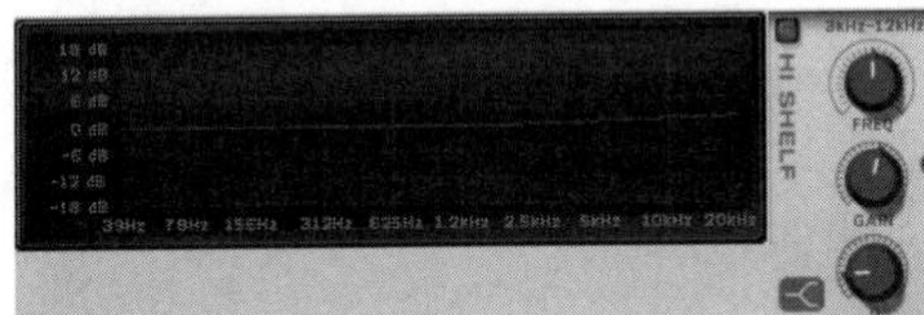

Figure 11.6 Raise the Hi Shelf band 2 dB.

Mastering EQ examples

Though the MClass EQ is fairly easy to use, it's worth mentioning that it specializes in correcting slight imbalances.

In this example, we'll use the Hi Shelf band to boost high frequencies, adding some definition to a dead-sounding mix.

To boost high frequencies:

1. Start your song and set the MClass Equalizer Bypass switch to On.
2. Enable the Hi Shelf band.
3. Set the Freq knob between 3 kHz and 12 kHz.
4. Boost the Gain knob to 2 dB (**Figure 11.6**).

   This is not a drastic boost, but it can give a mix some presence without sounding tinny.

✔ Tip

- A temporary, exaggerated boost or cut in Gain can help while you dial in frequency and Q settings.

Q dip

Here's an example that compensates for too much low midrange in a muddy-sounding mix. We'll use the Lo Shelf "Q dip" to both boost the low frequency and cut a thin band before the midrange.

To separate lows from mids:

1. Start your song and set the MClass Equalizer Bypass switch to On.
2. Enable the Lo Shelf band.
3. Set the frequency between 60 Hz and 116 Hz.
4. Boost the Gain knob to about 2 dB.
5. Nudge the Q knob to the right until you get a slight cut in frequency at the end of the curve slope (**Figure 11.7**).

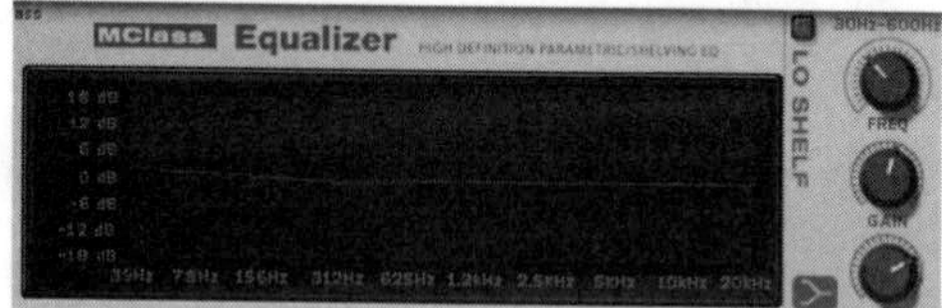

Figure 11.7 This slight dip below 0 dB is caused by a high Q value and helps separate the lows from the midrange.

Figure 11.8 Set the MClass Stereo Imager Bypass switch to On.

Figure 11.9 Use the X-Over Freq knob to separate low and high signals.

Figure 11.10 The Lo Band Width knob determines the stereo image of the bass.

Figure 11.11 Enable the Solo Lo Band button to concentrate on bass adjustments.

Using the MClass Stereo Imager

The name may cause you to think this effect creates a stereo file from a mono one, but this is not what the MClass Stereo Imager does. Instead, it splits the audio into low- and high-frequency bands, and allows you to make each more mono or more stereo.

The most common use for a stereo imager is to make the low end more mono. This tightens up the bass and adds punch.

Increasing the stereo width for the high band can also "open up" the sound. However, widening is more unpredictable than narrowing, and depends largely on the character of the mix being processed.

To narrow the bass:

1. Start your song and set the MClass Stereo Imager Bypass switch to On (**Figure 11.8**).
2. Use the X-Over Freq knob to select a frequency at which to divide the signal into low and high bands (**Figure 11.9**).
3. Turn the Low Width knob counterclockwise to narrow the stereo image for the bass (**Figure 11.10**).
4. Enable the Solo Lo Band button to hear just the low frequency output (**Figure 11.11**), and adjust the X-Over knob as needed.

Usine the MClass Compressor

The MClass Compressor introduces separate input and output gains, a "soft-knee" compression option, an adaptive release setting, and a sidechain input that can be used for de-essing or ducking (which we'll discuss more in "Using Sidechains" later in this chapter).

Used judiciously, heavy compression can help you keep your dynamics uniform, and mild compression can make more of what's going on in your music audible.

Let's dial in a compression setting typical for mastering a mix with strong signal levels, that only needs slight dynamic processing before going to CD.

Compressor Terms

Input Gain Boosting the incoming signal—this can be useful if you want more extreme compression on a low-level signal, as it pushes more signal past the threshold setting.

Threshold Determines the volume level at which *reduction* happens. When the threshold is crossed, the compressor responds by lowering the volume. Incoming signals below this level are unaffected.

Ratio How much a signal is reduced when the threshold is crossed: 1:1 means no reduction, and (infinity):1 means that no signal is allowed to cross the threshold at all.

Attack Time lapse between when the threshold is exceeded and when compression starts. Long attack values are good for percussive sounds, as they don't reduce sharp attacks, but keep average volume under control.

Release The time it takes for the compressor to stop compressing after the signal crosses below the threshold again. Long release times can help smooth compression on individual tracks like vocals, but can cause lower-level signals to get lost.

Output Gain Useful for making up gain lost during compression. For example, if the Gain meter shows the signal is being reduced by -4 dB, then a good "make-up gain" output setting would be +4 dB.

Figure 11.12 Set the MClass Compressor Bypass switch to On.

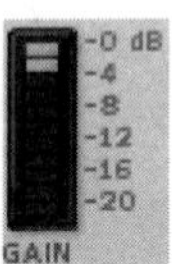

Figure 11.13 The Gain meter shows 3 dB of gain reduction.

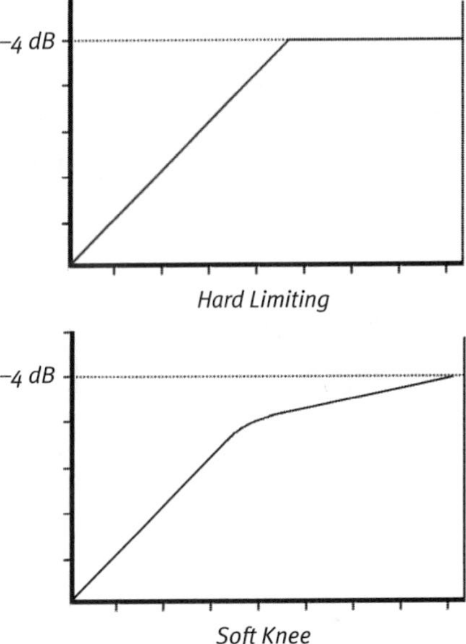

Figure 11.14 Hard limiting (a ratio of infinity-to-1) sounds much sharper than soft-knee compression, but doesn't affect anything below threshold.

To set up compression:

1. Start your song and set the MClass Compressor Bypass switch to On (**Figure 11.12**).
2. Set the Threshold knob so that the highest peaks in the song are triggering the compressor.

   Green indicator lights will appear in the Gain meter when the compressor kicks in.
3. Set the Ratio knob so that the loudest sections of the song get about 3 dB of reduction in the Gain meter (**Figure 11.13**).
4. If you find you're using a high ratio like 10:1, activate the Soft Knee button. This will start compression earlier, before the signal reaches the threshold level, but implement it more gradually for a less drastic sound (**Figure 11.14**).

Breathing and Pumping

Both breathing and pumping are signs of compression overuse. If either happens, try reducing the release time, backing off the ratio setting, raising the threshold, or all of the above.

"Breathing" High compression and make-up gain combined can raise the average signal level so background noise starts becoming audible between peaks.

"Pumping" This occurs when the compressor is so high it begins functioning like an amp envelope, and the rising and falling volume of the compressor upstages the louds and softs of the music.

Using the MClass Maximizer

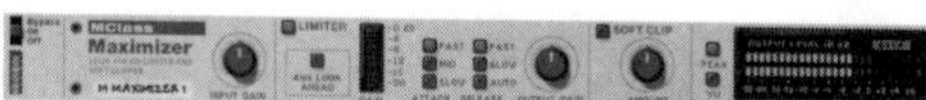

Figure 11.15 The MClass Maximizer is a limiter/compressor.

Although you don't want too much compression, you still want to ensure that no distorting peaks are getting through the mastering process. For this task you need a special kind of compressor, called a *limiter*. This acts as a gatekeeper at the end of your mastering chain.

Figure 11.16 Activate the limiting on the Maximizer.

The MClass Maximizer is a limiter/compressor designed to sit between you and the vast void into which your music will journey once it leaves your hands. It has the highest detail of level metering available in Reason and it is easy to use.

Figure 11.17 Set the Input Gain amount.

To limit your final mix:

1. Start your song and set the MClass Maximizer Bypass switch to On (**Figure 11.15**).
2. Activate the Limiter enable button (**Figure 11.16**).
3. Use the Input Gain knob to adjust the basic volume of your mix (**Figure 11.17**).
4. Activate the Look Ahead button (**Figure 11.18**). It introduces a delay of 4 milliseconds, which increases the Maximizer's resolution for detecting and dealing with tiny peaks.

   There is no penalty for using it, and it should always be used if you are boosting your signal a lot at the input gain stage.
5. The Output Gain should be set to 0 dB (the default), though it can go as high as +12 dB. The maximum value for digital audio is 0 dB (**Figure 11.19**).

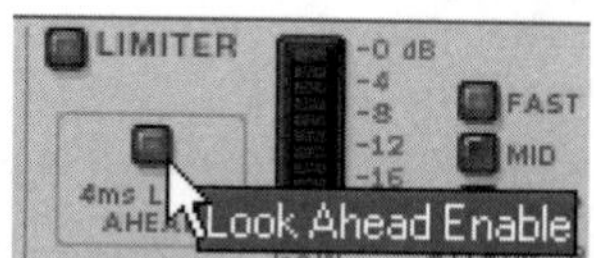

Figure 11.18 The Look Ahead function increases your protection against peaks.

Figure 11.19 The Output Gain knob is set to 0 dB by default, and must remain there for digital audio.

Figure 11.20 Setting the Attack switch to Fast with Look Ahead enabled gives you brick wall limiting.

Figure 11.21 Set the Release switch to Auto for adaptive limiting.

Figure 11.22 If you enable Soft Clip, you must also increase the Amount.

6. Set the Attack switch to Fast (**Figure 11.20**), especially if you are using the Maximizer at the end of your mastering chain. When Look Ahead is enabled, the Fast setting will give you total peak protection, or *brick wall limiting*.
7. The Release switch sets how long the limiter takes to stop limiting peaks.

   Set Release to Auto if you want the Maximizer to intelligently adapt to the sound (**Figure 11.21**).
8. Enable Soft Clip to protect against hard clipping distortion (**Figure 11.22**).

   If the soft clip Amount knob is set to 0, hard clipping may still occur, so make sure you turn it up when using this feature.
9. Set the meter response mode: Peak mode is the fastest, and will show small peaks; VU mode will show the average levels.

Creating a Multiband Compressor

How much compression you can use is all too often determined by the low frequencies coming from the kick drum and the bass in your mix.

Enter the *multiband compressor.* A multiband compressor is just a series of compressors, each assigned to a different frequency range—sort of like a multiband equalizer with compression added.

Though Reason doesn't really have a multiband compressor, you can set up your own using stereo imagers to split your signal into different frequency bands, then passing them to multiple compressors. Though it isn't as easy as using one compressor, it can be much more useful in mastering your music.

The stereo imager has an additional set of stereo outputs that can be set to output either the high or low band. This allows you to output the low and high signals separately. You can further narrow the bands by chaining an additional stereo imager to one or both of the output signals.

To split low- and high-band outputs:

1. Select your song's hardware interface and create an MClass Stereo Imager.
2. Use the X-Over Freq knob to set your low-band range (**Figure 11.23**).
3. Activate the Solo Lo Band button (**Figure 11.24**).

   Now the audio outputs will pass only the low-band signal.

Figure 11.23 Specify the low-frequency range with the X-Over Freq knob.

Figure 11.24 The Solo Lo Band button sends only low frequencies out the main outputs.

Figure 11.25 Set to Hi Band, the Separate outputs will send out only high-frequency signal.

Figure 11.26 Send frequencies above 340 Hz to another stereo imager to be split again.

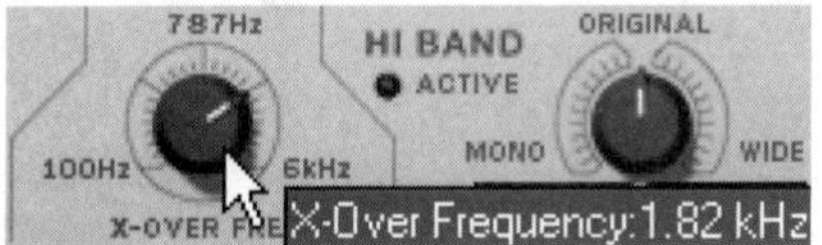

Figure 11.27 Split the high frequency again in Imager 2 with the X-Over Freq knob.

Figure 11.28 Switch the Separate outputs on Imager 2 to Hi Band.

4. On the back panel, set the Separate Out switch to Hi Band (**Figure 11.25**).

   This will make it so the separate outputs contain only the high-band signal. If you only need two-band compression, you can stop there, but we'll continue and set up a third band.

5. Hold Shift and create an additional stereo imager.

6. Run the Separate output from the first stereo imager to the Audio Inputs of the new one (**Figure 11.26**).

   Since this signal is already split, it contains only frequencies from about 340 Hz to 6 kHz.

7. Set the X-Over Freq knob on the new imager to split the high-frequency input (**Figure 11.27**) and enable the Solo Lo Band button.

   Now the main audio outputs of this stereo imager will contain just the frequencies from 340 Hz to the X-Over knob value.

8. On the back panel of the second stereo imager, set the Separate Out switch to Hi Band (**Figure 11.28**).

   The Separate outputs will pass only the frequencies above the X-Over knob value.

Now that the frequencies are separated, we can pass each to its own compressor, then save the whole setup as our very own multi-band compressor.

Figure 11.29 Create a Line Mixer and three MClass Compressors.

To create a three-band compressor:

1. Hold Shift and create a Line Mixer and three MClass Compressors (**Figure 11.29**).
2. Cable the low-band output from Stereo Imager 1's audio outputs to the audio inputs of Compressor 1 (**Figure 11.30**) and connect Compressor 1's audio outputs to Channel 1 of the Mixer (**Figure 11.31**).

   Rename this compressor Lo Band.

Figure 11.30 Connect the low-band signal to Compressor 1...

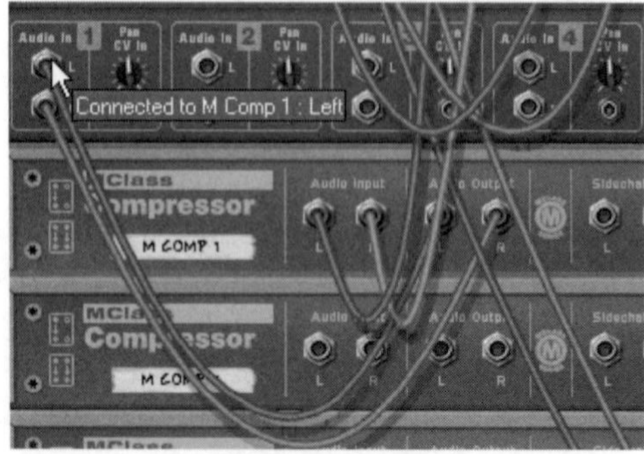

Figure 11.31 ...and then send it to the Mixer.

Figure 11.32 Connect the mid-band signal to Compressor 2...

3. Cable the low-band output from Stereo Imager 2's audio outputs to the audio inputs of Compressor 2 (**Figure 11.32**) and connect Compressor 2's audio outputs to Channel 2 of the Mixer (**Figure 11.33**).

   Rename this compressor `Mid Band`.

4. Cable the high-band output from Stereo Imager 2's Separate outputs to the audio inputs of Compressor 3 (**Figure 11.34**) and connect Compressor 3's audio outputs to Channel 3 of the Mixer (**Figure 11.35**).

   Rename this compressor `High Band`.

continues on next page

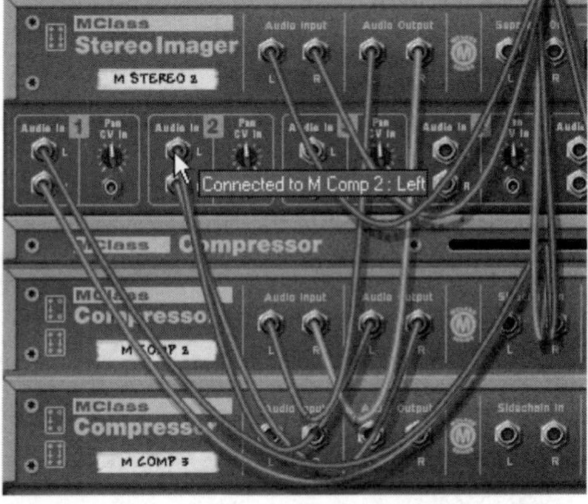

Figure 11.33 ...and then send it to the Mixer.

Figure 11.34 Connect the high-band signal to Compressor 3...

Figure 11.35 ...and then send it to the Mixer.

5. Select the Line Mixer, both Stereo Imagers, and all three compressors and use the Edit > Combine command (**Figure 11.36**).

   All the devices are now enclosed in a self-contained Combinator.

6. On the back panel, connect the Master Output of the Line Mixer to the From Devices input of the Combinator (**Figure 11.37**).

7. Cable the Combi Output to inputs 1 and 2 of the hardware interface (**Figure 11.38**).

   Now you can set different compression for each of the three bands.

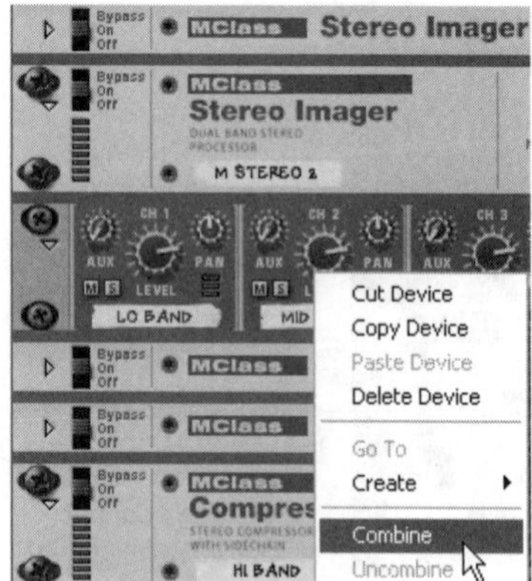

Figure 11.36 Save the multiband compressor as a Combi patch to use it on other songs.

Figure 11.37 Hook up the Combi Line Mixer.

Figure 11.38 Cable the Combinator as a mastering device at the end of the signal path.

Figure 11.39 Split any signal you plan to sidechain if you want to keep a copy in the mix.

Figure 11.40 Route a signal back to the Mixer.

Figure 11.41 Route a split copy to the Compressor sidechain input.

Using Sidechains

Sidechaining means compressing one signal using another as a trigger. The MClass Compressor has sidechain inputs that allow you to use sidechaining methods such as *ducking* (in which the presence of one type of sound causes another to *duck* in volume to make room) and *de-essing* (in which spikes caused by vocal *s* sounds are isolated using an EQ and then used to trigger compression of the voice track).

For example, say you have a bass and a kick drum that are sharing the same frequency band, and, despite all your efforts at separating them using EQ and mixing, the bass continues to overpower the kick. Instead of sacrificing the bass sound, one workaround is to set up an MClass Compressor to duck the bass down a few dBs when the kick drum is playing.

To set up sidechain ducking:

1. With your song loaded, create a Spider Audio Splitter and split the audio output signal from the kick drum (**Figure 11.39**).

   We need to route a split "copy" signal into the compressor if we want to keep the original in our mix.

2. Holding Shift, create an MClass Compressor and route one split kick drum signal from the Spider to the original destination—the Mixer (**Figure 11.40**); send the other split to the sidechain inputs of an MClass Compressor (**Figure 11.41**).

continues on next page

3. Now cable the audio outputs from the bass to the audio inputs of the Compressor (**Figure 11.42**).
4. Cable the Compressor output to an open Mixer channel (**Figure 11.43**).
5. Set the ratio according to how hard you want to limit the bass sound while the kick is playing (**Figure 11.44**).

   If you want smooth limiting, try a lower ratio and a lower threshold.
6. Set the threshold at approximately the level to which you want your bass to duck.

   If you are setting the ratio high, the threshold dB value will be close to the amount of cut (**Figure 11.45**).
7. Try soloing your bass channel and then adding the kick drum to hear the effect.

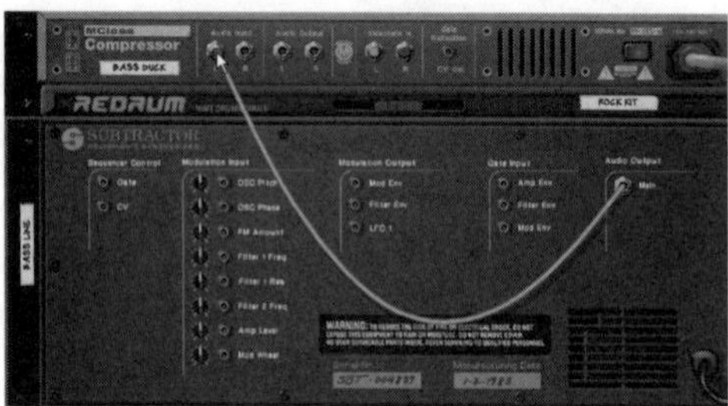

Figure 11.42 Route the signal we want to duck into the Compressor audio inputs.

Figure 11.43 Send the compressed signal back to the bass channel of the Mixer.

Figure 11.44 For hard limiting, set the ratio high.

Figure 11.45 The threshold level is the duck amount for high ratios (soft knee and low ratios don't duck as low).

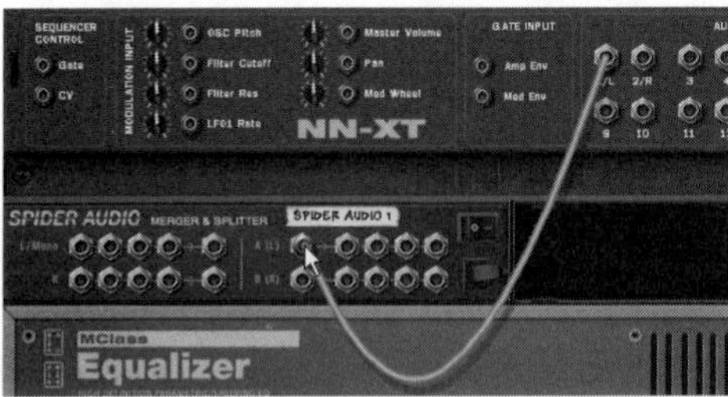

Figure 11.46 Split a signal before sidechaining it.

Figure 11 .47 Pass one copy of a signal to the Compressor and another to the EQ.

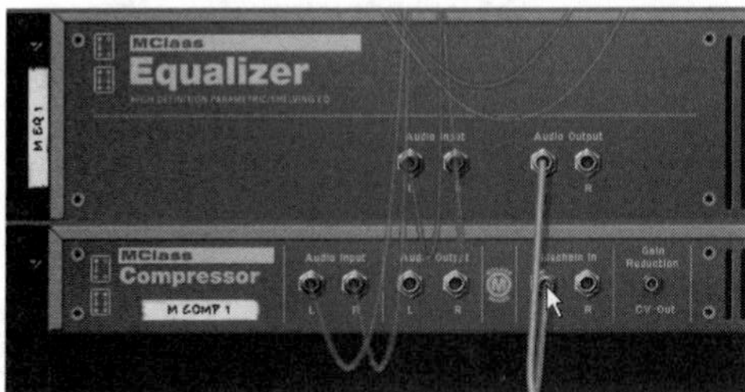

Figure 11.48 Sidechain the EQ output.

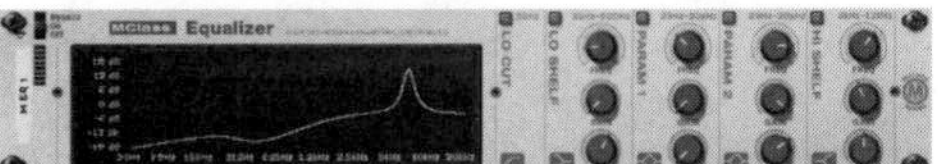

Figure 11.49 A sidechain signal with everything filtered out but a thin band of sibilant frequencies will only trigger the Compressor when an *s* or similar sound is present.

De-essing

Though de-essing is more common in studios that handle voice recording, you may find yourself using vocal samples that need some cleaning up. A typical de-essing setup requires a sampler, an EQ, and an MClass Compressor.

To set up de-essing:

1. Create a Spider Audio Splitter and split the output from the sampler that is going to be playing the voice files (**Figure 11.46**).
2. Create an MClass Compressor and MClass EQ (or MClass Suite); send one split from the Spider to the Compressor's audio inputs and another split to the audio inputs of the EQ (**Figure 11.47**).
3. Cable the outputs of the MClass EQ to the sidechain inputs of the MClass Compressor (**Figure 11.48**).
4. In the EQ, boost the frequencies between 5 kHz and 10 kHz and bring all the other frequencies down as far as possible (**Figure 11.49**).

   Since the Compressor responds to high levels, cutting out all but the frequency band you want to compress ensures that only the *s* sibilant frequencies will have enough gain to trigger the Compressor.
5. Set the Compressor threshold to the level at which you want to limit your sibilants.

   Set it slightly lower if you plan on using soft knee or low ratio settings.
6. Play your loop and tune the EQ and Compressor as needed.

✓ Tip

- Enabling the Solo Sidechain button and moving the Freq knob around at high gain can help you figure out what frequency and Q values you need to tune the effect.

Outputting Your Song

When you're done mastering, it's time to save your final song. The simplest way is to use the Export Song As Audio File command discussed in "Saving Your Work" in Chapter 4, "Getting Started."

However, if your song contains custom patches and samples, you need to make sure they're available the next time you open the song. Although you could create your own ReFill to make sure they're all there (see "Creating Your Own ReFills" in Appendix B, "Resources"), if you just need to archive a song using a few original patches and samples, creating a self-contained song is much easier. To do this you just need to set the song *self-contain* settings.

To save a self-contained song:

1. Choose File > Song Self-Contain Settings (**Figure 11.50**).

   This will bring up the Song Self-Contain Settings dialog box with a list of all the referenced sound files for the song.

2. Click Check All to include all the referenced files (**Figure 11.51**).

3. To remove sounds, select them in the Song Self-Contain Settings dialog box, and click Uncheck.

4. Click OK.

   Now whenever you save your song, it will contain all the referenced sounds.

Figure 11.50 Use the Song Self-Contain Settings to make sure your song won't be missing any parts.

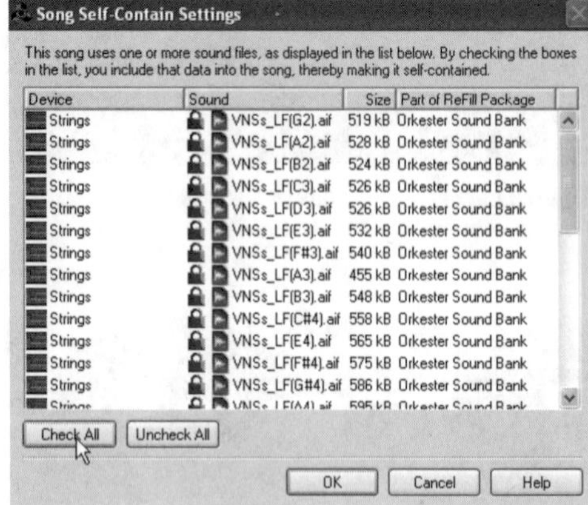

Figure 11.51 It's a good idea to include all referenced files, though if you're using only Factory and Orkester resources, it's not necessary.

✔ **Tips**

- If you're using only patches and sounds from the Factory and Orkester banks, self-contain settings don't have any effect.
- It is much easier to keep track of your files *before* you save your work. That way, you can decide to reorganize your library's folder structure later and not have to see the Missing Sounds dialog box when you open a song.

Managing Sounds

Protect against accidental loss of work! Any time you use patches from a variety of sources, it's a good idea to look at the Song Self-Contain settings and make a note of what sounds your song needs.

For example, if your song requires an obscure ReFill you downloaded from a shareware site, make a note of it and back up a copy of the ReFill when you archive the song to CD or DVD. That way, if you forget and throw the ReFill out, or take your work to another computer, you can still boot the song properly!

Finding missing sounds

The Missing Sounds dialog box will help you find or replace any missing files required by a song or patch.

To find missing sounds:

1. Songs or patches using missing refills will launch the Insert CD dialog (**Figure 11.52**). Click Browse to launch the browser or Cancel to bring up the Missing Sounds dialog.
2. In the Missing Sounds dialog box (**Figure 11.53**), click Search & Proceed to start an automatic operation, Open Dialog to search manually, or Cancel to abort.
3. The manual search window has several options:
   - ▲ **Download ReFill** This handy feature opens your Web browser to the ReFill's URL so you can download it again (**Figure 11.54**).
   - ▲ **Replace / Search In** This opens the Reason browser so you can find a compatible or duplicate sound to use instead.
   - ▲ **Search Locations** This will automatically search your local drives for the missing sound.

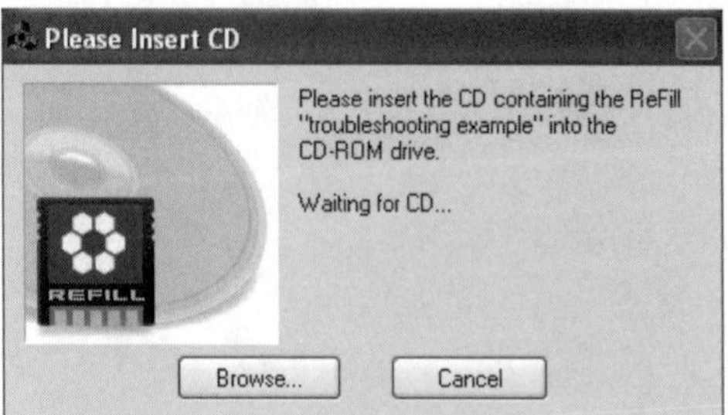

Figure 11.52 The missing ReFill dialog box asks for the CD the sounds are on. To manually search your local system, click Cancel.

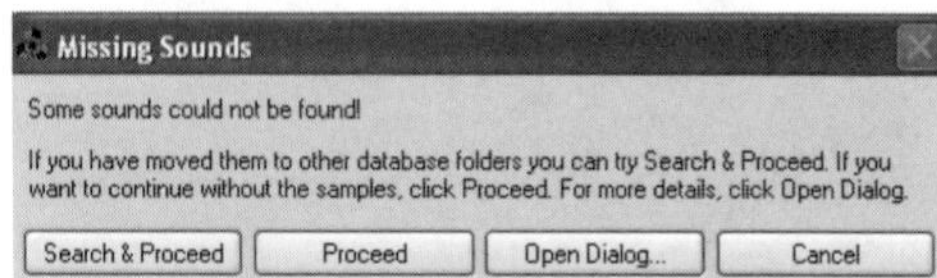

Figure 11.53 Searching for files referenced by an old song is much harder than keeping track of them before you save!

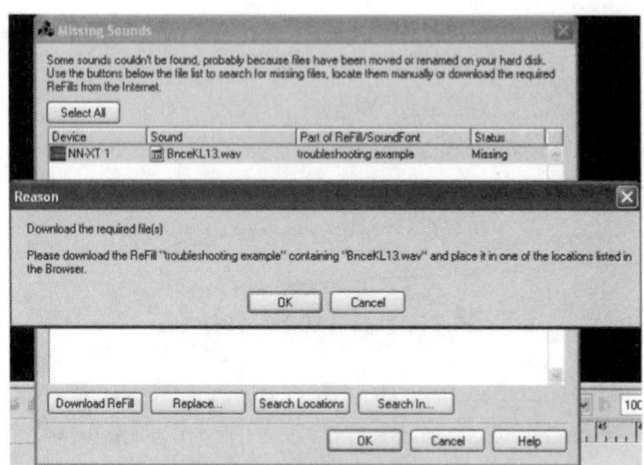

Figure 11.54 If you've lost a ReFill, Reason can help you find and download it again.

A

ReWire, ReCycle!, ReBirth

In addition to Reason, the folks at Propellerhead Software make several other audio-related products. Though you don't necessarily need them to use Reason, they all enhance your virtual studio.

The ReWire technology, which is built into Reason, allows it to work seamlessly with many other audio applications. Reload and ReFill Packer (covered in Appendix B, "Resources") are both free to registered Reason owners and enable you to create your own patches and ReFills. The ReCycle! and ReBirth programs are stand-alone applications that can be used with or without Reason.

Reload

Offered free to registered Reason owners, Reload converts Akai sample CDs into ReFill format. You can download it from the Propellerhead Web site (www.propellerhead.se), as long as you're logged in as a registered user.

To convert an Akai sample CD:

1. Launch the Reload program.
2. The first time you launch Reload you'll be asked to provide a serial number. This number is mailed to you when you register Reload. It is also stored at the Propellerhead site under My Account > My Registered Products.
3. Reload will prompt you to insert an Akai sample CD. Insert the CD you want to convert.
4. Choose whether you want to create NN-XT patches or whether you want Reload to create NN-XT patches and build them into a ReFill (**Figure A.1**).
5. If you choose to create patches, Reload will ask you to pick or create a destination folder (**Figure A.2**).

   or

   If you choose to create a ReFill, Reload will ask you to choose or create a destination folder. This folder must be empty or you will get an error message (**Figure A.3**).
6. Reload will begin converting the CD (**Figure A.4**). This can take anywhere from 5 minutes to an hour, depending on your CD and processor speeds.

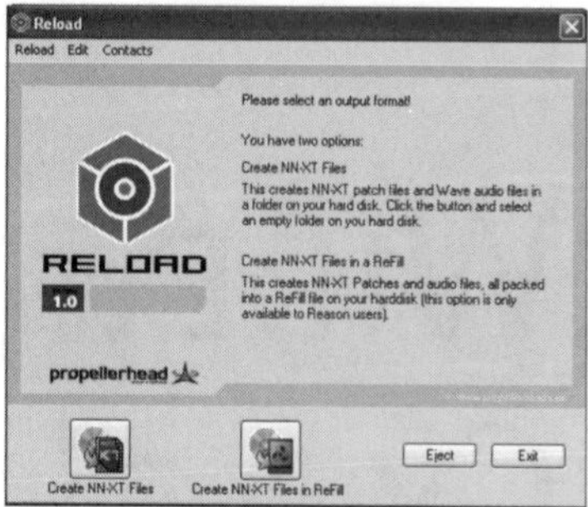

Figure A.1 Choose either a folder or ReFill format.

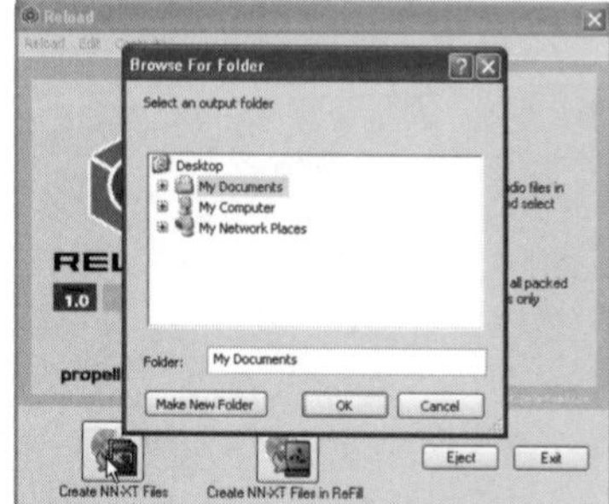

Figure A.2 Choose a destination folder for your patches.

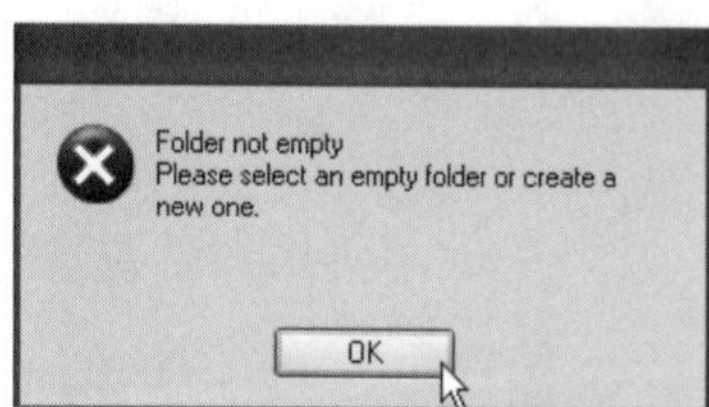

Figure A.3 ReFills need an empty folder.

Figure A.4 Use Reload to convert an Akai CD into a ReFill.

RELOAD

Figure A.5 ReWire allows Reason tracks to be recorded in other programs; it currently permits 64-track bussing using the hardware interface back panel.

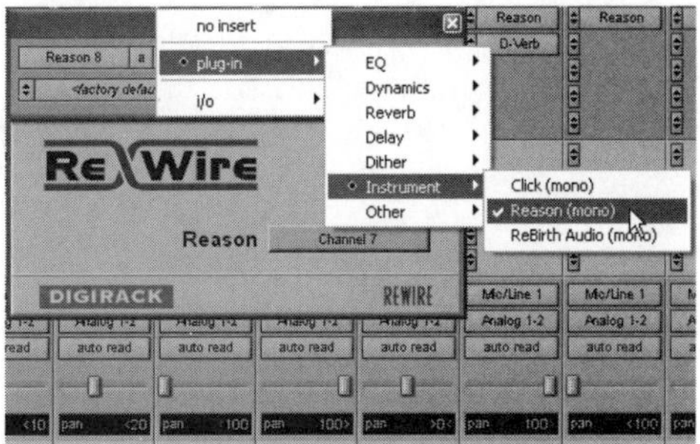

Figure A.6 Reason audio can be sent to a Pro Tools mixer channel using the insert function.

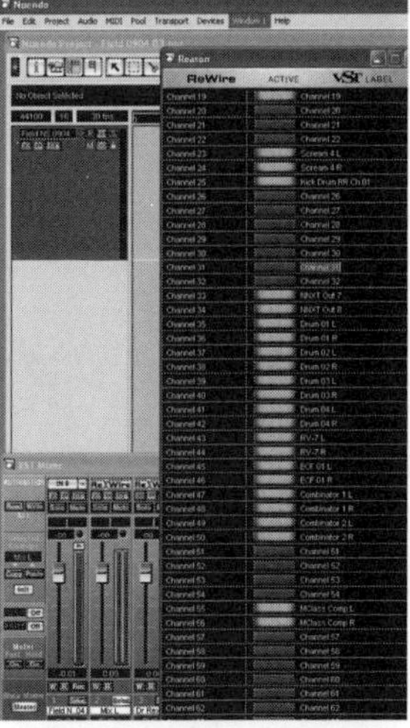

Figure A.7 Steinberg's Nuendo multi-track recording software shows the 64-channel ReWire bus that integrates Reason painlessly into the domain of audio recording and post-production.

ReWire

Your Reason hardware interface makes it possible to run up to 64 separate audio signals out of Reason and into multi-track software like Acid or Pro Tools (**Figure A.5**). The software technology that allows you to do this is called ReWire, and it is supported by most major audio software on the market.

Though Propellerhead has mentioned plans to expand ReWire2 to 256 channels, no further word has been announced as of the writing of this book.

How ReWire functions depends on the recording software. In Digidesign's Pro Tools, any audio signal routed through Reason's hardware interface can be brought up in the Mixer window channel strips as *inserts* (**Figure A.6**).

In Steinberg's Nuendo, a 64-channel input/output window allows you to enable and disable audio inputs coming from your Reason hardware interface (**Figure A.7**).

When routing audio to another program, Reason's mixing features are less important, as most of the mixing happens where the live recording is taking place.

ReCycle!

Hopefully this book has given you an idea of how versatile slice files are both as ways of creating rhythmic sample patches and as ways of mixing up beats and morphing music loops. If you want to make your own loop files and use them without tempo restrictions, you'll need ReCycle to do it.

ReCycle lets you create your own Rex files (.rx2), the most common and simplest way to expand your Reason sound library. With ReCycle you can slice loops into Rex files automatically or manually. It includes a variety of sensitivity knobs, gates, and equalization and gain tools to tune the loops (**Figure A.8**).

ReCycle can open up your existing loop library, allowing you to preserve a loop's character regardless of tempo. It can also exaggerate or add new effects to old sounds. The latest version, 2.1, supports 24-bit audio and can be purchased from the Propellerhead Web site for $249.

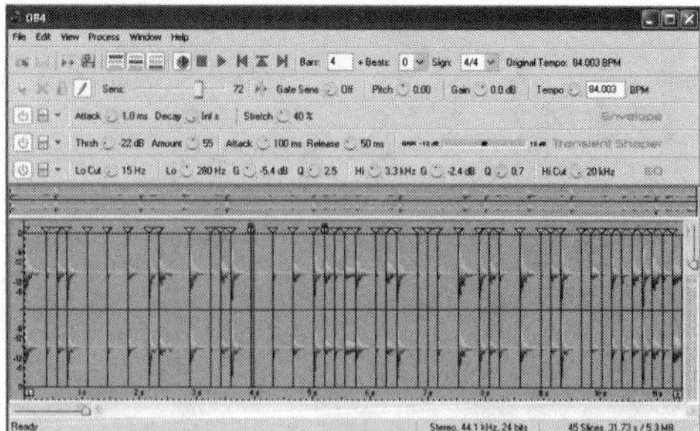

Figure A.8 The ReCycle! interface includes many tools to help you make your own slice files.

Figure A.9 The ReBirth techno micro-composer is still a favorite of professionals.

Figure A.10 Reason's ReBirth input machine gives ReBirth a back panel.

ReBirth

Released in 1997, ReBirth was Propellerhead's first virtual drum and bass synth program. This techno micro-composer program is still used professionally today (**Figure A.9**). It remains the only TB-303 bass line synth, TR-808 and 909 drum machine emulator on the market.

Reason brought ReBirth users a long-awaited back panel with the ReBirth input machine (**Figure A.10**). This rack device connects all the separate (and mix) audio signals from ReBirth and makes them available in your Reason song or any ReWire project.

The ReBirth update costs $69 and can be purchased at the Propellerhead Web site, though the full program cannot be. Replacement drum sounds and customized skins are available to registered users for download.

B

Resources

Now that Reason has been around for a few years, things are really starting to get interesting. As digital audio programs continue to become more cross-compatible with each other, new possibilities open up all the time.

There's a thriving international community of composers working with Reason on projects ranging from garage bands to Hollywood films. Here are just a few sites that I found helpful in my work on video games and during the writing of this book. By the time this book is in the stores, there will be many more.

If you have ideas or find useful sites, feel free to email me at joe@lyfordaudio.com.

Information sites

www.propellerhead.se Register with Propellerhead and use their forums to learn more about what others are doing with this versatile, open-ended program.

www.peff.com Kurt Kurasaki has been an evangelist for ReBirth and Reason since the beginning. His site is a great place to find useful Reason and ReBirth links, news, resources, and ReFills.

www.soundonsound.com This magazine posts articles on every audio subject and is an invaluable resource for anyone interested in learning more about music production.

Reason forums

www.futureproducers.com A place for composers to share ideas and information.

www.reasonstation.net A place to get ReFills to use with Propellerhead's Reason and to hear from other Reason users.

www.reasonfreaks.com Another long-standing forum for Reason users.

Samples and ReFills

www.analoguesamples.com A great place to download samples of hard-to-find/expensive analog synths to put in your sampler.

www.lapjockey.com/ljhome.htm

www.timespace.com/reason.asp

www.reasonrefills.com

www.reasonbanks.atw.hu

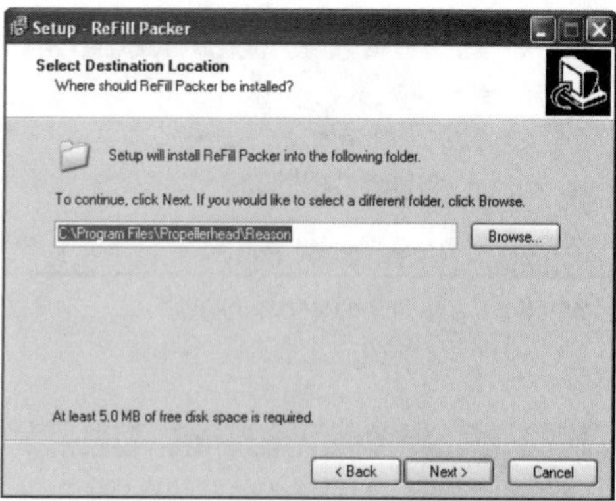

Figure B.1 Select a destination in the setup wizard.

Creating Your Own ReFills

As we've seen, ReFills are Reason sound banks compressed into one file. Most third-party sound developers now publish their libraries in ReFill format, and shareware ReFills are easy to find on the Internet.

You can make your own ReFills using the ReFill Packer application. This is recommended if you need to archive a lot of material, since ReFills save space and are secure from alteration.

ReFill Packer is free to registered Reason users and can be found in the Reason > Download section of the Propellerhead Web site (you will need to log in or register to enter).

To install ReFill Packer:

1. Download the 3.0 version file `RefillPacker_pc.zip` (Win)/ `RefillPacker_mac.zip` (Mac) from the Propellerhead site and unzip the file.
2. On a Mac, the `ReFillPacker.dmg` should automatically mount when unstuffed (if not, double-click to mount the disc image) and you can simply copy the files (`ReFill Packer`, `ReFill Packer Documentation`, `Sample Folder`, and `Template Folder`) into your `Reason` folder.

   or

   In Windows, double-click the program Install ReFill Packer to launch the setup wizard.
3. Select an install location and click Next (**Figure B.1**).

continues on next page

4. A dialog will ask if you want to install to the Reason folder that already exists on your drive (**Figure B.2**). Click Yes.
5. Choose whether you want to create a desktop alias and click Next.
6. Click Install to finish the installation. The install wizard will extract files and display a progress bar.
7. When installation is complete, click Finish (**Figure B.3**).

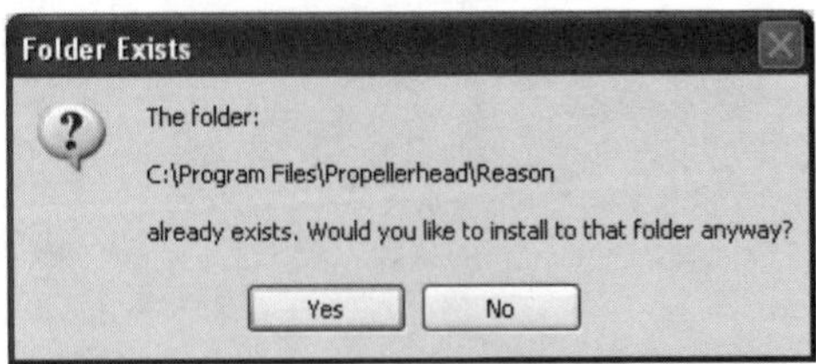

Figure B.2 Install to the Reason folder.

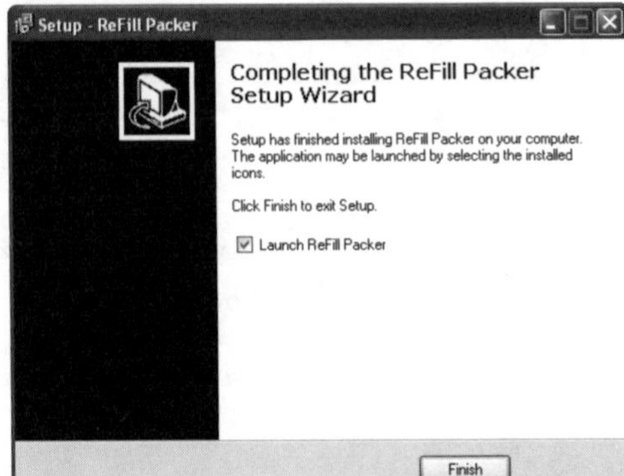

Figure B.3 Finish the installation.

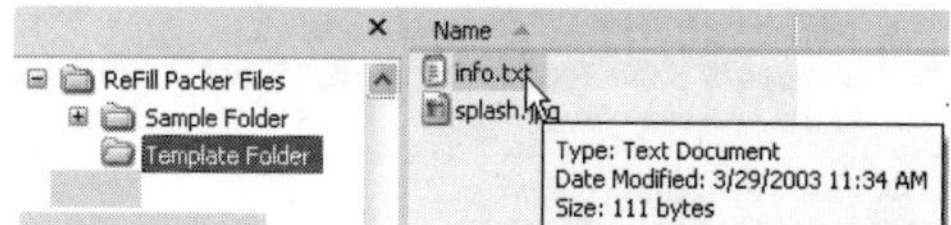

Figure B.4 The info.txt file contains information about your ReFill, and is necessary in order to name the file.

Deciding what to pack

A ReFill can't be unpacked or repacked into another ReFill. This is good for protecting your work, but it means you need to keep your folders organized and know which patches and samples are ones you've created.

Before running ReFill Packer, have all your sampler patches and samples organized so they are self-contained, and don't reference other ReFills. This doesn't have to be a problem, especially if the external ReFill references point to either the Factory or Orkester bank.

If a patch isn't self-contained, Reason will require the presence of other ReFills in order to load it.

To prepare a ReFill folder:

1. Find the `Template Folder` you installed with ReFill Packer, make a copy of it wherever you want to create your ReFill, and rename the copy with your ReFill's name.

   This folder will be the source for all the files, patches, and directories in your ReFill, though the actual ReFill file will be saved elsewhere.

2. In the source folder you created, you should see two files: `info.txt` and `splash.jpg` (**Figure B.4**). Make these files writable so that you can customize your ReFill. In Windows, right-click and select Properties from the context menu, then uncheck the Read Only box. Mac users, select a file and press Cmd+I, then open the Ownership & Permissions tab of the Info window and select Read & Write from the pull-down menu.

continues on next page

Both files are required by ReFill Packer, and must be present in the source folder. The `info.txt` file stores the actual name of your ReFill plus copyright and author information, and `splash.jpg` is the image that comes up in the browser whenever this ReFill gets loaded.

3. Open the file `info.txt` in a text editing program and type in the information you want to include in your ReFill (**Figure B.5**).
4. Make your own image to replace `splash.jpg`. It must be 64 × 64 pixels and named `splash.jpg`. With any other name or size, ReFill Packer will return an error message (**Figure B.6**).
5. Copy into the folder all the files, patches, and directories you want in your ReFill.

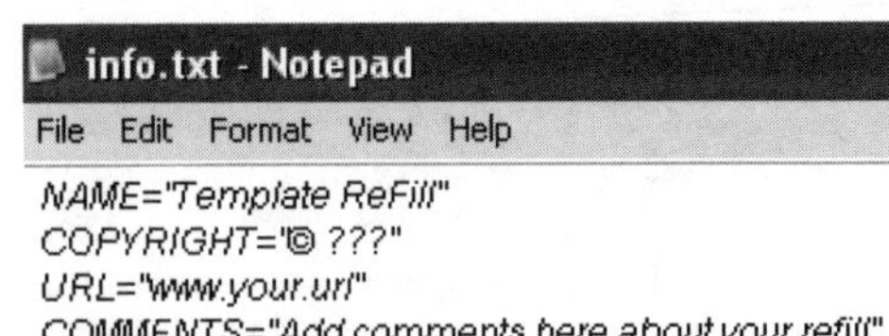

Figure B.5 Use any text editor to change the info.txt file and name your ReFill.

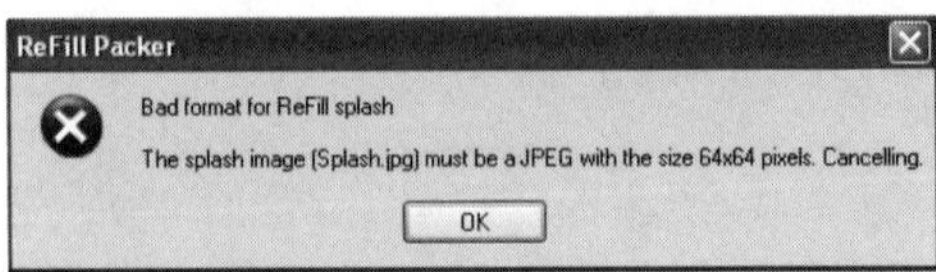

Figure B.6 Make sure your splash.jpg image is 64 by 64 pixels in size!

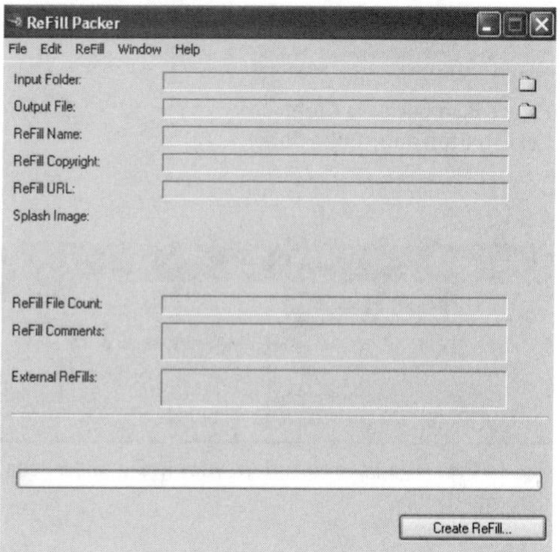

Figure B.7 Set your input and output folders in the main ReFill Packer screen.

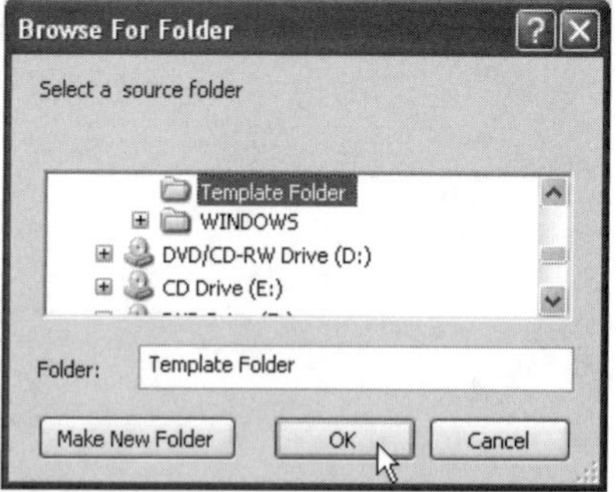

Figure B.8 The input folder is where the files for your ReFill are stored.

Figure B.9 The output file is where you want your new ReFill to go when it's packed.

Now you're ready to run ReFill Packer.

To create a ReFill:

1. Launch ReFill Packer.

   You'll see an input/output information screen (**Figure B.7**).

2. Click the folder icon next to the Input Folder field and choose the ReFill folder you prepared (**Figure B.8**).

   Remember the *input* folder is the *source folder* where your patches and sounds are coming *from.*

3. Click the folder icon next to the Output File field and select where you want ReFill Packer to put your new ReFill (**Figure B.9**).

   Remember that you've already set the name of the ReFill in the `info.txt` file, so you're simply choosing a save location.

continues on next page

4. Click Create ReFill (**Figure B.10**).
   ReFill Packer will now start building your ReFill.
5. If your ReFill references other ReFills, the program will pause to alert you and give you a choice to abort or continue (**Figure B.11**). If you choose to continue, the external ReFills referenced will be displayed in the External ReFills field (**Figure B.12**).

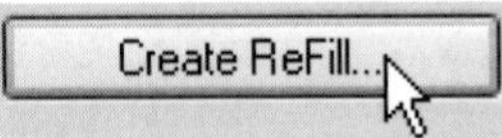

Figure B.10 Click the Create ReFill button and you're done!

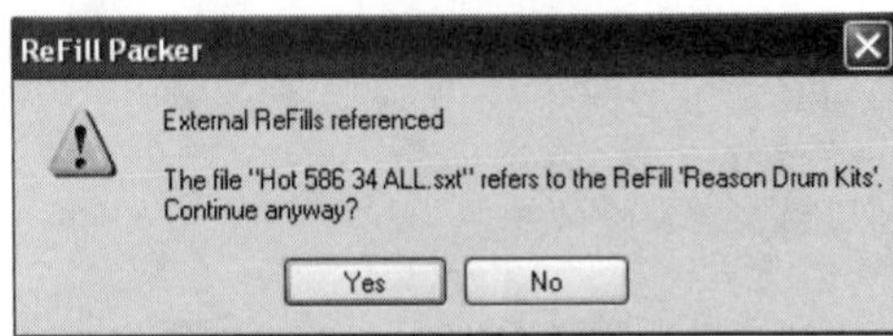

Figure B.11 If you see this alert, your ReFill references external ReFills.

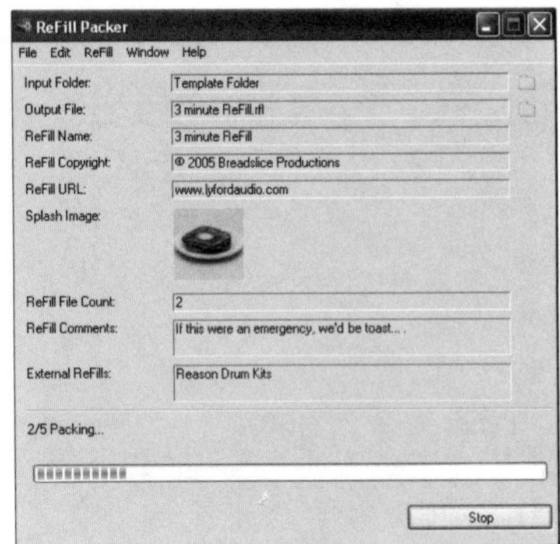

Figure B.12 The External ReFills field shows any outside references in your ReFill.

INDEX

INDEX

M

N

O

P

Q

R

S

T

U–V

W–Z